The Flourishing Lawyer

A Multi-Dimensional Approach to Performance and Well-Being

Heidi K. Brown

AMERICAN BAR ASSOCIATION
ABA Publishing

Cover design by Elmarie Jara/ABA Design

Printed in the United States of America.

26 25 5 4 3 2

Library of Congress Cataloging-in-Publication Data
Names: Brown, Heidi K. (Heidi Kristin), 1970- author.
Title: The flourishing lawyer : a multi-dimensional approach to performance and well-being / Heidi K. Brown.
Description: Chicago, Illinois : ABA Publishing, American Bar Association, [2022] | Includes index. | Summary: "This book is about how all of us can thrive-in good times and in arduous periods. This book is about focusing on more dimensions than just our intellect so we can be prepared for, and rise to, challenges like the ones we have been navigating since Spring 2020"--Provided by publisher.
Identifiers: LCCN 2021061081 (print) | LCCN 2021061082 (ebook) | ISBN 9781639050949 (board) | ISBN 9781639050253 | ISBN 9781639050956 (epub)
Subjects: LCSH: Practice of law--United States--Psychological aspects.
Classification: LCC KF300 .B755 2022 (print) | LCC KF300 (ebook) | DDC 340.023/73--dc23/eng/20220204
LC record available at https://lccn.loc.gov/2021061081
LC ebook record available at https://lccn.loc.gov/2021061082

Discounts are available for books ordered in bulk. Special consideration is given to state bars, CLE programs, and other bar-related organizations. Inquire at Book Publishing, ABA Publishing, American Bar Association, 321 N. Clark Street, Chicago, Illinois 60654-7598.

www.shopABA.org

Contents

Also by Heidi K. Brown

The Introverted Lawyer: A Seven-Step Journey Toward Authentically Empowered Advocacy

Untangling Fear in Lawyering: A Four-Step Journey Toward Powerful Advocacy

The Mindful Legal Writer: Mastering Predictive and Persuasive Writing

The Mindful Legal Writer: Mastering Predictive Writing

The Mindful Legal Writer: Mastering Persuasive Writing

Fundamentals of Federal Litigation

Preface

It's 8:26 a.m. on Day 133 of my pandemic experience.

It's Day 1 of this book project.

One hundred and thirty-three days ago, I hopped on the New York subway, relatively cheery, on my way to a boxing lesson with my trainer Lou in the Chelsea neighborhood of Manhattan. That evening, New York began locking down.

I stocked up on groceries and my favorite Spanish red wine. I abruptly shifted to teaching my legal writing course at Brooklyn Law School online. I am the most technologically inept human on the planet, but I went *all in* preparing to teach. I purchased a good webcam, ring light, and microphone. I jumped into Zoom training. I experimented with then-unfamiliar electronic features like the "hand-raise" and "chat" functions, and (dreaded) breakout rooms.

As a proud introvert (I mean, I wrote an entire book called *The Introverted Lawyer*), locking down solo felt like a breeze . . . at first. I fell into a relatively comforting routine: wake up, make coffee, write for two hours, teach, watch Governor Andrew Cuomo's daily press conferences, exercise in my kitchen, write a bit more, concoct something edible for dinner (my cooking abilities are worse than my tech skills), escape into a Spanish-language Netflix show, sleep, get up, repeat. Working out became a major highlight of my day. In the early weeks, to give my overloaded brain a break, I'd leave my apartment, try not to touch anything in the hallways, and descend eleven flights of stairs to exit the building, avoiding elevator encounters with other humans. I ran (in a sweaty mask or bandana) to Brooklyn Bridge Park, along the promenade into the neighborhood of DUMBO. Reaching the Manhattan Bridge, I'd circle back past the courthouses and the law school, return to my apartment building, force myself to expend a bit more energy trudging up eleven flights of stairs, and ultimately collapse on my couch.

Two months in, bored with running and annoyed by knee strain, I ordered a stand-up heavy boxing bag from Everlast. It arrived . . . unassembled. I built it myself, like a piece of Ikea® furniture. I filled the base with gallon after gallon of water from my kitchen sink. I screwed the pieces together with an Allen wrench, slashing my hand in the process. When the bag finally stood fully assembled in my kitchen, I felt victorious. I punched it each day. I gave it an appreciative pat each night.

Back in January of 2020, two months before the pandemic hit New York, I sent my publisher a proposal for this new book, *The Flourishing Lawyer.* My previous book, *Untangling Fear in Lawyering: A Four-Step Journey Toward Powerful Advocacy,* had been out for a year. I hankered to write a new one. I'm happiest when I'm writing. I also love hearing from readers of *Untangling Fear* and its prequel, *The Introverted Lawyer,* who share with me their stories and triumphs of grappling with introversion, shyness, social anxiety, and performance fears in law school and practice. Noticing themes and patterns in the Instagram and LinkedIn messages and emails I received from readers, an idea for a new book began percolating: one about how we—as law students and lawyers—can do more than just *survive* the profession but rather *thrive* in it, by understanding and cultivating more dimensions of ourselves than just our intellect. As is my custom when I have an idea budding, I first wrote a piece for the *ABA Journal* analogizing lawyers to athletes and other performers like singers, musicians, actors, or dancers.[1] In the article, I mused about how we don't seem to stigmatize most athletes or performers who seek help with mental, emotional, and physical challenges affecting performance. So, why do we do that (or at least, we have in the past) to law students and lawyers?

Pre-pandemic, my "big plan" for this book was to dive into the six dimensions of lawyer well-being identified in the 2017 Report of the National Task Force on Lawyer Well-Being:[2]

- Physical
- Emotional
- Social
- Spiritual
- Occupational
- Intellectual

Next, I planned to immerse myself in sports and performance psychology books by great coaches (and writers) like Phil Jackson, the former coach of the Chicago Bulls basketball team (in the Michael Jordan era) and the Los Angeles Lakers (in the Kobe Bryant era). I figured I'd craft a formula for us—as members of the legal profession—to take better care of ourselves (and one another) by investing in all six National Task Force dimensions, not just the intellectual or occupational domains that tend to dominate our attention.

Then I read the book *Flourish*, by Dr. Martin E. P. Seligman.[3] Dr. Seligman is one of the founders of the field of positive psychology and Director of the Positive Psychology Center at the University of Pennsylvania. In *Flourish*, Dr. Seligman outlines a well-being theory comprised of five elements, using the mnemonic PERMA:[4]

- **P**ositive emotion
- **E**ngagement
- **R**elationships
- **M**eaning
- **A**ccomplishment

I got excited to study these concepts too. I wondered . . . do they intermingle with, overlap with, or expand the six dimensions identified in the National Task Force report? Do they override or supplement the techniques implemented by sports and performance coaches to help athletes and performers succeed on the field or in the arena and lead happy, healthy, fulfilling lives? My Big Plan was to synthesize all that and apply it to what I know *personally* from surviving (but struggling to thrive in) three decades in the legal profession: three years of law school, nearly two decades of practicing law in the hard-hitting field of construction litigation, and thirteen years of teaching law.

Then the pandemic hit, and our world changed.

Law school shifted online. Many educational institutions switched to a pass/fail grading system for the Spring 2020 semester. Some law firms canceled or postponed students' summer internships; others thankfully transitioned to remote settings. Bar exams spun into chaos: some states insisted on clinging to in-person test conditions; at least one jurisdiction issued a last-minute postponement; several switched to online formats with onerous electronic "surveillance" rules to prevent cheating; petitions for "emergency diploma privilege" circulated. Meanwhile, law offices adjusted to work-from-home dynamics. Some delayed employment start dates for recent law school graduates. Others implemented layoffs or salary reductions.

Interestingly, despite all this turmoil, some law students, lawyers, and law offices thrived.

This book is about how *all of us* can thrive—in good times and in arduous periods. This book is about focusing on more dimensions than just our intellect so we can be prepared for, and rise to, challenges like the ones we have been navigating since Spring 2020.

As I sit down to write on Day One of this new book project, the future of the legal profession, our country, and the world, is unclear. That can feel scary. But it's also incredibly exciting. We literally can reinvent the legal profession—for the better.

Normally when I embark upon a new book project (this is my seventh book), I can visualize the arc of the book from start to finish. I scurry off to an office supply store and buy large pink and orange Post-it® notes. I write concepts for chapters in Sharpie ink and stick the Post-it notes to the windows of my New York apartment. Sipping morning coffee and staring at the Post-it notes, I move them around, rearranging their chronology and progression until the "story" flows from beginning to end. My book's infrastructure—its skeleton—usually crystallizes before my eyes. Then, I sit down and write it. I love author Steven Pressfield's advice from his motivating book on the creative process, *Do the Work*: "Get the first version of your project done from A to Z as fast as you can. Don't stop. Don't look down. Don't think."[5] My usual process is writing five pages a day, two hours each morning as soon as I wake up, for as many days in a row as it takes to generate the first draft.

For this book, I had a plan. I also had a detailed chapter-by-chapter book proposal.

The pandemic changed this book for me. I know this book needs to exist. But as I type these words today, on Day One, I can't picture it yet. I'm not sure where it will take me . . . us. And while I love not having a set agenda when I travel, being wholly and completely devoid of a writing plan has never felt like a winning approach to meeting a manuscript deadline. But I'm going do something completely out of my comfort zone. I'm going to let this book tell me what it wants to be, and what it wants *us* to be when we emerge from the pandemic, anew.

In case you might be thinking, "Oh, she just has pandemic writer's block," respectfully, I wish that were the problem. It's not. During the first 100 days of lockdown, I wrote every day. I dipped a toe into the online platform of Medium for the first time and launched a blog series called *Monday Minute* about cultivating our mental health while sheltering at home. I wrote a travel essay about my last trip before lockdown—a pilgrimage to find the band U2's Joshua tree, the *actual tree* in the California desert photographed by Dutch photographer Anton Corbijn which became the emblem of U2's 1987 *The Joshua Tree* album. That essay prodded me to reprise a half-written travel memoir manuscript I forgot I had started; I found the manuscript on an old laptop and added six chapters about solo adventures through Peru, Australia, Vancouver, Mexico, Rome, and Argentina. For work, I finished a law review article about gender-neutral pronouns entitled *Get with the Pronoun*.[6] I penned a book chapter (for someone else's book) about how quiet students actually can thrive in remote learning.

Nothing is blocking my writer flow. I just can't close my eyes and envision the end product of this book . . . yet. This one feels different. *Everything* feels different.

This is unsettling yet a tad thrilling. It's a new sensation for me as a writer to cede control. It's also illustrative of this pandemic. We don't know what the future of our profession, our society, or the world looks like. And that's okay. All we can do is consciously resolve to build strength now so we can handle whatever comes our way in the future. Positive psychologists call this *buffering*—when we accrue mental, physical, and emotional assets in the present to help us reduce or soften the impact of future challenges.[7] Social psychologist Dr. Barbara Fredrickson champions our ability to actively *broaden-and-build* our existing reserves of personal resources to handle future stressors.[8]

Through the chapters of this book, we will explore who we are and who we want to be as members of the legal profession and as humans. We will learn how we thrive as individuals, and how we can fortify multiple dimensions of our personas. Armed with this new information, we will be better prepared to anticipate and move through difficult future predicaments and dilemmas with clear heads, resolute minds, and strong bodies.

So . . . let's do this.

I am going to trust my writing system and do the work. I'm going to put words on paper every day, and watch this book tell me what it wants to be. *For us.* If you've read any of my stuff before, you know that I believe in vulnerability, transparency, and openness about our personal struggles in order for us to grow individually and help one another. In *The Introverted Lawyer*, I reflected on my experiences growing up as a minister's daughter, not trusting my voice as a law student, and grappling with overwhelming anxiety as a litigator in three aggressive law firm environments. Through writing that book, I found my voice—a quiet but impactful one. Next, in writing *Untangling Fear*, by listening to and transcribing my (negative) mental soundtrack, I discovered that my fears of judgment and criticism in law school and law practice echoed primal fears from childhood, adolescence, and early adulthood of rejection, exclusion, and unworthiness. Writing those two books changed my entire approach to working and living. I finally rejected outdated and inaccurate messages about perceived "weaknesses" and rewrote my mental soundtrack with accurate reminders about my strengths. I realized how solidifying my physique (through boxing lessons, for example) ignites and bolsters my mental and emotional power. I finally stood up to bullies in my past—professional and personal. I disentangled guilt from shame. I exhumed years of unspoken hurt, anger, outrage, and sadness. And in the end, I figured out who I want to be. I'm not totally there yet. But I will never go backwards.

You helped me get to this place. Writing is concurrently exhilarating and terrifying. Over the years, as many writers probably do, I have received correspondence criticizing my work. A law professor publicly characterized some of my work as "pablum." (That one stung. Also, I had to look up the word "pablum" to make sure I knew exactly how badly I was being insulted.) I gave a Zoom talk to a law school class in a different state recently and the host asked me, "How do you handle harsh criticism like that Letter to the Editor in response to your latest *ABA Journal* article?" I responded, "I don't know which letter you're referring to because I stopped reading online reviews of my work." And then I spent the next three hours ruminating about what that critic possibly wrote. (Later, I breached my no-reading-negative-comments policy, asked my publisher to send me the critique, read it, and decided the guy had completely missed my point, and I felt okay about that.)

You remind me every day that this work matters. When I hear from readers through Instagram, LinkedIn, or emails, I am invigorated knowing that our collective work—to improve ourselves and our profession—deeply *matters.* We must keep going. So, here's the plan. We are going to navigate our way to post-pandemic lawyering *together.*

In addition to being a book about shoring up multiple dimensions of our well-being, this book likely is going to narrate a tale of adventure for me as I evolve as a writer, exploring new internal terrain. Thank you for accompanying me on this expedition.

Three major life events frame this new book and its detour from my usual writing process. Ten days into pandemic lockdown in New York City, I turned fifty. Instead of venturing off on a solo trip to Rome (my favorite place in the world and where I wrote the initial draft of the manuscript for *Untangling Fear*) as originally planned, I celebrated in my first Zoom happy hour with eight of my closest friends (after a two-hour Zoom faculty meeting). Then, I miraculously figured out how to AirDrop a YouTube video of a U2 concert in Berlin onto my TV and staged a solo dance party in my living room. It was one of the best (and weirdest) birthdays of my life.

Two months later, I received epic news: I was accepted into the Master of Applied Positive Psychology (MAPP) program at the University of Pennsylvania, led by Dr. Seligman (author of the book *Flourish* mentioned earlier) and his incredible team. As I spent my (first) pandemic summer engrossed in online boot camps on "excellence in remote teaching," striving to gain sufficient skills to provide an awesome educational experience for my new 1L law students in the fall of 2020, I also geared up to be a student again—at fifty years old.

A month after receiving my Penn acceptance news, to be physically closer to my friends, I moved from my Brooklyn apartment to Chelsea, the first neighborhood I called home when I moved to New York City twenty years ago. Moving during the pandemic was simultaneously stressful and therapeutic. In the early months of COVID lockdown alone in my tiny Brooklyn apartment, I sat on my living room floor amid boxes and clutter, sifting through a lifetime of possessions and memories. I waded through cartons of old letters and photographs from past relationships (some reflected in my earlier books). I repackaged and relabeled containers for storage, writing notes to myself like, "OK, you can still hang onto this, but do not open again until 2030." I purged my closets, perplexed at double-edged guilt: on one hand, I own too many clothes, yet on the other hand, I lamented letting go of items I had spent money on yet had barely worn. Moving day was tension-filled: the movers arrived mask-less and late (an unfortunate complication in New York City where my move required intricate choreography of elevator reservations in two buildings situated in two different boroughs). I took the subway for the first time in months, transporting four scraggly houseplants to my new home which I had rented sight-unseen. Over two wholly unproductive work weeks, I unpacked and organized a much smaller living space.

Today, on Day One of this book project, I sit on my couch in my new dwelling, air conditioning cranking—a shield against predicted 98-degree temperatures outside. I am surrounded by my favorite belongings: a record player; black-and-white U2 lithographs on the walls; framed pictures of vivid graffiti I've captured on trips to Portugal, Dublin, Amsterdam; every book I have read in the last 20 years; my boxing bag (this time, its large basin filled with books instead of gallons of water). I designated my kitchen table for Zoom teaching; a tufted futon for reading, researching, and grading papers; and my white Ikea leather couch for writing. In this quiet, comforting space—the pandemic raging outside—this book will emerge and bloom.

So, let's begin together. What does it mean for us to *flourish* as members of the legal profession? The Oxford Dictionary defines "flourishing"—in verb form—as:[9]

- "growing or developing in a healthy or vigorous way, especially as the result of a particularly favorable environment."
- "waving (something) around to attract the attention of others."
- "working or at the height of one's career during a specified period."

Merriam-Webster defines the verb as "to grow luxuriantly," "to be in a state of activity or production," or "to reach a height of development or influence."[10]

In *noun* form, the Oxford Dictionary defines a "flourish" as "an instance of suddenly performing or developing in an impressively successful way," or "fanfare played by brass instruments."[11]

I like how the word *flourish* encompasses quiet and patient growth but also triumphant sights and sounds—like waving a vibrant flag around and blaring trumpets and tubas in jubilant celebration. We will do both. First, we will consciously tend to multiple dimensions of our well-being, cultivating individual strengths and environments in which we can thrive—through good times and tough stretches. Then, we will vigorously wave jazz hands and crash cymbals, or fist-bump and cheer, in revelry and appreciation for our growth.

There is no playbook for what the legal profession "should" look like after the pandemic. Let's write our own scripts. Let's redefine what it means to be a "success" in law school and legal practice. Let's cultivate deeply healthy souls as law students and lawyers and other contributors to the profession. Let's be open, honest, and vulnerable with our personal stories. Let's push back against outdated hierarchy, bullying, lack of civility, and harmful iterations of cancel culture. Let's bang the drums of change, clap our hands loudly, close our eyes, dance like crazy to our own songs. And let's embrace quietude and silence when we need to pause.

This book is for all of us. While of course I want everyone who is already "doing well" to keep doing well, this book is also for the underdog. If you've ever been told, "You can't do that," or "You don't have a chance," or "You should aim for something else," or "Just get over it," or "Just do it," or "Fake it till you make it," or be something that you're not, or be something you don't want to be, this book is for you, for us.

I have no interest in perpetuating hierarchy and exclusion. I aspire to greatness for *all* of us—however we define greatness for ourselves. A life and career that you deem great for *you* likely will differ from what I decide is great for *me*. That's the cool part. We get to carry each other into our individual zones of awesomeness.

Safety Theme!

To write this book, I read approximately 34 books and more than 100 articles written by a bunch of smart people who are experts in their fields: psychology, health care, sports, medicine. A theme that emerged from pages and pages of reading was *safety*. I don't mean "safe spaces" (a term that gets an unfairly bad rap from people who, for some reason, like to make fun of millennials). I also don't mean "playing it safe." I mean the necessary feeling of trust and security in our own bodies, minds, relationships, and environments, for us to function well.

It took me a long time to realize that my extreme performance anxiety throughout law school, practice, and my early days of teaching stemmed from feeling wholly unsafe. I needed to do the scary thing of ploughing the soil of my upbringing to discover that I feel unsafe when persons in positions of authority or power (educational, occupational, relational, spiritual) dangle carrots of manipulation and wield sticks of judgment. I feel unsafe and scared when others get to decide whether I'm worthy of inclusion and acceptance . . . when they rank me. Of course, I realize that my version of feeling unsafe is different from individuals who grew up without physical safety, food security, adequate shelter. Nonetheless, each one of us has a story of safety and unsafety that matters deeply here.

In researching my prior books, I became frustrated with the conflicting messages our society promotes about fear. On one hand, we constantly are told, "Just face your fears!" Each day on Instagram, we are badgered, "Do something every day that scares you!" or "If your dreams don't scare you, they're not big enough!" OR, we are advised that fear is good for us; it's motivating; it means we care. I've heard law professors and lawyers admonish, "If you stop being scared, it's time to leave the law." So, under such a framework, we seem to be relegated to three choices: (1) come off the factory line, ready and raring to spar; (2) be scared all the time but pretend we're not; or (3) quit. No. Just no.

I think we need to adjust our attitude toward safety, understanding that it is through a deep sense of personal and collective safety that we can be our bravest, most daring, and most adventurous. As Dr. Bruce D. Perry and Oprah Winfrey note in their book, *What Happened to You? Conversations on Trauma, Resilience, and Healing*, "A child in an environment where they feel loved and safe will choose to leave their comfort zone."[12] I believe the same is true for adults.

As we embark on this self-discovery expedition, let's explore the thoughts, feelings, physical sensations, people, activities, and environments that instill in us a fundamental sense of safety. Let's also identify what jeopardizes and rattles our perception of safety. Then, with this enhanced awareness, we can intentionally step into training and performance scenarios that involve risk, and maybe a bit of thrill, adventure, and awe.

I'm ready for what's next. Are you? Let's do this together.

> *There is no reason to write a book*
> *unless the process of doing so changes the author's life.*
>
> John Ratey and Richard Manning[13]

> *You hunker down in the cellar of your heart,*
> *and when the debris stops falling from the sky,*
> *you crawl back out and behold the new day*
> *and the rest of your golden life.*
>
> Michelle Tea[14]

Acknowledgments

Lou: Thank you for always treating and training me like a real fighter and for teaching me to breathe and trust. You are the most thoughtful, empowering, and creative educator I have ever had.

My Penn MAPP family, especially Kym, Cheryl, Grace, Erin, Paige, Karen, Kathy, and Britt: Thank you for being bright lights of unconditional love.

My Brooklyn Law School research assistants (Slay, Hadel, and Josie) and my research librarian, Loreen: Thank you for your diligence and enthusiasm in tracking down the zillions of resources I needed for this project. I could not have crafted this book without you. And thank you especially to Slay for meticulously checking ALL my citations.

Brooklyn Law School's marketing, public relations, and events teams, especially Peggy, Clorinda, Rose, Dominick, Amy, Conor, Michael, Liz, and Chris: Thank you for all your support and help in spreading the word about well-being in the legal profession. And thank you especially to Amy for converting my crazy ideas into creative graphics.

Kelly: Thank you for constantly reminding me that we are the muse, the queen, the goddess, the warrior, the magic . . . that we see in each other.

Jenn: Thank you for being a shining star of brilliance and hilarity. I can't wait to see you transform our profession.

Flora: Thank you for cultivating space for us to grow and support one another as artists.

All my students and readers: Thank you for helping me find my life's meaning and purpose, and for trusting me with your stories.

Jenna, Lauren, Susan, Jess, Melissa, Todd, Julie, Ernest, Lucinda, Jodi, Cecilia, Anna, Tim, Dana, and Maryellen: Thank you for letting me be your weirdo writer-y friend who needs boatloads of time alone but also treasures every nanosecond of our time together.

The teams at ABA Journal and ABA Publishing: Thank you for supporting my work and caring so much about getting the clarity of the message right.

My family: Thank you for understanding my need to roam and seek out experiences that "thrill, amaze, inspire," and for cheering me onward.

Clay: Thank you for being my introverted, kind, hilarious, brilliant, encouraging, caring, rock star best friend. Here's to helping each other flourish in our art and every dimension of our lives until and including when we are old and gray, eating gelato and drinking wine in our Italian villa, surrounded by rescue dogs and books and olive trees.

Introduction

I sit down to write today on the last Tuesday in July of 2020, the first day of the bar exam in states that stuck to a live, in-person test without pandemic-related postponement. Procrastinating, I briefly scroll Twitter. It's abuzz with complaints about the bar exam situation (#barpocalypse, some have dubbed it) and doom-and-gloom about how long it's going to take for things to get "back to normal." Dallying further, I check email. Some of my rising 2L students are writing me, bummed out that they didn't make law review or another journal, perplexed about why they weren't selected for the moot court team, frustrated with a perceived lack of feedback on how to improve. Other students write to share glimmers of excitement at applying a research or writing technique we learned in class over the past year to a real assignment in their remote summer internships. I skim a few emails from colleagues following up on issues raised in our most recent Zoom faculty meeting in which we spent hours brainstorming the "right" approach toward educating our students remotely in the upcoming fall semester. Some professors seek to stick to past practices—lecturing, cold-calling (calling on students without advance notice), grading on a curve.

I can't help but think: What if we refuse to go back to the way things were—in legal education and practice? What if we take this opportunity to rip the whole thing down and start fresh? A clean canvas. What if we create a new training model without unhealthy (and outdated) hierarchies and survival-of-the-fittest Hunger Games? How fun would it be to design classrooms in which every student feels included because we offer multiple channels of "participation" instead of just one-dimensional Socratic teaching? What if we change and broaden the definition of "success" in law school—crafting abundant pathways toward achievement of individual ambitions rather than doubling down on externally imposed goals? What if we stop putting so much pressure on every student to make law review or try out for advocacy teams that seem to funnel everyone toward a similar communication style? What if we defuse unhealthy and unnecessary competition and speak openly about cultivating greater awareness of personal strengths and motivational drivers, to learn collectively how everyone can thrive?

Also, what if law offices were to stop evaluating job applicants primarily on law school rankings, grade point averages (GPAs), and other traditional accolades and instead prioritize consideration of candidates' emotional intelligence, positive attitude, optimism, flexibility in the face of challenges, and healthy communication skills? What if, instead of enabling (and grooming) bullies and jerks, we finally call them out and hold them accountable? What if we refuse to applaud disdain, incivility, and misused cancel culture and instead learn how to have hard conversations and treat one another with respect?

Such a world sounds beautiful—and doable—to me.

Like my other books, I want this one to focus on positive evolution and offer practical solutions to real problems we experience as a profession. But before we get to the stuff of goodness and flourishing, it helps to *name* the challenges. An "airing of grievances" of sorts, like the ritual of the holiday Festivus, featured in the TV show, *Seinfeld.*

This pandemic has illuminated some cracks in our profession, including:

- The antiquated nature of entrenched hierarchies in legal education and law practice.
- A misguided scarcity mindset.
- The fallacy of the notion that there is "one pathway" to success as a law student and lawyer.
- The myth of the infallibility of the "successful" lawyer.
- The flawed expectation of office face time and 24/7 connectivity.
- The prevalence of bullying, gaslighting, and lack of civility.
- The dangers of "shame culture" or some versions of "cancel culture" (e.g., Twitter culture).
- Damage to the "soul of the law."[15]

I love the lyric by Canadian singer and poet, Leonard Cohen, "There is a crack, a crack in everything. That's how the light gets in."[16] Instead of throwing a shroud over the cracks in our profession and pretending they don't exist, let's let the light in. Japanese *kintsugi* artists ("kin" for "golden," and "tsugi" for "repair") use liquid gold or silver to mend fractures in pottery. Instead of trashing a broken bowl, vase, or pitcher—deeming it unfixable—kintsugi artists accentuate the "scars" using precious metal as binding, ultimately unifying broken fragments into a more beautiful object than the original.

This is our chance to acknowledge cracks in our profession, but instead of just complaining about them, we can mend these fissures in an intentional and artistic way, generating a more powerful version of our professional community. This is also an opportunity to engage in forward-thinking *prevention* by asking, *How can we strengthen ourselves as individuals and as a collective to ensure we can rise to each occasion in inevitable future challenges, instead of faltering?* Rather than waiting until we are in our next crisis, or in pain, or until our wounds are too deep or unfixable, let's look ahead. Let's figure out what we can do to *prevent* calamities and anguish. To do so, we must take a hard look at our profession, starting from where it all begins: the moment that aspiring lawyers first walk through the doors of our law schools.

> *Let light shine through the cracks*
> *in the armor of your staunchest beliefs.*
>
> Jonathan Lockwood Huie

LET'S REDEFINE "SUCCESS" IN LAW SCHOOL

As unpleasant as it is to revisit the angst I experienced as a law student (and wrote about extensively in *The Introverted Lawyer* and *Untangling Fear*), I'll share a few highlights (or lowlights) of my story in hopes that mine might resonate with yours and illuminate why the myth of "one successful lawyering path" is dangerous. And trust me, I don't use that word lightly.

As an undergraduate at the University of Virginia, I was a happy and good student. I loved college. I pursued classes in French, Italian, and Russian. I double-majored in French and Foreign Affairs. I dabbled in psychology and anthropology classes. I earned Dean's List, Phi Beta Kappa, and Distinguished Major honors, and graduated with a strong GPA. I took the Law School Admission Test (LSAT) without having the extra money for a test prep course and not having a clue why I needed one. Other than the "logic games" section of the standardized test (which still confounds me as to how it was even remotely related to the actual practice of law), I did not fare well. I applied to the University of Virginia School of Law and was accepted, perhaps on my high GPA and reference letters from my undergraduate professors, one of whom also taught at the law school (thanks, Professor Turner!). But that mediocre LSAT score haunted my psyche. My classmates all seemed to have aced the test and talked about it continuously—the first marker of "success" in our chosen pathway toward lawyering. The (not so healthy) competitive tone was set early.

In my undergraduate foreign-language classes, I never was afraid to speak aloud. I readily ventured answers to my professors' questions in near fluent French, and very amateur Italian. The law school classroom was a different story. I felt like I had time-traveled into a colosseum scene in the film *Gladiator.* Terror gripped me from Day One and held on. At 21 years old, I sat in my large Socratic-style lecture classes paralyzed with fear and enveloped in a blanket of unworthiness.

Each night, I pored over my assigned readings, trying to make sense of the unfamiliar terminology. I couldn't understand why French verb tenses, Italian idioms, and the Russian alphabet hadn't intimidated me, but legal phrases like *collateral estoppel, indemnity*, and *res ipsa loquitur* made me dizzy.

Highlighter ink stained my hands as I fell asleep with Contracts and Civil Procedure textbooks in my bed. Each day, I drifted down the hallway of the law school building like a zombie. My classmates chattered in clusters outside each classroom, already seemingly adroit with legal rules, theories, and lingo. Inside the classroom, time stood still as I prayed my professors would not call my name. When they did cold-call me, I froze. My face flushed crimson, a fiery blush broadcasting my fear to my classmates and teachers. Though I was prepared for class, I was terrified of looking stupid. I was petrified of their judgment, rejection, and exclusion. In every performance moment, my brain failed to deliver the substantive information I obsessively studied each night in preparation for class. I carefully crafted meticulous checklists of rule elements and flowcharts of procedural steps, keeping them at hand's reach on my desk, but when asked by my teachers to regurgitate the simplest of concepts, my class outlines seemed as clear and organized as a Jackson Pollock painting.

Not one of my professors acknowledged the perceived scariness of the classroom. Not one paused to explain that the law was a new language—analogous to those I loved studying in college—and that it was okay if it took some of us longer than other classmates to grasp it. Not one teacher said, "Hey, here is why I ask these particular questions in class in this way," or "Hey, it's perfectly alright if you don't know the exact answer to my question in class; you've done the reading so let's talk about what you do know and I'll get you there. Let's help you stay in the conversation." Instead, law school seemed to be a game everyone else was playing, enjoying, and winning. It felt as if they had garnered access to a secret set of rules and vocabulary. In my first set of 1L finals, I remember having to go to the library in the middle of a test to look up the word "notwithstanding" in a dusty dictionary because I couldn't make sense of how the word affected the essay question.

For some reason, my law school released one fall semester grade—the one from our 1L small section class (Criminal Law)—weeks before the rest of our large lecture course grades. I received a C+, the worst grade I had ever gotten in my life. My roommate got an A+. To this day, I still don't know why she and I talked about our scores. For weeks before I received my other 1L grades, I cried. I berated myself. I catastrophized. *You're too dumb for law school. You don't belong. You're going to fail out. No one is ever going to hire you. You're going to be broke.* I went home and spent my winter break hidden under a cloak of shame, embarrassment, and fear.

When the rest of my fall 1L grades came out, I did fine. Not stellar, but fine. I wiped the tears off my cheeks and heaved myself off the couch. I took a deep breath and dove back into second semester. I vowed not to talk about grades with anyone. I kept my headphones on, blasting Nirvana songs to drown out the din of my eager classmates bantering in the school hallways about their prospects of making law review and landing BigLaw summer jobs.

Then came the next peer-pressure rite of passage: forcing myself to try out for the moot court advocacy team. While classmates wouldn't stop talking about the oral argument tryouts, I worried I would be deemed even more of a law school loser if anyone found out that getting up in front of people and arguing while judges interrupted me with questions was literally the last thing I wanted to do . . . *ever.* In my legal writing class, however, I had loved writing my very first brief (which doubled as the subject matter of the looming oral argument). In fact, writing that brief is the first memory I have in law school of feeling in "flow"—a concept coined by psychologist Dr. Mihaly Csikszentmihalyi (pronounced "cheek-sent-me-high").[17] "Flow" is "the state in which people are so involved in an activity that nothing else seems to matter."[18] Csikszentmihalyi says that "[t]he best moments usually occur when a person's body or mind is stretched to its limits in a voluntary effort to accomplish something difficult and worthwhile."[19] (We'll delve lots more into the awesome experience of *flow* later, in Chapter 4.)

I loved my legal writing class. Unlike my other classes which seemed all survival-of-the-fittest to see who could most impress the teacher in rapid Socratic volley, my writing assignments afforded me unparalleled space to think. I could sit quietly with the statutes and case law and let them talk to me. Through *writing* about the law (instead of answering spontaneous questions about it in front of eighty peers), I finally started to *see* elements of rules muster into neat checklists. I could visualize "balancing tests" of different legal factors, like weights on a measuring scale. I loved the process of crafting and retooling arguments, choosing words and phrasing that conveyed logic and persuasion. Writing about the law was heaven. Talking about it (out loud before I was ready) was hell. Instead of delivering an oral argument to a panel of moot court judges, I just wanted to deposit my beloved brief in a dropbox and be done with the whole thing.

While my classmates vigorously debated the nuances of their moot court arguments, rehearsing in coteries on the law school lawn, I worried there was something wrong with me. *If I don't already feel eager to argue and fight about legal issues, does that mean I'm not cut out for this profession?*

I vomited in the restroom before my moot court tryout. In the mock courtroom, two minutes into my oral argument, a 3L student-judge interrupted me with the first question. In response, I stammered, "I don't know." I don't remember anything after that, except that in the judges' debrief, one advised, "You need to stop twirling your hair." I stared down at the outline I'd carefully crafted from the brief I could recite by heart. My cheeks burned. I wanted to flee.

When our spring grades came out, it was déjà vu. I received a C+ in Constitutional Law. I did fine in my other classes. I did not even bother participating in the write-on competition for law review. I still didn't even know what law review was.

Earlier that spring, I had found a quiet carrel in the library and made a list of 100 law firms in Northern Virginia and Washington, D.C. I sent my résumé to the 100 firms. I landed a summer associate position at a boutique litigation firm that happened to specialize in construction law.

My first summer job at the construction litigation firm breathed new life into me. If the firm noticed those two C+ grades on my transcript, or the lack of law review or moot court accolades, they didn't seem to care. They never once mentioned any of those items. I loved the legal research and writing projects doled out by the partners. Every time a partner summoned me to his office to talk about (and periodically praise me for) my writing, my nerves started jangling again. But I began to find my niche in the law that summer. I enjoyed, and was good at, poring over factual documents, analyzing statutory rules, finding case law, and crafting persuasive arguments to resolve our clients' complex legal conflicts. While other summer associates were light-years better at public speaking, mingling at networking events, and exuding confidence, my gift was research and writing. My law firm cared about our work ethic and our ability to write, think through complicated problems, and interact with our intense and demanding clients during document reviews and strategy meetings. For three blissful months, no one talked about grades, law review, or moot court.

At the end of the summer, I returned to school for my 2L year. My insecurity bloomed anew. The students on law review and the moot court team roamed the corridors like the in-crowd in high school. I hid in the shadows.

For the next two years, I let those blips on my transcript—and my lack of identification with any of the traditional law school "clubs"—define me in my interactions in the classroom and the hallways. I felt less than. I wasn't less than. I had a lot to contribute. Yet, for two years, I unnecessarily dimmed my shine because of two three-hour tests and one unpleasant oral argument.

If I could go back 30 years, sit my 21-year-old self down, and have a candid conversation about *grades*, this is what I would say:

> Your grades absolutely don't define you. Yes, it's okay to be bummed out or frustrated about a less-than-ideal grade, or excited about a good one. But they have nothing to do with who you are as a person and who you will be as a lawyer. Yes, they are pieces of information. But YOU get to decide how to use that information.

Instead of viewing grades as yardsticks of measurement against my peers, I should have simply considered them indicators of how my brain processes different types of legal concepts. If I could go back to my 1L and 2L years, perhaps I could have noticed that I did well in classes that had definitive *rules* that could be broken down into *elements* or *factors*. I liked Civil Procedure. I liked Uniform Commercial Code classes. I even liked Tax! In contrast, I struggled in classes in which the professor focused and tested heavily on abstract theory.

Using my grades in Criminal Law and Constitutional Law as *information* rather than a *judgment* of my intelligence or worthiness, perhaps I could have approached future theory-based classes better armed with this knowledge. I could have worked with my professors to try to transform abstract theory into more tangible "rules" that my brain could process and apply more effectively.

Also, instead of regarding those two blotches on my transcript as "scarlet letters" of unfitness for the profession, I could have evaluated my report cards for clues about intellectual activities and curiosities I enjoyed. Instead of crying about Criminal Law and Constitutional Law, I should have surveyed my transcript to see if any patterns emerged about academic tasks I relished and in which I felt in "flow." I could have used my law school grades to discern that I love researching, writing, and thinking, and I do NOT love classroom scenarios in which I am expected to (and evaluated at least in part based on my ability to) argue or engage in vigorous and spontaneous debate about abstract concepts without time for reflection. I forced myself into 2L and 3L classes I thought I needed to take because everyone else was clamoring to enroll in them. In retrospect, I should have pursued more writing and reflection-oriented classes and sought out more courses that fostered my authentic educational, intellectual, and personal development.

I wish someone in legal education had said to me—out loud—that grades do not define our law school journey or our long-term career trajectory. *It's time to say it out loud.* Yes, the gatekeepers of some traditional markers of "success" in law school and some employment decision makers use grades as a selection mechanism. But we don't need to buy into or continue perpetuating that limiting construct. In fact, we can reject it. We can insist upon a more holistic and 360-degree evaluation of our ability to contribute in legal arenas. As a 1L, I judged myself so harshly about those two less-than-ideal Criminal Law and Constitutional Law grades that I considered myself unworthy of certain law school groups and postgraduation jobs. I was wrong. I brought a lot to the table beyond grades: keen listening, creative problem solving, a passion for legal writing, a fierce work ethic, a collaborative mindset. I wasted a lot of time in school treating myself like I didn't belong.

Together, in this book, we will embark on an adventure of self-discovery, to investigate how we learn and thrive as *individuals*, and how we can help each other do so. As my favorite band sings, "We're one but we're not the same. We get to carry each other."[20]

After my successful 1L summer associate job, the firm invited me back for my 2L summer. I ended up working at that firm for six years after graduation. I was very cerebrally fulfilled and happy in my work for *most* of those years, minus some major life stressors in working for a particularly hot-tempered partner and trying, and ultimately failing, to sustain my post-law-school marriage to my long-term college boyfriend—my most formative relationship, which lasted 12 years. Eventually, my marriage imploded. The end was (mostly) my fault. Devastated and adrift, I quit my job (a year shy of my partnership vote), left everything I knew and loved, and moved to New York to start over.

Manhattan kicked me around like a Hacky Sack for a bit (its version of tough love for many newcomers). I tried to adjust to big city life, my stomach perpetually tied in a pretzel knot of regret and shame. Needing money, I landed a BigLaw job and a snazzy office in Tower Two of the World Trade Center. Shellshocked by grief as I continued to navigate the aftermath of my divorce amid the chaos of New York, I spent many dazed hours staring out the thin windows of my WTC office, fighting back tears and flinching every time I heard my supervising partner yelling into his speakerphone in the office next door. Nearly a year into that job, I took what I thought was going to be a brief leave of absence to clear my muddled head. I flew to Greece for a mini-vacation and was traveling on a connecting flight home from Frankfurt when the pilot diverted our plane to Gander, Newfoundland, in Canada.

9/11 happened during my flight.

Canadians fed, clothed, and took care of me—and 6,000 other stranded travelers—for five days. I slept in borrowed clothes on the floor of a middle school classroom. Ultimately, Lufthansa flew my fellow passengers and me back to Germany because the airspace between Canada and the United States was still closed. I landed in Frankfurt, ate a McDonald's cheeseburger and fries at the airport with two guys on my plane, turned around, and boarded the first flight back home. My law firm—extremely lucky not to have anyone perish that awful day—relocated to midtown and tried to recover financially and emotionally. I never went back to that job.

I took a few months off to process the officiality of my divorce, the trauma of 9/11, and the realization that my deep sadness over leaving my marriage, which culminated in me stepping away from my law firm work to try to heal, had kept me out of the towers that day.

I began treating myself like a bohemian New York writer. I stayed up late obsessively watching CNN for news coverage about Osama bin Laden, then wrote till 2:00 or 3:00 a.m. I penned cathartic reflections about the demise of my relationship, but also started writing chapters of my first law book, a nuts-and-bolts guide for junior attorneys about civil procedure and federal litigation. I slept as late as possible, took walks or roller skated by the Hudson River, and wrote all afternoon.

My savings dwindling again, I dove back into the law firm world and joined a small boutique litigation firm as a brief-writer—my ideal lawyering role.

One of the numerous life lessons I've learned through my circuitous employment journey is that grades are not the end-all-be-all predictors of "success." My grades did not hold me back from moving to New York at the age of thirty, starting over, and landing a job in BigLaw. Nor did they hold me back from switching firms again, and ultimately transitioning from law practice to legal academia. I've taught for 13 years at three law schools. I direct a Legal Writing Program. I received tenure a month before I turned fifty. I have published a plethora of law-related articles. This is my seventh book. I promise you: You do not need to have a perfect law school GPA and be on law review or the moot court team to be a "success" in our profession.

My point is: We must insist on a new (inclusive) definition of "success" in law school. If we are doing the hard work and are committed to our studies and to ensuring we can ethically represent our future clients, we deserve to be here. Our LSAT score does not permanently define us. Neither do our grades. Even if we encounter disappointments in these markers (and we are allowed to be bummed out about them), we have the power to refuse to let them dictate our future. If we want to work in BigLaw, or join an in-house counsel team, or do a judicial clerkship, or work in public interest or for a particular government agency, or switch practice areas entirely, we absolutely can do it. We just need to take control over our career paths, and acknowledge that some opportunities might take us longer than others to land. So what? We'll get there eventually.

To nurture my creative spirit and multiple dimensions of my well-being, I'm a big devotee of two practices designed by author Julia Cameron and described in her life-changing book, *The Artist's Way*:[21]

- **Morning Pages**: three pages of long-hand, unedited journaling every morning to clear out brain clutter
- **Artist Dates**: weekly adventures to rouse our inner artist, such as museum visits, quests to find cool street art, or unscripted playtime with tools like paints or a disposable camera

Before the pandemic, I took myself on an Artist Date to see the musical *Jagged Little Pill* on Broadway, inspired by Alanis Morissette's music. Scoring a cheap, last-minute ticket, I sat in the front row of the theater so close to the stage, I could see the actors' eyes sparkle. During the show, I heard a song I don't think I previously knew. The lyrics pushed me to reframe that memory of receiving my 1L grades: "That I would be good even if I got the thumbs down."[22] I was good then, even though I didn't feel like it, and I'm good now. *We* are good.

LET'S PULL THE PLUG ON BULLYING AND INCIVILITY

When I started my full-time job as a 24-year-old, first-year associate at my Virginia law firm after graduating from law school and taking and passing the bar exam, I was eager and excited. I had married my long-term college boyfriend a few months earlier. I drove to work on the Washington, D.C. beltway in my Jeep Cherokee, dressed in cute pastel suits with short skirts (inspired by the television show *Ally McBeal*). I decorated my office with my University of Virginia diplomas and my bar admission certificate.

I loved spending hours in the firm's law library, turning the thin parchment pages of the burgundy case books, jotting notes from the loose-leaf binders containing the Code of Federal Regulations. When beckoned, I scurried to the partners' offices, furiously scribbling instructions for research assignments on yellow legal pads. I stayed late many evenings, handwriting drafts of memoranda and briefs, leaving them overnight for the word processing team to type. I'd arrive the next morning to find the printed pages on my chair for editing.

My first few years of practice, I felt important and valued. I experienced joy and zest in my work. Research and writing remained my forte. Two of the founding partners—both with powerful litigation personas softened by kindness and humor—left markups of my written work on my desk with notes like "Excellent!" and "Your writing stuns me!" Public speaking and confrontation still rattled me, but I was working on it.

While my fellow associates angled to take depositions and argue motions in court, I preferred quietly crafting and drafting arguments in my office. But the firm prodded all of us into the performance arena early. I flew to St. Louis to take my first deposition of an insurance claims adjuster. Though I had spent days fashioning strategic questions and fastidiously organizing folders of exhibits, I was nervous and felt like I had no idea what I was doing.

In response to our requests for production of documents, the insurance company had denied the existence of any claim evaluation manuals. In my deposition, a ferocious blush ravaging my cheeks, I read a question from my outline.

> Me: "Sir, do you have access to any claims adjuster manuals?"
> Claims Adjuster Deponent: "Sure, I have a ten-volume set on my desk. Want me to go get them?"

That was my first deposition "win."

As I moved up the associate ranks, the stakes of our cases intensified. As did the tempers of some of the people in charge. In the three law firms that employed me over the course of my career—the medium-sized boutique firm where I started, a BigLaw firm in Manhattan, and a small 10-lawyer firm—I learned a great deal, intellectually and strategically, from many lawyers with compassionate dispositions and integrity. But I also absorbed my share of verbal blows from other attorneys with nasty tempers, volatile personalities, and abusive streaks. One called me an adjective that begins with F and a noun that begins with C when I questioned one of his directives. I've dodged car keys, binder clips, staplers, and highlighters that others have hurled across conference rooms. I've been yelled at for trying to go home at night to tend to my crumbling marriage. Fellow associates, paralegals, court reporters, legal assistants, couriers, and I endured lots of screaming, swearing, and stomping when things didn't go particular lawyers' way. I've sat across deposition and negotiation tables from senior attorneys using aggressive body language, sarcasm, and rude dismissiveness to try to intimidate me (and others). They'd see me—young, female, inexperienced, my blush incontrovertible evidence of my nerves—and gear up for torment. *Game on,* the glint in their eyes conveyed.

Over the years, if ever I admitted this stuff got to me, the advice relayed to deal with such behavior was, "Toughen up. Grow a thicker skin." We collectively excused the day-to-day volatility. *They're eccentric rainmakers. They've just got strong personalities. They're results-driven. They're just under a lot of pressure. They're having marital problems.* Or we convinced ourselves that this was "zealous advocacy." This is what the clients expected.

For two decades, I thought I was just weak. That I needed to be tougher, louder, meaner. That I needed to mirror the behavior of those lawyers to be good at my job.

I wasn't weak. And I didn't need to be like them to be a good lawyer.

Sometimes I think about that young, hard-working, smart, quiet girl that got excited to put on her suit every day and eagerly dive into the next brief, the new case, the novel intellectual challenge. And I'm sad that so much joy and zest for lawyering were extinguished so early in her life and career because she didn't know how to stand up for herself and make all that manipulation and exploitation stop.

In this book, we're going to explore and cultivate our strengths, acknowledge and appreciate our worth, and learn how to stand up for ourselves and others (especially in Chapter 8 when we specifically discuss how to defuse bullies). Let's make our profession better. Borrowing from the great boxing champion Muhammad Ali, let's empower ourselves to stand tall and convey: "If you even dream of [bullying] me, you'd better wake up and apologize."

LET'S BE BETTER COMMUNICATORS

Law is a field of words, yet often lawyers are tragically poor communicators, listeners, and feedback providers. Our profession hinges upon effective conveyance of information, to and from clients, judges, jurors, colleagues, the public, and our counterparts on the other side of the deposition or negotiation table, but on many occasions, we fail to model productive dialogue with one another. Of course, some lawyers are excellent communicators. But as a community, we have vast room for growth.

As a young associate, I frequently (and perhaps mistakenly) believed I was expected to, more or less, read some of my supervising attorneys' minds regarding my assignments' scope and timeline. "Just get it done," often seemed to be the mandate, without much elaboration. I felt stupid asking clarifying questions, like I was annoying the busy partners with my insufficient knowledge base and lack of decision-making discernment. Further, while I loved writing—client opinion letters, contracts, briefs—my bosses would sometimes send drafts back to me with vague notations in the margins like, "beef up." *Um, how exactly? I've included all the beef I found, but ok.* In the early years of practice, I spent lots of time guessing which direction to take on a project, rather than amplifying my voice and asking concise but thoughtful queries that would have optimized the pace, and augmented the quality, of my work.

Another communication gap that, for me personally, took a greater toll was never knowing when it was okay to call it a day (or more accurately, a night) and go home. I constantly stressed out over whether, the moment I finally decided to extinguish my desk lamp and end my workday, a partner would stride into my office with an "urgent" project that allegedly needed to be completed by 9:00 a.m. Or if I at last planned a long-overdue vacation with my husband in the early years of my practice or in later years with friends, some "emergency" would arise in one of the firm's cases. In my experience over nearly two decades working in three law firms, communication about what situations or tasks were really exigent or pressing was not great. Everything seemed like a five-alarm fire. It wasn't.

Constructive feedback also is not the strong suit of some supervising attorneys. I once heard a law firm partner declare, "I'll never tell you what you are doing right. Your *job* is to do things right. I'll only tell you what you are doing wrong." Obviously, that type of feedback ethos is demoralizing and soul-depleting. Not in the slightest bit motivating or invigorating.

Feedback when intermittent strategic or logistical mistakes inevitably occurred in our complex area of practice, or when we received an adverse substantive result in a case, was even worse. Lots of yelling, throwing of objects, slamming of doors. I cringe even as I write this, thinking back to how many minutes of every day I braced myself waiting for the next barrage of fury over something that was often wildly beyond our control.

Communication among lawyers (and law professors) about differences of opinion over legal issues (for example, on social media) likewise could use some improvement. Conversations are often riddled with sarcasm and snark. Sometimes it feels like we are engaged in a battle of wit to see who can use the fanciest words to craft the subtlest yet harshest insult to someone's intelligence, writing style, or ideas. Yet we wrap ourselves in the veneer of "rigor" or "candor" to dismiss legitimate objections to such tone or alarm bells of potential harm. This kind of stuff chips away at our soul.

As a young lawyer, I did not know how to articulate what type of communication, direction, and feedback I needed as a learner of complex new subject matter, procedure, and strategy. So worried about disappointing or irritating the erratic partners, I kept legitimate questions corralled inside my head. Further, I did not know how to assert myself when behavior or speech toward me or others seemed unacceptable or not conducive to producing our best work product. I also lacked the strength to draw healthy boundaries when I ultimately needed to go home after billing a ridiculous number of hours in one day, or needed rest and recovery after going all-out for weeks or months in a series of depositions or trial prep. Instead, I thought my career had to be all-or-nothing. On multiple occasions, I chose *nothing*—leaving jobs instead of communicating what would have helped me (and possibly other associates) thrive.

We absolutely can enhance our communication skills without reducing the intellectual and substantive rigor of our profession. We can amplify our voices with authenticity and integrity. Together, in this book, we'll talk about how to engage in productive dialogue one on one and in groups. We'll learn a technique called active-constructive responding (ACR).[23] We'll also explore some cool methods of improving our listening and making space for others to express perspectives and ideas, such as "constructivist listening"[24] and perspective-giving and -taking.[25]

By enriching our communication skills as law students and lawyers, inevitably we will perform better individually and collectively. We will foster inclusive dialogue in which more voices are heard. And we will be able to assert what we need to thrive, not just today or tomorrow, but over a lifelong trajectory as healthy members of our profession.

LET'S MORE DEEPLY DEFINE THE MEANING OF "CHARACTER AND FITNESS" TO PRACTICE LAW

Over the years, many of my students have asked me to complete "character and fitness" affidavits or affirmations in support of their applications for admission to various state bars. Of course, I readily oblige. But each time I fill out the form, a question nags at me: In law school and practice, do we adequately pause to think and talk about what *character and fitness to practice law* truly means to us as individuals and as a community, or what it should or could mean? We check boxes and scurry through forms and paperwork, but are we devoting sufficient time—in law school and practice—cultivating layers of good character and nurturing different dimensions of fitness? What does it truly mean to have *character*? What does being *fit* really entail?

The pandemic evoked another question: Does our profession's continued reliance on the traditional bar exam as a rite of passage for purported intellectual *fitness* to practice law make sense?

Prior to the pandemic, I'd never been a bar exam abolitionist. I like rules and standards. I like studying. And I don't mind academic tests, even though standardized tests are not my jam. But the handling of the 2020 administration of the bar exam during the extraordinary circumstances of the pandemic jarred me out of complacency toward considering other viable pathways for ensuring intellectual readiness for the profession.

Let's face it: our profession bungled many of the logistics of the 2020 bar exam. Numerous graduating students experienced the trauma of extended pandemic lockdown in the spring, the completion of their final semester of law school isolated from their classmates and teachers, and postponement of graduation celebrations. Normally, after graduation, these future members of our profession would have entered a two-month period of intensified study for the bar exam. Bar prep courses are designed with this finite number of weeks in mind, appropriately pacing review and memorization of substantive rules, and scheduling practice multiple choice questions and essays, to maximize retention of knowledge. There is a science and pedagogy to this learning and studying process.

In 2020, on top of enduring the stress of health, financial, and other issues related to the pandemic, our graduates had to study for this monster test under a cloud of constantly shifting guidelines in many jurisdictions on when, where, or how it would occur.[26] Some states stuck to in-person July tests with questionable social distancing measures (at least according to Law Twitter). Other jurisdictions postponed the July test—at least one notifying students of rescheduling only a few days before the exam was to go forward—jerking students around on timing and information about in-person versus online administration. Some jurisdictions enforced seemingly absurd rules (chock full of explicit and implicit bias) to prevent cheating (camera surveillance for online tests; restrictions on feminine hygiene products in live tests). We didn't seem to learn much of a lesson the first time around either; electronic glitches during the July 2021 exam added yet another layer of unnecessary stress onto many test-takers.

Throughout the mayhem of 2020, bar prep counselors scrambled to adjust learning processes and timelines for memorization and practice tests to accommodate a prolonged study duration for students whose exams were postponed from July into the fall. Meanwhile, many graduates attempted to push forward in their daily study routines without the security of jobs, as some employment start dates were deferred and hiring cycles frozen.

A few jurisdictions, including Washington, D.C., Utah, Oregon, Washington, and Louisiana, embraced a one-time "diploma privilege" in light of the pandemic, granting permission for law school graduates to practice law *without* taking the bar exam, under particular guidelines such as completion of a certain number of hours of supervised practice.[27] Other states granted temporary permission for law school graduates to practice law under supervision of a licensed attorney, but did not eliminate the requirement of eventual bar passage.[28] Washington, D.C., Utah, Oregon, Washington, and Louisiana returned to requiring law school graduates to sit for the bar exam in 2021.

Some jurisdictions comprise exceptions to the national norm requiring bar passage. Wisconsin does not require state bar applicants to pass a bar exam, instead relying on academic qualifications and character and fitness assessments.[29] New Hampshire offers an honors program in which up to twenty-four bar applicants take simulation courses and submit a portfolio demonstrating acquisition of key lawyering competencies; a bar examiner follows each student's work over a two-year period, reviews the final portfolio, and certifies to the board of bar examiners that the student has completed the state bar's admission requirements.[30] In early 2021, the California Supreme Court approved a plan to permit bar-takers who *narrowly failed* the bar exam to apply for admission to the bar after performing 300 hours of supervised legal practice, without retaking the test.[31]

In 2021, Oregon launched a task force to explore alternatives to the bar exam, including development of an "experiential pathway" for law students who study in-state, and a supervised practice pathway for out-of-state students.[32] In early 2022, the Oregon Supreme Court unanimously voted to approve the proposal for alternative pathways, and directed the Oregon Board of Bar Examiners to establish new committees to develop implementation concepts and plans.[33] Minnesota also announced a study of potential new pathways into the profession by 2026 (the year that changes to the bar exam are expected to go into effect).[34]

I'll let others debate the merits of scrapping the bar exam altogether (or flesh out the nuances of providing alternative routes to practice), but in the meantime, I suggest we think more deeply about what it really means for us—as law students and lawyers—to have the appropriate *character* and *fitness* to practice law. Our profession seems to regard character and fitness as assets we either inherently have or don't have at a particular point in time (i.e., like checking a box on a form). We don't seem to view character as something we can define, analyze, study, and *develop* in law school and shape further in practice as our work increases in complexity and we encounter novel challenges.

We also could stand to adjust our view of fitness. Fitness is a multi-dimensional lifelong pursuit. Athletes and performers work on their fitness constantly, from myriad angles; we can, and should, as well.

Let's look at some state bars' definitions of character. New York vaguely requires each bar applicant to be "a person of good moral character and possesses the general fitness requisite for an attorney and counselor-at-law."[35] Jurisdictions such as Alabama, Arkansas, and the District of Columbia do not seem to precisely define "character" either. In 1985, Professor Deborah L. Rhode published an article in *The Yale Law Journal* characterizing historical character and fitness standards this way: "The prevailing assumption appeared to be that bar standards were self-evident; if the applicant had a character and fitness problem he 'should know it.'"[36] California and Washington add *some* details, referring to "good moral character" as including "qualities of honesty, fairness, candor, trustworthiness, observance of fiduciary responsibility, respect for and obedience to the law, and respect for the rights of others and the judicial process."[37] Other states focus instead on character *deficiencies*, listing grounds for *exclusion* from bar membership. In fact, Texas states that the purpose of the "good moral character" requirement is to *exclude* people from the profession who are likely to cause injury to clients, obstruct justice, or violate rules of professional conduct.[38] Kentucky and Vermont likewise reiterate the *exclusionary* purpose of the moral character requirement.

Um, OK. But in law school and practice training (and perhaps also in pre-law programs at colleges and universities), what if instead of leaping to exclusion and barriers to entry, we talked more openly about how to *cultivate* traits of character and fitness in the context of our complex legal arena—where we often are confronted with ethical and moral challenges that test even the strongest character or the most "fit"? How about we consider how to *enrich* the layers of our character as law students and lawyers so we can be sure to exercise good judgment and make wise decisions, especially when the "right" choice is not 100% clear?

We all know we should strive to be good people, especially when others are entrusting their lives, businesses, and futures to us. And one would hope that such "goodness" would come naturally. But I think we can deepen our understanding of how to sculpt our character and how to augment our fitness—for both life and lawyering.

For context, let's peer back at the historical origins of the concept of evaluating aspiring attorneys' character and fitness to practice law prior to their admission to the profession.

Derek Davis, former Executive Director of Harvard Law School's Center on the Legal Profession, wrote a helpful article contextualizing the backstory of the profession's current character and fitness requisite for legal practice, traceable to the late eighteenth century.[39] (Rhode's *Yale Law Journal* article provides an eye-opening, detailed historical account.[40]) Reacting to public outcry against lawyers' "blood-sucking practices,"[41] jurisdictions began imposing character and fitness requirements; Massachusetts apparently mandated references from ministers![42] Various state bars began evaluating applicants' "virtues" (such as honesty) and individuals' life experiences (like criminal misdeeds) that allegedly could call one's character into question.[43]

In 1878, seventy-five lawyers from twenty states and the District of Columbia established the American Bar Association.[44] One of the association's early mandates was to formalize professional standards and criteria for occupational competence.[45] By the early twentieth century, many states had instituted bar examination boards.[46] The National Conference of Bar Examiners formed in 1930.[47]

Today, every state bar applies some version of a character and fitness standard.[48] Proponents of the standard offer two reasons for its existence: (1) fostering "a sense of professionalism," qualifying the legal profession "as a distinct field of professional conduct," and (2) protecting the public.[49] Character and fitness questionnaires typically inquire into applicants' educational history, job history, criminal record, financial record, military record, litigation history, and health—though these combinations vary from state to state.[50] Many states require character references in addition to the applicant's character and fitness questionnaire or affidavit.[51] In addition to such documentation, in forty-eight states, bar applicants must pass the Multistate Professional Responsibility Exam, demonstrating the requisite knowledge of the Model Rules of Professional Conduct.[52]

In Rhode's 1985 article, she spotlighted three realities:

- "Throughout its history, the moral fitness requirement has functioned primarily as a cultural showpiece. In that role, it has excommunicated a diverse and changing community, variously defined to include not only former felons, but women, minorities, adulterers, radicals, and bankrupts."[53]
- "Although the number of applicants formally denied admission has always been quite small, the number deterred, delayed, or harassed has been more substantial."[54]

- "We have developed neither a coherent concept of professional character nor effective procedures to predict it. Rather, we have maintained a licensing ritual that too often has debased the ideals it seeks to sustain."[55]

Has much changed since 1985?

In recent years, critics have questioned the propriety of intrusive questions in character and fitness forms about a bar applicant's mental health diagnosis and treatment, addiction counseling, debt load, social media activity, and immigration status.[56] Some jurisdictions (including Arizona, California, Connecticut, Illinois, Massachusetts, Michigan, Mississippi, New York, New Hampshire, Virginia, and Washington) have led the way toward removing or substantially altering questions about applicants' mental health on the character and fitness forms.[57]

Historians recount how "the character and fitness requirement arose out of a [perceived] need to defend the integrity of the profession and protect the public from substandard practitioners."[58] To me though, this stance sounds, well, *defensive* and *deficit-focused.* What if we flip this around now and focus our attention on positive action and strengths—identifying good character traits that we aspire to cultivate in members of our profession, then teaching law students and lawyers how to build and develop those traits, plus spot and champion them in others?

Six months into the pandemic, I began gearing up for a five-day immersive orientation week launching the coursework for my Master of Applied Positive Psychology (MAPP) degree at the University of Pennsylvania—to be administered remotely for the first time in the history of the program. Two of my assigned foundational MAPP readings nudged me to begin thinking about lawyers' character and fitness in a different way. The first: an excerpt from *The Autobiography of Benjamin Franklin.*[59] In the passage, Franklin described a personal development project. He started by listing 13 virtues, and then constructed a system for cultivating one virtue at a time before moving on to the next one. Keeping in mind that he wrote this list in the 1700s, these are the virtues he aspired to nourish:[60]

- Temperance: exercising moderation in eating and drinking
- Silence: speaking only when necessary to bestow a benefit; avoiding trivial dialogue (*my introverted self perked up at this one!*)

- Order: organizing objects and time well
- Resolution: having a solid plan and following through
- Frugality: spending money with the intention of doing good; avoiding waste
- Industry: being efficient
- Sincerity: speaking without deceit
- Justice: avoiding doing harm or withholding aid to others
- Moderation: avoiding extremes
- Cleanliness: exercising good hygiene in body, clothing, and home
- Tranquility: avoiding overreacting to common or routine happenings
- Chastity: engaging in intimacy only with healthy intent and purpose for self and others
- Humility: mirroring the behavior of Socrates (*another of my personal favorites!*)

Franklin resolved to attend to one virtue at a time, one per week for 13 weeks, then start again at the beginning of his list.[61] He kept a chart, tracking positive moments and identifying areas he wished to improve. Each morning, he asked himself, "What good shall I do this day?"[62] In the evenings, he reflected, "What good have I done today?"[63] Later musing on his system, he conceded that he obviously never achieved the impossible goal of "perfection," but he enjoyed the endeavor of working on himself.[64] In the end, he emphasized, in particular, that he was proud of how he had nurtured the virtue of *humility*.[65]

The second MAPP reading that seemed to jump up and down in a tantrum on my couch, demanding attention, was an excerpt from Plato's *Apology* about Socrates's trial.[66] Prosecutors had charged Socrates with two offenses: (1) allegedly corrupting the youth of Athens by challenging them to ask and answer lots of questions about life, and (2) failing to show enough reverence to the Greek gods. In my *Introverted Lawyer* book, I confessed that I owed Socrates an apology. For two decades, I had been mad at him for inventing the Socratic method—at least the way I understood it (and still often see it used) in law school. When I read the book *Socrates Café* by Christopher Phillips though, I changed my mind;[67] I wished I could have had Socrates as a friend. I liked discovering that his motto was "know thyself"—a phrase inscribed on the entrance to the Temple of Apollo in Delphi, Greece. Socrates is basically the brand ambassador for "intellectual humility." He never thought of himself as, or pretended to be, the smartest guy in the room. Instead, he roamed the streets and markets of Athens asking questions, seeking to learn more about himself and inspire others (including youthful citizens) to do the same.

In the excerpt from Plato's *Apology* we read for MAPP, Socrates declared, "I have no wisdom, small or great."[68] He emphasized that, unlike many of the politicians, poets, and artisans he queried in his daily conversations, "I neither know nor think that I know."[69] Chucking ego out the window, he didn't pretend to be omniscient or brilliant. Instead, he was self-aware enough to decide and assert that his purpose in life was to seek "to persuade every man among [us] that he must look to himself, and seek virtue and wisdom."[70] Further, rather than focusing on the negative, he highlighted how we can effect positive change: "The easiest and noblest way is not to be crushing others, but to be improving [our]selves."[71]

Wow. *Not to be crushing others.*

Motivated by Ben Franklin and Socrates, I have an aspiration. What if we adjust our traditional ways of assessing law students' and aspiring attorneys' character and fitness to practice law? What if we stop regarding the concepts as measurable finitely at one point in time—when we apply to law school, or when we apply to be members of state bars—and instead regard character and fitness as something we can teach, learn, nurture, and hone—in ourselves and one another. Like Franklin and Socrates. Our current practice seems to focus on rooting out character "flaws" as perceived barriers to entry to the profession: past mistakes, financial missteps, struggles with mental and emotional health perhaps due to illness or difficult life events like divorce or loss. Obviously, some truly egregious issues could warrant denial of admission. But, in general, what if we focus energy on identifying and then cultivating *positive* character traits—starting from the moment we apply to law school (or even in pre-law programs), as we begin our studies, continuing through each year of our legal education, and again as we transition to practice, and on an ongoing basis thereafter, for years and decades of our professional arc?

Throughout this book, together we'll explore multiple dimensions of our character and fitness to practice law. We can *teach* and *learn* character in the context of living and lawyering. Additionally, we can redefine fitness, and then develop lawyering fitness regimens that will help us thrive—as individuals and lawyering communities—not just today but for decades to come.

REDEFINING FITNESS: LET'S TREAT OURSELVES LIKE SCHOLAR-ATHLETES OR SCHOLAR-PERFORMERS

The Oxford English Dictionary defines *fitness* in a few ways:[72]

- "the condition of being physically fit and healthy"
- "the quality of being suitable to fulfill a particular role or task"
- "an organism's ability to survive . . . in a particular environment"

Growing up, I never thought of myself as an athlete.[73] I dreaded gym class. I still have nightmares about the Presidential Physical Fitness Test: those sit-ups, that flexed arm hang, the 600-yard dash. During my undergraduate and law school years, I reluctantly played intramural softball, cajoled onto the field by enthusiastic classmates. Skittish after taking a foul ball to the chin, I flinched every time anyone hurled the ball toward me. Nonetheless, I always rather envied the students known as scholar-athletes—those who excelled in class and on the field.

Sports and fitness seeped into my life slowly. At my first law firm, partners and associates often jogged outdoors together during lunch. I remember gasping for air running up a hill while updating a partner on the status of our latest discovery requests. We worked hard, billed copious hours, and clocked many miles. Over the past two decades, I edged into the New York City spinning craze. Now, I run a few times a week in a nearby park and train twice a week with my boxing coach, Lou. During the pandemic, I ordered and assembled an Everlast stand-up boxing bag in my apartment. Now, on rainy days, I punch it to clear my head and work up a sweat. As I wrap my knuckles in stretchy fabric and slide my boxing gloves onto my hands, I finally feel like a "real" athlete. When I work out, and for hours thereafter, I feel strong, motivated, formidable, and healthy—mentally, physically, and emotionally. And it's gotten me thinking. What if I had treated myself like a "real" scholar-athlete (or scholar-performer) when I was a stressed-out, anxious, and fearful junior attorney?

Athletes and performers (musicians, singers, dancers, actors) do not just focus on the talent or skill that draws glory on the field or the stage, such as the ability to throw, catch, hit, or kick a ball; the facility to execute a triple flip off a balance beam or on the ice; or the capacity to generate that perfect reverberating guitar echo or hold that powerfully endless note of a song. Real athletes and performers—and their employers and coaches—attend to numerous other facets affecting individual and team performance. These drivers include emotions such as fear, anxiety, and self-doubt; challenges like ego or temper; the realistic need for rest and recovery; the ability to process feedback and critique; and the capacity to rebound from losses and mistakes.

Let's think for a moment about the six dimensions of lawyer well-being identified in the National Task Force's report: occupational, intellectual, emotional, spiritual, social, and physical.[74] When I reflect on my experiences at three law firms over two decades in law practice, I recall attending to my *occupational* and *intellectual* growth. On the occupational side, I loved the legal research and writing aspects of my job and developing as a writer and problem-solver. I loved poring over factual documents, analyzing statutory rules, finding case law, and crafting persuasive arguments to resolve our clients' conflicts. I enjoyed pushing myself to grow as an effective networker and business developer, albeit an introverted one.

On the intellectual side, I thrived while seeking to develop a deeper understanding of the nuances of the doctrine and rules in my area of practice: construction law. Every case required us to learn something new about complex contractual relationships, engineering and architectural designs, even the effects of different soils beneath building foundations. I realize, however, that I routinely neglected the physical, emotional, spiritual, and social aspects of myself. Notwithstanding the lunchtime 5Ks at my first firm, my body, brain, mind, and spirit fell into seriously bad shape.

What if we could up our collective game, improve our output, exceed our benchmarks, *and* enjoy multi-decade legal careers by treating ourselves like scholar-athletes or scholar-performers? What would happen if we made a conscious effort as individuals and as a legal community to tend to more fitness dimensions than just our occupational and intellectual selves?

My dad was an avid Chicago Bulls basketball fan when Phil Jackson was the team's coach. I remember hearing about how Jackson integrated mental, emotional, and spiritual dimensions into his coaching to get the best out of his team—as individuals and as a cohesive unit. Pro golfers such as Tiger Woods have worked with mental coaches, as have Olympic gymnasts, including Simone Biles. Adam Clayton, bass player for the band U2, has shared in interviews that his pre-performance routine involves exercise and clearing his head. He is known to visit art galleries in cities where the band is playing—nurturing his cultural and artistic dimensions. We don't seem to stigmatize athletes and performers for attending to their mental, physical, emotional, artistic, creative, or spiritual health. (Indeed, high-profile athletes like gymnast Simone Biles, tennis player Naomi Osaka, and swimmer Michael Phelps have generated initial media buzz and some critique by those who misunderstood or lacked empathy for what they were going through, but thereafter have been held up as models of authentic strength for being transparent about mental health issues.) Unfortunately, our profession has (at least in the past) stigmatized law students and lawyers who have needed or asked for help in some of these dimensions. Let's end that.

As lawyers, we are performers, and frankly, we are athletes in a sense. We perform difficult and complex tasks, activities, maneuvers, and interpersonal dances every day. Our jobs can be cognitively, mentally, emotionally, spiritually, and physically taxing. Instead of regarding a desire to tend to these layers of ourselves as a "weakness," let's consider what occupational and intellectual powerhouses we all could be if we cultivated our physical, emotional, cognitive, spiritual, and social health.

Business as usual in our profession isn't working as well as it could—from a health and well-being perspective at least. Let's shake things up. Let's add new dimensions to our training, coaching, development, and growth. Let's try business as *unusual.* Let's experiment with perceived contrasts and juxtapositions. NFL athletes Steve McLendon and Lynn Swann took ballet lessons to become better football players. Boxer Vasyl Lomachenko credits traditional Ukrainian dance lessons for his fierce footwork. A few months ago, my boxing trainer Lou used salsa music to teach me how to find a cadence in my punches. He urged, "Slow down. Be patient. Listen. Feel and trust your own rhythm." (A couple weeks later, I applied that same advice in a negotiation and was wildly surprised by the result.)

Let's break the stereotype model of what "success" looks like in our profession. Let's acknowledge the unique combination of strengths that each of us brings to the profession and also brainstorm imaginative solutions to help individuals work through periodic personal challenges. When pro golfers suddenly develop the "yips" in their putting, do their managers yell, "Just fix it!"? No, they get a putting coach and work on mechanics, routine, breathing, focus, and trust. Did Simone Biles's coaches chide, "Just do it!" when she developed a case of the "twisties" and lost a sense of where she was in the air during high-flying events like the uneven bars and vault during the 2021 Olympics? No. She took a (very public) pause (exhibiting supreme class in staying and cheering on her teammates), regained her equilibrium, and won a bronze medal on the balance beam. Instead of telling anxious or fearful junior lawyers to "Just get confident!" or admonishing struggling public speakers or legal writers to "Just do it better!" let's contemplate nontraditional resources to work through challenges and draw out untapped strengths in multiple personal dimensions.

Dr. Andrew George Wood, a sports psychologist in the United Kingdom, wrote an article organizing stressors affecting athletes into helpful categories; Dr. Wood's frameworks are readily analogizable to stressors we experience as law students and lawyers. Dr. Wood identified three sets of stressors that athletes encounter: competitive, organizational, and personal.[75]

Competitive stressors include training for competition (including the need to practice, hone, and execute specific techniques), pressure to win or succeed, and dealing with opponents.[76]

Organizational stressors affecting athletes' performance include:

- Training environments
- Conflict and ambiguity in roles in sports organizations
- Cultural and political issues affecting organizational structure and climate
- Lack of social support in interpersonal relationships
- Career and performance development issues such as insecurity of position and income[77]

Additionally, Dr. Wood described how lifestyle and financial pressures—home life, relationships, fiscal responsibilities—constitute **personal** stressors that can affect athletes' performance.[78] Dr. Wood recommended that athletes (and coaches) first *understand* these different stressors and then *adopt* effective strategies for addressing each issue during training. Repeatedly implementing such strategies in training, athletes can learn to trust their training in performance moments.

Dr. Wood further demarcated three categories of *stress responses*:[79]

- **Physiological**: our heart rate hastens, we sweat, our muscles tense, our breathing becomes labored
- **Cognitive**: we perceive stimuli around us, we dig into the archives of our memories, we make decisions
- **Emotional**: we experience emotions like fear, anger, and resistance or exhilaration, joy, and empowerment

Stressors	Stress Responses
• Competitive • Organizational • Personal	• Physiological • Cognitive • Emotional

These frameworks for understanding different types of stressors that affect athletes, and natural responses thereto, are helpful for us as law students and lawyers. As part of developing our *fitness* to practice law, we can commit to enhancing our ability to recognize different types of *stress triggers* (competitive, organizational, personal) and our automatic stress *reactions* (physical, mental, emotional). We can establish training systems in which we bolster multiple performance dimensions—not just our intellectual or occupational domains. Like athletes and performers, we can tweak and adjust our training regimens, tailoring them to our individual needs and goals. Then, ultimately, when we step into performance arenas and encounter these stressors, we can pause, acknowledge our training, *trust* our training, and activate routines and rituals that will fuel our success. Conversely, if we remain blind to our stress triggers and habitual physical, mental, and emotional stress responses, or don't learn how to trust our training, we might vault into, and become locked in, a state of overwhelm; our performance will suffer.

We don't need to be elite athletes, famous rock stars, or CEOs to treat ourselves (and one another) like scholar-performers. We can challenge and inspire each other to attend to multiple fitness dimensions on a daily, weekly, or monthly basis. Let's notice the effects that our investment in different well-being domains have on our lawyering performance moments—in presentations, negotiations, depositions, oral arguments, conflicts, collaborations, moments of faltering, and ultimate triumphs.

This endeavor does not have to be expensive or time-consuming. It does have to be deliberate, intentional, and inclusive—like Ben Franklin's and Socrates's approaches. By collectively insisting on a more dimensional approach to development and performance, we can flourish as individuals and a community. As Penn MAPP graduate Anne Brafford points out in her helpful Well-Being Toolkit for Lawyers and Legal Employers, "Well-being is a team sport."[80]

A CALL TO ACTION

As we hopefully begin to descend the mountain of this pandemic, dust ourselves off, and assess where we are as a profession and a society, let's reimagine ourselves. Let's let go of past practices and jettison lazy messages like "but, this is the way we've always done it." Let's start fresh. Let's rethink. Let's build a healthier, happier, better functioning, more civil profession. As we embark on this journey through this book together, here are some starter thoughts:

- Let's (inclusively) redefine what it means—to us as individuals and a community—to have the requisite *character* to practice law.

- Let's channel Socrates's mantra to "know ourselves," get to know our character strengths, discover how to cultivate our character, and learn how to spot and value strengths in others (that may be different from our own).
- Let's contemplate physical, mental, emotional, spiritual, social, occupational, and intellectual dimensions of *fitness* to practice law.
- Let's begin to regard ourselves as scholar-athletes or scholar-performers, understanding that—like athletes and performers—we must tend to multiple dimensions of well-being rather than just focusing on the "skill or talent" that brings us glory in the legal arena.

This pandemic has unearthed many truths, including that we cannot afford to take health (in any form) for granted. I'm excited to team up with you as we rediscover and reshape ourselves and our profession. Let's carry each other.

> *I am not reinventing myself. I am going through the layers and revealing myself. I am on a journey, an adventure that's constantly changing shape.*
>
> Madonna

"Know Thyself" Reflection

COAXING, AND COACHING, OUR INNER ATHLETE OR PERFORMER

Let's heed Socrates's advice a bit and get to know ourselves. Do you have a favorite athlete? Or if sports aren't your thing, which performers do you admire? Is there a singer, an actor, a musician, or a dancer you like a lot? Who do you follow on Instagram, perhaps for inspiration?

As you already know (and I know this will induce a few eye-rolls . . . please bear with me), I'm obsessed with the Irish band U2, and I also take boxing lessons. And I was a late bloomer on both counts.

All the cool girls in my high school in the late 1980s milled the hallways in R.E.M. and U2 t-shirts. I was unequivocally *not* part of their in-crowd. While U2 music got me through two rough relationship splits in my twenties and thirties, I did not see the band live until 2009. It was my first year teaching legal writing at a California law school. Appalled that I had never been to a U2 concert, a law professor colleague took me to my first show at the Rose Bowl in Los Angeles. While my coolly composed friend swayed serenely back and forth to each song, I felt like I'd been struck by lightning. That show electrified every nerve ending in my body.

Two years later, I moved back across country to New York and began following a U2 cover band called Unforgettable Fire around the city. At their gigs in small venues, I'd worm my way close to the stage. If I squinted my eyes enough, fake Bono looked like the real one, and the drummer resembled Larry Mullen, Jr. Afterward, I'd wend my way home in lower Manhattan, my ears ringing after two hours of jumping up and down next to thundering speakers.

In 2015, weary of presidential election drama and craving adventure, I skipped Thanksgiving and flew to Ireland for the first time, clutching an overpriced resale ticket to U2's iNNOCENCE + eXPERIENCE tour at Dublin's 3Arena. That weekend, on a U2-themed walking tour (yes, I went *all in*), I met two American girls—Michele and Renee—who have been attending shows together for decades since college in Louisiana. Arm-in-arm, we belted out lyrics at two nights of concerts in Dublin. Over three days, I met and bonded with fans from all over the world. Since then, I have seen U2 play more than twenty-five times—in five U.S. cities and five foreign countries. It's a layer of my life and persona that makes me happy and inspires me. Michelle, Renee, and I can artfully wedge a U2 reference into any mundane conversation. We could be chatting about politics, bagels, coronavirus vaccines, or Himalayan sea salt, and one of us will interject, "Hey, circling back to the band for a sec, remember that time Bono improvised a lyric and . . ."

Why am I telling you this?

Because as law students and lawyers, we are performers too. We train in school and in practice, we perform, and then we continue honing our training. I find that, through observing how performers I admire approach their art and craft, I learn how to give myself higher *regard* in my own work. This past February, I enrolled in my friend Sarah's online workshop on somatic (bodily) awareness as exploratory research for some of the physical aspects of well-being that we'll explore later in this book (in Chapter 5). In the first session, Sarah led us through a body scan. While we noted sensations up and down our physical frames, she asked us to give ourselves *regard,* which she defined as "one of the most healing things we can offer ourselves; it's saying to ourselves, *I see you.*" I like the word *regard.*

In 2015, during U2's iNNOCENCE + eXPERIENCE tour, each time Bono introduced a song called *Iris*, he first gave *regard* to his mother Iris who died when Bono was fourteen. Each night during that tour, Bono whispered into his microphone, "She left me an *artist.*" Like many phrases Bono utters, those five words were like the tip of a match slowly scraping along the striker of a matchbook, ultimately igniting a fire in me. An urgent boost of energy to give myself regard as an artist. To untangle my fear. To be my own muse.

Bono's homage to his mother paving the way for him to identify as an artist echoes the band's song lyric: *Iris standing in the hall. She tells me I can do it all. . . . Don't fear the world. It isn't there.*

Don't fear the world. I wish someone had told me that.

If I ever encounter Bono again when he's not on stage (he was mere feet away from me *twice* but a few more gregarious fans elbowed me out of the way to garner his attention), I want to tell him, "Thank *you* for making *me* an artist." In observing *his* artistry, I feel empowered to create my own art.

In fact, I admire all four members of U2 for the way they cultivate their multi-dimensional personas. Of course, I love their music. Their lyrics etch like graffiti into the folds of my memory. I get goosebumps listening to some of their older songs, hearing the reverberation of The Edge's fingers sliding along his guitar strings. Few things parallel the elation I feel while jumping up and down at a U2 concert somewhere in the world, surrounded by strangers from multiple continents, watching as the band members exchange grins and laughter. These four guys have worked together literally for 45 years; Bono refers to the band as their "first and only job" since they were teenagers. Grown men now, their love and respect for each other abound on stage. In a brilliant prescient financial maneuver, they decided from the beginning to split all earnings equally. They demonstrate how much they value their families and spouses, often featuring their kids on album covers and acknowledging their wives in the audience.

The four guys give back to humanity—in countless individual and collective ways. Bono cofounded ONE (a global movement to extinguish poverty), and (RED) to end HIV/AIDS. Bass player Adam Clayton works with musicians and artists in addiction recovery. Early in the pandemic, the guys donated €10 million to COVID-19 relief efforts and another $1.5 million toward workers in the live music industry facing pandemic-related economic hardships. Drummer Larry Mullen, Jr. donated $100,000 to the Navajo & Hopi Families COVID-19 Relief Fund. Guitarist The Edge spearheads environmental causes. In each show, the band highlights global humanitarian missions and human rights initiatives. They don't take their fame and wealth for granted. At the end of each show, Bono always expresses gratitude to the audience, saying, "Thank you for giving us a great life."

I also love how the four guys nurture creative pursuits outside of music. Bono loves to create art. He sketches human figures, scribbling lyrics, quotes, and poems around the faces. (Some fans sport tattoos of Bono's doodles.) I mentioned earlier how Adam visits art galleries before gigs in the cities where the band is touring. Larry has explored acting, starring in the 2011 film *Man on the Train.* The Edge has tried (with much opposition and criticism) to design and develop a community of eco-friendly homes in California. I'm intrigued by how the guys' cultivation of other interpersonal dimensions has enhanced their music—their primary art form and occupation.

What if, as law students and lawyers, we did something similar?

Until I wrote *The Introverted Lawyer,* I had always mostly done the safe thing (except my divorce and moving to New York City when I was nearly broke, both of which were wildly unplotted and scary life decisions). For the bulk of my life, I followed the path I thought I was supposed to take. I trudged through law school, landed the law firm job(s), climbed the partnership track, jumped through performance hoops, tried to please my bosses . . . and for what exactly? I did the safe thing while never actually feeling safe. I would have been a much more profoundly impactful lawyer much earlier if I had recognized and honored my inner artist—the writer and creator in me who is not afraid to be adventurous and exploratory in getting to know myself.

So, let's take a moment right now and ponder, *Is there a favorite musician, singer, actor, dancer, or athlete who inspires you to tap into your (perhaps undiscovered) authentic persona?* Who motivates you to be, or to discover, *you?*

I also love boxing. Growing up, I'd hear critics describe boxing as a brutish, thuggish sport, but I never saw it that way. I'd stay up late watching reruns of Muhammad Ali fights, enamored with the way he danced around the ring smiling at the world. I was fascinated by his poetic metaphors for boxing training and life. Other fighters intrigued me as well, the way they pulled themselves from nothing—no money, no stability, sometimes no shelter—and devoted every ounce of energy to becoming the best boxer they could be, studying the physics of angles, energy management, eye-hand coordination, patience. The sport is so much more than two people hitting each other. Fighters and trainers call it "the sweet science."

I visited the Muhammad Ali Center in Louisville, Kentucky. I began reading about Ali: his conversion to Islam; his name change from his birth name, Cassius Clay; his conscientious objection to the Vietnam War; his refusal to be drafted; the criminal charges levied against him for draft evasion. He was stripped of his boxing titles. He didn't fight for four years. But then he came back.

I admire his work ethic and his ability to stand up for what he believed. I also love how he cultivated his artistic and creative side. He wrote spoken word poetry. He painted. He dabbled in acting. He was a philanthropist and a humanitarian. Like many famous athletes, Ali's track record with women was not saintlike. But his efforts to motivate us to improve our society are indelible.

Like my obsession with U2, my close personal relationship with boxing solidified mid-life. In 2016, I started taking group boxing lessons in Brooklyn, signing up for a numbered heavy bag hanging from rafters in a dimly lit gym, punching with flimsy rented gloves until my knuckles bled. When my favorite trainer parted ways with that fitness studio, I followed him and started taking one-on-one lessons in an authentic downtown boxing club in the Tribeca neighborhood of Manhattan. In 2019, I started working with a new trainer, Lou. Training with Lou has changed my life.

Boxing training is the most physically difficult activity I have ever attempted. And I'm fanatical. I wish I had started training when I was in my twenties instead of my forties (and now my fifties). But hey, better late than never.

As I write this, I'm still avoiding indoor gyms in New York due to the pandemic. Lou meets me in a nearby park twice a week. He teaches me how to wrap my hands the right way so I can curl my fingers into a fist. He laces up my gloves and guides me through drills. As my glove hits his leather mitt with a satisfying *smack-crack,* he meticulously and patiently corrects my form. "Don't fall in love with the sound," he instructs. He teaches me proper body mechanics: straight jabs, hooks thrown from hips rather than elbows and shoulders, uppercuts tracking proper angles.

"Short steps, long punches. It might seem counterintuitive but good boxers don't pull away from a fight; they lean into it." Every training session with Lou doubles as a life lesson. Sweat pours down my steamy red face. My muscles scream. I gasp for air. And I am happy. Full of zest. And awe at life.

Lou treats me like a "real" fighter. I *am* a real fighter.

When Lou thinks I am ready to be pushed beyond "mitt work," he slides his own gloves on his hands—but intentionally backwards so he has less control and power—and we spar. I'm 5′4″ and he's 6′4″. He dances, bobs, and weaves—artfully—barely expending an ounce of energy yet causing all my punches to miss. I keep striving to connect my glove to his body. He senses panic in my widened eyes. He reminds me to breathe. He throws punches (lightly with his backwards gloves) and I experience what it's like to have a fist flying at my ribs. I strain for oxygen and realize I've been holding my breath again, a nervous habit . . . one that always has had the ability to trash all my performances, intellectual or physical.

My struggle to catch my breath routinely and quickly translates to fear. Whenever Lou reads terror in my eyes, he reminds me to return to a cadence of simply breathing. *In. Out. Trust my system. Trust my body.* When we trained indoors before the pandemic, he'd play salsa music or hip-hop to distract my racing brain with the simplicity of rhythm. Now when he senses I'm annoyed with myself, my inner critic ranting at my windedness or inability to grasp a new punch combo, he changes things up. He hands me an RMT® (Rotational Movement Training) rope, demonstrating how to wield it like a lasso. "Close your eyes. Don't force anything. Let the energy of the movement of your hips move the rope." I do close my eyes. As I swing the rope through the air, creating invisible infinity symbols and figure-eights, my stress and self-doubt and trepidation release into the New York ether.

The whole thing is brilliant, and I love every minute of it.

Boxing has added a layer to my persona that I like a whole lot. I used to not like myself very much.

There are many times in my current job as a law professor and presenter at legal conferences around the world when my public speaking fear (which I have worked really hard to wrangle through writing *The Introverted Lawyer* and *Untangling Fear*) commandeers my brain. But then I remind myself, I didn't die in a 90-minute boxing session yesterday in the park when it was 98 degrees outside and Lou was pressing me through round after round of punching, and my red face was drenched with sweat—so, I'm not going to die if I open my mouth and say something at a faculty meeting, even if I don't say it perfectly or someone criticizes me. Boxing trains my brain as much as it trains my body. It helps me realize that I am actually safe; there is no way Lou will let me run out of breath or have a heart attack. And when I realize I am safe, I can be my most daring.

So, let's do this. Think about an athlete or performer (singer, musician, actor, dancer, comedian, etc.) who you admire or who inspires you. Reminder: Athletes and performers do not just focus on the skill or talent that brings glory on the stage or in the arena. They cultivate their mental, physical, and emotional stamina (and other dimensions) to be able to handle a variety of situations. They also seek help from people who know more about those topics than they do. For instance, athletes and performers spend time thinking about, and ask for help with:

- Learning their physical, mental, and emotional mechanics.
- Developing individualized routines and rituals.
- Incrementally taking basic skills to more advanced levels.

- Processing and learning from mistakes.
- Managing feedback and criticism.
- Unpacking performance anxiety or stage fright.
- Carving out time for rest and recovery before the next performance.
- Figuring out their nutrition and sleep.

When gymnasts, skaters, or skiers fall, sometimes they need help getting over the fear toward getting out there and doing the same task again. When football or tennis players hurt themselves, they rehab their injuries, and then they untangle fear toward future harm. When musicians or dancers fall on or off the stage (U2's guitarist, The Edge, literally fell *off* a stage during the 2015 iNNOCENCE + eXPERIENCE tour), they get back up.

We do not tend to judge athletes and performers for seeking help in these realms. In fact, I think it's cool to read about the myriad dimensions these individuals work on daily, or throughout their training weeks. It's interesting (and inspiring) to learn about their everyday regimens. Choreographer Twyla Tharp wrote a book called *The Creative Habit: Learn It and Use It for Life* in which she describes her day-to-day mental and physical routines and how she starts every new artistic project. Using the reassurance of ritual to squash self-doubt, she tells herself, "I've done it before. It was good. I'll do it again."[81] We can do the same.

Let's start by giving ourselves *regard.*

Notice When the Universe Gives Us Regard

As we begin to identify athletes, performers, or other artists who inspire us, and we start to give ourselves *regard*, let's be open to noticing signs from the universe that we are *seen* . . . symbols or markers out there in the world that we *exist* and we are on our own *right track.*

After I received both doses of the Moderna vaccine and finally finished an extraordinarily complex academic year during the pandemic, both as a teacher and a master's program student, I booked a solo trip to Split, Croatia, to really begin digging into writing and editing this book manuscript. Being in a different cultural environment always helps me enter and stay in *flow* as a writer—that state in which challenge and skill meet in equipoise, time and space seem to disappear, and we feel energized and exhilarated.[82] (We also can feel thoroughly wiped out when we emerge from a flow zone! In 2018, I wrote the first draft of *Untangling Fear* in Rome and loved every minute of my creative process, though each writing session consumed a ton of mental, physical, and emotional energy.)

My daily routine for getting writing done in Split was: wake up, make a pot of coffee, scribble three pages of Julia Cameron's recommended Morning Pages[83] in my journal to expunge all the annoying feelings of travel guilt that creep into my psyche, write for two hours, go hike or run to get some exercise, then do a cultural outing. One afternoon during a side trip to Dubrovnik, walking along the cobblestones of an ancient fortress, I stopped to gaze down at the Adriatic Sea lapping at a dock below. Small boats in various states of repair lay askew on the shore. I caught a glimpse of a single letter and number spray-painted on a metal grate next to a boat resting on pilings. The letter and number said: *U2*.

I laughed out loud. I mean, why on earth did that particular letter and that particular number appear in that particular boatyard? I sat there for a minute and just marveled in awe at the life I have created since I left my last law firm job. I teach. I box. I travel. I write. All things that personify who I am at my core.

Eventually, I tugged myself away from the graffitied message that seemed specifically scribbled for me and resumed walking along a coastal pathway. I tucked into a beach bar restroom to wash my dusty hands. Inside, on the wall, a mural of Muhammad Ali stared back at me, one arm defiantly hooked in a victory gesture. *Keep going, champ. You've got this.*

That night, I didn't sleep great. I loved my Airbnb with the corner of an ancient Roman temple jutting out of the bedroom wall, but the acoustics were about as soothing as New York's Times Square. Every passing footfall woke me up. Cathedral bells rang at the crack of dawn. In the morning, I got out of bed, brewed coffee, plowed through my daily two-hour writing quota again, and trudged a couple miles to find a COVID PCR testing site, planning for my next travel move. I had rented a house in Tenerife, in Spain's Canary Islands, to continue working on this book, but getting there was incredibly complicated. Again, I felt pangs of guilt, self-indulgence, even shame—my usual go-to emotions when I start to doubt myself.

Sleep-deprived and frustrated with the rocky writing session I had that morning, I set out on a hike up a hill in Split called Marjan. As sweat began to fleck my cheeks, I noticed I was ruminating . . . catastrophizing about travel logistics. *Will the airline accept my overweight luggage full of research books? Why am I not just heading somewhere less complicated? Maybe I should just go back home instead? Nobody else is taking this much time "off" to write.*

Just then, I walked into what seemed like a cloud of honeysuckle. The amazing smell was almost overpowering. Simultaneously, I heard a song bouncing over the stone wall of a garden along the hiking path. *It's a beautiful day. Don't let it get away.* Lyrics from my band. Again, in Croatia of all places. I laughed. I decided to stop worrying, and instead give myself *regard.*

I told myself, *OK, it's a beautiful day. Don't let it get away by worrying about travel glitches that are not likely to happen because you have researched and planned your next geographical move to the nth detail. Don't let it get away by feeling guilty or shameful about taking time away to heal from this traumatic year and work on a project that you're excited about and that you know needs this kind of solitary focus to get done. Trust your creative system. It works.*

Hike this hill, inhale this Croatian honeysuckle air, listen to the waves of the Adriatic tumble onto the rocks, and put one foot in front of the other. This trip, and this writing project, are about you and your well-being. Everything else is a side show. Now, move it.

Start giving yourself *regard.* Start noticing signs and symbols that remind you of what excites and energizes you. And then begin stepping into your power.

Part I

EDGING INTO THE EUDAIMONIC TURN

Before we start digging into multiple dimensions of our personas and well-being, I'll share a few principles I've learned in studying positive psychology that may help us frame our self-discovery adventure through a lens of strength and zest. (An organization called the VIA Institute on Character defines *zest* as vitality, excitement, enthusiasm, and energy.)[84]

Eudaimonia is a Greek word (*eu* for good, and *daimon* for soul or self) that encapsulates the array of experiences, objects, and ideas that foster human flourishing.[85] According to Professor James Pawelski, director of education at the Positive Psychology Center at the University of Pennsylvania, scholars across a multitude of disciplines—such as psychology, medicine, neuroscience, economics, and theology—are spearheading an endeavor called the *eudaimonic turn*, a shift in attention away from focusing on brokenness in our world toward the study of individual and collective well-being.[86] An interesting initiative called the "positive humanities" is an interdisciplinary collaboration between the field of positive psychology and the humanities.[87] The humanities, which include domains such as music, art, literature, culture, religion, languages, philosophy, history, and *law*, present rich opportunities for individuals and communities to explore and nurture positive ideas, feelings, and behaviors that can contribute to human thriving on a global level.

Sometimes I wrestle with law's inclusion in the definition of the humanities. Law is a field of words, yet roots and derivations of the term *humanities*—human, humanity, humaneness—often can appear to be a low priority of our profession. Humanity, or the state of being human, can get lost in a morass of seemingly all-or-nothing rules, winners and losers, systemic injustices, ossified hierarchies, and intellectual elitism. Synonyms of humanity, such as kindness, graciousness, politeness, consideration, philanthropy, likewise can seem absent in many layers of the legal system. Toxic competition and some hurtful forms of cancel culture persist. Incivility and bullying abound.

Our legal arena could use some coaxing into the eudaimonic turn.

What if, instead of thoroughly exhausting ourselves unearthing, or stirring up, problems around every corner, we also invest (and replenish) energy in fostering *good*? While obviously our profession grapples with myriad problems and challenges that need addressing, instead of ruminating solely about brokenness, violation, harm, and damage, let's devote attention to cultivating the good that each of us can bring to law and to humanity. Let's steer into law's eudaimonic turn.

CHAPTER 1

The Field of Positive Psychology: A Booster Shot for Human Flourishing

In the spring of 2021, at the same time I was wrapping up my studies in my master's program in applied positive psychology at the University of Pennsylvania, COVID-19 vaccine rollouts were proliferating to places around the globe. To me, the vaccine and positive psychology share analogous purposes. Instead of merely *treating* the symptoms of an insidious virus or disease forever, scientists innovate vaccines as protective shields—to *prevent* future harm and foster conditions conducive to human thriving. Similarly, one of the goals of the relatively new field of positive psychology is to help individuals, communities, and institutions bolster resilience in the face of ongoing and future stressors *and* stimulate mental, emotional, and physical health globally.[88] Just over 20 years ago, the founders of positive psychology undertook a scientific adventure: while mainstream psychologists focused on treating, healing, and repairing damage, disease, pathology, and illness, positive psychologists began investigating complementary pathways toward prevention, growth, and human flourishing.[89]

When laypersons hear the term positive psychology, they might mistakenly equate it with self-help, or assume the field pushes an unrealistic "sunshine and rainbows" mentality. However, positive psychology distinguishes itself from self-help based on its researchers' commitment to developing and relying upon scientific studies and data.[90] To develop empirical support for techniques that can foster well-being in individuals, groups, communities, and institutions, positive psychologists invent and test processes for achieving desired outcomes; these initiatives are called *positive interventions*.[91]

I'll share a bit of the history of positive psychology first, with the aim of laying a foundation for how we—as members of the legal profession—might activate our own eudaimonic turn. By embracing positive psychology principles that resonate with each of us as individuals, we can learn how to better navigate the normal ups and downs of life and lawyering, and ultimately flourish.

HISTORY OF POSITIVE PSYCHOLOGY

In the early 1900s, a psychologist named John B. Watson popularized a theory of psychology called *behaviorism* based on the principle that all human actions are merely a function of responses to stimuli.[92] Behaviorists studied human actions, which they deemed observable, rather than thoughts or feelings, which they adjudged unobservable.[93] Before World War II, the field of psychology focused on three objectives: curing mental illness, augmenting human productivity, and discerning and cultivating high talent.[94] After World War II, the science of psychology concentrated on healing disease, repairing damage, and attending to pathology.[95] During this era, psychologists tended to regard human beings as passive vessels needing assistance from more educated influencers in order to change.[96]

In the 1960s and 1970s, psychologists like Carl Rogers[97] and Abraham Maslow[98] articulated a different theory of psychology called *humanism.* Humanists advanced the principle that human beings are not, as the behaviorists believed, simply "billiard balls, doing poorly or well depending on what other billiard balls happen to have ricocheted into them."[99] Humanistic psychologists began championing self-actualization—the process in which we as individuals actively strive to make the most of our potential.[100] Humanists believe that personal development continues throughout the long arc of our lives.[101] We are constantly changing, evolving, learning, and growing.[102]

In 1996, Dr. Martin Seligman (whom we call Marty in our Penn master's program) was elected president of the American Psychological Association (APA). Thereafter, he boldly announced the development of a new field of psychology—positive psychology—as one of his goals.[103] Seligman highlighted the fact that psychologists after World War II had devoted substantial intellectual focus to human problems and their remedies.[104] He sounded a call for a fresh direction of study about what is *right* with people, that is, human goodness and excellence, rather than continuing to view human beings as fragile and flawed.[105] He contended that the psychology of the prior six decades was only half the story.[106] He advocated that psychological treatment should not merely fix brokenness; it should cultivate the best in individuals as well.[107]

Importantly, Seligman characterized positive psychology as an intended *complement* to mainstream psychology, not its substitute.[108] Early positive psychology researchers surmised that systems and processes designed to help override negative emotions, thoughts, and behaviors likely differed from those that could effectively augment positive feelings, ideas, and actions.[109] In his role as APA president, Seligman outlined an ambition to engage researchers and practitioners in a study of what makes life good, what *health* really means, and what individuals seek out when not struggling or downtrodden.[110]

In 2000, Seligman and his friend and collaborator, Dr. Mihaly Csikszentmihalyi (developer of the concept of *flow* mentioned earlier, and which we will dive into in Chapter 4), cowrote an introduction to an edition of the scholarly journal *American Psychologist*, continuing to hone the definition of positive psychology.[111] At the time, they sought to distance positive psychology from the field of humanism, concerned that humanism (and its perceived self-help tenor) lacked scientific grounding.[112] Seligman and Csikszentmihalyi also worried that humanism's emphasis on the *self* risked short-changing the much-needed development of collective well-being.[113] (However, in my view, well-being often needs to start within *self* before we—as individuals—can effectively help each other, groups, and communities cultivate well-being.) Notably, in 2019, Seligman apologized to humanistic psychologists for conflating humanistic psychology with fuzzy self-help approaches, and for not fully crediting Maslow with planting the initial seeds of positive psychology through humanism.[114]

In their article, Seligman and Csikszentmihalyi defined positive psychology as a science devoted to the study of three realms:[115]

- **Past, present, and future positive subjective *experiences*:**
    - Past: well-being, contentment, and fulfillment
    - Present: happiness and flow states
    - Future: optimism and hope
- **Positive individual *traits*:**
    - "the capacity for love and vocation, courage, interpersonal skill, aesthetic sensibility, perseverance, forgiveness, originality, future mindedness, spirituality, high talent, and wisdom"
- **Positive groups and institutions**:
    - Civil virtues
    - Structures and systems that foster improved citizenship, such as: "responsibility, nurturance, altruism, civility, moderation, tolerance, and work ethic"

Instead of continuing to fixate on narratives of human survival and endurance in the face of hardship and adversity, the founders of positive psychology planned to study how humans thrive in non-adverse circumstances.[116]

Seligman and Csikszentmihalyi further heralded the need to shift to a *prevention* model rather than clinging to a treatment paradigm.[117] Simply treating disease, labelling weaknesses, or fixing damage after the fact does not prevent the next calamity. Instead, positive psychologists embarked on a quest to investigate human strengths and competencies that, when intentionally cultivated, could serve as buffers against the impact of future life challenges.[118]

Seligman and Csikszentmihalyi called this a "redirecting of scientific energy" toward a science dedicated to strength and prevention.[119] They also emphasized the field's commitment to developing reliable and valid tools to measure outcomes.[120]

From that point, over the next 20 years, positive psychology bloomed into the scientific investigation of optimal human functioning and how to build positive qualities in individuals.[121] Its mission is to enhance the lives of all people, not just those grappling with illness or disease.[122] In Seligman's words, positive psychology is the study of "what we choose for its own sake."[123] Another friend and collaborator of Seligman's, Dr. Christopher Peterson, described positive psychology as the scientific inquiry into what makes our lives most worth living.[124] Its subject matter is well-being; its measure is human thriving; its ultimate goal is to augment human flourishing.[125]

The concept of flourishing combines two well-being avenues: **hedonic** (feeling good) and **eudaimonic** (functioning well).[126] Hedonic well-being, or just feeling good, is not sufficient for a life of robust well-being.[127] We also need to function well, embodying eudaimonia. Eudaimonia is not a fixed state or an end goal but rather an enduring, dynamic process in which we actively and continuously cultivate multiple dimensions of personal well-being.[128] As we endeavor to nourish a life of flourishing, we can seek to minimize or extinguish debilitating components of the human experience while amplifying the presence of bolstering support systems.[129]

Interestingly, Peterson stated that the original goals of the field of positive psychology were to *describe* and *explain* how humans flourish, rather than to *prescribe* or *direct* how people should live their lives.[130] He indicated that the field was prescriptive only in identifying three topics that *should* be researched: (1) positive experiences, (2) positive individual traits, and (3) positive institutions.[131] Peterson asserted that the essential task of positive psychologists was to present objective facts about each phenomenon researched so individuals and communities could make informed decisions about which aims to strive for in different conditions.[132]

From its origins and in its current iteration, positive psychologists are quick to point out that positive psychology is not about chasing happiness—the unrealistic "sunshine and rainbows" approach. Life can be hard; obviously, we all encounter challenges, setbacks, and disappointments. In fact, positive psychologists emphasize that we actually cannot flourish without appropriate doses of negativity.[133] Emotions and experiences that are perceived or classified as negative provide helpful framing around positive emotions and experiences, shaping "the good life."[134] (We'll explore that notion later when we delve into our emotional well-being dimension in Chapter 6.) Researchers have clarified that while the "first wave" of positive psychology may have seemed laser-focused on the positive, the "second wave" accentuates the important interplay between the positive and negative aspects of life.[135]

ONE POSITIVE PSYCHOLOGY WELL-BEING FRAMEWORK: DR. MARTIN SELIGMAN'S PERMA

In the early stages of the positive psychology field, Seligman proposed a framework for human flourishing comprised of three pathways:[136]

- **The pleasant life** (experienced through positive emotions, or hedonic "feeling good")
- **The engaged life**
- **The meaningful life**

Seligman later supplemented these three concepts by adding **relationships** and **achievement**, creating a five-part well-being framework called PERMA (**p**ositive emotions, **e**ngagement, **r**elationships, **m**eaning, **a**chievement).[137] In the PERMA framework, positive emotions engender hedonic happiness; they broaden our awareness of how we feel about past, present, and future experiences, and help us accrue lasting personal resources for tackling the next life challenge.[138] Engagement occurs when we fully immerse in activities we enjoy, temporarily relinquishing conscious fixation on emotions, the self, time, and space; this is Csikszentmihalyi's *flow* state.[139] Relationships help us foster positive states such as love, camaraderie, and belonging.[140] Meaning derives from one's sense of mattering and purpose in life, when we fuse with something bigger than ourselves.[141] Finally, accomplishment springs from active pursuit and achievement of goals that are intrinsically important to us, mastery of skills and competencies, and perseverance through challenges.[142] (As we work through different dimensions of well-being in later chapters, consider using Appendix A as a tracker as we explore the different components of PERMA together.) Positive psychologists have developed activities—called positive interventions—that can help us cultivate the different components of PERMA.

WHAT ARE POSITIVE INTERVENTIONS?

As Pawelski points out, the word *positive* derives from Latin words (*pono, ponere*) which mean "to put," "to place," "to set up," and "to build."[143] Positive psychology practitioners construct positive interventions: simple intentional acts we can undertake that have potentially complex ripple effects. Positive interventions are activities that positive psychology practitioners design, individuals perform, and researchers can measure and evaluate, with the goal of augmenting individual and collective well-being.[144] Interventions are brief in time (they can occupy minutes, hours, days, or weeks rather than months or years), simple in instructions and steps, and self-administrable.[145] The word "intervention" comes from the Latin *inter* (between) and *venire* (come). Positive interventions gently *come between* us and natural human tendencies that may cause us to stumble. Interventions can generate intentional friction—disrupting unhelpful habits in thinking, feeling, and doing—then help pave a road toward well-being.

Mitigating negative thoughts, emotions, and behaviors is important, yet insufficient to nurture sustainable well-being.[146] Interventions aim to amplify positive cognitions, feelings, and actions.[147] Interventions equip us with a durable array of tools to deploy for prevention and growth.[148]

Five components usually comprise positive interventions: (1) an activity, such as writing, thinking, speaking, or moving; (2) an active ingredient—a "new" approach to the activity, such as focusing on our breath or untangling negative thoughts; (3) a target system—the psychological, emotional, spiritual, physiological, or social dimension we wish to shape at the time; (4) a target change—the toggling of a lever (i.e., making an incremental adjustment) in the chosen domain; and (5) a desired outcome.[149] Directly positive interventions aim to preserve and maintain, or promote and increase, a preferred state.[150] Indirectly positive interventions seek to mitigate and decrease, or prevent and avoid, a dispreferred state.[151]

Pawelski offers a useful analogy to explain two approaches within positive psychology: green capes and red capes.[152] When we adopt a "green cape" approach in exploring ourselves through a positive intervention, we aspire to grow desirable states of being and we take concrete action to do so.[153] Alternatively, other times we may seek to lessen undesirable conditions; there, we take a "red cape" approach, noticing and shining a spotlight on problems and working toward solutions.[154] Pawelski describes positive psychology as a reversible cape approach to a flourishing life: we need a balance of mending cracks (red cape) and cultivating growth (green cape).[155]

To qualify as positive, an intervention must be positive in its point of application (i.e., not in an acute or crisis scenario) *or* in its method (i.e., a green cape approach), or *both.*[156] Interventions that are *neither* positive in point of application *nor* in method do not qualify as positive interventions in this context, but instead remain part of the repertoire of mainstream psychology treatments.

Viewed through a different lens, positive psychology interventions can be positive in one, two, or three of the following dimensions: (1) topography: helping individuals cultivate positive qualities, the best things in life, or what makes life worth living; (2) target population: making evidence-supported techniques for flourishing accessible to all individuals, not just people in crisis; and (3) processes: growing and building, rather than healing brokenness, damage, or injury.[157] If an intervention is not positive in at least one dimension—topography, target population, or process—it is not a positive intervention.[158]

Positive interventions work in at least four powerful ways: (1) they invite us to pause and listen to feedback from our bodies on how we process thoughts, sensations, emotions, feelings, and stimuli; (2) they elucidate our power to calibrate new thoughts, emotions, feelings, actions, and physical movement; (3) they champion our uniqueness—nudging us to define individualized notions of "the good life"; and (4) they teach us optimized and efficient habits, practices, routines, and processes to boost and multiply positive feelings, cognitions, and behaviors.

Throughout our self-discovery adventure in exploring multiple dimensions of well-being, I'll share some positive interventions that I learned about in my MAPP studies, and that have worked for me to "know myself," as Socrates urged.

IS WELL-BEING MEASURABLE?

The field of positive psychology offers scientifically validated tools to measure the effects of positive interventions on both our hedonic and eudaimonic well-being.[159] For example, scientists have developed tools to measure:

- Emotion (also called "affect") or mood[160]
- Satisfaction with life[161]
- Subjective happiness[162]
- Subjective well-being[163]
- Eudaimonic well-being[164]
- Overall flourishing[165]

Positive psychology practitioners also have developed instruments to measure specific attributes, such as gratitude[166] and optimism.[167] The website www.authentichappiness.org offers free access to many of the major well-being assessments. Exploring some of these tools and instruments can be helpful as we begin to "know ourselves."

STEPPING INTO OUR EUDAIMONIC TURN—AS INDIVIDUALS AND AS A LEGAL COMMUNITY

Have you ever been on a walk or a hike, or meandering through an unfamiliar city, suddenly felt the urge to take a different pathway or route, and then stumbled upon an amazing sight, or cool view, or wild experience you never would have stepped into if you hadn't taken that uncharted turn? Let's veer onto a new road.

> *Do not go where the path may lead.*
> *Go instead where there is no path and leave a trail.*
>
> Ralph Waldo Emerson

Chapter 2

Let's Get to Work Cultivating Our Multiple Dimensions

We sell ourselves short if we default to one or two of our personal dimensions. As we've noted, athletes and performers who we admire and who inspire us cultivate dimensions of their persona that go well beyond the singular skill, talent, or ability that draws glory on the stage or in the arena. We can do the same. Together, let's explore the six dimensions of lawyer well-being outlined in the 2017 National Task Force Report, but let's also add four more for consideration. The report lists these dimensions:[168]

- **Physical**
- **Emotional**
- **Social**
- **Spiritual**
- **Occupational**
- **Intellectual**

I'd love to add a few more into the mix:

- **Artistic/creative:** even if we believe we don't have an artistic or creative bone in our body, we can take time to experiment with, immerse ourselves in, and surround ourselves with art and creativity in some form
- **Cultural:** exposure to different cultures and ways of life—through travel, food, music, architecture, art, ritual—expands our thinking; here, we'll also explore the concept of "cultural humility"
- **Moral/ethical:** the law might seem—on its face—as a dichotomy of "right" and "wrong" but it's often the plentiful fuzzy areas that affect our well-being; here, we'll delve more deeply into cultivating our character

- **Caring and caregiving:** let's deepen our understanding of what it means to have healthy empathy and compassion for others (and ourselves); let's establish and honor boundaries; let's learn how to recognize trauma and vicarious trauma in ourselves and others and hold space for trauma processing

In 1759, Voltaire wrote, *"Il faut cultiver notre jardin."*[169] *We must cultivate our garden.* We have the power to begin tending to our individual well-being *today.* By doing so, we inevitably will create positivity ripple effects in our relationships and communities, ultimately improving well-being on a societal and global level. I'm excited for us to get to work!

WHY MULTIPLE DIMENSIONS MATTER

As author and lawyer Stewart Levine pointed out, "Serving others is a lawyer's job. Being fit yourself is a necessary foundation for taking care of others."[170] Levine defined "optimum fitness" for lawyers as incorporating "physical fitness, mental clarity, emotional stability, and a spiritual foundation that will enable [us] to take care of clients, colleagues, and the community [we] serve."[171] He suggests that fit lawyers can differentiate themselves from less-fit ones.[172] (Indeed, Professor Jarrod Reich likewise makes the economic case for the connection between attorney well-being and robust business development.[173])

Some state bars have begun acknowledging multiple dimensions of well-being and fitness as components of attorney competence to practice law. For example, my home state, the Commonwealth of Virginia, includes this comment to Rule 1.1 (the rule on attorney *competence*) in the Virginia State Bar Rules of Professional Conduct:

> *A lawyer's mental, emotional, and physical well-being impacts the lawyer's ability to represent clients and to make responsible choices in the practice of law. Maintaining the mental, emotional, and physical ability necessary for the representation of a client is an important aspect of maintaining competence to practice law.*[174]

Vermont includes the same language in Comment 9 to Rule 1.1 in Vermont's Rules of Professional Conduct.[175] Further, Rule 1.1(b) of California's Rules of Professional Conduct defines "competence" as not only "learning and skill," but also "mental, emotional, and physical ability reasonably necessary for the performance of such service."[176]

Our days are chock full of work and personal responsibilities. Countless emails, meetings (now ubiquitously on Zoom!), projects, deadlines, appointments, and engagements loom. It might not seem like we have time to think about, let alone work on, *ten* different realms of personal development. However, this does not have to be time consuming or costly. Remember Ben Franklin's methodical approach and Socrates's invitation to "know thyself" mentioned in the Introduction to this book? If we set up a system to first consider what each of these dimensions means to us, and then activate simple steps of enrichment within each dimension, one at a time, we can steer ourselves onto a eudaimonic pathway toward becoming healthier, happier, and more fulfilled in our work and personal lives. By enhancing our awareness of the benefits of each of these dimensions, and then learning how to nurture them through *realistic, small chunks of committed time* (and activities like positive interventions), we set ourselves up for an abundance of flourishing. This is a gift to ourselves, one another, our clients, and ultimately our profession.

If you are feeling overwhelmed by the prospect of working on ten dimensions, let's start simply by using the chart below to consider which well-being domain (or domains) resonates with you first, or perhaps a bit more than the others. In John Ratey and Richard Manning's book, *Go Wild*, they talk about "the lever effect."[177] They credit Dr. Beverly Daniel Tatum, president emerita of Spelman College, for highlighting the term "lever" to refer to an initial catalyst that can set us onto a path toward enhancing our well-being on a broader level. Dr. Tatum's initial lever was *sleep*.[178] Starting by working solely on her sleeping habits, she eventually evolved toward focusing on her nutrition, and subsequently improving her physical movement. Ratey and Manning suggest nature as an example of another potential initial lever; beginning with the basics of getting outside more can lead to increases in bodily movement (our physical dimension), appreciation of beauty (our artistic/creative dimension), and interaction with other humans (our social dimension).[179] We don't have to do everything at once. Just like I tell myself when starting a new book project, *I don't need to (and can't possibly) write 400 pages at once. Set up a system of increments. Start with one manageable task. Take your time. Watch the increments build and grow into something whole. Trust your system.*

Consider using the chart below to first ponder the ten dimensions and see which one (or ones) ignites an initial spark of interest. Let's start there. Then we can craft our own personal development project, like Ben Franklin's described in the Introduction to this book. We can choose a realistic duration of time to explore each dimension—A week? A month? We can adopt a routine or system for learning *first* (i.e., reading the chapter devoted to that dimension) and then engaging in activities and exercises designed to enrich that dimension and teach us about ourselves. When we feel ready, we can switch to another dimension for the next designated time period (i.e., a week, month, or other duration). Once we have worked through all ten dimensions, we can start again at the beginning.

One (gentle) recommendation . . . Even if physicality, bodily movement, exercise, or sports are so *not* your thing, please consider starting with the **physical dimension** anyway. Many of the concepts we'll explore in the physical well-being dimension will help us establish workable routines and practices for nurturing many of the other dimensions. (Plus, some of the science stuff related to enhancing our awareness of our physical selves—our *somatic intelligence*—is really cool and illuminating.) It's time we start treating ourselves like scholar-athletes or scholar-performers and using our bodies to power our brains and minds! I've organized the chapters in a sequence that makes the concepts flow chronologically and build upon one another. So, you could just work through each dimension in the order in which the chapters progress. But, I am all about encouraging our authenticity, so . . . *Please, do you.* You can approach the dimensions in any order that works for you. Make this self-exploration adventure *yours.*

WELL-BEING SELF-DISCOVERY PLANNING TOOL

Working on our well-being is not an overnight endeavor. But that's what makes it fun. We get to take our time exploring, investigating, and learning new techniques and practices that will help us live happier, healthier, more fulfilling lives for years to come. At the same time, this process does not need to occupy a huge chunk of our busy daily, weekly, or monthly calendars. If we approach this initiative thoughtfully, we can construct a workable plan to integrate our well-being self-discovery quest into our lives in a seamless way, and ensure that we look forward to each twist and turn of the adventure.

As I mentioned, I (gently) recommend we start with the **physical dimension**, simply because the concepts we'll learn there will serve as foundational knowledge for the exploration we'll do in the other dimensions. However, this is *your* odyssey. You do *you.* Consider using the chart below to identify (1) the dimensions you are most drawn to delving into ASAP; (2) those you are intrigued by but want to pursue *after* focusing on others first; and (3) those you are not quite ready to immerse in but will get to eventually. You can decide to devote a week or a month (or even some randomly selected time frame like 9.2 days!) to the first dimension, and see how that timeline works for you, and then adjust the time periods thereafter, to allocate a realistic and reasonable amount of time for development of each dimension. There is no right or wrong way to embark on this voyage.

In the space next to each dimension in the wheel on page 16, assign the dimension a 1, 2, or 3 based on the following prompts (you'll likely have a few 1s, a few 2s, and a few 3s; this process will help us construct a chronology of dimensions to nurture; and of course, we can always edit our sequence!):

Assign the dimension a **1** if your current feeling toward exploring that part of your persona sounds like **one** of these:	YES! I already rock at this dimension—so this feels like a nice comfort area to start with and nurture further **OR** I'm not so familiar with this dimension but I am super-intrigued and can't wait to explore this aspect of myself **OR** I know this is an aspect of myself I often put on the back burner, but I'm feeling ready to bolster it! Let's do it.
Assign the dimension a **2** if your current feeling toward exploring that part of your persona sounds like **one** of these:	I haven't really ever thought about this aspect of myself. Sounds intriguing but let's do this one *after* I've pursued a few others first **OR** I already feel pretty good (or healthy) in this aspect of myself although I do want to cultivate it even more, so let's focus on some other dimensions first.
Assign the dimension a **3** if your current feeling toward exploring that part of your persona sounds like **one** of these:	Um, this one feels scary (or less pleasant) right now. I'll circle back when I'm ready, after I've bolstered a few other dimensions **OR** I already feel really good (or healthy) in this aspect of myself, so let's focus on a lot of other dimensions first.

Once you have ranked your 1s, 2s, and 3s, let's prioritize the 1s. Rank them 1A, 1B, and so on, in the order you'd like to sequence them. You can do the same with the 2s and the 3s (and we can always revisit and adjust the chronology). Below the wheel on page 16 is a key indicating the book chapter that corresponds with each dimension.

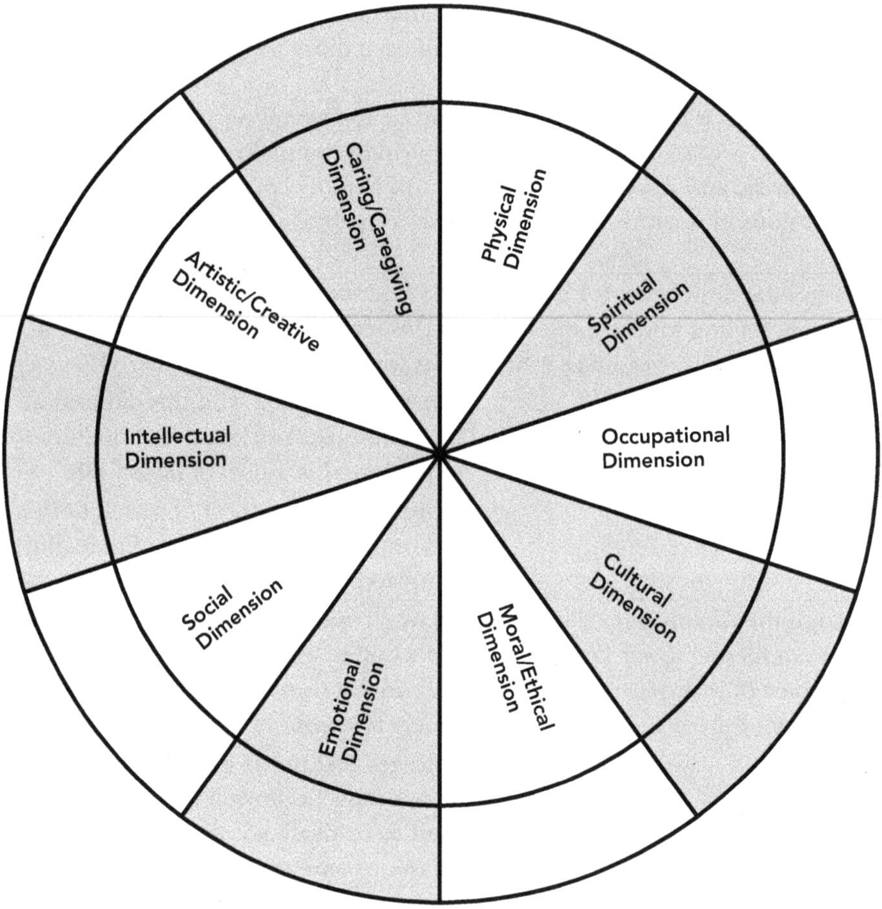

Dimension	Book Chapter	Sequence for Focusing on the Dimensions (1A, 1B, 2A, 2B, 3A, 3B, etc.)	Time to Focus on This Dimension (One Week? One Month? Other?)
Physical	5		
Emotional	6		
Artistic/Creative	7		
Social	8		
Cultural	9		
Spiritual	10		
Occupational	11		

Dimension	Book Chapter	Sequence for Focusing on the Dimensions (1A, 1B, 2A, 2B, 3A, 3B, etc.)	Time to Focus on This Dimension (One Week? One Month? Other?)
Intellectual	12		
Moral/Ethical	13		
Caring/Caregiving	14		

Hurray! Now, we are almost ready to begin. Just two more things to consider and contemplate before we leap in!

Don't ever feel like your best days are behind you.
Reinvention is the purest form of hope.
Make today your best yet.

Phil Wohl

Part II

AWARENESS AMPLIFIERS

Before we dive into our first dimension (or pull our first well-being "lever," to use Ratey and Manning's suggested terminology[180]), I'll flag a few positive psychology concepts that may help us enrich our work in each dimension. Let's call these *awareness amplifiers*. This entire endeavor is about knowing ourselves better, enhancing our self-awareness, and using those insights to augment our lawyering training and performance.

As Christopher Phillips, author of *Socrates Café*, explains, Socrates's inquisitive "know thyself" approach "aim[ed] to help people gain a better understanding of themselves and their nature and their potential for excellence."[181] Phillips refers to the Socratic method in this context as "a way to seek truths by your own lights."[182] Phillips says that, "by becoming a better questioner, by rekindling your love of questioning, you likely will develop a better sense of who you are, who you can be, where you are, why you are, and how you might want to chart a new course for yourself."[183] Indeed, "Socrates enabled those with whom he engaged in dialogues to descend into the depths of *their own* souls and create *their own* life-affirming ethic."[184]

Three positive psychology concepts invite us to get to know ourselves on a deeper level so that when we begin to nurture and cultivate each well-being dimension, we can more astutely notice and activate healthy thoughts, feelings, and behaviors that will help us flourish as individuals:

- **Character strengths**
- **Flow**
- **Grit**

Because these concepts relate to multiple dimensions of well-being, we'll explore the basics of each principle a bit first, and then we'll tie them to particular dimensions as we progress through each domain.

Find out who you are and do it on purpose.

Dolly Parton

Chapter 3

Awareness Amplifier #1: Crafting Character through Flexing Strengths, Like Muscles

In thinking about our character in the context of "character and fitness" to practice law, we can begin to view ourselves not as stiff cardboard-cutout caricatures, but as evolving and malleable sculptures we can shape with intention. Positive psychologists indicate that character strengths *can* be cultivated.[185] Like playwrights or screenwriters, we can *craft* our character!

WHAT ARE CHARACTER STRENGTHS IN THE CONTEXT OF POSITIVE PSYCHOLOGY?

Positive psychologists define character strengths as valued traits that radiate in, and from, our ideas, emotions, and behaviors.[186] Each of us has a unique persona configured from an array of strengths we possess in varying degrees.[187] Humans are not defined by a single strength, but by our amalgam of strengths.[188] In getting to know our character strengths (which are both stable *and* pliable), we can lay stepping stones toward a life of well-being.[189]

HOW DO WE IDENTIFY OUR CHARACTER STRENGTHS?

If we don't even know where to start in identifying our character strengths, we are not alone.[190] Studies indicate that two thirds of us have "strengths blindness," that is, lack of awareness of, or clarity about, our character strengths.[191] To discover our strengths and appreciate how they make us extraordinary, we can start by taking an assessment called the VIA Survey of Character Strengths.[192] The letters in the acronym VIA originally stood for the Values in Action Inventory—a psychological assessment developed by the VIA Institute on Character, "a non-profit organization dedicated to bringing the science of character strengths to the world."[193] Now VIA is a standalone term connoting the *pathway* connecting scientific research on character with individual practice in cultivating one's strengths, leading to self-discovery.[194] I love the linguistic connection to the Italian word for street: *via*!

The researchers who designed the VIA Survey (Seligman and Peterson, in collaboration with fifty-five scientists)[195] created an umbrella framework comprised of six *virtues*: fundamental human qualities revered by philosophers throughout the ages. The six virtues encapsulated in the VIA and defined in more detail on the VIAcharacter.org website are **wisdom**, **courage**, **humanity**, **justice**, **temperance**, and **transcendence**.[196] Next, the VIA Survey (a free, online, easily accessible instrument) identifies twenty-four character strengths situated within the six virtues.[197] After we take the assessment, a report delivers our "strengths profile," listing our strengths in order from one to twenty-four. The profile also shows each strength's corresponding *virtue*. In reviewing the profile, we can discern different groupings of our strengths, such as:

- Signature (top) strengths
- Middle strengths
- Lower strengths[198]

Middle strengths support and bolster signature strengths.[199] Dr. Ryan Niemiec, known as the world authority on the science of character strengths, explains that our lower strengths are not weaknesses; they just don't energize, excite, or come as easily for us as our signature strengths.[200]

Strengths can be *tonic*, which means we showcase them on an ongoing and steady basis, or *phasic*, that is, they ebb and flow as we encounter different life events.[201] Our character strengths are different from our talents (activities we naturally perform well), skills (trainable actions), interests (our passions), resources (our access to external scaffolding), and values (what we treasure).[202]

The VIA Institute on Character groups the twenty-four character strengths within the six virtues as follows (and the website—VIAcharacter.org—provides helpful descriptions of each strength):[203]

Virtue	Character Strengths
Wisdom	Creativity Curiosity Judgment Love of Learning Perspective
Courage	Bravery Honesty Perseverance Zest
Humanity	Kindness Love Social Intelligence
Justice	Fairness Leadership Teamwork
Temperance	Forgiveness Humility Prudence Self-Regulation
Transcendence	Appreciation of Beauty and Excellence Gratitude Hope Humor Spirituality

HOW DO OUR SIGNATURE STRENGTHS MAKE US EXTRAORDINARY?

It's a fun moment when the online VIA Survey reveals our signature strengths; these are identified by VIA's algorithm as our Top 5, but really include all strengths that have the same raw scores as the Top 5 on the VIA scale.[204] While the basic VIA report is free on the VIA Institute on Character's website, there is a more detailed report available (for a fee) called the Total 24 Character Strengths Report, which shows raw scores.[205] According to Niemiec, a 1.0 difference in two strengths' raw scores likely indicates a meaningful differentiation between them, for example, distinguishing a signature strength from a middle strength.[206] I love thinking about the uniqueness of our signature strength configuration (like our autograph or fingerprints). There are 5.1 million constellations of Top 5 signature strengths![207]

A strength earns the *signature* moniker because it is an aspect of our persona that we embrace fully; we love that part of ourselves; we get excited about using the strength and crave opportunities to do so; we continuously find new ways to flex the strength in creative ways and projects (even if people try to hinder our use of it); engaging the strength invigorates rather than depletes us; and we relish the joy and zest that arises from its deployment.[208] Notably, one study in New Zealand showed that people who were highly *aware* of their strengths were nine times more likely to be flourishing, and people who *used* their strengths were eighteen times more likely to be flourishing.[209] Wow!

IS IT POSSIBLE TO FLEX A STRENGTH TOO MUCH OR TOO LITTLE?

Sometimes, we can flex our strengths too much (overuse) or too little (underuse) when addressing a situation.[210] We might *overuse* a strength by misjudging a situation's needs, misinterpreting context, or being stuck in a pattern of relying on one strength while forgetting others.[211] We might *underuse* a strength simply because we have not nurtured or practiced a particular skill enough, we lack mindful awareness of our power or an impetus to act in a situation, or we fear being judged if we activate the strength.[212] To assess whether we might be overusing or underusing a strength, we can consider whether our deployment of the strength negatively affects us or people we care about.[213] Both the VIA Total 24 Report (the more detailed report offered for a fee) and an article by Niemiec offer helpful illustrations of overuse and underuse of the twenty-four strengths in the VIA Survey, and describe optimal uses of each strength.[214]

As we begin to explore our ten well-being dimensions, we'll get to know our strengths more deeply and contemplate how we can use them to enhance our well-being (and help other individuals flourish). We might consider alternating between *capitalization* (practicing strengths we already know how to optimize) and *compensation* (fine-tuning strengths we either overuse or underuse).[215] We also can activate *towing* (using a higher strength to boost—or tow along—a lower one) or *tempering* (using a balance-oriented strength—like humility or perspective—to modulate an overused strength).[216]

As we work through different well-being dimensions in later chapters, consider using Appendix B to keep track of the various character strengths and virtues we explore together.

Exercise #1

Let's Get to Know Our Character Strengths as We Craft Our Character (and Fitness) to Practice Law

Just as fitness exercises like cardio workouts and lifting weights help us build stamina and muscle, positive psychologists indicate we can engage in deliberate practice to understand our strengths, flex them in optimal ways, and ultimately shape our character. Consider engaging in the following exercises to explore your character strengths:

- Take the free VIA Survey on the VIAcharacter.org website.
- Looking at the results from the VIA Survey of Character Strengths, what are your Top 5 "signature" strengths?

  ____

- Read the description of each of your signature strengths on the VIAcharacter.org website, found at www.VIAcharacter.org/character-strengths.
- Write your Top 5 signature strengths on a Post-it® and stick it on your laptop or someplace visible in your home and office!
- The VIA situates our character strengths within six virtues. Which of the six virtues do your signature strengths showcase?

  ____

- How did you feel when you discovered your signature strengths? Were there any surprises? ____
- How did you feel when the VIA revealed your "lower" set of strengths? (Remember, these are not weaknesses; as Niemiec points out, they simply do not excite, energize, or come as easily for us as signature and middle strengths.) Were there any surprises? ____

Character strength researchers suggest a variety of exercises to help us flex our strengths. (Dr. Ryan Niemiec and Dr. Robert McGrath wrote a useful book called *The Power of Character Strengths: Appreciate and Ignite Your Positive Personality*, that describes each strength, and offers activities for nurturing them.[217])

Two exercises involving character strengths that might be helpful in our well-being amplification adventure are *writing* and *strength-spotting*.

Exercise #2

Noticing and Writing about Our Character Strengths

Embracing Socrates's maxim—getting to know ourselves—one way to explore our character strengths is through writing.[218] One exercise proposed by Niemiec is to set an alarm at various moments in our days or weeks to prompt us to pause and write about a strength we just deployed in a situation, and how the strength worked in the context in which we used it.[219] Studies indicate that reflective writing can help transform present values into future desired behavior.[220]

Further, we can use writing as part of a Strengths Practice Model proposed by Niemiec called Aware-Explore-Apply.[221] In A-E-A, we enhance strength awareness and application through three mechanisms:[222]

- **Aware:** noticing, naming, and describing a strength
  - The VIA website[223] and the more detailed Total 24 Report offer helpful language defining each strength; we can experiment with this "strengths vocabulary," writing about how we used a specific strength.
- **Explore:** journaling about the effects of activating a strength
  - We can write about thoughts, feelings, and actions associated with our use of a particular strength.
- **Apply:** reflecting on how we could amp up the strength's role in our daily life
  - Researchers suggest activities like using a signature strength in a new way each day for a week.[224]

Consider trying the A-E-A model this week: notice a strength, write about it, and choose an activity in which you can deploy it again.

Exercise #3

Strength-Spotting, in Ourselves and Others

Next, as we increase our fluency with the language of character strengths, we can practice strength-spotting in ourselves and others, using another of Niemiec's models called SEA:

- **S**potting a strength in ourselves or others and labeling it
- **E**xplaining how we observed the strength in action
- **A**ppreciating the strength by articulating its value and meaning to us[225]

This week, let's practice strength-spotting and SEA—in person (in the moment) or in writing (through a positive text message, email, social media post, or handwritten note).

By helping one another craft our character in this way, we also can kindle *positivity resonance*[226] (a concept coined by Dr. Barbara Fredrickson, which we will explore more fully in our emotional well-being dimension in Chapter 6). Positivity resonance can occur when two individuals generate and augment positive energy in one another through three intertwined actions: [227]

- A two-way exchange of positive emotions: warmth and openness
- Synchronous moments: mirroring one another's physical behavior, such as smiles, body language, and other verbal and nonverbal expressions
- Mutual investment in one another's well-being

My VIA Total 24 Character Strengths Report identifies my signature strengths as perseverance, curiosity, zest, creativity, and love of learning! (Also, my #6 strength—hope—yielded the same raw score of 4.5 on the VIA scale as two of my Top 5 strengths: creativity and love of learning.) I find it interesting to notice if our signature strengths are spread out across the six virtues, or if they cluster within just a few of the virtues. My Top 5 signature strengths relate to only two of the six virtues:

- Wisdom: my strengths of curiosity, creativity, and love of learning
- Courage: my strengths of perseverance and zest

The VIA Total 24 Character Strengths Report also provides a helpful Expression Map laying out four quadrants to help us understand whether our strengths are **interpersonal** (reflecting how we relate to others) or **intrapersonal** (focused within ourselves), and **mind-related** or **heart-related**.[228] Three of my five signature strengths fit squarely in the intrapersonal/heart quadrant of the Expression Map: zest, curiosity, and creativity (with two of my other highly ranked strengths—hope and appreciation of beauty—nestled therein as well). My mind-related signature strengths of perseverance and love of learning also lean toward the intrapersonal realm. As an introvert, I do spend a lot of time reflecting inward.

So, what are your Top 5 signature strengths? Which virtues do they represent?

You cannot dream yourself into a character;
you must hammer and forge yourself one.

James A. Froude

CHAPTER 4

Awareness Amplifier #2: Finding Flow and Getting Gritty

Two other positive psychology concepts screaming for application to legal education and practice are *flow*, the concept coined by psychologist Csikszentmihalyi,[229] and *grit*, a research focus of psychologist Dr. Angela Duckworth.[230] It's particularly exciting to contemplate how flow and grit can work together in the context of enhancing our healthy training and performance as members of the legal profession.

FLOW

Flow is a state in which we lose temporal and environmental awareness while engaging in an activity.[231] Time and the outside world seem to disappear or transform as we fully immerse in a task. Peterson describes flow as "the coming together of a person and an environment."[232] He says, when we are in flow, "The sense of self as a social actor is lost."[233] Flow requires an optimal balance between challenge and skill.[234] If the challenge exceeds our skill level, flow likely is impossible. Likewise, if the task is too easy and our skill level surpasses the challenge, no flow.

The legal profession is notorious for creating situations marked by an *imbalance* between challenge and skill. We often encounter a juxtaposition of unrealistic deadlines, impossible expectations, and insufficient practical training. A wild imbalance between challenge and skill prevents us from entering flow. Let's change that!

GRIT

Duckworth and her colleagues define *grit* as perseverance and passion for long-term, high-level goals.[235] People with grit work—with stamina—toward such objectives, achieving lower-level goals along the way.[236] Gritty individuals possess four powerful psychological assets:

- Genuine interest in pursuing endeavors
- Disciplined practice
- The ability to articulate a purpose behind their initiatives
- Hope—a belief that effort yields change[237]

Gritty people invest not only more, but better, time in personal growth.[238]

Gritty humans engage in *deliberate practice*.[239] As explained by cognitive psychologist, Dr. Anders Ericsson (who studies how experts hone high-level skills), deliberate practice involves five actions:

- We deconstruct a larger performance goal into smaller components
- We select one stretch sub-goal at a time
- We focus attention and effort on stretching our skills to accomplish the sub-goal task
- We welcome feedback
- Then, we repeat the sequence on the same or a different task[240]

Unlike in flow where challenge and skill meet in equipoise, in deliberate practice, the challenge before us typically exceeds our skill level at that moment. Our growth and evolution require us to adopt good new *habits*: simple, accurate, sequential, consistent, and efficient movements that we execute over and over until they become second nature.[241]

Healthy Habits

Habits are, in essence, sequential chain reactions.[242] One domino falls and hits the next domino, and so on. Good habits involve simple, accurate, and efficient movements.[243] Individuals make better choices when we adopt easier decision-making processes.[244] By getting to know ourselves and observing how our brains, minds, and bodies function, we can identify flawed habitual processes that generate waste or excess and deplete precious energy resources. In healthy habit formation, we reduce unnecessary attention paid to each falling domino, and minimize mental and muscular exertion between movements. We learn to repeat simple and sequential behaviors, consistently for a duration of time, with minimal thought.[245] Instead of intellectually vetting each movement before advancing to the next, we simply hit the start button and trust our practiced sequence. By eliminating pauses, interruptions, and detours in our thinking and reactions along the way, we become more efficient. We free up our energy to achieve our greatest potential.[246] We learn how to consciously steward energy, wisely investing our psychological and physiological capital.

After we've engaged in deliberate practice of a particular new task for a while, ultimately, challenge and skill attune into balance—that is, we may realize we have once again entered a state of flow. Our gritty deliberate practice can lead us to flow moments—an exciting prospect! A gritty person who invests time in understanding these concepts ideally can oscillate between periods of deliberate practice and flow. We first engage in the hard work of practicing and honing skills; then, by enhancing self-awareness and engaging in reflection after episodes of task-oriented activities, we recognize when our newly acquired skills helped us meet a fresh challenge and enabled us to enter a flow state. After each flow episode, our self grows in complexity.[247]

People with grit seize upon this awareness of heightened self-complexity and keep moving forward, choosing the next skill to expand. The fun rush we feel after an episode of flow can motivate us to select another grit goal or subgoal. Indeed, as Peterson describes, our flow activities "eventually lose their magic unless the bar is raised to meet our changes in expertise."[248] Undulating between deliberate practice and flow, we—as gritty humans—can continue moving along our continuum toward long-term goal achievement.

FOSTERING FLOW

Researchers have spent a lot of time studying the concept of flow in the context of disciplines like sports, music, and dance, tracking the relationship between peak performance and flow.[249] We might easily imagine Olympic athletes, violinists, pianists, ballet dancers, or artists like Picasso transcending time and space when they enter their flow zones. But flow is not reserved for elite athletes and performers, or famous artists, or experts in a field.[250] As members of the legal profession, we can cultivate our own flow states.

As a writer, often during one of my designated two-hour morning writing sessions, I lose sense of time and space. Ultimately, I look up from my laptop, delirious and disoriented, my hair wild like Medusa, my face flushed. I'm famished. Sometimes I forget where I am. That's flow for me.

When have you experienced flow?

A flow state involves nine components:[251]

A balance between the challenge and our skill level • A task that requires effort • We have the requisite skill to complete the task	
A clear goal for the activity or work session	
Unambiguous and immediate feedback • Interestingly, this can be in the form of *inner* recognition that we are doing well or excelling at the task • Feedback does not need to be from an external source[252]	
An ability to concentrate on the task at hand • Appropriate uninterrupted time to immerse in the task • Ability to tune out everyday distractions	
A sense of control over the steps needed to accomplish the task	
A merging, or blurring of boundaries, between action and awareness	
Loss of self-consciousness or self-judgment • Safety in letting go of concern for how we are perceived	
Time transformation • Time can seem to speed up or stand still	

<table>
<tr>
<td>An "autotelic" experience
• Autotelic comes from the Greek words auto for self and telos for goal[253]
• A self-contained activity[254]
• The activity serves a purpose in itself
• It does not require an external or outside purpose or reward—engagement in the activity is the reward</td>
<td></td>
</tr>
</table>

Deliberate practice and *flow* share some characteristics like clarity of goals, concentration, and feedback; however, the point of deliberate practice is to *stretch* skills, while in flow, our skills already match the challenge. In flow, self-doubt and self-scrutiny are supplanted by recognition and trust that we have honed the appropriate skills (through deliberate practice) to handle the task.

Researchers reviewed seventeen studies of flow states in elite sports and compiled a list of ten factors that can facilitate, prevent, or disrupt flow in performance:[255]

- Internal states:
  - Focus
  - Motivation
  - Physiological arousal levels (which we will learn about in Chapter 5)
  - Thoughts and emotions
  - Confidence
- Environmental and situational conditions:
  - Surroundings (i.e., noise, light, temperature, distractions)
  - Interaction with (and dependence on) other individuals (like teammates or opposing teams/players)
- Behavioral factors:
  - Preparation
- Feedback
- Performance

As we embark on this adventure to study multiple dimensions of our well-being, let's begin to notice when we feel like we are in states of flow, and also when we feel tugged out of states of flow. We can learn what circumstances, routines, and training or performance rituals can help us cultivate personal flow states more often.

An outside observer might mistakenly characterize flow as effortless: for example, basketball star Stephen Curry sinking one impossible three-point shot after another; Monet transforming globs of oil paint into a masterpiece; a rockstar holding a note of a song for an extra-long transcendent moment; a litigator delivering a powerful closing argument. However, strenuous exertion, practice, and unrelenting discipline during our deliberate practice sessions enable such flow moments.[256] While some individuals might accidentally fall into occasional flow, cultivating a life peppered with flow episodes requires self-awareness and diligent preparatory work. We gotta get and stay gritty.

Exercise #1

When Are You in Flow?

Think about a moment or experience in your life—either personal or professional—in which you may have experienced *flow*. If you're not sure whether you've ever experienced flow, that's fine too! As we navigate each of our ten dimensions of well-being, you may find that engaging in a new experience activates a skill that enables you to rise to a challenge in a way that transports you into flow. For now, let's run through the checklist of nine components of flow:

- Is there an activity you engage in—in your personal life, or law school or law practice life—which feels challenging but for which you know you possess the skill to handle the tasks involved?____________________
  - What makes the activity challenging? ____________________
  - What skills do you possess to enable you to tackle the challenge?

    ____
- Is there a definitive and concrete goal to achieve when you engage in the activity for a duration of time? (e.g., a certain number of pages to write, a particular distance to run, a wall to paint, a specific object to construct)

  ____
- When you engage in this activity, are there moments when you realize along the way that it's going well, or that you are executing the skills necessary to move forward, or that the project you're working on is materializing before your eyes? This is immediate, internal *feedback* that contributes to the flow state.

  ____
- When you engage in this activity, are you able to block out the rest of the world and concentrate for a particular duration of time? How many minutes or hours?

  ____
- Do you feel a sense of control over the steps needed to accomplish your task?

  ____
- Do you sometimes or often lose a sense of time while you are performing the activity? ____________________
- Do you lose a sense of hyperawareness of the space or environment around you?

  ____
- Do you find that you have suspended self-judgment or self-consciousness, at least temporarily?____________________

- Does the activity serve a purpose in itself, such as enjoyment, satisfaction, creation of something tangible from nothing? In other words, do you feel a sense of accomplishment from the activity itself, regardless of any external reward or feedback?____

Based on these criteria, have you experienced flow? If so, what did it feel like for you?

____

Now let's consider deliberate practice. Remember that deliberate practice involves (1) deconstructing larger performance goals into smaller components, (2) selecting one stretch sub-goal, (3) focusing attention and effort on stretching skills to accomplish the sub-goal, (4) obtaining and processing feedback, and (5) repeating the sequence. What skills do you tend to deliberately practice that enabled you to enter this flow state?

____

Would you like to cultivate flow states more frequently in your personal life or work? I know I would! We'll experiment with some strategies for priming our bodies, brains, and minds for flow as we move through our ten well-being dimensions.

BECOMING ENERGY-EFFICIENT TO CULTIVATE FLOW

Instead of chasing isolated flow moments, we have the power to identify, curate, and commit to intense but healthy relationships with flow-generating activities.[257] To do so though, we must learn how to optimize our energy. Cultivating an energy-efficient state is a feat I struggle with all the time in my boxing lessons and when gearing up for public speaking performances.

Whenever we step into a task, we naturally get bombarded with information and data from myriad internal and external sources. Our brains and bodies have limited bandwidth for effectively processing stimuli. Too many stimuli overload our system. At each encounter, we have a choice. We can perceive new input as a threat and let it disrupt our consciousness, undermine our goals, and disorganize the self—precipitating what Csikszentmihalyi calls "psychic entropy."[258] Or, we can sharpen our attention, reject distractions, and focus for the optimal duration that the task requires.[259] We can learn to control and prioritize the countless stimuli competing for attention in our consciousness. We can get better at saying, "I refuse to waste energy on unproductive thoughts or activities." If we let our thoughts tangle in disorder, our ideas pile up like suitcases on a TSA conveyor belt. Instead, we can learn how to greet new stimuli and efficiently assess: *Is this worth the risk of casting me into disorder? Or, is this an amplifier of my goals?* This single query can free us to steward our psychic energy, investing it all in flow.[260]

As we study our multiple well-being dimensions, we'll increase our awareness of how to transform inefficient and wasteful thinking and behavior into efficient, sequential, and automatic processes. Many daily life struggles involve uneconomical thinking and behavior. When we worry or ruminate, we waste energy stopping and starting, moving in fits and starts, running in circles, getting nowhere. When we engage in unhealthy habits, our energy diffuses and dissipates rather than fueling us directly toward our goals. In doing this work to get to know ourselves, we will learn how to *attack* waste and excess. We'll start to find our "sweet spot" in energy exertion: not too much, not too little, but the optimal amount to flourish in each personal and professional scenario we undertake. We'll learn how replace energetic chaos with intentional order. We'll convert unproductive disordered thinking into ordered links in a simplified chain. We'll automatize some of our mental processing and subsequent behavior, making choices easier and clearer.

Identifying environments and tasks that enable us to enter flow, and then choosing surroundings and activities that facilitate flow, can help us find our *meaning*, or our calling.[261] According to Dr. Jeanne Nakamura and Dr. Mihaly Csikszentmihalyi, "Every flow experience has the potential for meaningfulness."[262]

HOW IS FLOW DIFFERENT FROM A CLUTCH STATE?

In high-stakes sports competitions, we may have heard athletes referred to as "clutch" players. While flow can be an enjoyable (or at times blurry) state in our training or performance during which boundaries of time and space disappear, clutch is different. Sometimes, we encounter a performance moment in which we know the stakes are high, all eyes are on us, and we need to execute a particular task or skill—*right now.* We amp up our game, and we deliver. That's clutch. I believe, if we engage in gritty deliberate practice *and* learn how to generate more flow states in our training, we'll also be able to yield more clutch performances.

Researchers describe the clutch state as "superior performance that occurs under pressure circumstances."[263] In a clutch state in the context of sports, an athlete recognizes a pressure scenario, is prepared to experience temporary stress, appraises the outcome as important, and knows how to channel the right amount of energy in the moment to achieve success.[264] While flow states allow for exploration and experimentation, clutch states demand conscious effort, precision, intensity, and awareness.[265] In clutch states, we identify a specific challenge, laser-focus on a fixed objective, and activate tangible steps we have rehearsed a zillion times in deliberate practice to accomplish the goal.[266] While researchers describe flow as a state of *optimal* arousal, clutch is a state of *heightened* arousal, that is, an expenditure of an intense amount of energy for a short duration of time necessary to achieve a desired outcome.[267] (In this context, arousal means "a state of physiological alertness and readiness for action."[268])

As we get to know ourselves on a deeper level—physically, mentally, emotionally, spiritually, and more—we'll learn how we can move through different phases of growth in training and performance, engaging in gritty deliberate practice, and entering flow and clutch states.

Be the flow.

Jay-Z

Part III

LET'S THRILL, AMAZE, INSPIRE— OURSELVES AND OTHERS

Now comes the fun part. Discovery. Experimentation. Investigation. Exploration. Creation. Invention. Reinvention.

No pressure. No expectations. Just expansion of our self-knowledge.

My mom once gave me a silver bracelet inscribed with the words *thrill, amaze, inspire.* I'm so sad that I have no idea where that bracelet ended up—probably lost in one of my dozen moves. It was one of my favorite gifts of all time. As we step into the process of exploring ten dimensions of well-being, let's be open to experiencing new thrills, being amazed, and getting inspired. Again, I recommend starting with our **physical** dimension, only because we'll learn numerous concepts, themes, and strategies in that realm that will lay a foundation for growth in other dimensions. But this is your adventure. Please forge your own path. The chart below can help you design the order in which you step into each well-being dimension. I'm excited for our expedition!

Well-Being Dimension	Book Chapter	Sequence Number (1A, 1B ... 2A ... etc.) (from the chart we used in Chapter 2)
Physical	5	
Emotional	6	
Artistic/Creative	7	
Social	8	
Cultural	9	
Spiritual	10	
Occupational	11	
Intellectual	12	
Moral/Ethical	13	
Caring/Caregiving	14	

Chapter 5

Our Physical Dimension

Our bodies are apt to be our autobiographies.

Frank Gelett Burgess

In this chapter, we will learn about:

- Somatic intelligence
- *Pre*habilitation
- Eustress and hormesis
- Homeostasis and allostasis
- The vagus nerve
- Catabolic and anabolic systems
- Individual zones of optimal functioning (IZOF)
- Mechanisms of somatic perception: neuroception, proprioception, interoception, and exteroception
- Appraisal
- The power of routine and ritual

If you're like me, before doing this work, you may never previously have considered yourself to be a "real" athlete. You might not even like sports, physical activity, or breaking a sweat! Or maybe you love working out. Or perhaps you navigate or grapple with limitations on bodily movement. No matter the extent or nature of your relationship with your body and its mechanics, in this chapter on the physical dimension of well-being, we will channel our favorite athletes and performers. We will get to know numerous aspects of our physical bodies and how we are built to handle stressors. Then we will set up (inclusive and realistic) training strategies we can rely on and trust in performance moments. We will learn how an enriched understanding of our bodies can power our brains and minds.

When I was writing *The Introverted Lawyer* and *Untangling Fear*, to finally comprehend the physical manifestations of my extreme public speaking anxiety, I needed to start with the basics: conducting a physical inventory. When anticipating a stressful public performance, or each time I stepped into one, I surveyed my body and began to notice—really for the first time ever—the sequence of my automatic physical reactions and responses to stress, anxiety, and fear. I observed that when I encounter (or even imagine!) a perceived threat, my body initially reacts by trying to get small. My shoulders cave inward. I cross my arms and legs. I hunch down. It's as if my body is trying to become invisible so I can slink or roll right out of the room. Next, my cheeks and neck flush. My blush fires up. I overheat. My heart jackhammers against my ribcage like a caged animal. I can't get enough air. My head hurts. I sweat. Overall, I'm a hot mess.

Reading a pile of books about the biology of fear, I realized my body's automatic response—though designed to protect me—was not conducive to good, let alone peak, performance. To remedy this, I needed to get to know the inner workings of my body and how I could use my physicality to enhance, instead of hinder, my delivery of substantive and intellectual content. I needed to learn, and be inspired by, the connection between strengthening our physical bodies and bolstering our brains and minds. Together, let's get somatically intelligent.

GETTING SOMATICALLY INTELLIGENT: THE PHYSICALITY OF *FITNESS* TO PRACTICE LAW

The pandemic has prodded us to become more aware of our bodies. Perhaps we are more hyperalert to odd physical sensations, or coughs or sneezes, that prior to 2020 we would have shrugged off. We've adjusted to breathing through masks. We pay more attention to how close in proximity our physical bodies are to other humans. Without access to our gyms or usual workout routines during initial lockdown, some of us experimented with new forms of physical movement. Or maybe we didn't move as much as we usually do. Throughout 2020, my iPhone had this annoying (and judgmental) habit of reminding me how many more steps per day I had walked the same time of year in 2019. I wanted to scream at it, *Dude, I know!*

Your body may have fought (and beat!) COVID-19. I am grateful that our bodies fight for us.

Our bodies are remarkable organisms.

As law students and lawyers who spend so much time in our heads, many of us may take our physical bodies for granted, perhaps deprioritizing the *physicality* of our fitness to practice law. Some of us might even feel like our bodies hold us back at times, like in pivotal performance moments when we need our inner power most.

Throughout my time in law school, law practice, and the early years of my law professor career, whenever I experienced anxiety or stress in performance scenarios, I felt as if my body betrayed me. It wasn't until I started studying how our bodies naturally react to the sensations of stress, anxiety, and fear that I realized my body was actually trying (albeit ineffectively) to help me. It sensed a threat and leapt into self-protect mode, just not in a way that benefited the intellectual, occupational, or emotional dimensions of my performance.

For years, I forced myself to apply the not-so-helpful mantras of "Just do it!" and "Fake it till you make it," barreling into performance scenarios with zero self-awareness. I hoped (futilely) that eventually my body would become bored of being so reactive all the time and just get over it already. Ultimately, I learned that our bodies don't pause to deftly discern the difference between a potentially serious threat to our physical safety (like an ominous shadow in the ocean while we are snorkeling) or a likely manageable emotional threat (like negative judgment by our peers). Our bodies simply are programmed to react—fast. The cool thing is though, if we get to know, appreciate, and understand our bodies' automatic biological responses to perceived threats, we can consciously recalibrate our breathing, posture, thinking, and feeling, and then steer our bodies and brains onto a different course toward enhancing our performance in pivotal lawyering (and life) moments. This enhanced bodily awareness is called **somatic intelligence**. Rather than letting our physical reactions become stress-activating events themselves (like my blush exacerbating my mental and emotional angst), we can learn how to commandeer control—to "stay and play," as expert in human performance optimization and former figure skater, Dr. Gloria Park, puts it.[269]

For those of us who are laypersons when it comes to medicine, we may have dismissively used the term *psychosomatic* to refer to physical discomfort or ailments that have mental or emotional root causes rather than organic origins like an injury or infection. The term does not need to have a negative connotation though; rather, it can highlight the important influence our mind can have on our body. This relationship is a two-way street; a counterpart perspective—a *somatopsychic* one—prompts us to study the effects of our body on our mind.[270] By enhancing our understanding of our bodies, we can use our physicality to bolster the mental and emotional aspects of our performance.

The field of *somaesthetics*—developed by a philosophy professor named Dr. Richard Shusterman—invites us to become somatically intelligent, starting with revering our bodies as our most important instrument.[271] Shusterman points out that musicians, actors, dancers, and artists study how their instruments function; we too must learn how our essential tool—our body—operates, to get the most out of it.[272] Shusterman says that thinkers like philosophers and scholars (and thus, law students and lawyers) can do better work if we enhance our awareness of, and ability to regulate, our "somatic instrument of thought."[273] The body plays a key role in our thinking, feeling, and doing.[274] Instead of letting our bodies and brains react reflexively and wildly, we can use somatic (bodily) awareness to eliminate inefficient actions (physical and mental) performed out of impulse and inattention, and ultimately enhance self-regulation and performance.[275] (Remember Csikszentmihalyi's concept, discussed in Chapter 4, of becoming more efficient in how we steward psychic energy to foster *flow*? Similarly, here in studying our physical dimension, we can learn to recognize and regulate bodily responses to stress, anxiety, and fear that end up wasting precious energy.)

As we begin to regard ourselves as athletes or performers and dig into our physical well-being dimension, the following chart explains some terms and terminology we will explore that will help us better understand our bodies and enhance our somatic intelligence.

*Pre*habilitation[276]	Instead of waiting for an injury, illness, or medical emergency to nudge us to take care of our bodies, we can implement the sports/medical concept of *pre*habilitation: preemptive training strategies designed to prevent future harms from occurring. In *pre*habilitation, we deter rather than treat.
Eustress[277]	Eustress (*eu*: Greek for *good*) is a waystation between stress and distress. Everyone encounters stress, but we can decide whether to teeter off the precipice into distress, or intentionally linger in a productive eustress zone.
Homeostasis[278]	Our body continuously goes through a normal thermostatic process of stabilizing our heart rate, blood pressure, breathing, and other bodily functions.
Allostasis[279]	When we encounter stressors, our body proactively ramps up various processes, and our internal systems undergo normal fluctuations, with the goal of returning us to homeostasis.
Allostatic Load[280]	Over time though, if our systems are operating *inefficiently*, we can suffer metabolic wear and tear from the cumulative effect of the physiological burden sustained by our body in its effort to adapt to stressors.
Individual Zone of Optimal Functioning (IZOF)[281]	Each of us has an IZOF—a zone (like eustress) in which we are at our preferred performance arousal level (not overly amped up or jittery but also not numb). We can train ourselves to notice states of arousal, recalibrate stress responses, and toggle into our IZOF.

Neuroception[282]	Our body engages in a process of assessing whether new stimuli qualify as safe, potential threats, or definitely dangerous.
Proprioception[283]	Our body gleans sensory input from our external surroundings (i.e., objects, space, depth) and translates such information to enable us to move body parts via "motor reactions."
Interoception[284]	Our body keeps tabs on its internal state, garnering useful information from organs like our heart (heartbeat), lungs (respiration), and stomach (hunger).
Exteroception[285]	Our body registers stimuli outside ourselves, through senses like sight, smell, hearing, and touch.
Hormesis[286]	We can intentionally engage in low- to medium-dose stress experiences to help us build strength and *improve* resistance to future damage, injury, and panic. Exercise and novel experiences (like travel!) are forms of hormesis!
Arousal Reappraisal[287]	Good news! We have the power to reframe physiological responses to stress as *beneficial* rather than inhibitory to our performance.

We don't need to be elite athletes or famous performers to learn about and begin to apply the foregoing concepts in our lives as law students and lawyers. We *all* have bodies; therefore, we *all* can become somatically intelligent.

Let's start with the concept of ***pre*habilitation**.

ADOPTING A "PREHABILITATION" MINDSET

We've probably all heard the term *rehab*ilitation. Dictionaries define "rehab" as "the action of restoring someone to health or normal life through training and therapy after imprisonment, addiction, or illness."[288] The sports and medical worlds offer a different—forward-thinking—concept: *pre*habilitation. *Pre*hab serves at least three roles in sports and medicine:

- Athletes can engage in preemptive, preventive exercise methods to reduce the risk of future injury.
- Medical professionals can prescribe movements or exercises to patients *prior to* surgery to bolster strength before they encounter the stress of an operation.

- Medical professionals can instruct patients on how to enhance their functional capacity *before* surgery to withstand the stressor of inactivity after an operation.[289]

In prehab, we identify potential imbalances, weaknesses, or vulnerabilities that could later bloom into injuries[290] or that might prolong recovery after an invasive intervention like surgery.[291] In a prehab regimen, athletes, for example, focus on strengthening muscles around joints that could become vulnerable to injury because of repetitive or intense activity. We think and look *ahead* with the aim of *preventing* future injuries or harm, rather than retroactively treating such issues once they materialize. (This reminds me of one of the goals of the field of positive psychology: prevention, that is, building strength now as a *buffering* mechanism against future stressors.)

What if we were to apply the sports/medical concept of *pre*habilitation to the legal profession? Instead of waiting until legal community crises occur (burnout-related ethical lapses, addiction, the tragedy of suicide), what if we start implementing preemptive strategies to prevent injuries and harms from occurring—to ourselves and others? What if we identify potential imbalances and vulnerabilities that could manifest into future challenges, and then get to work bolstering our internal and external support networks now?

Dr. P. Z. Pearce is a recently retired doctor of sports medicine who treated athletes for four decades. Pearce is an avid proponent of prehabilitation as a way to lower the risk of injury or harm to athletes.[292] According to Pearce, a good prehab process involves first assessing an athlete's flexibility and strength, and then teaching athletes the fundamentals of basic training and injury prevention.[293] Interestingly, Pearce notes that 70% of all sports injuries result from overuse of body parts (muscles, joints, limbs), which he classifies as "certainly the most preventable" cause of athletic harm.[294] He emphasizes that athletes can avert injury by learning about, identifying, and remedying training errors *before* they materialize into problems.[295]

When we conjure images of hard-working and committed athletes or other types of performers, we might imagine them engaged in nonstop training. However, Pearce emphasizes that an effective training program has a simple ethos: we intentionally and mindfully stress a system; then we afford ample time for rest and recovery to allow the system to adapt to a higher level of function.[296] He explains that training can take two forms: engagement in short intense thrusts of movement (anaerobic) or longer sessions of endurance work (aerobic).[297] Either way, productive training requires interim periods of sufficient rest to necessarily allow for physiological adaptation.[298] The proper cycle is NOT go, go, go, go, go, until we drop. Rather, the proper cycle is: stress a system, rest, recover, adapt, repeat.[299]

Importantly, the concept of prehabilitation does not need to be limited to *physical* training; it can (and should) also apply to the development of *mental* fitness and psychological resilience in athletes and performers, and therefore—in my opinion—law students and lawyers.[300] The American Psychological Association (APA) defines psychological resilience as an individual's capacity to adapt *in healthy ways* to stressors and challenges.[301] As we will explore together later in this chapter, in constructing individual and collective *pre*habilitation regimens, we can learn how to evaluate and "appraise" perceived challenges in healthy ways, and develop physical, mental, and emotional techniques that we practice repeatedly, building protective layers against the negative effects of future stressors.[302]

One interesting research study in the context of sports psychology focused on the relationship between anxiety and shoulder injuries sustained by South African rugby players.[303] An article describing the study noted how previous researchers had analyzed linkages between biological, physical, environmental, and technical risk factors and rugby injuries; however, the role of psychological factors in injury development remained largely unexplored.[304] The South Africa study emphasized how coaches and talent scouts design rugby training programs to produce bigger, stronger, faster, and more talented players, yet some surprisingly forget to integrate injury *prevention* strategies, such as prehabilitation.[305] The study—which included 112 rugby players—found a link between anxiety and shoulder injuries, noting that anxiety can lead to muscle tension, narrowing of attention, and tightening of shoulders during rugby tackling maneuvers.[306] Only 54% of the players in the study who reported a shoulder injury had adhered to any sort of prehabilitation program.[307] The authors of the study suggested that future training programs should incorporate anxiety management techniques.[308]

Carving out some time to analyze where we might experience future "pain points" in our studies, work, and personal lives, we can construct a law version of prehab. Then, we can begin to strengthen *all the muscles* surrounding our most vulnerable joints. Instead of just continuing to flex, stress, and overstrain our intellectual and occupational muscles, we can develop multiple dimensions of well-being that can help us do our jobs (and life) better. Let's develop training systems and routines that we can trust and rely on in performance moments when we inevitably will encounter stress. Through *prehab*, we look ahead.

LET'S GET TO KNOW, AND STEP INTO, OUR EUSTRESS ZONE

I first learned the word **eustress** when I read the book *The Mindful Athlete: Secrets to Pure Performance,* by sports psychologist George Mumford, when I was writing *Untangling Fear.*[309] Mumford was an aspiring college basketball player, but injuries shifted his life onto a different trajectory. Now he works as a mindfulness and sports performance expert, advising athletes on issues affecting their health and well-being. He helps athletes connect their sports training regimens to game-day action and delivery. In Mumford's book, he describes the conscious choice we can make when we encounter an external stressor:

> *Life is all about the stimulus that we experience in the world and the way we interpret that in our minds. We can* react *to this stimulus in various knee-jerk ways—with anger, agitation, anxiety, fear, craving, doubt, guilt—or we can* respond *to this stimulus by getting still.*[310]

Mumford provides a helpful distinction among stress, distress, and what Dr. Hans Selye, author of *The Stress of Life,* defined as *eustress.*[311]

In his 1956 book, Selye distinguished between stressors and stress.[312] A stressor is a spark, a catalyst, a demand, or a provocation, while stress is our *reaction* to the stressor.[313] Likewise, Dr. Richard Lazarus (a psychologist who rose to prominence in the 1960s) defined stress as "a pattern of negative physiological states and psychological responses occurring in situations where people perceive threats to their well-being, which they may be unable to meet."[314] Further, "stress is a particular relationship between the person and the environment that is appraised by the person as taxing or exceeding [their] resources and endangering [their] well-being."[315]

A professional development and educational organization in the United Kingdom called the WJEC (formerly the Welsh Joint Education Committee) similarly describes a stressor as "a stimulus resulting in a positive or negative response to a specific situation. It produces both physiological and psychological symptoms."[316] As a reminder, "physiological" refers to the way our *body* works; "psychological" relates to our *mental* and *emotional* states. Consideration of all three dimensions—body, brain, and mind—is essential for us to understand how we function optimally (or suboptimally) in the face of stress.

In the mid-1970s, Selye introduced the concept of *eustress* as a state that differs from distress.[317] The *eu* in the word comes from the ancient Greek for *good, well, pleasant,* or *true.*[318] Eustress is a waystation between stress and distress.

We all experience stress. Law students and lawyers (and other members of the legal profession) wade through stress almost daily. As Mumford points out, "When stress is persistent, unresolved, and cumulative to the point of being chronic—whether that stress is physical or emotional—it becomes distress."[319] Lingering in protracted distress can lead to mental health issues such as anxiety or depression.[320] Likewise, distress is taxing on our physical bodies.

Mumford's book highlights Selye's eustress as a conscious and positive alternative to distress. He says:

> *Eustress, on the other hand, enhances physical and mental functions through such things as strength training and challenging work. This is the "good" kind of stress. Eustress can be described as that space between where we are and where we want to go—or that place between our comfort zones and the fringe of our discomfort zones.*[321]

Mumford explains that when we drive our physical bodies beyond our comfort zones in exercise, bodily movement, or sports conditioning, we feel physical manifestations of the exertion: we breathe more heavily, our hearts thump faster, we perspire, we might even sense a few pangs of muscle strain.[322] If we approach the physical challenge mindfully—armed with the knowledge that we actually can handle it—our bodies adjust, and we get physically stronger. Mumford says that, "In this way, we set down new neural pathways while increasing our physical skills."[323] Not only are we toning or building muscle, we are changing our brain. We are building self-trust.

The fear of being *unable* to handle a situation or, on the flip side, the knowledge we *can* navigate it is the important part here and determines whether stress turns into distress or eustress. The WJEC explains the difference between these two operational zones in the context of sports performance (which we can analogize to lawyering performance). The WJEC indicates that distress "is a negative form of stress and in extreme cases causes anxiety and apprehension. It tends to be detrimental to sporting performance."[324] In contrast, eustress "is positive and gives a feeling of fulfilment and arousal. It can increase focus, attention, and skill level. Some athletes actively seek and need stressful situations."[325] Thus, an athlete (and likewise, a law student or lawyer) in a state of distress typically cannot perform at peak levels because the body, brain, and mind are laser-focused on the amorphous blob of stress that seems all-encompassing—rather than the surmountable training or competition hurdle before them. In contrast, someone in a state of eustress feels motivated and energized to tackle the challenge. Through becoming somatically intelligent, we can develop the capacity to choose eustress over distress.

As noted on the website Mentalhelp.net, eustress is a beneficial, positive zone to linger in during training and performance because:

- We learn to trust that the discomfort from our exertion is a temporary state of being and will not last forever.
- We remind ourselves that we possess myriad coping mechanisms to move through the stress interval.
- This realization motivates rather than overwhelms us.
- We consciously channel our energy into focusing on tangible steps to execute the given task(s).
- We notice—in real-time—how our coping skills are working.
- We feel excited and empowered.
- Our performance improves incrementally.[326]

Eustress can spark physical, emotional, and psychological growth. It also can cultivate the experience of pleasure, help us notice what gives meaning to our life, and inspire us to optimistically approach complex challenges with a solution-oriented mindset.[327]

Let's contrast that with a state of distress, in which:

- We feel anxious, worried, or concerned.
- We are convinced this phase will persist for a long time, maybe forever.
- We doubt our coping abilities, or forget that we have them at all.
- We feel mental and physical discomfort, possibly even pain.
- Our performance deteriorates.
- Other mental and physical challenges emerge.[328]

Psychiatry professor and author (and one of my favorite lecturers in my master's program in positive psychology at Penn), Dr. John Ratey, echoes these principles. He emphasizes how eustress activities (like exercise or physical movement) heighten our ability to effectively process physical and mental sensory input.[329] We get better at noticing sensations that previously might have freaked us out, instead framing them as positive and helpful. For example, we may formerly have associated a rapid heartbeat, sweat, and faster breathing with anxiety or fear, but when we feel those sensations during exercise or physical movement, we start to realize we generated them through an activity *we* initiated, can control, and can ride out successfully.[330] We learn to trust our breathing and our ability to regulate our systems. If we engage in eustress activities on a regular basis—through an intentional prehabilitation regimen—we get better at more lucidly and accurately assessing, and then either discarding or untangling, perceived threats.[331]

Mumford draws parallels between physical development (through exercise and bodily movement) and mental growth:

> *The same is true of our ability to push ourselves mentally. Mentally we can train ourselves to be comfortable with being uncomfortable, to feel calm in the midst of chaos and stay in the eye of the proverbial hurricane.*[332]

Through enhanced self-awareness gained by exploring our eustress zone, we can increase our tolerance for temporary discomfort because we know and trust that it will subside.[333]

Importantly, Mumford advises that, in training, "[o]ur bodies work best when we push them in small increments. If we push ourselves too far, eustress can become distress."[334] Thus, for us, instead of barreling blindly into lawyering scenarios with a "just do it" or "fake it till you make it" mentality, we can learn how to toggle into, and ultimately thrive in, states of eustress, rather than floundering in states of distress. We'll do this by first reflecting; we'll conduct a physical inventory (see Exercise #2 at the end of this chapter), observing how our bodies naturally react to stress. Then, we'll get to know our sliding scale of different stress zones. These zones will differ for all of us and will range from unchallenged boredom, to healthy challenge and growth, to unhealthy overload and potential trauma. As Mumford counsels, we can treat the experience of stepping into productive eustress as "a continuous incremental process of romancing [our] discomfort zone."[335]

As members of the legal profession, we often understandably feel stress—as individuals and a community. Like Mumford's athletes though, we can strive to understand the great potential of the eustress zone. With proper guidance and boundaries, we can push ourselves physically and mentally, not to a point of distress (which can cause us to lose hope and self-trust), but instead into a zone of transformation. We grow by experiencing discomfort during training challenges and recognizing that we are not in peril but instead are safely strengthening and improving.

As we start to regard ourselves as scholar-athletes or scholar-performers, let's play in our different zones, familiarizing ourselves with how we move between the phases of stress, eustress, and distress. Let's enhance our self-awareness of the physical, emotional, and mental signs of too little "good" stress (boredom), too much "bad" stress (distress), and the "just right" ratio that pushes us into enough intensity that we grow (eustress). By getting to know our physical, emotional, and mental stress responses, we can *choose* to linger in states of *eustress* instead of catapulting into *distress*. We can decide whether to teeter off the precipice into *distress*, or intentionally revel in productive *eustress*. Sounds empowering, right?

THE HOMEOSTASIS-ALLOSTASIS DANCE

We might remember from high school science class that **homeostasis** is our body's state of internal balance.[336] Our body constantly strives to maintain this steady condition.[337] The word homeostasis derives from Greek words for *same* and *steady*.[338] In homeostasis, numerous physiological measures—such as body temperature, oxygen, heart rate, blood pressure, hunger, and thirst—hover at optimal levels.[339]

Stressors are external forces that jostle us out of homeostasis.[340] When that happens, our body initiates a *stress response* in an effort to restore homeostasis.[341] While animals launch the stress response only when they are *actually* knocked out of homeostasis, Dr. Robert M. Sapolsky, author of *Why Zebras Don't Get Ulcers: The Acclaimed Guide to Stress, Stress-Related Diseases, and Coping*, points out that humans can activate the stress response merely by *anticipating* a disruption to our homeostasis.[342]

Stress scientists Dr. Peter Sterling, Dr. Joseph Eyer, and Dr. Bruce McEwen have expanded our understanding of homeostasis through introducing and studying another concept: **allostasis**. Researchers define allostasis a bit paradoxically in that it signifies our body's ability to restore constancy or stability through the act of change.[343] *Allo* derives from the Greek for *other* or *different* or *variable*.[344] Allostasis represents our body's natural ability to calibrate physiological levers to adjust to changing environmental conditions and ultimately return us to homeostasis.[345]

Stressors naturally disturb homeostasis, prompting our bodies to adapt.[346] Our body launches a three-step process that scientists call the general adaptation syndrome.[347] Selye—whom Sapolsky refers to as "one of the godfathers of stress physiology"[348]—outlined three phases of our stress response: alarm, adaptation (also called resistance), and exhaustion.[349] In the alarm stage, our bodies and brains register the stressor. In the adaptation stage, allostasis kicks in; ideally, our bodies respond to and deal with the stressor, then work toward reestablishing homeostasis.[350] If stress persists and lingers, however, we can enter a phase of exhaustion.[351] This is the not-so-good zone where stress-related ailments germinate and grow.[352]

Sapolsky urges us to understand that the ramifications of an overactivated (or inefficient) stress-response system can wreak more damage than the stressor itself.[353] If we constantly allow our bodies to spring into the act of allostasis (even in circumstances that don't warrant such a taxing physiological response), eventually this causes metabolic wear and tear, which researchers call **allostatic load**.[354] Allostatic load is the cumulative metabolic wear and tear our bodies sustain due to recurrent cycles of allostatic stress responses, and inefficient ramping up and winding back down of our physiological systems.[355] In addition to chronic stress, major life events also can contribute to allostatic load.[356] (The trauma of my divorce, compounded by 9/11 the same year, in addition to moving twenty-five times in 50 years likely has exacerbated my allostatic load.)

As scholar-athletes and scholar-performers, we can begin to learn about, pay attention to, and actively address situations and habits that compound our allostatic load, so we can avoid inadvertently fostering a breeding ground for anxiety, depression, and illness.[357] Encouragingly, we don't have to be scientists or medical professionals to educate ourselves about our stress-response system and start engaging our bodies, brains, and minds to work *for* us (rather than against us).

LET'S LEARN A BIT MORE ABOUT THE MECHANICS OF OUR STRESS RESPONSE

As Sapolsky explains, we have both a *voluntary* nervous system and an *autonomic* nervous system.[358] Our voluntary nervous system instigates conscious physical acts, such as greeting someone COVID-style with an elbow bump or punching a boxing bag with a gloved hand. In contrast, our autonomic nervous system initiates reflexive operations, such as blushing and sweating.

Our autonomic nervous system has sub-channels. One part of the autonomic nervous system, called the *sympathetic* nervous system, is activated by stressors; another part, called the *parasympathetic* nervous system, is suppressed by stressors.[359] Stanley Rosenberg, author of *Accessing the Healing Power of the Vagus Nerve: Self-Help Exercises for Anxiety, Depression, Trauma, and Autism,* explains that the autonomic nervous system is tightly linked to our emotional state, which in turn shapes our reactive and responsive behavior.[360] The origin of the term *sympathetic* in this context is attributed to a Greek physician, surgeon, and philosopher named Galen, who influenced many scientific disciplines, including anatomy.[361] Galen described nerves and organs working together, as in *sympathy,* leading to the naming of the sympathetic nervous system.[362]

During a stress response, our sympathetic nervous system releases hormones called epinephrine and norepinephrine (the American equivalents of the British terms adrenaline and noradrenaline).[363] The adrenal gland secretes other hormones called glucocorticoids.[364] Glucocorticoids activate neurons in the brainstem and incite sympathetic arousal.[365]

Ideally, once a stressor has passed, our parasympathetic system takes over and begins to mellow us back out.[366] An important nerve called the vagus nerve (described a bit more in the next section of this chapter) begins to slow down our heartbeat.[367] We return to a state of calm.[368]

If the threat to our safety is real, we want our systems to kick into gear like this—this natural rise and fall is a good thing. However, if we put our bodies through this physiological roller-coaster ride in situations wholly unworthy of such an effortful response, our systems eventually suffer. As Sapolsky emphasizes, the stress response is designed to equip our body to immediately and explosively expend energy to address real and concrete physical threats.[369] But when we allow *psychological* stress to overactivate our physical stress response, this all-systems-go exertion can be wasteful and depleting.

Sapolsky explains that a moderate amount of stress stimulation can improve memory and learning.[370] (This brings to mind our productive eustress zone!) However, if we blast right into severe stress scenarios (distress), memory falters.[371] Sapolsky cautions that severe and prolonged stress detrimentally affects learning, and even more significantly, our immune system's functioning.[372] Rosenberg echoes this principle; if our professional or personal lives keep us dialed up to a constant stress state, even in the absence of present threats or bodily danger, problems grow like weeds.[373] (That's why amping up our somatic self-knowledge is an awesome way to *prehab* and be forward thinking about how we tackle stress encounters!)

LET'S GET TO KNOW OUR VAGUS NERVE

Rosenberg explains that cranial nerves, spinal nerves, and parts of our brainstem work together to form our autonomic nervous system.[374] We have twelve cranial nerves.[375] One of them—called the **vagus nerve**, whose name derives from the Latin *vagus*, which means *vagrant* or *wanderer*—meanders through the body from the brainstem down into the chest and abdomen, managing many of our organs.[376] When I read in Rosenberg's book that the vagus nerve stimulates the lungs (respiration); the heart (circulation); the stomach, liver, pancreas, and intestines (digestion); and the kidneys (elimination),[377] I laughed out loud because the rhyming reminded me of a list of nouns in one of my favorite U2 songs: *Desperation, dislocation, separation, condemnation, . . . Let it go.* (I love this lyric so much, I have it tattooed on my ribs, translated into Italian.) Because the vagus nerve reaches into and touches so many body functions, it plays a key role in helping us maintain and reestablish homeostasis.[378] Some scientists refer to this tool as our "vagal brake"—our ability to slow everything down and find ease again.[379]

In 1994, a scientist and psychiatry professor, Dr. Stephen Porges, introduced a concept called the polyvagal theory.[380] Prior to the emergence of Porges's polyvagal theory, the general belief was that our autonomic nervous system had only the two channels: our sympathetic system, which ramps up in response to stress (which we commonly refer to as our fight-or-flight state),[381] and our parasympathetic system (associated with the vagus nerve), responsible for returning us to a state of calm.[382] Porges, however, identified a third autonomic circuit. His polyvagal theory delineates *two* branches of the vagus nerve: the ventral branch and the dorsal branch.[383] The ventral branch facilitates a state of relaxation, peaceful rest, a feeling of well-being, and an ability to engage socially.[384] The dorsal branch, in contrast, metabolically shuts us down, putting us in a depressed state.[385] When we are frozen or paralyzed with fear, the dorsal branch is running the show.[386] The dorsal represents the *freeze* mode of the fight-flight-freeze response. Porges's theory invites us to get to know and embrace the ventral vagus circuit in our parasympathetic system; the ventral branch can elevate us out of chronic overactivation of our sympathetic (fight-or-flight) response, and out of dorsal shutdown/freeze states.[387] Notably, the ventral vagus circuit activates and thrives when we feel *safe*.[388] Porges uses the term "vagal tone," analogous to muscle tone, to describe the quality of our ability to deploy our vagal brake.[389]

afety
heme!

Porges also invented the term **neuroception** to define our body's process of assessing whether new stimuli qualify as safe, potential threats, or definitely dangerous.[390] Encouragingly, as Rosenberg points out, we can improve the accuracy of our neuroception by getting to know our bodily senses and learning how to ground ourselves when we encounter unfamiliar stimuli.[391] (We will learn more about the differences between neuroception and other modes of sensory perception like **proprioception**, **interoception**, and **exteroception** in a bit, and how we can tie all these functions together, choosing to linger in productive eustress zones, instead of distress.)

Life obviously is a box of stressors. Unless we encase ourselves in Bubble Wrap, we inevitably will encounter stimuli that potentially activate our sympathetic system (fight-or-flight) or send us into a dorsal freeze. However, Rosenberg offers words of reassurance: each time we consciously reboot our ventral vagus state, or what he calls a state of social engagement in which we feel emotionally and physically *safe*, our autonomic nervous system becomes stronger, more resilient, and more able to bob and weave at the next series of punches thrown at us by life.[392] We can train ourselves to be ventral vagus victors.

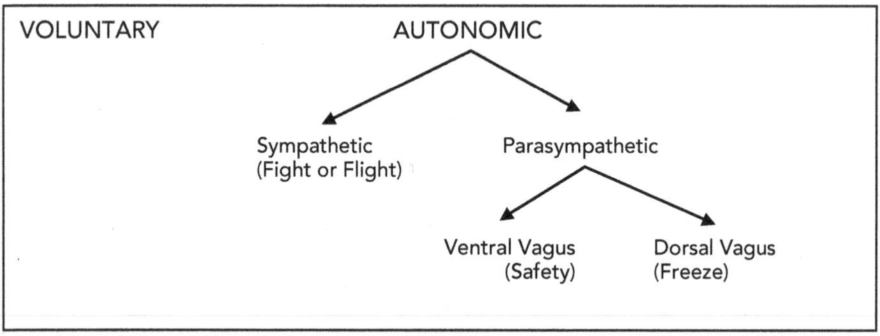

NERVOUS SYSTEM PATHWAYS

WHAT IS HEART RATE VARIABILITY?

Rosenberg indicates that when our nervous system is humming along optimally, the length of time between consecutive heartbeats varies naturally; in other words, the normal ebb and flow of our emotions, changes in breathing patterns, hormonal fluctuations, and rise and fall of blood pressure lead to inconsistencies in the durations between sequential heartbeats.[393] This is called heart rate variability (HRV).[394] Ideally, we want high HRV: a robust level of variation in the time intervals between heartbeats. If we have high HRV, it apparently means the ventral branch of our vagus nerve is operating well.[395] On the flip side, if our autonomic nervous system tends to linger in a fight-or-flight stress state, or a depressed state of dorsal activity, we have less variation in time intervals between heartbeats (or low HRV).[396] A low HRV means we tend to loiter in one state. If we have a low HRV, "it's a sign that the body is under stress and the vagus nerve has been temporarily put on the bench."[397] (If this concept seems confusing, don't worry; the concept of high variability being "good" still seems very counterintuitive to me too.)

A company called Elite HRV explains:[398]

> *Generally, a low HRV (or less variability in the heartbeats) indicates that the body is under stress from exercise, psychological events, or other internal or external stressors. Higher HRV (or greater variability between heartbeats) usually means that the body has a strong ability to tolerate stress or is strongly recovering from prior accumulated stress.*

Caroline Williams, author of the book, *Move! The New Science of Body Over Mind*, indicates that researchers have connected high HRV with these health benefits:

- Improved working memory
- Enhanced capacity to focus
- Emotional steadiness
- Less risk of anxiety and depression
- Stronger ability to manage blood sugar levels
- Improved ability to suppress inflammation[399]

She emphasizes that "[i]ncreasing vagal tone is not about never getting stressed, but having a flexible system that can return to normal as quickly as possible afterwards."[400]

Interestingly, we can check our HRV through a chest strap heart monitor or other device that connects to accompanying apps that analyze the data. (I bought an electronic device (a ring) with an app that measures my HRV, but mine appears to be alarmingly low![401] Even though I feel like I practice flexibility by working out so much and returning to baseline levels of physiological arousal—and I feel pretty emotionally relaxed these days—it's possible I am not taking enough breaks for recovery from exercise, eustress activities, and perhaps less overt stressors.)

WHAT'S THE DEAL WITH STRESS HORMONES?

Let's add one more layer of learning about our bodily responses to stress before we start talking about action plans: hormones. Two categories of hormones—**catabolic** and **anabolic**—and the balance between them, determine whether our bodies operate in destructive or restorative zones.[402]

As we now know from Sapolsky's and Rosenberg's explanations summarized earlier in this chapter, our sympathetic nervous system kicks our fight-or-flight response into gear. In response to a stressor, the sympathetic nervous system unleashes hormones such as epinephrine, norepinephrine, and cortisol to launch what are called *catabolic* processes.[403] Catabolic systems—a term that derives from the Greek word for *throwing down*—break complex components into simpler ones; in the context of stress, catabolic processes split molecules into energy.[404]

On the flip side, our parasympathetic nervous system releases a different set of hormones, such as growth hormone, insulin-like growth factor (IGF-1), and insulin.[405] These hormones activate *anabolic* processes.[406] Anabolism—which derives from the Greek words for a *mound* and *throwing objects up*—is the process of synthesizing or putting simple components together to build more complex structures.[407] Our anabolic processes foster relaxation, digestion, storage of energy, and healing.[408]

Catabolic hormones, particularly cortisol, and anabolic hormones battle one another.[409] Our body is constantly engaged in a tug-of-war, or a dance, between catabolic and anabolic processes.[410] We need catabolic hormones to survive.[411] But if we exist in a chronic stress or arousal state, our catabolic hormones (especially cortisol) exact a toll. This is the allostatic load we discussed earlier. We become less equipped to adapt to future stressors in healthy ways.[412]

When our catabolic processes ramp up to handle a true stressor, thereafter we want our anabolic processes to wind us back down to a relaxed state. Health psychologist Dr. Elissa Epel and her colleagues describe an "ideal or tight allostatic system" as one that smoothly and flexibly transitions from high-arousal to low-arousal states, rolling with the given circumstances.[413]

Interestingly, medical professionals can measure our ratio of anabolic to catabolic hormonal levels when we are in a resting state.[414] Scientists refer to this as the growth index.[415] If our anabolic-to-catabolic ratio shows a positive growth index, this indicates that we exist in a state of low allostatic load, good health in terms of stress management, and thriving.[416] There, our stress-response system is functioning effectively and efficiently, and we are accruing resources to handle future stressors.[417] Conversely, as we have discussed, chronic stress heightens our allostatic load, decreasing our efficacy and economy in responding to future stressors.[418]

So, what can we do about this? Encouragingly, Epel and her colleagues suggest two potential avenues for fostering allostatic flourishing: (1) intentional exposure to short-term stressors we know we are equipped to handle, and (2) purposeful periods of relaxation, that is, episodes of consciously reduced arousal.[419] Short-term, intermittent, properly managed stress can prompt the body to engage in the catabolic-anabolic dance, recover, and foster "tight allostasis."[420] (Again, in contrast, chronic and poorly managed stress overtaxes the catabolic system, exacerbating allostatic load.)[421] Additionally, time to recover from one stress event before tackling another one is essential for our bodies to replenish our resources.[422]

I find it intriguing, and reassuring, that we don't need (and in fact shouldn't try) to eliminate all stress from our lives. Like athletes intentionally stress muscles to break them down initially so they can build back better and stronger, we too can benefit from intentionally engaging in manageable-dose stress scenarios (also called **hormesis**, which we'll dive into next) with a mindset toward initiating short-term catabolic processes followed by enhanced restorative anabolic processes.[423]

WHAT IS HORMESIS?

I'm excited about the term *hormesis*. Like many of the other terms we are learning, the origin of this word is also Greek, meaning *rapid motion, eagerness, impelling*, and *urging on*.[424] Epel defines hormesis as a short-in-duration, low-to-moderate-dose stressor that can generate positive physiological and psychological reactions.[425] (Sounds similar to eustress!) Exercise is a perfect example of a hormetic intervention.[426] Another example is intentional exposure to contrasting temperatures: Imagine jumping from a hot sauna into a cold plunge pool, and then back again. Further, Epel suggests that novel experiences that require us to tap into coping mechanisms, apply knowledge, and master challenges, and that result in a sense of achievement or accomplishment also count as hormesis.[427] (This makes me think of solo travel experiences!)

Throughout the (first) pandemic winter, many days I jogged solo on a small track at my neighborhood park, the lone person braving New York's frigid temperatures. My cheeks frozen, tiny ice flecks clinging to my eyelashes, the crisp fresh air invigorated me. At the time, I didn't realize this was a double dose of hormesis: exercise and the shock of cold air.

Epel explains that hormetic stress, in a moderate and controlled manner, yields the benefits of "housecleaning," rejuvenating our cells and igniting growth of new neural pathways.[428] These mild to moderate stressors spur our cells to adapt, relatively quickly.[429] A hormesis episode does not revert the body back to normal; it delivers a better, stronger version of our self.[430] Here's the sequence: we mildly to moderately stress the body; our adaptation response kicks in; the body reacts, building scaffolding around areas that feel challenged; the body heals, and grows.[431] After, when we pause to notice how quickly and effectively we recovered from the short-term stressor, we begin to trust that we can do so again. (Again, this sounds like eustress!) This iterative process helps us develop plasticity for survival and thriving.[432]

Hormetic High-Fives

Mildly to moderately intense exercise and bodily movement can shift us into a hormesis zone. There, we navigate the rise and fall of stress arousal symptoms and learn to trust that we can handle such temporarily taxing physical, mental, and emotional responses, ultimately riding through the hormesis experience successfully. As Epel and her colleagues encouragingly point out though, other novel experiences that require us to tap into coping mechanisms, apply knowledge, master challenges, and acknowledge a sense of achievement or accomplishment also count as hormesis.[433]

For me, that's solo travel.

A New York City sound jolted me awake—again. I glanced at the clock. 3:26 a.m. *What on earth is driving this new iteration of chronic insomnia? Stress? Has the pandemic finally taken its toll on my psyche?* As an introvert, I thought I had the whole working-from-home thing nailed. Throughout the (first) wild pandemic academic year, I juggled my usual 800 balls in the air, but mid-April 2021, some began dropping—loudly and sloppily. The end of the semester rapidly approached. I kept telling myself, *Just grade two papers a day . . . Get through those three or four more dreaded Zoom meetings a day . . . Remember to eat . . . Don't worry, you'll finally sleep this summer.*

In early May, as I scrolled through countless emails from people already pressing me to make decisions about the fall semester (I screamed at my computer, *For the love of God, can't we just catch our breath from the spring semester first?!*), it finally hit me: I was completely and utterly burned out. Like *epically* fried, to my core. Not since 2001, when my divorce and 9/11 trauma brought me to my knees, had I felt this raw.

I pushed myself to finish grading earlier than usual, and then I did the only thing I knew would breathe fresh life into me. I researched every location around the globe that would accept vaccinated Americans. A rule-follower, I scrutinized the wildly confusing COVID protocols for various destinations. And then I booked a one-way ticket to Croatia—a gift to myself for surviving the academic year. And a rebellious declaration that I needed to begin treating myself like a writer again. I craved time, space, quietude, and independence to hunker down and get to serious work on this book. Navigating complicated COVID PCR test timing (absurdly long waits for results, bumping up against 72-hour travel validity windows) added a smidge more to my stress level. But the moment I held a KLM boarding pass in my hand, I knew everything was going to be okay.

After switching planes in Amsterdam, I landed in the Croatian city of Split. Croatian border patrol photographed my vaccine card, asked about my accommodations and departure date, and then administered that lovely ch-chunk sound of the stamp hitting my passport. *I was in!*

I spent 11 days exploring the history and culture of Split, practicing my one Croatian word (*hvala*, which means *thank you*), taking day trips on ferries to local islands like Hvar and Braĉ and a longer ride to Dubrovnik, where I stayed two nights. I hiked, toured vestiges of ancient Roman temples and amphitheaters, and ate delicious whole grilled fish doused in olive oil and lemon. On the tenth day, I found my way to a clinic for my sixth COVID PCR test (after accidentally waiting in the vestibule of a Botox clinic and sipping the cappuccino they graciously offered me before we all realized I was in the wrong place). I obtained the test results in English later that day, and the following morning, I boarded a flight to Barcelona (via Vienna). When I finally arrived at my hotel in Barcelona for a one-night stopover, having shown my passport and test results three more times, I felt like I'd won the show *The Amazing Race*. The next afternoon (before my PCR test results expired), I hopped on one more flight to Tenerife in the Canary Islands, where I had rented a one-bedroom house to spend a month writing this book.

Here's where hormesis kicked in. Because of the house's remote location in a banana grove overlooking a volcanic black-sand beach on the Atlantic Ocean, far away from public transportation, I needed to rent a car. This might not sound like a big to-do for most people, but I've lived in New York City for 20 years, no longer own a vehicle, and happily take the subway or walk everywhere. The last time I sat behind the steering wheel of an automobile was Thanksgiving before the pandemic hit, when I flew to Norfolk, Virginia, and then needed to drive another two hours to visit my family in North Carolina's Outer Banks. At the Tenerife airport, I gingerly slid my driver's license and credit card through the half-moon in the glass barrier between the Autoreisen clerk and me. I tried to exude cool competence, like I operate motor vehicles in foreign countries all the live-long day. With barely a glance, he handed me the keys to a Citroën. As I heaved my suitcases (laden with research books) into the trunk of the car and nestled into the driver's seat, I murmured a silent *thank you* to my dad, who'd taught me how to drive stick shift on a beat-up, rusted-out Volkswagen Beetle when I was sixteen. Learning how to drive a car with manual transmission and a temperamental clutch and sticky gears had armed me with at least one helpful tool for getting myself to my Tenerife house in one piece. I activated my iPhone GPS (shelving concerns for the astronomical cell phone bill that likely would await me upon my return to the United States) and entered the address for the house. I remembered that the homeowners had sent me precise latitude and longitude coordinates via WhatsApp, but I mused, *Why on earth would I need those details if I have the address?*

I shifted into first gear, listened to my GPS's voice Americanize the Spanish names of roads, and I exhaled. *Enjoy every minute of this adventure, babe. You've earned it.* I navigated the curvy two-lane highway away from the airport fine, watching the orange sun begin to set over lovely green mountains. I practiced downshifting and upshifting through the road's arcs. GPS led me to a roundabout. Instructed me to take the third exit. *Uno. Dos. Tres. Wait, which one's the third exit?* My Citroën circled the roundabout again. I re-counted, prayed I chose the correct route, veered onto a smaller road, and then found myself on an even narrower one-lane road flanked by stone walls. No visible street names or house numbers. Only banana trees, bougainvillea, cactus plants, and me—feeling the initial familiar pangs of panic. *What if another car comes from the other direction?!* My GPS started speaking Spanish, then English, then told me I had passed my destination. *But there is nowhere to turn around?* The road descended further toward the ocean, deeper into fields of banana trees. The sky purpled. The road opened up slightly to reveal a parked pickup truck and four guys sitting on the ground, chilling and drinking beers. I slammed the brakes so as not to plow into them. My car stalled.

I decided to input the actual latitude and longitude coordinates of the house into the GPS. The GPS admonished me to backtrack. I restarted the Citroën and orchestrated a five-point turn to point my car back up the hill. The guys waved. After a few hundred feet, the GPS declared, *You have arrived at your destination.* I HAVE NOT ARRIVED—I AM IN THE MIDDLE OF A BANANA FIELD! My heart knocked at my ribs. I inched the car further up the hill, stalled once more, gently restarted the engine somehow without rolling the vehicle backward into a concrete wall. I wound my way around the twists and loops of the road, and ended up back at the main road. *Do not freak out. Turn around and try again.* I maneuvered the car in the correct direction and slowly descended the serpentine hill once more. I recognized a pile of broken cactus pieces I had passed a few times, and then suddenly noticed a bamboo gate between two white terra cotta planters. The entrance to the property I had seen in the owners' photographs! No house number in sight. I pulled into the driveway. The owners had been waiting for me and opened the mechanized gate. A gorgeous, tan, smiley Spanish woman named Marta waved happily at me. I exhaled again. *You made it, babe. Remember U2's lyric: Don't fear the world. It isn't there.*

Marta gave me a quick tour of the property, handed me the keys to my writing cottage, and bid me a great night's sleep. I poured a glass of chilled Canarian white wine and sat on my veranda just as the sun dunked into the Atlantic. It took me a solid hour to truly calm down. As I watched 6-inch lizards engage in standoffs with sweet-looking cats (one extroverted and one introverted) and butterflies and dragonflies dart across the wicker sunbed, I smiled at the realization that my entire post-semester travel adventure thus far had been an exercise in hormesis. I grabbed a new journal that my Penn classmate Grace had gifted me for my birthday, its leather cover adorned with orange koi fish and blue flowers, and began to list the stress-induced **physical** sensations I had felt so far on the journey:

- Chest pangs worrying about delayed COVID PCR results that could have prevented my departure from New York and then again from Croatia (but didn't)
- A headache about possibly not having the right paperwork for border patrol in multiple countries (I did)
- Shortness of breath when renting the car, driving it, stalling on the twisty hill, feeling lost

My heart had thumped rapidly. My forehead was so sweaty, I had worried I would set off alarms at airport temperature check machines. My hands had trembled as I gripped the steering wheel of the rental car so tightly.

Next, I made a list of **mental** and **emotional** messages that had churned: *Why are you putting yourself through this? You could have done something easy like go to Vermont?! What on earth gives you the right to take all this time "off" to write a book; you've got umpteen other work responsibilities? You're being so selfish. Also, you probably read the Amsterdam/Croatia/Vienna/Spain/Canary Islands websites wrong?! Ugh, you have the worst sense of geographical direction too!*

But then, I made the most important list—I catalogued the skills and competencies I had tapped into to get myself to an incredibly wild and natural destination where I could carve out the time and space to rest and write this book:

- My ability to thoroughly research flights, interesting Airbnbs, travel protocols, and COVID rules
- My interest in spending time in locations where not many Americans go
- My desire to immerse in languages besides English
- My organizational skills in having all my paperwork in order for multiple border controls (Amsterdam, Croatia, Vienna, Barcelona, Canary Islands)
- My physical stamina for hauling four pieces of luggage through multiple airports
- My patience in navigating three different airlines' luggage rules
- My ability to drive a stick-shift car
- My bravery in driving a car in a foreign country after not having driven *at all* for a year-and-a-half
- My capacity to self-regulate and realize that it's okay if I'm lost; I'm not going to be stuck in the middle of a banana farm forever; I'll eventually find where I'm supposed to be
- My self-awareness about when I need to take a deep breath and trust myself and my coping systems
- My self-awareness to notice when my shame and guilt triggers are pressed, and to activate my coping systems (journaling, exercise, my two-hour-a-day writing process) to remind myself why I am here, that I deserve this retreat to work on my art and myself, and that I am not doing anything wrong by taking the time and space I need
- My badassness in being able to do all this solo

The 13 days of travel to and from Croatia culminating in my safe arrival in Tenerife constituted a hormetic experience. Yes, at times, I felt stressed. But I was able to unlock my stockpile of resources to solve sundry problems. In the end, my body and brain reestablished a relaxed state. And then I got to enjoy the sensation of being proud of what I had achieved. And over the subsequent month, I reaped the rewards of new life experiences I never would have had access to if I had taken the safe route and stayed home. I also added a piece of evidence to my memory bank that I can retrieve the next time I feel trepidation toward another adventure.

What hormetic or eustress experiences can we dive into (with awareness) this week? And when we emerge from them, let's give ourselves hormetic high-fives!

WHAT IS OUR INDIVIDUAL ZONE OF OPTIMAL FUNCTIONING?

I find it encouraging to learn that there is not a one-size-fits-all model of eustress or hormesis, or any of these concepts. Each of us is a unique individual, and our brains, minds, and bodies process stimuli differently from person to person. Indeed, a Russian sports psychologist named Dr. Yuri Hanin discovered that the circumstances and conditions under which different athletes deliver their best performances depend upon *individualized* optimal states of arousal.[434] (Remember that arousal here means "a state of physiological alertness and readiness for action."[435]) In other words, the most favorable states of arousal for prime performance differ from athlete to athlete.

In his early studies, Hanin used an assessment tool called a State-Trait Anxiety Inventory to evaluate relationships between athletes' state anxiety and performance levels. [436] (In psychology, a *state* is a temporary or situational thought, feeling, or behavior whereas a *trait* is a more stable and lasting characteristic or habit.[437]) Later, Hanin expanded his research beyond anxiety to consider a variety of emotional states that could influence athletes' performance, such as alertness, anger, excitement, exhaustion, and many more.[438] Hanin developed a concept called the **Individual Zone of Optimal Functioning**, or **IZOF**, which he defines as the personal setting and condition in which each athlete performs at their peak.[439] When athletes' emotional states fall outside their optimal zones, that is, arousal levels are either too intense or not intense enough, athletic performance typically declines.[440] Hanin's research suggests that athletes should identify and study their *own* IZOF rather than comparing themselves to benchmarks of other athletes.[441] Coaches and trainers can teach athletes about performance arousal states; help them better understand and interpret mental, emotional, and physical reactions that affect training and performance; and instill techniques for entering and staying in IZOF when performance counts.[442]

Like athletes and performers, we too can explore our IZOF—as law students, lawyers, and other members of the legal profession. Instead of trying to mirror what everyone around us is doing, let's get somatically intelligent and construct individualized training routines that will help us tap into our IZOF and ultimately perform at our best.

INTERLUDE: A WORD ON SLEEP

I'm probably the last person in the universe who should be giving advice about sleep. I have chronic insomnia. Every night, I try to do everything "right," sleep-wise. I make sure my bedroom is as cold as a meat locker. I stop looking at computer, phone, and TV screens at least an hour before I go to bed. I leave my phone in the kitchen all night. I take one melatonin tablet. I dab peppermint oil on my forehead—another effort to feel cool instead of perpetually hot. I usually fall asleep okay under a weighted comforter. And then, like clockwork, I'm wide awake at 3:26 a.m. Often unsuccessful at falling back to sleep, I get up, shuffle like a zombie to the kitchen, grab my phone, slide back in bed, and try listening to guided meditations on the app Insight Timer. Sometimes I can finally drift back asleep around 5:00 a.m. and I wake up again around 7:00 a.m.

I used to freak out about not sleeping. I'd lie in bed worrying about how tired and headachy I would be the next day. I'd begin imagining issues that didn't exist: political dramas at work, health concerns, relationship dilemmas. Everything seems worse at 4:00 a.m. But then I read a different perspective about sleep in Ratey and Manning's book, *Go Wild.*

Ratey and Manning start off by referencing research by Dr. Robert Stickgold—one of the world's leading sleep researchers—indicating that "for every two hours [our] brain spends taking in information during the day, it needs an hour of sleep to figure out what that means. If [we] don't get that hour, [we] don't figure it out. The difference between being smart and wise is two more hours of sleep a night."[443] Ratey and Manning also mention Dr. Antti Revonsuo, another sleep researcher, who describes sleep not as a "retreat to helplessness, but rather a functioning part of our learning process when the brain works through problems and devises solutions."[444] Sleep researcher and anthropologist Dr. Carol Worthman cautions that sleep deficiency resembles stress, increasing cortisol.[445]

Stickgold says we all need 8.5 hours of sleep out of every 24 hours.[446]

Of course, when I first read this information, I thought, *Well, 8.5 hours of sleep sounds epic, but how on earth do we make that happen?*

Ratey and Manning offer an encouraging perspective about sleep: they say we don't need to crash out for exactly 8.5 hours in a row every night to be "good" sleepers. They urge, "Irregularity is okay. So are naps. A sense of safety is critical."[447] In their book, I learned about a sleep pattern called "second sleep" described in historical writings from preindustrial Europe; people apparently would go to bed early, wake up in the middle of the night for a few hours—when they would interact with other human beings!—and then go back to sleep.[448] Minus the interacting-with-other-humans part, this is my life!

Dr. Daniel Lieberman, author of the book *Exercised: The Science of Physical Activity, Rest and Health* and expert in human evolution and health, acknowledges that sleep provides needed rest but he indicates, "we don't actually need to sleep to save energy, repair tissues, and otherwise recuperate; we could just sit still."[449] Indeed, he describes sleep as a process of "flush[ing] out the cobwebs left behind by the day's experiences."[450] But, like Ratey and Manning, Lieberman takes the pressure off us to get the prescribed dosage of eight (or Stickgold's 8.5) hours of solid, uninterrupted sleep each night. (I find this to be a relief, because that is literally impossible for me to achieve!) He identified Worthman as the source of the research revealing that, prior to the Industrial Revolution, it was normal for people to wake up in the middle of the night for an hour or more.[451]

Lieberman acknowledges that many of us are sleep deprived. But instead of sounding alarm bells of concern about lying awake in the middle of the night, he suggests we focus on balancing rest, exercise, and physical activity, and understanding our patterns of sleep and wakefulness.[452]

So, I'm no sleep expert. But I've started paying attention to when I am tired, letting myself go to sleep then (if logistically possible), and not stressing out if I'm not able to sleep 8.5 solid hours in a row. Some of the same electronic apps that measure HRV can also track our sleep patterns, providing helpful information and suggested modifications regarding sleep timing and other conditions. Since I started tracking my sleep with the same ring and app that monitor my HRV, I'm realizing that I do get a decent number of hours of sleep per night, just not all in a row. This discovery has made me feel better about sleep in general.

LET'S GET TO WORK: FOUR SOMATIC INTELLIGENCE STRATEGIES

Some empowering news: Even if we have overly hyped-up stress-response systems (our sympathetic nervous system) or tend to wallow in a dorsal vagal state (our parasympathetic system), we have the power to do something about it. Educating ourselves, we can get proactive and adopt a prehabilitation regimen. Rosenberg advocates that we start by enhancing our knowledge about how to influence our autonomic nervous system so we can more readily transition out of fight-or-flight or dorsal vagal (freeze) states back into ventral vagal (socially engaged) states.[453] We can purposefully toggle into eustress and hormesis zones, notice the rise and fall of our physiological stress responses, and begin to identify our IZOF. Researchers indicate that we can nurture a state, or perhaps a practice, of enhanced allostasis by improving our methods of **appraising** stressors and then activating healthy coping techniques.[454] Enhanced allostasis helps us buffer against detrimental effects of catabolic stress responses and reap the benefits of anabolic and restorative physiological systems.[455]

Accordingly, four practical strategies for cultivating our physical well-being dimension include:

- **Somatic self-discovery** through enhanced bodily awareness
- Purposeful engagement in movement-oriented **eustress** and **hormesis** activities (i.e., experimenting with riding out the rise and fall of arousal responses in activities like exercise, physical movement, and other exertions of energy)
- Adoption of healthy **appraisal scripts** (i.e., realistically and positively framing stimuli and stressors)
- Development of training **routines** and adoption of effective coping **rituals** we can activate in training and performance moments[456]

Let's work toward reducing our allostatic overload.[457] Our goal can be to nurture our systems such that we optimally engage in allostasis, recover rapidly from acute stress scenarios, and exist at a healthy resting level of physiological arousal.[458]

Strategy #1: Somatic Self-Discovery Through Enhanced Bodily Awareness

We might previously have thought that many of our bodily systems operate outside of our conscious control. However, we have the power to increase our awareness of how our internal and external mechanics and processes (and the signals and signs they deliver) affect our thoughts, emotions, and feelings. We can start by exploring **proprioception**, **interoception**, and **exteroception**.

Earlier, we briefly touched on Porges's concept of *neuroception* through which our brain registers a stimulus and determines whether it is safe or poses a threat to our welfare.[459] Throughout a regular day, our body uses many other working parts and systems to assess how things are going outside, inside, and all around us:

- **Proprioception**: our body detects and senses where it exists in the space immediately around us—through balance, equilibrium, weight distribution, and movement
- **Interoception**: our body keeps tabs on its internal state, garnering information from organs like our heart (heartbeat), lungs (respiration), and stomach (hunger)
- **Exteroception**: our body registers and gathers information from stimuli outside ourselves, through senses like sight, smell, hearing, and touch

An initial strategy for becoming somatically intelligent is to learn how these perception mechanisms work, begin to pay closer attention to them, and become more attuned to how our body affects our thoughts, emotions, and performance. Notably, advocates for enhanced somatic intelligence regard "the body as not just something to be treated or cured," but rather as a helpful instrument of well-being.[460] I love Williams's message about our physicality: "[I]t's essential to remind yourself that you are not a brain on legs, but a fully integrated mind-body beast."[461]

Enhancing Proprioceptive Understanding

The term *proprio* derives from Latin, meaning *one's own.*[462] In the early 1800s, Sir Charles Bell, a Scottish surgeon, anatomist, and artist (among his many other vocations), identified a sixth sense, called the muscle sense, that supplements our senses of sight, hearing, smell, taste, and touch.[463] Later, in the early 1900s, Sir Charles Scott Sherrington, a British neurophysiologist, introduced the term **proprioception**, along with **interoception** and **exteroception**.[464] Researchers define proprioception as a neural process in which our body gleans sensory input from our external surroundings and translates such information to enable us to move body parts via "motor reactions."[465] Throughout our day, we rely on signals generated by our hands, feet, arms, legs, skin, muscles, and joints to help us navigate the space around our bodies.[466] Proprioception is at work when we are able to find our way across our bedroom in the dark without slamming into furniture. Likewise, proprioception is the mechanism that allows us to perceive where our hands approximately are located in space if we close our eyes and extend our arms out to our sides; we do not need to see our body parts to sense where they are.[467] Proprioception enables us to discern the general positioning of our arms and legs underwater even if we cannot see below the surface. Williams explains that "[t]hrough proprioception, we instinctively know where we are, how we are moving, and where our body begins and ends."[468]

When I first learned about proprioception in some of the literature I was reading as research for this book, I suddenly began hearing the term everywhere. First, I heard two fitness trainers use the term to refer to how our bodies naturally strive to rebalance themselves if we stand on one leg or step off a curb at an odd angle. A Penn classmate who conducted a Zoom "energy break" during one of our course sessions mentioned proprioception when she asked us to close our eyes, swing our arms back and forth, and notice that we could still sense our limbs in the air around us even though we could not see them. I liked learning that the most fundamental purpose of the instrument of proprioception is to stabilize and safeguard the body.[469] Proprioception prompts us to contract muscles to hold ourselves upright and not careen into fellow passengers on a swaying subway car.[470] Proprioception enables us to regain balance and control of our bodily movements, adjusting weight and posture, for example, if we hit an icy patch on a sidewalk.

So, you might be asking yourself, how is proprioception relevant to law students and lawyers? Well, apparently, we can train and improve our proprioceptive sense![471]

Some of us might think: *I have a terrible sense of balance,* or *I have slow reflexes.* Proprioception actually makes me ponder (analogously) my deplorable sense of *direction,* of where I am in topographical space. I refer to myself as "geographically challenged." I have the hardest time discerning east from west, and north from south. (This is why I love living in Manhattan where streets are numerically sequenced.) When I am wandering foreign cities, inevitably if the correct route to get to my intended destination is to turn right, my instinct is to turn left. For those of us who are not great at sensing where we are, or feel like we don't have the best control over our balance, we might be tempted to shrug our shoulders, sigh, and say, *Well, this is just who I am.* But researchers indicate that there is such a thing as proprioceptive training. We can enhance our perception and awareness of how our bodies function in the space around us. Greater awareness can lead to augmented confidence in our ability to control how our bodies interact with our environment, especially when we encounter stressors. Proprioceptive understanding also can help us build trust in our own bodies—as a stanchion of safety and support.

Reinforcing our prehabilitation theme, researchers have used proprioceptive training as a method of injury *prevention*; for example, exercises like standing on one leg with closed eyes or balancing on a wobble board can help lower the risk of first-time or recurrent ankle sprain.[472] Other researchers have reported the successful use of proprioceptive training to help people improve motor function after an injury.[473] Acupuncture, vibration, and magnetic or thermal stimulation are other ways to enhance proprioception.[474] While individuals certainly can seek the guidance of physical therapists and medical professionals to design proprioceptive training regimens, there are basic exercises we can engage in on our own to nurture our proprioceptive sense and build strength, balance, and joint stability. For example, proprioception trainers recommend movements like balancing on one leg or doing squats on a single leg.[475] (Links to proprioceptive training activities suggested by experts can be found in Exercise #3 at the end of this chapter.)

Now that I know what proprioception is, I try to notice moments throughout my day when proprioception is definitely at work as my body moves through space and interacts with my surrounding environment. I notice when the floor of my shower feels a little slippery, yet my feet naturally adjust their grip to stabilize me, once again helping to protect me from injury. I notice when I'm able to steady myself on one leg when I'm sliding on a pair of sweatpants or a single shoe. I notice when I wake up in the middle of the night and I'm able to walk to my freezer to add ice to my water glass without illuminating the lights. During my trip to Tenerife in the Canary Islands where I worked on the first draft of this book, I noticed how my feet, ankles, calves, knees, quads, and hips shifted and adjusted to keep me from falling over when I tried to enter the ocean on a rocky beach but was unable to see the numerous different-sized stones below the water's surface. Enhanced proprioceptive awareness has helped me appreciate my body more, as an instrument of power, safety, and support.

For the next few days, try to notice when *your* proprioception kicks into gear. Enhancing our proprioception is one component of our endeavor to become somatically intelligent.

Perhaps the most exciting application of proprioceptive training is its potential to help us engage our bodies to manage our thoughts and emotions in healthier ways. Charles Darwin[476] and William James[477] (the latter is known as the father of American psychology) laid the groundwork for the scientific understanding that emotions arise from bodily responses to stimuli. Dr. António Damásio, a Portuguese neuroscientist and neurologist, has built on this concept, studying how our bodies gather information through proprioception (and interoception) and convey this data to our brain. Damásio explains how "consciousness begins as the feeling of what happens when we see or hear or touch."[478] He expands on William James's idea "that during an emotion, the brain causes the body to change, and that the feeling of emotion is the result of perceiving the body's change."[479] Damásio distinguishes emotions (which he defines as a "collection of responses, many of which are publicly observable") from feelings ("the private, mental experience of an emotion").[480] He adds a third step: our becoming aware of our feeling of the particular emotion.[481] Damásio posits that, if we work on enhancing our awareness of how our motor behavior interacts with and affects our emotions, we can intentionally use our bodies as instruments of emotional regulation.[482] Damásio says that "[c]onsciousness is valuable because it introduces a new means of achieving homeostasis."[483] In other words, better attunement to the relationship among our bodily movements, thoughts, and feelings can help us engage in more *efficient* allostasis to return us to homeostasis after we encounter stressors.

Researchers refer to proprioceptive awareness as *consciousness* of our limbs and joints in space, our muscles' ability to tense and relax, and our capacity to move, balance, and adjust our posture. There is a field of psychotherapy—dance and movement therapy—specifically designed to guide individuals in experiencing different emotions through intentional patterns of movement and posture adjustments.[484] Practicing varied facial expressions, postures, and bodily movements can help us consciously connect proprioceptive input with particular emotions.[485] Researchers point out that, because our bodies perpetually exist in some sort of posture—sitting, standing, walking, running, twisting, lying down, curling up in a ball, hugging, high-fiving—getting to know how our posture can affect our emotions can be eye-opening and empowering.[486] Proprioceptive training can help us retool unhelpful postures and reflexive physical habits that impede well-being.[487] We can learn, for example, whether muscle tension in particular areas of our body signals feelings of fear or anger.[488] Or, we might recognize and begin to deconstruct bodily habits that restrict movement, worsen tension, and spike pain.[489] Conscious bodily movement (through exercise, for instance) is another pathway toward emotional self-regulation.[490]

Inclusion alert! Researchers emphasize that individuals with limited motor capabilities are not at all excluded from these opportunities for self-discovery. Movement and somatic therapists can use motor imagery and mental simulation instead of motor execution to link imagined movement with desired emotions.[491]

Overall, by better understanding proprioception and how our bodies' movement in space affects how we feel, we can enhance our conscious relationship with our emotions.[492] Intertwining this increased somatic intelligence with the work we'll do in cultivating our emotional well-being dimension (in Chapter 6), we can magnify opportunities for flourishing.

"Proprioception of the Mind"

In seeking to better understand the concept of proprioception, I came across a paper written by Debra Ann Fowler, cofounder and executive director of an LGBTQ+ education initiative called History UnErased, Inc. Fowler wrote a piece entitled, *Proprioception of the Mind: Balancing Science and Spirit through Emotional Intelligence*, for her Master of Arts in Teaching program at the School for International Training in Vermont. Not only did the title of her paper intrigue me, she captivated me further with her inclusion of a portion of a quote by William James (the father of American psychology whom I'd been reading a lot about in my MAPP program at Penn). The full quote reads:

> *Even if the day dawns in which it will not be needed for fighting the old heavy battles against nature, muscular vigor will still always be needed to furnish the background of sanity, serenity, and cheerfulness to life, to give moral elasticity to our disposition, to round off the wiry edge of our fretfulness and make us good humoured and easy of approach.*[493]

This call to action to nurture our "muscular vigor" once again seems to connect the vitality of our bodies with the vibrancy of our minds. Indeed, Fowler characterized her interesting concept of "proprioception of the mind" as our ability to "tap into the auspicious synchronicity between the mind and the body."[494]

Fowler described proprioception of the mind as an instrument teachers can use to enhance their "attunement" to their students.[495] Reiterating the definition of proprioception—our "unconscious attunement of where the various regions of the body are located at one time"—she asserted that great teachers should have an analogous sense of where students are in their learning.[496] Fowler reinforced how "proprioception works to correct our balance if we suddenly experience a disruption to our equilibrium—communicating with our muscles before our conscious mind understands the disruption."[497] (This reminds me of allostasis kicking in when an external force jostles us out of homeostasis!)

Fowler equated proprioception of the mind to an antenna that helps us (or in her context, teachers) synthesize neurological responses, emotional intelligence (paying attention to others' cues and energy), life experience, intuition, and empathy to serve others.[498] Like the researchers mentioned above, Fowler believes that proprioception "can be sharpened."[499]

This is exciting stuff. Noticing and honing our proprioception can help us become somatically intelligent—more attuned to what is going on around us and how stimuli affect our thoughts, feelings, and behaviors.

Enhancing Interoceptive Understanding

Turning now to a different angle of physiological perception, **interoception** is our body's ability to perceive sensory information from *inside*, specifically from organs like the heart (our heartbeat), the lungs (the oscillation of our breathing), our stomach (whether we are hungry or satiated), and our autonomic nervous system activity (whether we are feeling on edge or calm).[500] Like proprioception, we can improve interoception by enhancing our awareness; here we focus on the functioning of our *internal* body systems and the signals and signs they generate.[501] Similar to proprioception, researchers tie interoceptive awareness to productive regulation of our emotions.[502] Science writer David Robson provides a helpful summary of Damásio's theory that tending to our proprioception and interoception can play an important role in augmenting our emotional awareness:

> *[Damásio] proposed that emotional events begin with non-conscious changes in bodily states, called "somatic markers": when you see an angry dog, for instance, and your muscles tense or your heart begins to race. This physiological reaction occurs before you are even aware of the emotion, and it is only when the brain detects the alteration to the body's internal state, through interoception, that we actually experience the feeling and allow it to shape our behavior.*[503]

Through improved interoceptive awareness, we can more accurately identify and evaluate physiological cues that arise during stressful scenarios and subsequently launch healthy emotion regulation strategies.[504] As Williams points out, "the better a person is at sensing their internal state, the more likely they are to take action to put things back into balance—to seek out rest or to get away from someone who gives them a bad 'gut feeling,' for example."[505]

Researchers have developed measuring tools to assess:

- Our interoceptive **accuracy**: this is objectively quantifiable, like our ability to count our own heartbeats
- Our interoceptive **sensibility**: this involves how we subjectively experience internal sensations, and our belief that we can perceive internal cues
- Our interoceptive **awareness**: the relationship between our objective interoceptive performance (our accuracy) and our understanding of what that information means[506]

For example, in an assessment called "the heartbeat detection task," individuals silently count their heartbeats while an electrocardiogram counts them as well.[507] This tool helps us gauge our ability to accurately detect sensations from our heart. As Robson writes, "It is only by listening to the heart, it seems, that we can take better care of the mind."[508] Further, a 32-item self-report questionnaire called the Multidimensional Assessment of Interoceptive Awareness (MAIA)[509] evaluates eight categories of internal bodily awareness:

- **Noticing:** being cognizant of bodily comfort, discomfort, and neutrality
- **Not distracting:** not avoiding or shrugging off aches, tenderness, discomfort, or pain
- **Not worrying:** not ruminating over aches, tenderness, discomfort, or pain
- **Attention regulation:** maintaining appropriate levels of focus on bodily sensations
- **Emotional awareness:** being attuned to linkages between bodily sensations and feelings
- **Self-regulation:** being able to adjust emotions by focusing on bodily sensations
- **Body listening:** actively gleaning insights from bodily cues
- **Trusting:** trusting one's body and regarding it as safe

Like proprioception, researchers have developed techniques for improving our interoception. One approach, called Mindful Awareness in Body-Oriented Therapy, or MABT, developed by Dr. Cynthia Price in the 1980s, teaches a three-part process:[510]

- **Awareness:** enhancing our *body literacy,* that is, our ability to identify and describe bodily signals and sensations
- **Access:** directing attention inside the body in order to notice, for example, the flow of breath as we inhale and exhale, or to observe how muscles feel when we tense and then release them
- **Appraisal:** reframing a new physical feeling or experience as productive and useful for our growth, helping us trust our bodies and feel a sense of safety

Another technique called Body Mind Centering also focuses on activities like discerning muscle sensations (i.e., movement, contraction, and release) or how our organs feel (i.e., whether we sense tightness, expansion, retraction, vibration).[511]

Again, while individuals can and should certainly work with therapists and medical professionals to engage in therapeutic interoception techniques, there are basic exercises all of us can access and undertake to augment our awareness of our internal systems' functioning. One involves simply focusing on the internal movement of our breath.[512] We can pay attention to our breath, learn how to notice and release tension in areas of the body, and ultimately relax the nervous system.[513]

Researchers have compiled a set of accessible interoception tasks for children with autism and attention-deficit/hyperactivity disorder: noticing arousal levels during and after exercise, clenching and releasing one's fist, finding and checking one's pulse, deep breathing, and more.[514] Further, South Australia's Department for Education offers a website of educational resources about interoception and interoceptive activities designed for the classroom.[515] The Department's interoceptive activities invite us to focus on an internal bodily activity like breathing, pulse, temperature fluctuations, or muscle tension and notice that we have the ability to effect a change.

Resources to access interoceptive training activities can be found in Exercise #3 at the end of this chapter. Like proprioception, noticing and honing our interoception can enhance our somatic intelligence.

Enhancing Exteroceptive Understanding

A third pathway for enhancing our bodily awareness is through **exteroception**—the way our body registers stimuli outside ourselves, through senses like sight, smell, hearing, and touch. Exteroception education involves learning how to pay attention to bodily sensations that arise as we interact with external environments through these senses.[516] Researchers have used exteroception education to help individuals who grapple with chronic pain.[517] Similar to proprioception, by noticing emotions that arise as our body connects with the external environment and the space around us, we can identify unhelpful habits or emotions (perhaps like misplaced fear, guilt, or shame) that we associate with sensory stimulation, movement, or touch.[518] We can practice engaging with our environment *safely*, investigating environmental triggers of emotions, and adopting techniques and strategies for emotional regulation.[519]

Resources to access exteroception training activities can be found in Exercise #3 at the end of this chapter.

Strategy #2: Let's Get Moving

Moving our bodies can play a powerful role in nutrifying our brains and minds. Even if exercise is not your thing, or breaking a sweat is the last thing you feel like doing, let's embrace a fresh outlook toward incorporating at least some bodily movement into each day. Basic motion can yield helpful information about how our physicality can drive healthy thinking, feeling, and doing.

Positive psychologists regard physical activity as a monumentally impactful positive intervention.[520] Lest you think this means we need to sign up to run a marathon or announce to friends that we're gearing up to hike Mount Etna, it's important to clarify that physical activity in this context does not need to involve intense exercise or sports. Positive psychologists indicate that *any* episode of physical activity—defined as moving our bodies and expending energy above resting level—provides a cache of data about our power to affect our well-being.[521] Lieberman similarly defines physical activity as "any bodily movement produced by skeletal muscles that expends energy."[522] Even simple acts of movement (e.g., walking, stretching, dancing) furnish information—like positive emotions—useful for self-regulation.[523] Physical activity has a preventative function, can augment psychological well-being, and can improve quality of life.[524]

We've pondered the term *psychosomatic*, noting that our thoughts and emotions can influence our body's operations. Next, we considered the flip side, the *somatopsychic* connection between our physical well-being and the vibrancy of our thinking and feeling.[525] In the foreword to John Ratey and Eric Hagerman's book, *Spark: The Revolutionary New Science of Exercise and the Brain*, they quote Plato:[526]

> *In order for [humans] to succeed in life, God provided [them] with two means, education and physical activity. Not separately, one for the soul and the other for the body, but for the two together.*

I love this combination of education and movement. By educating ourselves about how our bodies work, and then applying that new knowledge via the simple yet intentional act of moving our bodies, we can foster flourishing.

Movement Is Good for Our Lawyer Brains

Ratey, with coauthors Hagerman (of *Spark*) and Manning (of *Go Wild*), deemphasizes physical aesthetics when championing the vital importance of bodily movement for our health. Instead, he spotlights the number one upshot of exercise—building and conditioning our brain.[527]

Let's start with some basic principles of the science of exercise. Our nemesis—toxic stress—erodes important links and connections between nerve cells in our brain.[528] We need good, strong, intact bonds between cells in order to learn and remember things.[529] Exercise reverses the erosive effect of stress on our brain neurons. When we move, our body opens the floodgates to a gush of neurochemicals and growth factors that bind brain cells together.[530] Our brain's infrastructure literally grows and strengthens—like a muscle.[531]

Neurotrophins are a family of proteins, also called *factors*, that help the neurons in our brain survive, function, and develop. Ratey is a huge fan of one neurotrophin in particular: brain-derived neurotrophic factor (BDNF). He calls BDNF "Miracle-Gro for the brain."[532] Here's how it works. Movement demands a reaction from both the body and the brain.[533] Exercise unleashes BDNF, which ignites cell growth as a response to the demands of movement.[534] BDNF helps neurons grow dendrites, synapses spark more connections, and myelin sheaths around these bonds thicken.[535] Do we want stronger, fitter, more powerful lawyer brains? According to Ratey, exercise is the key.

Indeed, scientists link exercise to tangible, "physical, measurable brain growth."[536] Researchers indicate that physical activity positively impacts neural systems engaged in attention, learning, and memory.[537] Studies have shown relationships among improved fitness, better task performance, and enhanced brain structure in brain areas tied to executive function.[538] Scientists have compared brain scans of fit and less fit adults; fit adults have more brain volume in their frontal, temporal, and parietal areas.[539] Exercise literally makes our brains bigger!

Also, remember the tug-of-war between our catabolic (destructive, and driven by cortisol) and anabolic (restorative) systems? Exercise reins in our cortisol levels.[540] It amps up regulatory neurotransmitters: serotonin, norepinephrine, and dopamine.[541]

"Train It and Trust It"

Yet another value of exercise is its trust-building factor. When we exercise or move our bodies, we are exerting control. We are consciously and intentionally stepping into a mild to moderate stress event, that is, eustress and hormesis. Ratey and Hagerman point out the significance of being able to predict and anticipate a positive outcome in exercise: we are honing and mastering new skills; we augment our confidence; we trust our ability to ride out the *safe* rise and fall of our stress response.[542]

Dr. Bob Rotella was the director of sports psychology at my alma mater, the University of Virginia, for two decades. In his book, *How Champions Think: In Sports and in Life*, Rotella references a helpful mantra: "Train it and trust it."[543] Rotella counsels athletes to develop a training system for practicing particular skills:

> *Learn the skill thoroughly so it's ingrained in your subconscious. Then, at the moment of performance, don't think about it. Trust that your subconscious brain will do its job.*[544]

Rotella cautions, "the trusting won't work if the training hasn't happened."[545] As part of our lawyering prehabilitation program, by incorporating a regimen of physical movement into our well-being training, we will garner powerful information about our bodies, brains, and minds. We will accrue trust that, as we sense the *safe* rise and fall of arousal intensity during episodes of physical movement, we are building strength and the knowledge that we will be okay when we encounter similarly intense physical reactions, thoughts, and emotions in the lawyering performance arena. In our prehabilitation work, we generate a positive track record of successful eustress and hormesis experiences. Later, when we step into real lawyering performance scenarios, we can trust our training, and deliver.

What Is the "Right" Dose of Exercise or Physical Movement?

Exercise does not need to occupy a significant amount of time in our lives to yield *eudaimonic* benefits. Researchers report that individuals have enhanced aspects of cognitive function, such as information processing speed and reaction time, through a short episode of exercise such as 30 minutes of running or cycling.[546] If you are new to, or hesitant about, exercise, it's perfectly okay to start basic. Health researcher Dr. Guy Faulkner and his colleagues emphasize that the most effective exercise dosage is the one that we personally enjoy and can realistically weave into our life routine.[547] Variety in activity and intensity can help us sustain our commitment.[548]

Notably, Lieberman titled his book *Exercised* because he believes we are too "exercised" (or "harassed, vexed, or worried") about what we are supposed to be doing, movement-wise.[549] He acknowledges all the conflicting advice we get about exercise dosage, and points out how "we fail to help people to exercise and then shame and blame them for not doing it."[550] He says "there is no optimal dose or type of exercise."[551] He reiterates, "Although there can be no optimal exercise prescription, physical activity nonetheless stimulates growth, maintenance, and repair mechanisms that build capacities and slow aging."[552] He boils down his dosage recommendation to this: "exercise several hours a week, mostly cardio but also some weights, and keep it up as you age."[553]

As we become more comfortable with exercise and movement, we might eventually embrace the recommendation of the American College of Sports Medicine and the American Heart Association that healthy adults should engage in 150 minutes of moderately intense aerobic activity a week and activate muscle-strengthening exercises two days a week.[554] Aerobic (meaning *with oxygen*) exercise is cardiovascular conditioning, which strengthens our heart and lungs. Anaerobic exercises (e.g., weightlifting, sprinting, jumping) are short and fast; our body uses energy already stored in our muscles.

If 150 minutes a week (perhaps 30 minutes a day five days a week, or 50 minutes three days a week) sounds like a lot, consider integrating movement into a different activity or experience you already enjoy. Do you like nature? Dr. Eva M. Selhub and biophilosopher Alan C. Logan, quoted in Ratey and Manning's book, *Go Wild*, call movement in nature "exercise squared."[555] Ratey and Manning talk about the concept of *biophilia*—our innate deep attachment to nature.[556] Walking or hiking outdoors can amplify the positive effects of movement. Or, if you like being around other people, Ratey and Manning indicate that group exercise or movement (in teams or outdoors) also can deliver a double-dip of effectiveness because we are activating arousal *and* social engagement; our hearts, bodies, and minds are stimulated at the same time.[557]

In 2003, Julia Cameron wrote a book called *Walking in this World: The Practical Art of Creativity*[558] in which she added another tool to her tried-and-true methods of Morning Pages (our three daily pages of longhand journaling) and Artist Dates (weekly excursions with our inner artist): Weekly Walks. She says, "Moving into our bodies, we embody the truth that as artists we are out to make a 'body of work.'"[559] She urges, "As we stretch our legs, we stretch our minds and our souls."[560] A cool thought: we could consider walks to be an on-ramp toward not only nurturing our physical well-being dimension, but also our artistic/creative dimension (Chapter 7) and our spiritual dimension (Chapter 10). Triple-whammy.

Being mindful that many individuals have movement limitations or may be nervous or fearful about exercising, I think Lieberman says it best:[561]

> Different [individuals] have different needs, and it is wrong and counterproductive to engage in body shaming or fitness shaming. Unfit [individuals], however, aren't best served by not being helped to exercise, because the benefits are substantial for everyone, especially those who are the least fit. The challenge is to support and assist everyone at every level nonjudgmentally and in ways and degrees they find acceptable and rewarding.

Also, Williams highlights how we can get creative in defining "movement" for individuals with motor limitations:

> [P]sychologists have found that a person's direction of movement influences what they think about. Moving forwards inspires thoughts about the future, while moving backwards brings back memories of the past. It doesn't even have to be actual, physical, movement—in lab-based experiments where volunteers

> watched a starscape that appeared to move either forwards or backwards, and even when they were asked to close their eyes and imagine moving in one direction or the other, the mere suggestion of motion was enough to direct the content of their thoughts.[562]

She encourages, "Whether on two feet, two wheels or some other means, get out and move."[563] She reiterates that "moving while focusing on the body provides many of the same benefits as high-intensity exercise but . . . can be done by anyone, young, old, able-bodied or less so."[564] Thus, "some sort of slow, quiet, and deliberate movement that is done with the express intention of listening in to your body" can comprise a successful "movement plan."[565]

Build in Rest Days

I have to admit, I'm not the best at resting. I feel guilty and edgy when I skip a day of exercise, like one day off is going to unravel years of investment of time and hard work. (Yes, dramatic, I know.) But all the literature says: we've got to stop, let our muscles rest, and watch them grow. As Ratey and Manning note, "Every runner knows you build strength on rest days."[566] Not only should we consciously seek to incorporate intentional bodily movement into our lives, we also must carve out time in our schedule for rest and energy replenishment.[567] As sports psychologist Dr. Michael Kellmann states, "a short-term planned sacrifice of recovery" can improve our future performance; he calls this "supercompensation."[568]

Interestingly, sports psychologists have applied the IZOF model not only to peak performance states but also to rest and recovery periods.[569] As we amp up levels of stress (even good stress like *eustress*), our bodies require increased recovery time.[570] Just like we can learn to toggle into healthy and productive eustress zones, we should experiment with our optimal states of rest and recovery, which likely will differ for each of us.[571]

In the sports context, researchers have developed the Recovery-Stress Questionnaire for Athletes (RESTQ-Sport), an assessment that helps measure athletes' recovery-stress states.[572] The ring I purchased that tracks my HRV and sleep also recommends optimal rest and recovery days. I'm not the best at listening to its advice yet! But it's a helpful reminder to take days off from training and working out, and let my body recover.

Strategy #3: Writing Appraisal Scripts

Dr. Richard Lazarus was a psychologist who wrote a book with Dr. Susan Folkman in the 1970s called *Stress, Appraisal and Coping.*[573] Lazarus explained the linkage between an action called **appraisal** and the phases of the stress-eustress-distress continuum. According to Lazarus, when we appraise a stressor as a potential threat of harm, we often can leap from stress to distress.[574] However, when we appraise a stressor instead as a *challenge* or an *opportunity* that we can manage by activating our coping resources, we can step into a productive state of eustress.[575]

Cognitive appraisal is a conscious process we can undertake each time we encounter a stressor. In appraisal, we assess (1) a situation's potential effect on our goals, (2) the demands of the situation, and (3) our coping resources.[576] Lazarus outlined two phases of appraisal. In primary appraisal, we interpret a stressor as either positive, dangerous, or irrelevant.[577] In this primary phase, if we determine that a stressor puts an important personal goal at risk, we might appraise a situation as a *threat.*[578] However, if we trust that our coping skills can help us meet the situation's demands, we might deem the situation a *challenge.*[579]

Next, in secondary appraisal, we more deeply evaluate how our personal resources can help us cope with the stressor and its ramifications.[580] A pivotal component of the appraisal process is our assessment of the level of control we can exert over the outcome.[581] If control is possible, we can launch action-oriented, *problem-solving coping* mechanisms.[582] If control is less realistic, we can instead adopt cognitive strategies to modulate our emotions (called *emotion-focused coping*) and, if necessary, accept the situation in a healthy way.[583]

Slightly different terminology echoes Lazarus's themes. Some researchers use the term *instrumental coping* to describe the act of taking direct action to address the nature and characteristics of the stressor.[584] Alternatively, we might invoke *palliative coping*: thoughts or actions that do not change the stressor itself but allow us to reduce emotional arousal levels, temporarily relieve the stressor's emotional impact, and feel better.[585]

The appraisal process yields different emotions.[586] Appraisals that characterize stressors as *threats* can ignite negative emotions like anxiety and fear, while *challenge* appraisals can generate a mix of negative and positive emotions, for example, blending nervous anticipation with excitement and wonder.[587] As we ride the wave of a stress scenario successfully, we might experience other positive emotional states, like relief, pride, inspiration, or a sense of accomplishment.[588] If the situation's outcome is unfavorable or incomplete, we might linger in negative emotional states, like frustration or confusion, unless we launch another appraisal loop.[589]

Dr. Jeremy P. Jamieson and his colleagues indicate that we also can practice reappraising the *sensations* of arousal during stressful situations as positive rather than negative.[590] We can remind ourselves that the arousal sensations we feel in our bodies (such as heightened energy) can actually be helpful to our performance.[591]

Epel and her colleagues tie a healthy appraisal process to enhanced allostasis.[592] Efforts to appropriately and realistically appraise everyday stressors as challenges we can handle (rather than insurmountable threats) can help us modulate the highs and lows of our stress arousal system, heighten the efficiency of our reaction-and-recovery process, and enhance our post-stress-event anabolic functioning.[593]

Other researchers use the terminology of *challenge* stressors and *hindrance* stressors.[594] If we label a situation as a challenge stressor (i.e., an opportunity to enter a eustress or hormesis zone), we are viewing it as useful to our achievement of a task and to our personal development.[595] In contrast, we might characterize an obstacle as a hindrance stressor if it poses a barrier to our completion of a task or to our personal development.[596] In a stress management paradigm called the holistic stress model, Dr. Bret Simmons and Dr. Debra Nelson indicate that we can amplify the positive effect of challenge stressors by "savoring" the experience of managing them, that is, approaching these stressors with curiosity and enthusiasm.[597] Business management professor, Dr. Matthew Blake Hargrove, and his co-authors point to Olympic athletes as examples of individuals who do not just cope with the physical, emotional, and mental demands of training and competition, but they actually savor, or delight in, the "eustressful" moments.[598] (Savoring is a big concept in positive psychology as well! We will dive into the act of savoring more deeply when we investigate our emotional dimension in Chapter 6).

Three pathways for savoring eustress (and hormesis) episodes include:[599]

- **Meaning:** tapping into how the challenge adds meaning or purpose to our personal or professional lives
- **Mindfulness:** paying attention to and noticing sensations in our bodies, brains, and minds when we anticipate, enter, and come out of a eustress experience
- **Energy management:** allowing for periods of rest after an intense eustress experience, to let its benefits generate and resonate

Notably, researchers suggest that the practice of savoring eustress episodes can cultivate *flow* states.[600]

Next time you engage in a eustress or hormesis activity, practice savoring it by activating the three pathways. For example, I might savor a boxing training session like this:.

Meaning	This boxing training session adds meaning or purpose to my life because: • It helps me understand my physicality, enhancing my somatic intelligence • I can practice getting control of my breathing and trusting that I can catch my breath • I activate my signature strengths of perseverance, curiosity, zest, and love of learning • I experience **flow** • I feel stronger—physically and mentally • I like being around my trainer because he is a positive person • Boxing informs my writing • I like interacting with other fighters and trainers in the exercise park; I feel connected to a community—something bigger than myself
Mindfulness	I notice physical sensations, thoughts, and emotions: • Breathing • Rush of energy • Physical and mental strength • (Positive) pride • Excitement that I achieved a **flow** state
Energy Management	I try to keep my schedule relatively clear of work or social engagements after a boxing session so I can relax, maybe write (another **flow** state), and let the "high" linger for as long as possible

In Exercise #6 at the end of this chapter, we will work on drafting our appraisal scripts.

Strategy #4: Routines and Rituals

Many athletes, performers, coaches, and trainers champion the importance of adopting, practicing, and activating routines and rituals as a core part of training and performance. Establishing a routine or ritual is especially helpful for us as we move through each dimension of our well-being amplification adventure. Choreographer Twyla Tharp has shared her approach for combatting feelings of resistance, panic, or fear when stepping into unknown creative territory, learning an unfamiliar skill, or embarking on a new project. She emphasizes the need to "establish some rituals—automatic but decisive patterns of behavior—at the beginning . . . when you are most at peril of turning back, chickening out, giving up, or going the wrong way."[601] Tharp says, "Turning something into a ritual eliminates the question, Why am I doing this?"[602] Routines and rituals help squash doubt. As Tharp says, rituals remind us, "I've done it before. It was good. I'll do it again."[603]

A training routine can be set up as a sequence of physical actions accompanied by cognitive and emotional behaviors that we undertake regularly and consistently.[604] We've all probably noticed athletes who execute the same series of movements every time they step up to the plate in a baseball game, or get ready to deliver a serve in tennis, or approach the balance beam in a gymnastics competition. Rotella calls this a "preshot" routine, like in golf.[605] In a preshot routine, athletes break down the mechanics of a performance task into a repeatable progression that they practice, practice, and practice in training. Rotella says, "A good preshot routine is both mental and physical."[606] When an athlete steps into a performance arena, they can't start thinking about all the past shots or all the future shots; as Rotella says, "There is only the shot to be played. There is only the present moment. . . . [The athlete relying on a good preshot routine] trusts that his body can execute the shot. He turns off the conscious brain."[607] When we practice a set of physical, mental, and emotional steps as part of our prehabilitation training, we learn to trust that the process works. Then, we can let our well-practiced sequence of movements carry us into and through performance moments.

Every time I start a huge new writing project like this book, the endeavor as a whole feels overwhelming. But I know that if I set up a daily routine and ritual, I can trust my incremental process and the work will get done. Yes, there will be periods of self-doubt, but instead of freaking out about worst-case scenarios—not meeting my publisher's deadline, writing a complete pile of junk, getting criticized, failing—I can rely on my daily system to keep moving me forward.

Roman Ritual

Today, I woke up in Rome, my favorite place in the world. I have five days left of this writing trip before I head back home to New York to spend the next few months revising and editing this book manuscript. When I woke up this morning, twinges of self-doubt began to percolate. *What if I can't get this content to make any sense? What if reentry into pandemic life back home in New York disrupts my writer flow? What if this whole project completely sucks?* Instead of wallowing (which I would have done five years ago), I got up and did my Morning Pages journaling (**Routine/ Ritual #1**). I then put on my running shoes. I walked to a café close to my hotel, ordered a caffè americano (practicing my Italian), sipped it while standing up at the bar like the Romans do, and then I went for a three-mile run by the Tiber River (**Routine/Ritual #2**). I ran on a footpath that curved along the riverbank, the murky green water of the Tiber flowing beside me. I ran beneath hundreds-of-years-old and thousand-year-old bridges. As I planted one foot in front of the other, I reminded myself, *One word at a time. One page at a time. Trust the writing process.*

After my river run, I circled back to my hotel, the icy air conditioning in my room a welcome refresher. As seagulls squawked and a cat mewed loudly outside, I set my timer for two hours of writing (**Routine/Ritual #3**). Two hours later, I emerged from the ether of my writing session, a bit delirious, and realized I had once again edged into *flow*. Then I went on Roman walkabout, searching for an artifact of culture or creativity to replenish my zest (**Routine/Ritual #4**).

Daily, I remind myself that this is my *prehab* and my *regard* for myself as an artist and a scholar-athlete. I am building stamina now, strengthening my lungs and honing my leg and arm muscles (through my jogs), and clearing my mind and brain of clutter (through my Morning Pages)—so when I inevitably experience another day when everything feels totally impossible, I will remember to trust my training and honor my system. I will rely on the truth that I stuck to my routines and rituals, bolstering my endurance to push through challenging times, and therefore I have robust coping mechanisms to handle each stressor.

Combining mental/emotional, physical, writing, and cultural rituals—the journaling, the run, the two hours on the clock, and then an artistic reward—I remind myself that the work gets done. The emotional work, the physical work, the intellectual work, the artistic work, the cultural work, the spiritual work. If we develop an individualized routine and a set of rituals that work for each of us, follow through on the sequence, and trust the process, growth will materialize before our eyes.

Routines and rituals also help us develop and then stick to our own training and performance plan without ruminating about what everyone else is doing. Remember Hanin's IZOF concept? The **I** of course stands for *individual.* An article in the Oregon State Bar Bulletin entitled *Fit to Practice*[608] mentions Michelle Rodd, an attorney and avid participant in the sport of Dragon Boat racing, a water sport involving vessels like canoes. Rodd uses the mantra "paddle your race" as a reminder that we can't control what everyone else is doing, or in her case "what's happening in another boat."[609] Rodd's routine is to trust the process, honor the race rules and parameters, put her paddle in the water, stay engaged, and allow the outcome to "take care of itself."[610] By adopting our own physical, mental, and emotional routines and implementing them during training and performance moments, we can learn to trust our systems and have faith that we have done everything we can to achieve a positive outcome.

As law students and lawyers, let's start exploring, developing, and adopting routines and rituals for our training and performance. When we wake up tomorrow morning, rather than barreling straight into the next cyclone of worry, anxiety, frustration, or agitation—out of habit or lack of awareness—let's pause. Let's adopt a prehabilitation mindset and begin setting up an individualized, realistic training regimen that works.

Treating ourselves like athletes or performers, let's pause to notice when and why our hearts beat faster, our pulses quicken, our muscles strain, our bones ache, or our chests rise and fall as we crave oxygen. Let's become somatically intelligent by studying the interplay among our bodies, brains, and minds. Let's get to know our stress-eustress-distress continuum. Instead of leaping into *distress*, let's hold on. Let's choose and seek out eustress and hormesis moments. Let's consciously engage with the discomfort, now with enhanced recognition and clarity of its powerful purpose and our safety and control. Let's interpret momentary unease as a signal of hope, optimism, and trust that we are growing and changing, as individuals and a community, through this shared experience. Here is a checklist to get us started.

Physical Well-Being Dimension Exercise #1

Prehabilitation Checklist

<table>
<tr><td>First, let's adopt and commit to a prehabilitation mindset, focusing on forward-thinking preventive training to prepare us for encounters with future stressors.</td><td></td></tr>
<tr><td>Next, let's commit to enhancing our somatic intelligence.
<ul>
<li>Let's start by taking a physical inventory—noticing and paying attention to our individual physical (and mental and emotional) responses to stressors. (See Physical Well-Being Dimension Exercise #2)</li>
<li>Next, let's investigate and experiment with our proprioceptive, interoceptive, and exteroceptive awareness. (See Physical Well-Being Dimension Exercise #3)</li>
<li>Let's pay attention to our breathing. Can we begin to trust the rise and fall of our breath to calm us down and enable us to perform better? (See Physical Well-Being Dimension Exercise #4)</li>
</ul></td><td></td></tr>
<tr><td>Next let's intentionally engage in eustress and hormesis, noticing and paying attention to our arousal states. (See Physical Well-Being Dimension Exercise #5)
<ul>
<li>When we encounter a stressor and sense our physiological (and cognitive and emotional) arousal responses, let's try to toggle into and linger in eustress, rather than barreling blindly into (potentially toxic) distress.</li>
<li>Let's get to know our individual zone of optimal functioning!</li>
<li>Let's practice savoring eustress and hormesis moments (identifying meaning and purpose; mindfully noticing how we feel; giving ourselves time to let the benefits sink in).[611]</li>
</ul></td><td></td></tr>
<tr><td>Let's pay attention to, and get to know, our optimal periods of rest and recovery.</td><td></td></tr>
</table>

Let's notice (and celebrate) when we experience flow states!	
Let's also notice (and celebrate) our clutch performances!	
Armed with all the foregoing knowledge, let's develop a training process for our overall daily/weekly approach to nurturing our well-being, as well as sequential routines and rituals for discrete training tasks. • Let's craft an appraisal script and practice using it when we encounter stressors. (See Physical Well-Being Dimension Exercise #6) • Let's be gritty! And engage in deliberate practice! • Let's practice breathing. • Let's develop a routine and ritual around our physical movement. (See Physical Well-Being Dimension Exercise #7)	
Let's also build time into our schedule to reflect on our routines and rituals and decide what we might tweak and adjust.	
Let's trust our training process in performance moments.	

Physical Well-Being Dimension Exercise #2

Conducting a Physical Inventory

To get better at stepping into, and reveling in, the eustress zone instead of leapfrogging into a distress zone, let's first heighten our awareness of how we naturally respond to stressors. This will be different for each of us. Let's start by paying attention to, and observing with curiosity, our bodies' physical adjustments and reactions (plus our accompanying automatic mental soundtrack and unique recipe of emotions). Obviously, our physical dimension is the focus of this chapter, but as somatically intelligent law students and lawyers, we'll notice how our physical responses interact with our thoughts and feelings.

The WJEC (formerly the Welsh Joint Education Committee) explains that "somatic state anxiety" refers to our physiological or physical stress responses, such as sweating or a rapid heartbeat, while "cognitive state anxiety" comprises the mental and emotional act of worrying.[612] Both are important to explore. In writing my books *The Introverted Lawyer* and *Untangling Fear*, I discovered two activities that helped me get to know my somatic and cognitive stress responses more deeply. First, in anticipation of, or at the moment I stepped into, a nerve-wracking lawyering scenario, I surveyed my body and noticed the sequence of physical changes that unfolded as I reacted to the stressor. Next, I began listening to the words of my mental soundtrack and transcribed them. I needed to identify the actual phrasing of the less-than-helpful messages I was telling myself about my abilities before I was able to overwrite that outdated script with accurate, up-to-date assertions.

So, you already know that I am an epic blusher. When I'm stressed, I also sweat, my heartbeat accelerates, and I forget to breathe. My physical frame caves inward: my shoulders hunch forward; I cross my arms and legs; my body seems to be trying to get small. The WJEC explains that if we associate our somatic responses with a feeling that we can't handle the demands of a task, our physical responses can exacerbate our cognitive and emotional reactions.[613] When I feel the first tingle of a blush prickle my cheeks and the first bead of sweat trickle down my neck, my negative mental soundtrack kicks in. *You're not good enough. Everyone's going to see you turning red. What are you even doing here?* Unless I stop the spin cycle, a disastrous downward spiral of self-doubt can whirl from there.

Here's a powerful message that the eustress zone can teach us: If we get to know our individual physical, cognitive, and emotional responses to stress, train ourselves to recognize them at their onset, and activate smart routines and rituals as part of our training system, we will realize (more quickly in each performance moment) that we *can* handle the scenario. And with each successful navigation of the natural rise and fall of our arousal responses, we grow.

So, as a first step here, let's enhance our somatic awareness. As you anticipate or step into your next lawyering performance moment, pause and conduct a physical inventory. What bodily responses do you notice?

Somatic Informational Resource	**Reactions/Responses That You Notice?**
Physical Frame: Shoulders, Arms, Legs, Hands, Feet, Spine, Neck, Head, Balance (Proprioception!)	
Skin: Temperature, Perspiration, Blushing, Tingling (Interoception! Exteroception!)	
Senses: Sight, Hearing, Taste, Smell, Touch (Exteroception!)	
Breathing (Interoception!)	
Heartbeat, Pulse, Shaking/Vibration (Interoception!)	
Stomach (Interoception!)	
Anything else?	

Now, transcribe the words of any less-than-helpful mental soundtrack you hear. It's okay if the language sounds a bit unpleasant right now. We will rewrite our soundtrack in our new appraisal script in **Exercise #6**.

____

____

____

____

What, if any, accompanying emotions do you feel alongside these physical changes and mental messages? ______________________________

We'll use this information as helpful insights as we work through the next few exercises.

Physical Well-Being Dimension Exercise #3

Somatic Self-Discovery

To enhance our somatic awareness, we can begin noticing the ebbs and flows of our internal systems throughout our day (**interoception**), information we gather through our senses of sight, smell, taste, hearing, and touch (**exteroception**), and when our sense of balance, equilibrium, and movement through space is activated (**proprioception**). As you go through each day over the next week, try recognizing and labeling moments of somatic perception. For example, lately I've been saying out loud, *Oh, that was proprioception*, when I notice that my body rebalanced itself when I got up too quickly from the couch, or when my ankle wobbled yet recalibrated as my wedge sandal caught briefly on a cobblestone. Or I'll acknowledge, *Oh, that was exteroception*, when I felt an abrupt temperature change in the water streaming from a shower head onto my skin. For me, noticing how much information my body delivers every minute of every day has heightened my appreciation for it, and my trust in it.

Let's consider engaging in activities that can expand our somatic awareness. Shusterman describes four *somaesthetic* approaches to studying how we use, perceive, and present our bodies:[614]

- **Analytic somaesthetics** explores theories of how mechanical factors like spine flexibility, neck rotation, and eye movement affect our interaction with the world.[615]
- Methods of **pragmatic somaesthetics** (e.g., diets, aerobics, dance, massage) teach us how to improve our experience and use of our bodies.[616]
- In **performative somaesthetics** (e.g., weightlifting, martial arts), we build strength and skill.[617]
- In **practical somaesthetics**, we can enhance well-being through disciplined, reflective practice in using our bodies, like yoga or tai chi.[618]

All these activities yield information helpful to increasing our somatic intelligence and appreciation for and trust in our bodies. Further, experts offer an array of activities specifically designed to help us explore our proprioception, interoception, and exteroception.

Exploring Our Proprioception

- A website called Healthline recommends basic balance, coordination, and movement control exercises to explore our proprioception, such as:
  - Balancing on one leg
  - Standing in a yoga "tree pose"
  - Lifting one leg to a 90-degree angle in "flamingo" pose
  - You can access these (and more) proprioception exercises at: https://www.healthline.com/health/fitness/proprioception-exercises#exercises

- A website called OpenFit offers a series of beginner, intermediate, and advanced proprioception exercises at: https://www.openfit.com/proprioception-exercises
- A Florida-based chiropractic practice offers additional proprioceptive exercises on its website: https://www.coxchirocare.com/doctor/chiropractor/chiropractic-West-Palm-Beach/the-treatment-plan/proprioception
- **Proprioception reflection:** As you go through your day, start to notice moments when your proprioception is in action. Do you sense your body rebalancing itself as you walk down a flight of stairs or start pedaling a bicycle? If you close your eyes, can you perceive where your hand, arm, leg, or foot is located in space without looking at it?

Exploring Our Interoception

- Dr. Emma Goodall and the Government of South Australia's Department for Education have created an Interoceptive Kit with numerous accessible exercises: https://www.education.sa.gov.au/sites/default/files/ready-to-learn-interoception-kit.pdf
- A step-by-step guide to exercises compiled by Dr. Goodall (focusing on exploring muscle tension, body temperature, pulse, and breathing) can be found at: https://gopsblog.edublogs.org/files/2018/10/Interoception-activities-zpoqlf-2j9btmb.pdf
- Occupational therapist, Dr. Kelly Mahler, offers Interoception Activity Cards (for a fee) that suggest accessible interoception-building activities: https://www.kelly-mahler.com/product/the-interoception-activity-cards/
- On a website called "He's Extraordinary: Tools for Raising an Extraordinary Person," author Nicole Day offers ten interoception exercises for kids (that adults can also explore): https://hes-extraordinary.com/9-interoception-activities-for-kids
- **Interoception reflection:** As you go through your day, start to notice moments when your interoception is in action. What signals, signs, and information are you receiving from your heartbeat, pulse, body temperature, breathing?

Exploring Our Exteroception

- A website called Mind Map Inspiration offers 25 exercises for noticing how we interact with the external world through our senses: http://www.mindmapinspiration.com/how-to-heighten-your-senses-mind-map-paul-foreman/
- Additionally, in 2021, author Julia Cameron published a book called *The Listening Path: The Creative Art of Attention*,[619] which recommends exercises to tune our sense of hearing.
- **Exteroception reflection:** As you go through your day, start to notice moments when your exteroception is in action. What signals, signs, and information are you receiving from your senses of hearing, sight, touch, smell, and taste?

Helpful Resources for Understanding Our Bodies and Enhancing Our Somatic Intelligence

- Book: Daniel Lieberman, *Exercised: The Science of Physical Activity, Rest and Health* (London: Penguin Books, 2021).
- Book: Stanley Rosenberg, *Accessing the Healing Power of the Vagus Nerve: Self-Help Exercises for Anxiety, Depression, Trauma, and Autism* (Berkeley: North Atlantic Books, 2017).
- Book: Robert M. Sapolsky, *Why Zebras Don't Get Ulcers: The Acclaimed Guide to Stress, Stress-Related Diseases, and Coping* (New York: St. Martin's Griffin, 2004).
- Book: Bessel van der Kolk, *The Body Keeps the Score: Brain, Mind, and Body in the Healing of Trauma* (London: Penguin Books, 2014).

Further, if you are interested in possibly pursuing dance/movement therapy, you can find credentialed therapists here: https://www.adta.org/find-a-dancemovement-therapist.

Physical Well-Being Dimension Exercise #4

Exploring the Basics of Better Breathing

Sapolsky reports that the mere act of inhaling *somewhat* activates our sympathetic nervous system.[620] By the basic act of exhaling, we do the opposite; we turn the key in the ignition of our parasympathetic nervous system, calling upon the vagus nerve to calm us down again. As part of our interoception work, we can garner information about our bodily sensations, thoughts, and feelings through the simple act of breathing.

I'm about as good a breather as I am a sleeper, that is, terrible on both counts. When I am nervous or stressed, my breathing is the first of my somatic functions to go awry.

When I was a kid, I took flute lessons. Anytime my flute teacher held a recital and I had to perform for fellow students and their families, my breathing became wild and erratic. Frenzied breathing is not exactly ideal for playing a wind instrument! For decades thereafter, my breathing issue plagued me in every intellectual performance in law school and law practice. I *still* grapple with breathing issues when I gear up for public speaking gigs, but my boxing trainer Lou goes to great lengths to teach me how to corral them.

During my boxing lessons, Lou can tell right away when I'm starting to freak out because I can't breathe. My eyes get panicky. He stops our punch series and calmly points out, "You're alternating between over-breathing and holding your breath again. Let's get you out of your head." He hands me an RMT® rope—a thick cord designed for rotational shoulder movement—and prompts me to wield it like a lasso into figure-eights and infinity signs. "Close your eyes. Breathe only through your nose right now. Just find your flow." I comply. I close my eyes. After a few seconds, I feel a breeze whirling along my skin (exteroception!), reminding me that there is air all around me and I'm not going to suffocate in the stifling New York summer heat. I sense my feet on the ground (proprioception!) in my badass high-top boxing shoes. I notice my heartbeat decelerating (interoception!).

After a minute or two, I open my eyes. *Ok, I'm still alive.* Lou extracts the rope from my hands. He slides my boxing gloves onto my fists. We resume.

In reading several books about breathing, I discovered that, for the bulk of my life, I've been approaching breathing all wrong. In the past, when I've felt that panicky sensation from shortness of breath, I've attempted to gulp deep breaths of air. Lou has noted that I over-breathe, which actually does not calm me down at all.

James Nestor, author of *Breath: The New Science of a Lost Art*, urges that "the air that enters [our] lungs affects every moment of [our] life."[621] He states, "How we breathe really matters."[622] He calls breathing "the most intimate connection to our surroundings."[623] He says, "To breathe is to absorb ourselves in what surrounds us, to take in little bits of life, understand them, and give pieces back out. Respiration is, at its core, reciprocation."[624] Williams similarly describes breathing as "literally taking inspiration from the environment and the subtle clues that it contains."[625]

Nestor provides an empowering view of breathing:

> *Breathing is an autonomic function we can consciously control. While we can't simply decide when to slow or speed up our heart or digestion, or to move blood from one organ to another, we can choose how and when to breathe.*[626]

Interestingly, Nestor indicates that breathing through our right nostril activates our sympathetic nervous system, while breathing through the left nostril calls up our parasympathetic nervous system.[627] He defines "the perfect breath" as "5.5-second inhales and 5.5-second exhales."[628] He also advises us to stop breathing through our mouths, and instead focus solely on **nasal breathing**.[629] Williams points out that nasal breathing "synchronizes brainwaves to the rhythm of the breath via sensory neurons at the top of the nose."[630]

Patrick McKeown, author of *The Oxygen Advantage*, emphasizes the detriment that chronic over-breathing poses to our health and performance.[631] He explains that it is "a common misconception that breathing in a larger volume of air increases the oxygenation of the blood."[632] He acknowledges, "Taking a large breath can actually feel good, even if it can actually be bad for you."[633] He explains that, when we over-breathe, we exhale too much carbon dioxide from the lungs, and remove too much of it from our blood.[634] Carbon dioxide "is the doorway that lets oxygen reach our muscles."[635] According to McKeown, "Maintaining a correct breathing volume ensures that the ideal amount of carbon dioxide remains in the lungs, blood, tissues, and cells."[636] Further, "As counterintuitive as it may seem, the urge to take bigger, deeper breaths when we hit the wall during exercise does not provide the muscles with more oxygen but effectively reduces oxygenation even further."[637]

Like Nestor, McKeown champions the value of breathing through our noses all day and all night.[638] He recommends we practice breathing that is "quiet, effortless, soft, through the nose, abdominal, rhythmic, and gently paused on the exhale."[639] This is quite a contrast to what he calls "stressed breathing" which "is faster than normal, audible, produces visible movements, and often involves sighs."[640]

To explore interoceptive awareness and the act of breathing, consider trying a "20 breaths" exercise crafted by Dr. Michael Baime: bringing attention to a single breath (one inhale and one exhale) as a standalone "event," then repeating that twenty times. Instructions can be found here: https://www.mainemed.com/sites/default/files/content/Twenty%20Breaths.pdf.

Let's try Baime's exercise while applying the slow, nose-breathing advocated by Nestor and McKeown. (Nestor and McKeown also offer numerous other suggestions for exploring the art of breathing in their books.)

Reflection: Try this exercise every day for a week. Do you notice any bodily sensations, thoughts, and feelings when you pause and take twenty breaths?

Helpful Resources for Enhancing our Breathing

- Book: Patrick McKeown, *The Oxygen Advantage* (New York: HarperCollins, 2015).
- Book: James Nestor, *Breath: The New Science of a Lost Art* (New York: Riverhead Books, 2020).

Physical Well-Being Dimension Exercise #5

Stepping into the Eustress/Hormesis Zone

As part of our prehabilitation training, let's experiment with our stress-eustress-distress continuum, and explore the factors (internal and external) that contribute to our IZOF. Can noticing our bodily sensations, thoughts, and feelings in training episodes help us consciously step into productive eustress, instead of barreling into distress? Can we observe the rise and fall of arousal sensations, and begin to trust our ability to navigate eustress (and hormesis) episodes successfully?

Stress	Eustress	Distress

What are some scenarios in our day or week that might qualify as opportunities to engage in eustress or hormesis?

1. ____________________
2. ____________________
3. ____________________

Exploring Eustress/Hormesis Through Exercise and Physical Movement

Exercise or physical movement offers a great opportunity to explore eustress and hormesis. If you're new to exercise or daily movement or possibly feeling resistant or hesitant, consider integrating movement into a different activity that you already enjoy.

- Do you like nature? Dr. Eva M. Selhub and biophilosopher Alan C. Logan, quoted in Ratey and Manning's book, *Go Wild*, call movement in nature "exercise squared."[641] Ratey and Manning talk about the concept of *biophilia*—our innate deep attachment to nature. By walking or hiking outdoors, we can amplify the effects of movement. Dr. Bruce D. Perry (who wrote a book with Oprah Winfrey about trauma) suggests movement and rhythm as a "therapeutic tool."[642] Like Ratey and Manning, Perry and Winfrey emphasize the amplifying effect of moving in nature: "[I]t's especially regulating if you can walk in nature. The sensory elements of the natural world bathe us with their own regulating rhythms."[643]
- If you like being around other people, Ratey and Manning indicate that group exercise or movement (in teams or outdoors) also yields a double-dip of effectiveness because we are activating arousal *and* social engagement; our hearts, bodies, and minds are stimulated at the same time.[644]

- In 2003, Julia Cameron wrote a book called *Walking in this World: The Practical Art of Creativity*, in which she added a third tool to her two tried-and-true, creativity-boosting methods of Morning Pages (three pages of longhand journaling each morning) and Artist Dates (weekly excursions with our inner artist): Weekly Walks. She says, "Moving into our bodies, we embody the truth that as artists we are out to make a 'body of work.'"[645] She urges, "As we stretch our legs, we stretch our minds and our souls."[646] The simple act of walking is a great place to start moving if you are new to, or hesitant to dive into, exercise as a form of eustress or hormesis.

As sports psychologist George Mumford writes in his book, *The Mindful Athlete: Secrets to Pure Performance*, exploring eustress is "a continuous incremental process of romancing [our] discomfort zone."[647] As we step into eustress and hormesis activities, let's reflect:

Physical Arousal Awareness: What physical sensations do I feel? (For example: Rapid heartbeat? Sweating? Shortness of breath? Muscle tension?)	
Mental Arousal Awareness: What is my mental soundtrack? (For example: *This is hard! I'm gasping for air! I'm hot and sweaty!* Or *Wow, this makes me feel strong!*)	
Emotional Arousal Awareness: What emotions do I feel? (For example: Frustrated? Excited? Motivated? Tired? Energized? Happy? Zesty? Unstoppable?)	
Post-Activity Rest and Reflection: As I moved through the activity, did I feel the rise and fall of arousal sensations, ultimately returning back to "baseline"?	
"Train It and Trust It": Did I realize that I survived the discomfort of the experience, such that I trust that I will survive another experience just like that one (or similar to that one)?	
Savoring Hormetic High-Five Moments: Let's recognize when we emerge from episodes of eustress/hormesis and give ourselves a "hormetic high-five"!	

Remember that, according to Dr. Elissa Epel, novel experiences that require us to tap into coping mechanisms, apply knowledge, master challenges, and acknowledge our achievement or accomplishment also count as hormesis. So, if exercise or physical movement feels too overwhelming or unrealistic as a starting point for you, consider other activities that foster eustress or hormesis opportunities: Solo travel? Learning a new performance skill?

Helpful Resources for Considering Exercise or Physical Movement (or even Travel!) as Eustress/Hormesis Opportunities

- Book: Julia Cameron, *Walking in This World: The Practical Art of Creativity* (New York: Jeremy P. Tarcher/Penguin, 2002).
- Book: Daniel Lieberman, *Exercised: The Science of Physical Activity, Rest and Health* (London: Penguin Books, 2021).
- Book: John J. Ratey and Eric Hagerman, *Spark: The Revolutionary New Science of Exercise and the Brain* (New York: Little, Brown & Company, 2008).
- Book: John J. Ratey and Richard Manning, *Go Wild: Eat Fat, Run Free, Be Social, and Follow Evolution's Other Rules for Total Health and Well-Being* (New York: Little, Brown & Company, 2014).
- Caroline Williams, *Move! The New Science of Body Over Mind* (London: Profile Books, Ltd., 2021).

Physical Well-Being Dimension Exercise #6

Crafting an Appraisal Script

Instead of reacting to stressors in a way that overactivates our sympathetic fight-or-flight response or sends us into a dorsal deep freeze, let's craft appraisal scripts that can help us toggle into, and stay in, productive eustress and hormesis zones. This script does not need to be chiseled into stone; it's a work-in-progress and can be edited and revised as many times as we need in order to shape one that works for us individually.

In writing *The Introverted Lawyer* and *Untangling Fear*, I needed to stop trying to *ignore* the annoying and unhelpful voice of my mental soundtrack and instead, first let her speak, really listen to the words, then decide to reject that outdated and inaccurate diatribe once and for all, and finally write a new script. In doing that work, I realized that whenever I anticipated or stepped into a lawyering performance scenario, I played these deflating words on a repeated loop in my brain:

> *You're going to fail. What are you even doing here? Why did you say yes to this? You're going to turn red and everyone is going to think you are a loser. You should quit. You don't deserve to be here. Just go away and hide. Nobody likes you anyway. You're such a weirdo.*

Not pretty. And this soundtrack had the lovely side effect of exacerbating my blushing, sweating, shortness of breath, and heart-thumping.

I had a decision to make. I could keep letting this voice run the show (and the associated negative emotions run roughshod over my body). Or I could acknowledge a new reality:

> *You've worked hard to be here. You know what you're talking about. You deserve to have a voice. You're prepared for this. You don't have to speak perfectly. Who cares if you turn red?! Remember author Erika Hilliard says, a blush "symbolize[s] the fact that life is coursing through you"![648] If you reach one person with your message, you've done your job. Also, you didn't pass out in a 90-minute boxing training session yesterday with Lou; you're not going to pass out now. Now go!*

I finally ejected the tired, old, negative soundtrack and replaced it with a helpful appraisal script I now activate in every performance moment.

My self-doubt messages still often initially creep into play. But through developing this new soundtrack, and adopting it as part of my prehabilitation training, I am able to notice more quickly when my body, brain, and mind are veering toward becoming stuck in the old unproductive negativity loop. I consciously recalibrate, remind myself to trust my training, activate my appraisal script, and step into each performance with enhanced fortitude.

Here are some appraisal questions we can ask ourselves when we anticipate or encounter a stressor:

Suggested Prompts	
Primary Appraisal: Is this stressor: • Positive? In other words, can I view it as a cool challenge? • Dangerous/threatening to my personal goals (or my safety)? • Innocuous or irrelevant? Is the stress generated by this situation low-dose, moderate, or severe? Is this stressor situation temporary? Or is it chronic or permanent?	
Secondary Appraisal (Part I) • **"Train it and trust it"** ◦ How have I substantively prepared for this performance moment? ◦ How have I physically prepared for this performance moment? ◦ How have I worked on my emotional strength to prepare for this performance moment? ◦ Have I experienced a situation recently in which I felt similar physical/mental/emotional stress responses (hormesis high-five moments!) and I remember that I rode them out and came out the other side fine?	
Secondary Appraisal (Part II) • **Control** ◦ What level of control do I have over the outcome of this situation? ◦ If I have a reasonable degree of control, what personal resources can I activate to take action right now and solve the problem? ◦ If control is less realistic, what steps can I take right now to calm my physical, mental, and emotional state to ride out the situation in a healthy manner?	

Post-Event Pause for Savoring
• How did this challenge add a layer of meaning to an aspect of my personal or professional life?
  ° Did I activate a character strength? (See Chapter 3.)
  ° Did I successfully trust my training?
  ° Did I learn something new—enriching my physical, mental, or emotional power?
• What new or familiar positive sensations, thoughts, or emotions did I encounter in my body, brain, and mind?	

These question prompts are just for starters, to get us thinking about how to *reframe* and *remind.* In our prehabilitation work, we can practice asking ourselves these questions in training moments, and assess which are most helpful, and which are not as constructive. Eventually, we can fine-tune a faster soundtrack to initiate quickly in performance moments, such as:

> *I feel the familiar physical sensations of eustress and hormesis! OK, I've prepared for this. I've trained for this—substantively, physically, mentally, emotionally. I've done the work. I deserve to be here. If I reach one person with my message, I've done my job. I'm going to trust my training, and ride the rise and fall of my arousal sensations. OK, let's do this!*

Physical Well-Being Dimension Exercise #7

Crafting Training and Performance Routines and Rituals

My friend Sarah, a somatic educator, suggests that we give ourselves *regard*, which she defines as "one of the most healing things we can offer ourselves; it's saying to ourselves, *I see you*." Can you *regard* yourself as an athlete, a performer, or even an artist on this somatic self-discovery adventure? Athletes, performers, and artists thrive on routines, rituals, and sequences.

Let's first develop an overall prehabilitation routine. Later, we can craft more focused sequences of actions for training in, and performance of, specific lawyering tasks.

Crafting a Prehabilitation Routine: Daily or Weekly

Activity	Schedule/Timeline
Strategy #1: Somatic Self-Discovery • Checking in with myself and conducting a physical inventory (see Physical Well-Being Dimension Exercise #2) • Exploring proprioception, interoception, and exteroception exercises (see Physical Well-Being Dimension Exercise #3) • Exploring some of Shusterman's somaesthetics activities (see Physical Well-Being Dimension Exercise #3) • Exploring breathing exercises (see Physical Well-Being Dimension Exercise #4)	
Strategy #2: Eustress/Hormesis • Intentionally stepping into eustress/hormesis activities (see Physical Well-Being Dimension Exercise #5) • Reflecting and savoring (hormetic high-fives!)	
Strategy #3: Practicing Appraisal • Adopting/crafting an appraisal script (see Physical Well-Being Dimension Exercise #6) • Activating the script in eustress/hormesis moments	

Example of an In-the-Moment Training and Performance Routine/Ritual/Sequence

The following step-by-step sequence can be used in preparing for, and participating in, lawyering performance activities like presentations, oral arguments, negotiations, difficult conversations, and so on:

- Conduct a quick physical inventory—noticing any interesting bodily sensations
- Activate an affirming appraisal script
- Breathe
- Physically recalibrate and stand or sit in an athlete's or performer's balanced stance (both feet planted on the ground, shoulders back, arms and hands open, spine straightened—allowing for productive air, blood, and energy flow)
- Trust your training
- Step into a well-practiced substantive/intellectual sequence

Individualize your routine: Before stepping into a training or performance moment, consider playing an inspiring song you like, or repeating a cool quote that embodies your persona, or channeling your favorite athlete or performer (perhaps the one you identified in our "know thyself" reflection at the end of the Introduction to this book). After the training/performance experience, take a moment to reflect and savor. What went well? What could "use more love" next time?

Helpful Resources for Establishing an Individualized Training/Performance Routine, and Regarding Ourselves as Athletes/Performers/Artists

- Book: Julia Cameron, *The Artist's Way: A Spiritual Path to Higher Creativity* (New York: Jeremy P. Tarcher/Putnam, 2002).
- Book: George Mumford, *The Mindful Athlete: Secrets to Pure Performance* (Berkeley: Parallax Press, 2016).
- Book: Steven Pressfield, *Do the Work* (Egremont: The Domino Project, 2011).
- Book: Bob Rotella, *How Champions Think: In Sports and in Life* (New York: Simon & Schuster, 2015).
- Book: Twyla Tharp, *The Creative Habit: Learn It and Use It for Life* (New York: Simon & Schuster, 2006).

Think with your whole body.

Taisen Deshimaru

CHAPTER 6

Our Emotional Dimension

To tell someone not to be emotional is to tell them to be dead.
Jeanette Winterson

In this chapter, we will learn about:

- The role of positive emotions in our well-being (Fredrickson's broaden-and-build and "upward spiral" theories of positive emotions)
- Appraisal scripts and optimistic explanatory styles
- Savoring
- Positivity resonance
- Capitalization
- Active constructive responding (ACR)

In the 1992 movie *A League of Their Own*, Tom Hanks' character—a coach to a women's baseball team—admonished a sobbing right fielder and barked, "There's no crying in baseball!"[649] I was knee-deep in my 1L year at the University of Virginia School of Law when that movie hit theaters. That line of the script might as well have been, "There's no crying in law school!" Yet I cried in private—over my Criminal Law and Constitutional Law grades, my moot court tryout debacle, my fear that I wasn't "cut out" for the profession. For many years of full-time law practice, I cried behind my closed office door, in restrooms, and in hotel rooms after what I perceived were "failures" in intense and often scary (for me) depositions and negotiations. While I'm a big believer in the catharsis of a good cry, those were so many wasted and unnecessarily depleting tears. At the time, I didn't know how to process emotions that were normal and often necessary but didn't feel good. I also didn't know how to amplify emotions that could be more conducive to my long-term well-being.

Like our physical dimension, one key to cultivating our emotional well-being is enhanced awareness. For much of our lives, we may have experienced emotions as reactionary—unconscious or automatic responses to life events. But studying and getting to know the differences among our emotions, what sparks each one, how they make us feel—*mentally* and *physically*—can be illuminating. For instance, it was eye-opening for me to learn the distinction between *guilt* and *shame*, that is, the difference between feeling I had *done something* bad versus feeling like I *am* bad. It was fun to identify activities that ignite my senses of *joy*, *wonder*, *marvel*, and *zest*, such as jumping up and down at concerts or meandering the streets of foreign cities solo. It was also useful to recognize and label resistance to certain scenarios as *fear*.

Dr. Bessel van der Kolk, author of the helpful book, *The Body Keeps the Score: Brain, Mind, and Body in the Healing of Trauma*, explains that the word *emotion* comes from the Latin word *emovere*, which means "to move out."[650] He notes Darwin's identification of the purpose of emotions as inciting *movement* in muscles in our face and body; apparently, emotions are designed to transition us back to safety and equilibrium. According to van der Kolk, this muscle movement transmits different signals to other human beings: *Leave me alone* or *I feel unsafe* or *I'd love your help* or *I'm eager to connect* or *I like being around you.*[651]

Here, in exploring the pivotal role of emotions in our professional and personal lives, we'll learn how different life scenarios ignite particular emotions in us along a spectrum, information that can help us self-regulate, toggling into our *eustress* zone, rather than catapulting into a *distress* zone. We'll study how emotions affect our thinking, feeling, and doing. We'll consider situations and people that spark positive emotions in us, and those that unfortunately can kindle negative or less constructive emotions. Through our prehabilitation work, we'll investigate techniques, rituals, and routines for amplifying positive emotions and for wrangling negative emotions appropriately. We'll practice, practice, practice. Then, when we step into performance moments or encounter challenging life events, we'll trust our training, and thrive. And we will savor it all.

DR. BARBARA FREDRICKSON'S BROADEN-AND-BUILD THEORY

First, let's lay the foundation for the scientific connection between positive emotions and well-being—earning positive emotions the pole position as the P in positive psychology's PERMA (**p**ositive emotions, **e**ngagement, **r**elationships, **m**eaning, **a**ccomplishment) framework. In the 1990s, Dr. Barbara Fredrickson studied the science of how positive emotions enhance our health and performance. Her research culminated in her **broaden-and-build theory.**[652] Fredrickson posits that positive emotions "open our hearts and our minds, making us more receptive and more creative."[653] Positive emotions help us develop new skills, deepen our knowledge base, forge new interpersonal connections, and discover new layers of our personas.[654] As Fredrickson puts it,

"[P]ositivity goes beyond self-talk. [It] infuses your mindscape and outlook, heart rhythms and body chemistry, muscle tension and facial expressions, and your resources and relationships."[655] She emphasizes that positivity does not just feel good; it changes the way we think and transforms how we contribute to the world.[656]

Fredrickson's broaden-and-build theory distinguishes the *narrowing* effect of negative emotions from the *expanding* effect of positive emotions. When negative emotions dominate our thinking, our capacity for idea generation shrinks.[657] In contrast, when we actively cultivate positive emotions in ourselves and others, our minds open to a wider array of possibilities, solutions, and opportunities. Fredrickson reports scientific studies that tie this "broaden effect" to heightened creativity.[658] Individuals in "broaden mode" are able to generate more solutions to perceived problems, identify a greater number of options for conquering challenges, and see the bigger picture in life.[659] Fredrickson explains:

> *Positivity literally expands your peripheral vision, allowing you to see more than you typically do. As positivity expands the scope of your visual attention, it also expands the conceptual connections you make. You come up with more and better ideas. And when you face problems, positivity makes your solutions better. . . . [Y]our positivity and your openness feed on and reinforce each other, creating a buoyant upward spiral within you.*[660]

Fredrickson describes this **upward spiral** phenomenon as "positivity and openness feed[ing] on each other, each reinforcing and catalyzing the other."[661]

Fredrickson emphasizes that, as we begin to notice how positive emotions drive openness to growth, and how this inquisitiveness can reciprocally ignite positive emotions, we accumulate tools in our well-being toolbox called "vantage resources."[662] These include:[663]

- Physical resources—physical skills, bodily vitality, energy
- Social resources—relationships with friends, family, work colleagues, mentors, romantic partners
- Intellectual resources—expertise, knowledge, problem-solving skills
- Psychological resources—creativity, optimism

As we accrue these resources, we learn to trust that they are available for us to access when we eventually hit speed bumps in our personal and professional lives.[664] Fredrickson's friend, Dr. Martin Seligman, underscores this point; he says, "Positive emotion does much more than just feel pleasant; it is a neon sign that growth is underway, that psychological capital is accumulating."[665] This psychological capital is like an emotional savings account; if we invest in strengthening our emotional well-being dimension now—through our *pre*habilitation training—we amass valuable assets in the bank that we can draw upon when we encounter challenges in our lives as members of the legal profession.

THE FRAMING ROLE OF NEGATIVE EMOTIONS

Importantly, Fredrickson—as a positive psychologist—does not dismiss or reject negativity or negative emotions; in fact, she emphasizes that "[n]egativity is important. Nobody can flourish without it."[666] She refers to negative emotions as "appropriate and useful" in certain life moments.[667] But for us to flourish as human beings, we can learn to situate negativity in a broader framework, with positivity playing a more dominant role. We also can learn to distinguish between appropriate and toxic negativity.[668] As Fredrickson explains, gratuitous negativity (embodied in the emotion of shame, for instance) is noxious.[669]

Indeed, negative emotions give us perspective and contrast, providing the necessary structural frame and tension to amplify positive emotions. Let's consider a weather analogy. I love the lyric by the 90s band Garbage: *I'm only happy when it rains. I'm only happy when it's complicated.*[670] That lyric is so *me.* I like thunderclouds, rain, fog, wind, and snow because they magnify my appreciation of sunny days. Philosophy professor Dr. Robert Nozick wrote about how some people want to earn their pleasures based on their actions and character.[671] I wish I had been aware of Nozick's work when, living in Laguna Beach, California, I felt like a weirdo because I was completely uninspired by the perfect daily weather. I might be the only person in history who was completely bored by Laguna's perfect "72 and sunny" climate. I yearned to earn my day. I crave edginess, grittiness, and imperfection to help me appreciate beauty.

Perhaps we can view certain negative emotions as providing valuable depth, shade, and nuance. Nozick distinguishes between a buoyantly happy life and one with value.[672] He says that a life of worth involves not just cheery moments, but shadows of grief, loss, and hurt. The hours in which we experience loneliness, pain, or sadness help us recognize and treasure contrasting flashes of joy, wonder, pride, inspiration, and connection.

Further, according to Peterson, negative emotions intermingled within otherwise positive circumstances can generate higher-order experiences that leave a deeper imprint.[673] A couple years ago, I slept in a car outside the Los Angeles Forum (a sports and concert venue) with two of my girlfriends to wait in line to grab front row General Admission spots at a U2 show. Leaning against the stage rail, with Bono singing directly at me—not another human soul between us, not even his bodyguard—I simultaneously felt exhaustion, sadness, long pent-up grief, human connection, alienation, exhilaration, revelation, wonder, and awe. The intense look on Bono's face made it seem like he was mad at me, though obviously that makes no sense. That concert moment was one of the loneliest yet most transcendent of my life. I use it as a frame of reference for subsequent life experiences that intertwine negative with positive emotions.

The interplay between negative and positive emotions during extreme challenges—such as the loss of loved ones, breakups, divorce, 9/11, economic depressions, natural disasters, pandemics—also can help us place subsequent experiences in context.[674] Past circumstances in which grief, fear, sadness, and regret intermingle with hope, gratitude, and love help us maintain perspective in the face of new difficulties. We can greet a new challenge and muse, "Well, this reminds me of _____. I was okay then; I'm going to be okay now."

Overall, the goal here is not to eliminate negative emotions. We can view them not as blemishes or imperfections but as essential to a life of flourishing. With that as a backdrop, Fredrickson offers us a powerful call to action: "Positivity is a choice."[675] So, let's get to choosing!

POSITIVE EMOTIONS CAN FOSTER A SENSE OF SAFETY

In her book *Positivity*, Fredrickson outlines ten positive states of being:[676]

- Joy
- Gratitude, which interestingly, she distinguishes from feeling indebted to others
- Serenity—those "deep sigh" moments of contentment or appreciation
- Interest—moments of possibility, mystery, or intrigue
- Hope—our belief that change is possible
- Pride—a sense of having achieved something socially valuable or having made a difference
- Amusement—laughter, fun, and delight
- Inspiration—moments when we transcend ourselves because someone or something motivates us to create, express ourselves, or take action
- Awe—moments when we transcend ourselves because we feel part of something expansive
- Love

She zooms in on these ten emotional states because they are the subjects of active scientific research.[677]

Peterson emphasizes that positive emotions like these are signals to our bodies, brains, and minds that we are safe.[678] (Here is our theme of **safety** again! Remember that, in studying our physical dimension in Chapter 5, we learned that a sense of safety is key to activating the ventral vagal circuit of our autonomic nervous system.) Even in the context of the emotion of awe, which Fredrickson indicates can teeter on the precipice of safety because we are intermingling negative and positive emotions, we do so in an ultimately positive way.[679] A feeling of safety stemming from positive emotions gives us room to expand, grow, try new things, venture fresh ideas, and experience new heights.

Two cool aspects of positive emotions are that: (1) they change how our mind functions and (2) we can cultivate them.[680] Fredrickson asserts that we have the power to actively increase our positivity.[681] How? Let's examine four techniques:

- Emotion exploration
- Appraisal scripts, engaging an optimistic explanatory style
- Ritual and routine
- Savoring

It's 3:26 a.m. and I am wide awake. Again. My air conditioning unit is rattling, pumping to keep my bedroom a chilled 68 degrees. Yet I'm sweating. I get up, make my way in the dark to my kitchen (yay, **proprioception**!), grab a glass of ice water and my cell phone, and return to bed. I click on the Insight Timer app. I listen to forty minutes of a meditation about "letting go." Still awake (#meditationfail), exasperated, hot, my annoying negative mental soundtrack starts to whir . . . *You're going to be exhausted . . . You're going to get a migraine . . . You're not going to be able to function tomorrow . . . Why can't you sleep well, like normal people? . . . How are you going to get all this work done? . . . You're weak . . .*

It's still dark outside. It's way too early to get up, make coffee, and go for a run.

I can't afford to let my mind derail me. I need to get some rest. I need to be able to get up at a reasonable hour and get today's manuscript pages done, plus fulfill a boatload of other work responsibilities. Somehow, I need to stop this self-doubt tornado from churning.

Oh wait, I remember now. I trained for this. I can regulate my emotions.

PREHABILITATION: EMOTION EXPLORATION

Grant Parr is a mental performance coach to athletes. He believes "[t]raining the mind is every bit as important as training the body."[682] He asks us to consider, "Why would the need for practice at training your mind be different than training any other part of your body?"[683] He urges that "mental preparation has to parallel physical preparation."[684] While it may seem that athletes focus more on the body while law students and lawyers concentrate more on the mind, we *all* need to integrate physical, mental, *and* emotional training to function at our best. This opportunity for exploratory education about our individual emotions presents a chance, once again, to "know ourselves," as Socrates encouraged.

Sports blogger Steve Koesterman highlights stressors faced by athletes, which interestingly parallel those encountered by law students and lawyers: "performance anxiety, energy/stress management, confidence issues, attention/concentration control, conflict management."[685] He points out that "[a]thletes tend to rely too much on their physical capabilities, ignoring the mental aspect of a given situation."[686] He cautions that "[a]thletes today can't afford to rely solely on their physical talents. Connecting the mind and body to produce an elite mindset to overcome internal and external distractions while performing is vital to success."[687] When we work on cultivating our emotional dimension, we set ourselves up well to tackle the unknown. As Parr emphasizes, "There's a huge difference between being scared of a situation because you know you've not done the work and simply being afraid because you have entered the unknown."[688]

When I am lying awake in the middle of the night and my brain begins to race ahead to everything that could go wrong the next day because I'm not getting enough sleep, my thoughts and emotions begin to swirl. Different emotions tangle and intertwine. I have a habit of confusing and conflating emotions when I am tired. Also, everything feels like the *unknown.* My go-to negative emotion is shame. Often, after a productive day of writing, work, and exercise, capped off with a fun night out with friends, I'll go to sleep in a positive mood—yet wake up in the middle of the night stressing out about my insomnia, my work, my (nonexistent) relationship status. Shame kicks in. I begin to feel like a bad person for taking this time to write, for major relationship mistakes I've made in the past, for needing so much time alone as an introvert. By doing this work we're exploring together, I've learned that in those moments, I need to first *recognize* the shame cycle in order to halt it. Next, I activate a healthy appraisal script. Then, I cultivate an *accurate* positive emotion that helps me stay on a healthy mental track until I have moved through the difficult moment (or until the sun comes up and everything seems a bit brighter).

We can't recognize what we don't know. So, let's first get better educated about our emotions. Let's start with the positive states compiled by Fredrickson: joy, gratitude, serenity, interest, hope, pride, amusement, inspiration, awe, and love. Let's spend a minute thinking about what each of these positive states of being means to us. What does it *feel like*—in our bodies—to experience these emotions? How does each emotion feel different from the next?

Joy:____________________________________

Gratitude:______________________________

Serenity:_______________________________

Interest:_______________________________

Hope:__________________________________

Pride:__________________________________

Amusement:_____________________________

Inspiration:____________________________

Awe:___________________________________

Love:__________________________________

Next, let's give some thought to emotional states that tend to feel "bad": anger, fear, jealousy, resentment, guilt, shame, loneliness, anxiety, nervousness, depression, rejection, numbness, grief, exhaustion. Let's spend a minute thinking about what each of these states of being means to us. How do these emotions *feel* in our bodies? How does one emotion feel different from the next?

Anger:_________________________________

Fear:__________________________________

Jealousy:_______________________________

Resentment:____________________________

Guilt:__________________________________

Shame:_________________________________

Loneliness:_____________________________

Anxiety:____

Nervousness:______________________________________

Depression:_______________________________________

Rejection:____

Numbness:____

Grief:____

Exhaustion:_______________________________________

Others?____

When we get to know our different emotions and get super-specific about how they *feel* in our bodies, we are better able to drill down to their roots. When I'm wide awake in the middle of the night, I often first feel sensations of fear (or lack of safety). I'm hot and sweaty. My heart starts beating fast. I feel shaky. Once I identify the emotion of fear, I ask myself, *What exactly am I afraid of? Rejection? Exclusion? Being judged? OK, and what exactly does that feel like? Not being worthy of love and care.* For me, when I drill down to the root of my fear, it ends up really being about shame. When I realize I'm really dealing with the emotion of shame, I can remind myself: *I am not a terrible person. This is just a deeply ingrained shame response that I can continue excavating and working through.*

Emotional Well-Being Dimension Exercise #1

Personal Emotion Education: Fredrickson's Positivity Portfolio

In her book *Positivity,* Fredrickson suggests an exercise (a positive intervention originally developed by Pawelski) that can help us explore and cultivate positive states of being.[689] This exercise also can be useful to teach us how to recognize *differences* between and among our various emotions.

In Fredrickson's Positivity Portfolio exercise, she recommends we first choose one positive emotion from her list of ten: joy, gratitude, serenity, interest, hope, pride, amusement, inspiration, awe, love. Next, she prompts us to collect physical items that invoke the chosen emotion, creating a "portfolio." Then, we dedicate a short duration of time (even 10 to 15 minutes is fine) every day for a week (or longer), to engage with the items while focusing on the chosen emotion, and observe what happens.

For my birthday the year before the pandemic began, my friend Jenn gifted me a box decorated with a blue, pink, and gold map of the world. I filled the box with stuff I love. Artsy cards from friends with encouraging notes written in loopy handwriting and song lyrics they know I like. Wrinkled ticket stubs and wristbands from U2, Madonna, and Red Hot Chili Peppers concerts. An expired passport checkered with ornate stamps. Postcards from art galleries in Málaga, Istanbul, San Francisco. Colorful coasters from restaurants in Rome and Cartagena. A piece of sea glass (a battered shard from an old beer bottle) plucked from a beach in Sicily. A sliver of crepe paper with the words, "Your intuition brought you here." Weirdly, an out-of-place photo of me (looking rather miserable) in my law firm office in Tower Two of the World Trade Center in early 2001. (I don't know how that picture ended up in the box!)

During the pandemic, I decided to try Fredrickson's Positivity Portfolio exercise. I chose the emotion of "awe." I grabbed my world map box to rediscover what was in it and see if it qualified as a good start to an "awe" portfolio. For a week, I spent 10 to 15 minutes every morning with my box while thinking about awe. I ran my fingers along the raised gold lettering on the box itself, identifying continents and oceans. I touched the bumps on a metallic, rose gold envelope inside. I gripped my Sicilian sea glass in my palm. I grazed the brushstrokes of a Cy Twombly painting on a postcard. As I meandered through travel mementos in the box, I remembered running my hands along a hand-carved wooden bed frame at an Indigenous Arts hotel in Vancouver. I heard the typewriter keys that Madonna clacked before the opening song of her *Madame X* tour. I smelled the musty books in the Dublin literary museum where I exchanged a few euro for a yellow caricature of writer Oscar Wilde.

Before the pandemic, travel had been a huge part of my personal and professional identity. I hopped on a plane a few times a month to deliver book talks and attend legal education conferences, but also to explore the world. When I travel, awe interrupts my constant need to accomplish something. I stop overthinking. I wander. My brain overflows with awe instead of the twenty-eight things on my to-do list. Spending time with my Positivity Portfolio first thing every morning, I was able to marvel at the world (and my life) in a different way during the pandemic than jumping on a plane. I felt calm. And for the next two hours of work immediately afterwards, I felt in a state of *flow*.

I started Fredrickson's Positivity Portfolio exercise the day before the nineteenth anniversary of 9/11. Contrasting the sad, lonely girl in the World Trade Center office picture in my box with the myriad layers of awesome life experiences I have had in the past 19 years—concerts, trips all over the world, new friendships, new jobs—invoked a tremendous feeling of awe. This feeling stayed with me throughout each day that I engaged in the exercise. I felt awe while teaching my remote law classes, running in a nearby park, breathing in the first whispers of fall weather, and exploring the flowers and art on New York's High Line pathway.

As part of our emotion education, let's spend some time getting to know the nuances of each of the ten positive emotions identified by Fredrickson. While seeking to cultivate positive emotions (as part of Fredrickson's broaden-and-build theory), we also can hopefully enhance our ability to distinguish different emotions from each other. Consider choosing a positive emotion from Fredrickson's list, collecting a portfolio of objects or items that invoke that emotion, and spend time with your collection for 10 to 15 minutes a day for a week. After one week, you could switch to a different emotion and create a new portfolio, and so on.

PREHABILITATION: APPRAISAL SCRIPTS (USING OPTIMISTIC EXPLANATORY STYLE)

Basketball coach Phil Jackson writes about emotional regulation in the context of sports. He describes the process of "quieting the endless jabbering of thoughts so that [our] body can do instinctively what it's been trained to do without the mind getting in the way."[690] He describes this process as "right action"—"the capacity to observe what's happening and act appropriately, without being distracted by self-centered thoughts."[691] He says, "If we rage and resist, our angry, fearful minds have trouble quieting down sufficiently to allow us to act in the most beneficial way for ourselves and others.[692] As we learned in Chapter 5 with regard to managing our physical responses to stressors, instead of letting our bodies, brains, and minds be commandeered by wild, knee-jerk, emotional reactions to perceived stressors, we can adopt a practice of healthy appraisal. By initiating **appraisal scripts** and sequences at the onset of emotional or physical arousal (in training), we can reassert control and execute mental, emotional, and physical steps that we know are beneficial for our well-being and our performance.

As we learned in Chapter 5 in the context of our physical well-being dimension, Lazarus articulated two phases of appraisal. In primary appraisal, we interpret a stressor—here, inciting emotional arousal—as either positive, dangerous, or irrelevant.[693] In this primary phase, if we determine that an important personal goal is suddenly at risk, we might appraise a situation as a *threat*.[694] However, if we trust that our coping skills can help us meet the situation's demands, we might deem the situation a *challenge*.[695]

Next, in secondary appraisal, we more intently gauge our personal resources and our ability to cope.[696] A pivotal aspect of the appraisal process is our assessment of the level of control we can exert over the outcome.[697] If control is possible, we can launch action-oriented, *problem-solving coping* mechanisms.[698] If control is less realistic, we can instead adopt cognitive strategies to modulate our emotions (called *emotion-focused coping*) and, if necessary, accept the situation in a healthy way.[699]

The appraisal process yields different emotions.[700] Of course, situations that we appraise as potential threats can ignite less-than-pleasant emotions, such as anxiety and fear, while situations we appraise as challenges can generate a mix of negative and positive emotions, for example, blending nervous anticipation with excitement and awe.[701] As we ride the wave of a scenario successfully, we might experience other positive emotional states, such as relief, pride, and a sense of accomplishment.[702] If the outcome is unfavorable or incomplete, we might linger in negative emotional states, such as frustration or confusion, unless we launch another appraisal loop.[703] One technique we can deploy as part of our emotion education—and as we craft our appraisal scripts—is understanding our "explanatory style."

Getting to Know Our Explanatory Style: Oxygenating Our Optimism

We all have a natural *style of thinking*. Scientists call this our *cognitive style*—the way we view the world.[704] Optimism and pessimism are familiar words in our vocabulary, but many of us may never have considered how these two approaches to evaluating life affect our mental, emotional, and physical health. We also may never have pondered whether we have the power to amp up our optimism. The good news is that, according to positive psychologists, we do!

Let's start with some definitions. An optimistic person expects good things in life.[705] In contrast, pessimists tend to wallow, expecting the next shoe to drop.[706] (In my twenties, I was a world-class pessimist and didn't even realize it!) Take a moment right now: Can you name one optimist in your life? How about one pessimist? Think about what language they use when describing their worldview: adjectives, nouns, verbs, adverbs. (My friend and I each have close buddies in our lives who we jokingly—and affectionately—refer to as "rays of sunshine" because they constantly send us doom-and-gloom text messages.)

How Do I Know If I'm an Optimist or a Pessimist?

Of course, it's easy to be optimistic when life is awesome and everything seems to be going right. The test of our optimism occurs, though, when troubles arise. Interestingly, optimists expect positive eventual outcomes even when things seem gloomy.[707] Why? Well, it comes down to different coping styles.[708]

Coping Styles of Optimists When Hitting Life's Speed Bumps	Coping Styles of Pessimists When Hitting Life's Speed Bumps
Set new goals	Try to escape the situation
Plan for the future	Distract themselves
Continue trying	Stop trying
Actively attempt to flex and adjust to stressful circumstances	
Engage in *problem-focused* coping: Seek to do something about the stressor (this is easiest with controllable stressors)	
Activate *emotion-focused* coping: Soothe distress and regulate emotional responses (this is easier with uncontrollable stressors)	
Engagement coping: Deal with the stressor or emotions head-on	Avoidance-coping: Seek to escape the stressor or emotions; redirect attention to other areas of focus

Are Optimism and Pessimism Hereditary? Are We Doomed to Our Fate?

Scientists refer to "dispositional optimism" as a *stable* attribute of personality.[709] However, researchers indicate that only approximately 25% to 30% of our optimism and pessimism tendencies are hereditable.[710] Environmental factors in our upbringing and early adulthood—such as socioeconomic status, academic and vocational training experiences, stability of employment, caregiver modeling—can drive dispositional optimism.[711] Notwithstanding nature and nurture, we have the ability to increase our optimism by noticing, and then adjusting, our schema (our patterns of thoughts and behavior).[712] We can seize *control.*

Why Should We Care? Because Optimism Is Good for Our Health and Well-Being!

According to the experts, optimism can enhance our health and well-being. First, research indicates that optimists are more likely to engage in proactive and preventative behaviors related to health and wellness, such as exercising, becoming knowledgeable about health risks, and minimizing dubious activities.[713] (Reading this book and doing our prehab work to cultivate our multi-dimensional well-being are acts of optimism!) Scientists have even linked optimistic behaviors to the ability to slow disease progression, reduce body fat, and stave off heart-related health issues.[714] Second, research suggests that optimists may be less physiologically reactive than pessimists to natural life stressors.[715] This can translate to less wear and tear on the body (remember our allostatic load?), better physical health, and enhanced longevity.[716]

Oxygenating Our Optimism: New Mental Exercises and Habit Formation

Researchers indicate that we have the power to boost our optimism through forming a habit of practicing healthy appraisal of situations and stressors.[717] In general, we form new healthy habits by repeating simple and sequential acts consistently for a duration of time.[718] To make optimism a habit, it helps to first notice the *words* we use to evaluate life events. Seligman explains that each of us has an *attributional style* or *explanatory style*—the way we classify the causes of prior outcomes.[719]

According to Seligman, the nature of our explanatory style depends on whether we view life circumstances as:

- Permanent or temporary
- Pervasive or situational
- Personally driven or externally influenced[720]

For example, pessimists tend to explain bad events as permanent (they will persist for a long time, or forever),[721] pervasive (the badness permeates our life),[722] and personal (we caused the outcome).[723]

As I mentioned, I was a world-champion pessimist in my teens and twenties. My friends called me "A-minus Brown." Every time I walked out of a test in high school or college, I was convinced I failed, the grade would tank my GPA, I'd never graduate or get a job, I'd be broke for the rest of my life and it was all my fault because I'm a deeply flawed human . . . Often, I'd end up with an A-minus, much to the annoyance of my high school and college friends. (Of course, my grades in law school were a completely different story.) Yet even the positive feeling associated with a good grade would not stay with me for very long.

Optimists explain negative events as impermanent (temporary), specific (limited to the situation at hand), and impacted by at least some external forces. Pessimists regard good events as impermanent (temporary), specific, and externally caused; optimists assess good events as permanent, universal, and internally driven.

Like Fredrickson's acknowledgment that not all negativity is bad, Seligman emphasizes that pessimism of course plays an important role at times: "Pessimism may support the realism we so often need."[724] Importantly, "[w]e can learn to choose optimism for the most part, but also to heed pessimism when it is warranted."[725]

Let's start paying attention to how we naturally categorize events as they unfold—under the permanent/pervasive/personal framework. Once we are aware of our natural tendency, we can make a concerted effort to appropriately appraise unfortunate situations or circumstances as temporary (impermanent and changeable), specific (unique to a particular setting or time), and external (not tied to a hardened "flaw" in us, but rather something we can change). Notably, when we identify external causes of negative events, we are not necessarily deflecting or blame-shifting in an unhealthy manner; instead, we are empowering ourselves to take charge of the next situation and effect positive change.

Emotional Well-Being Dimension Exercise #2

Let's Practice Oxygenating Our Optimism

- Identify a recent event that felt somewhat frustrating or unpleasant. ____________
- How did you react when it happened? Write down the words and language that appeared in your thoughts: ____________
- What emotions did you feel when it happened? Try to be as specific as possible: ____________
- Did you take any actions on the day that it happened? ____________
- Did you take any different actions on the day *after* it happened? ____________
- Did you reach out or talk to anyone about what happened? If yes, who? Why did you choose them? ____________
- Reflect on the words/language/actions you wrote above. Using the chart below, circle actions in either column that characterize your response to the event.[726]

Optimistic Tendencies	**Pessimistic Tendencies**
Actively highlight the positive	Only notice the negative
Spot opportunities and invitations to grow	Spot threats and downsides
Assert control over the situation (yet honor realistic boundaries)	Passively acquiesce and cede control to other forces driving the situation
Generate solutions and options	Ruminate and wallow
Stride into resolute action	Take the "ostrich" approach→avoid
Connect with others	Sequester from friends and family

- From the chart above, assess whether you currently have a tendency to lean toward a pessimistic or optimistic approach. Either is okay right now—because we CAN change our natural tendencies!
- Let's run the same scenario through a framework of optimistic questions:[727]

What benefit(s) could this circumstance possibly generate?	
What can I learn, or how can I grow, from this experience?	
What aspects of this circumstance can I direct/drive/control?	

What boundaries or limits on my ability to control the scenario can I embrace (so I am not wasting mental or physical energy on them)?	
What resources can I activate to make the situation better?	
What action-oriented steps can I take today?	
Who is the best person (or people) to help me focus on positive outcomes, solutions, growth, and forward movement?	

To make optimism a *habit*, we can repeat these queries each time we encounter a challenge.

Note: This optimistic approach to evaluating situations echoes some of the themes we identified in our appraisal script template that we developed in our physical well-being dimension in Chapter 5.

Appraisal Script Template

Suggested Prompts	
Primary Appraisal: Is this situation: • Positive? In other words, can I view it as a cool challenge? • Dangerous/threatening to my personal goals (or my safety)? • Innocuous or irrelevant? Is the stress/emotional arousal generated by this situation low-dose, moderate, or severe? Is this stressor/emotional arousal situation temporary? Or is it chronic or permanent?	
Secondary Appraisal (Part I) • **"Train it and trust it"** ◦ How have I substantively prepared for this situation? ◦ How have I physically prepared for this situation? ◦ How have I worked on my emotional strength to prepare for this situation? ◦ Have I experienced a situation recently in which I felt similar physical/mental/emotional arousal responses and I remember that I rode them out and came out the other side fine?	

Secondary Appraisal (Part II) • **Control** ° What level of control do I have over the outcome of this situation? ° If I have a reasonable degree of control, what personal resources can I activate to take action right now? ° If control is less realistic, what steps can I take right now to calm my physical, mental, and emotional state to ride out the situation in a healthy manner?	

PREHABILITATION: ESTABLISHING ROUTINES AND RITUALS

As we explore our emotions, and as we practice using our optimistic explanatory style and appraisal scripts when we encounter new scenarios, it helps to establish routines and rituals we can rehearse in training and activate in eventual performance moments. Parr emphasizes the power of "a repeatable process for an athlete, which will align with their thoughts and emotions."[728] Choreographer Twyla Tharp notes, "By making the start of the sequence automatic, [we can] replace doubt and fear with comfort and routine."[729] Another sports performance coach, Graham Betchart, echoes this theme, stating, "Repetition of your mindset creates retention of your mindset. Working on your mental game is like working on your shot. You have to practice and train daily. There is no quick fix with mental training. There is no overnight success."[730] Basketball coach Phil Jackson talks about how star player Michael Jordan relied upon routines and rituals in practice to bring his brain, mind, and body into alignment in the eventual game: "Rather than cloud his mind with negative thoughts, he [said] to himself, 'Okay, I've been here before,' and then trie[d] to relax enough to let something positive emerge."[731]

Routines and rituals are helpful for us in two ways in this context: (1) we can engage in daily or weekly routines and rituals to explore our emotional well-being dimension in *general*, and (2) we can develop a sequence of steps to activate our optimistic explanatory style and appraisal scripts when addressing specific emotionally charged situations. For example, to work on our emotional well-being generally, we can establish a routine or ritual for engaging in Fredrickson's Positivity Portfolio exercise, perhaps choosing a different emotion each week for a period of time. Additionally, we can adopt a routine or ritual for noticing which of Fredrickson's ten emotional states we encounter throughout each day.

Further, to work on regulating our emotions in specific scenarios, we can construct a sequence of actions to initiate when we encounter a stressor. For example, when I wake up in the middle of the night as I often do, my brain immediately boots up and begins listing all the things that could go wrong the next day. Not fun! I *could* allow myself to get sucked into this wasteful and depleting mental and emotional loop. OR, I can recognize when it's happening and activate a productive routine and ritual. My middle-of-the-night sequence for regulating my emotions goes something like this:

- *OK, it's the middle of the night. Remember, everything seems worse in the middle of the night. If you really are trying to solve a specific problem, you get **five** more minutes to think about this. If not, let's move on right **now**.*
- *We've trained for this.*
- *Inhale and exhale (activating nasal breathing discussed in Chapter 5).*
- *What emotion(s) are you feeling? [If the emotion is fear or anxiety, try to drill down and see if it is really your go-to emotion of shame. If so, remember you have a habit of heaping misplaced shame upon yourself.]*
- *Inhale and exhale.*
- *Let's activate an optimistic explanatory style and an appraisal script:*
    - *Is this situation permanent or temporary?*
    - *Is this situation 100% personal? Or can you identify external factors at play?*
    - *What character strengths can you activate?*
        - *Remember your signature character strengths! Perseverance, curiosity, creativity, love of learning, and most of all, zest!*
    - *Let's try to fall back asleep.*
    - *And if sleep doesn't happen, that's fine too. Let's just rest. Things will make more sense when the sun comes up.*
    - *Note: When I wake up, I do my Morning Pages and often a solution to the perceived problem materializes in my scribbles. Further, when I exercise later in the day, positive emotions edge out lingering self-doubt.*

PREHABILITATION: PRACTICING THE ACT AND ART OF SAVORING

One of the many tools Fredrickson offers for cultivating positive emotions is the act and art of *savoring*: pausing to give *regard* to positive moments and sensations, identifying and then lingering with what reaches in and touches our heart and soul. Fredrickson defines savoring as "considering good events in such a way that you willfully generate, intensify, and prolong your heartfelt enjoyment of them."[732]

How often do we race through life, blowing right past or through events, sights, experiences, and moments that thrill, amaze, and inspire us? How often do we stop to truly taste that bite of phenomenal pizza? Rewind that powerful lyric in that song? Stand in front of a cool piece of street art for five minutes to let the colors imprint in our memory? Stare at the sunset without feeling compelled to hashtag it on Instagram? Marvel at how our skin feels on that first perfect day between seasons when the weather transitions from hot to cool, or cold to warm? Inhale as we pass a neighborhood flower stand? Relish something we achieved in our work?

As we talked about in Chapter 5—in the context of savoring physical eustress episodes to amplify their impact—we can use three pathways to savor positive emotional experiences:[733]

- **Meaning:** tapping into how a moment, experience, or activity adds meaning or purpose to our personal or professional lives
- **Mindfulness:** paying attention to and noticing sensations in our bodies, brains, and minds within or after such a moment, experience, or activity
- **Energy management:** allowing for periods of rest to let positive emotions generate and resonate

As we barrel through our day today or tomorrow, let's try to notice moments that spark joy, gratitude, serenity, interest, hope, pride, amusement, inspiration, love, or awe. And then let's linger there for a bit. Let's practice savoring by activating the three pathways.

I recently experienced an awe moment. I was crossing the Ponte Sisto bridge in Rome, on my way back to my hotel after having dinner alone on my last night before flying home. A street performer was singing the song *Fix You* by the band Coldplay. I stopped on the bridge to listen. A lone seagull flew along the Tiber River below the bridge. A ferry boat floated by. Tourists holding hands dropped euro coins into the singer's open guitar case. I wanted to savor the moment. Later, I jotted these notes.

Meaning	Self-transcendent moments like these are why I travel. The song made me think of my friends. I recorded 30 seconds or so of the performance to share it with them.

Mindfulness	I paid attention to the sensations and emotions I experienced when listening to the song. Absorbing the sights and sounds on the bridge, I felt electrified. I felt wistful. I felt connected to the singer.
Energy Management	Back at the hotel, I watched and listened to the video recording a few times. I Googled the lyrics to remind myself of the song's meaning.

CULTIVATING EMOTIONAL WELL-BEING WHEN INTERACTING WITH OTHERS

Now that we are equipped with some tools for amplifying our *own* emotional well-being (emotion exploration, appraisal using optimistic explanatory style, routines and rituals, savoring), let's delve into how we can maintain and augment emotional well-being when interacting with others. Three approaches highlight the role of positive emotions in interpersonal interactions:

- **Positivity resonance**
- **Capitalization**
- **Active constructive responding (ACR)**

Fredrickson's Concept of Positivity Resonance

In addition to her broaden-and-build theory, which focuses on our individual well-being, Fredrickson offers another impactful lens illuminating the important role of positive emotions: the concept of **positivity resonance**.[734] Positivity resonance represents the ability of two individuals to generate positive energy in one another and cause it to grow. It works through three intertwined actions:

- Bidirectional exchange of positive expression, such as warmth and openness
- Biobehavioral synchronous moments, that is, mirroring one another's behavior, such as smiles, body language, and other verbal and nonverbal expressions
- Mutual investment in one another's well-being[735]

Positivity resonance has two prerequisites:

- A sense of safety[736]
- A sensory and temporal connection between two human beings, such as through eye contact, touch, conversation, shared laughter, smiles[737]

Fredrickson delivers an encouraging message: "Any moment of positivity resonance that ripples through the brains and bodies of you and another can be health- and life-giving, regardless of whether you share history together."[738] She mentions how "micro-moments" of positivity resonance accumulate and can be transformational beyond just the in-the-moment good feeling.[739] She says that positivity resonance can help us perceive things more clearly, make sense of past life experiences, and activate our creativity when problem-solving.[740]

Let's pause to think about how we act when we are around our relationship partners, friends, classmates, work colleagues, clients, and strangers. Around others, are we acting in a way that will help positive emotions resonate? Are we choosing to surround ourselves with individuals who make us feel physically and emotionally safe so we can then be adventurous? Do we help make others feel that way?

To cultivate positivity resonance for ourselves and others, Fredrickson suggests a micro-moment practice. Can we choose *three brief moments* today or this week to connect with other people?[741] In each of the three micro-moments, we can consciously practice:

- Opening our minds, hearts, and souls to the experience
- Offering attention toward the other person
- Helping the other person feel physically and emotionally safe
- Forging eye contact
- Considering our body language
- Staying present
- Communicating, listening, and sharing thoughts
- Openly exchanging feelings[742]

"Capitalization" Is Contagious

Another concept that has the potential to launch ripple effects of positive emotion in interpersonal exchanges is a communication technique called **capitalization.**[743] Positive psychologists call the act of sharing good news with another person, and the resulting magnification of the effect of the original positive experience, capitalization.[744] In describing a positive event to someone else (e.g., a good grade, a successful oral argument, a win-win in a negotiation), our positive emotional state can extend beyond the initial occurrence itself.[745] This might seem obvious, but the science of how it works is fascinating. Psychologists have conducted studies of the effects of sharing narratives of positive experiences or events with others. Results of these studies revealed that when we "capitalize" and share positive news with other people, we can increase positive emotions, well-being, and self-esteem to a greater degree than if we just experienced the positive event itself but didn't tell anyone.[746]

The success of capitalization, however, depends on the reactions of our dialogue partners.[747]

The Art and Beauty of Active Constructive Responding

Researchers created a measure called Perceived Responses to Capitalization Attempts (PRCA) to describe four ways in which we (and our conversation partners) react to positive disclosures or shared news:[748]

Active constructive responding (ACR)	Expressing eagerness, enthusiasm, or delight about a disclosed event, and actively following up with positive probing questions or reflections	Example: "That is SO amazing! I'm so excited for you. Tell me more. What's your first step?"
Passive constructive responding	Reacting supportively but in a quiet, subdued, understated, and succinct manner, halting engagement	Example: "Nice." *Then stares at iPhone.*
Active destructive responding	Accentuating negative implications of the disclosed event; demeaning the event	Example: "Yikes. That sounds like a ton of work. Are you sure you're up for that?"
Passive destructive responding	Ignoring the disclosure altogether; changing the subject	Example: "Ugh, I had the most stressful day."

Scientific studies indicate that ACR links to increased positive mood and emotions.[749] Conversation partners who practice ACR augment levels of trust, intimacy, and satisfaction within the relationship.[750]

Of course, some disclosures "require criticism or caution."[751] But learning about, practicing, and asking for ACR in our personal and professional relationships can help us enhance positive emotions and well-being for ourselves and others. As Peterson wrote, "a steady stream of 'constructive' criticism or tempered enthusiasm will take a toll."[752]

Our default communication style might depend on who we are speaking with at any given moment. For example, we might respond differently to our best friend's shared news of a positive event than a revelation from a family member, a work colleague, a romantic partner, or a stranger. It's important to consider relationship dynamics or circumstances that might initially obstruct good intentions to practice ACR. For instance:

- Natural emotions like insecurity, fear, or jealousy might nudge us to shut down or bristle at hearing someone else's good news, even from someone we love.
- We might have a pattern in a particular relationship of "playing devil's advocate" or pointing out potential risks or pitfalls.
- If the conversation partner has a history of reacting negatively to, or ignoring, our own capitalization attempts, we might unconsciously mirror that behavior in our interactions toward them.
- We might simply be having a stressful or exhausting day and feel too depleted to exert the energy necessary to amplify someone else's joy.

Nonetheless, like our appraisal abilities and our capacity for nurturing an optimistic explanatory style, we can hone our ACR skills. We can (gently) invite conversation partners to improve theirs as well. First, we can begin by listening to, and noticing, how friends, family members, classmates, romantic partners, work colleagues, and strangers respond to our efforts at capitalization. Do they:

- Uplift and amplify? (This is ACR.)
- Validate but extinguish further elaboration or expansion? (This is passive constructive responding.)
- Deflate by pointing out, or contriving, negative aspects of our news? (This is active destructive responding.)
- Deflect, reject, and disconnect? (This is passive destructive responding.)

Second, we can consider how we feel when we experience each response style, and realize that we may be making others feel that way if we deploy styles other than ACR. Third, we can notice how *we* respond to capitalization efforts by our friends, family members, classmates, romantic partners, work colleagues, and strangers. In doing so, we can discern our own response patterns. Fourth, we can transfer some of our learnings about optimism and character strengths to conversations. When listening to others share news, we can:[753]

- Actively focus on the positive in the disclosure.
- Celebrate how the disclosure showcases our dialogue partner's signature character strength(s), or use the conversation to spark a discussion about character strengths generally (for more on character strengths, see Chapter 3).
- Emphasize how the disclosure shows our dialogue partner's personal power and growth.
- Highlight the disclosure as an expansion of future possibility and potential.
- Use the disclosure to deepen our connection with the person.

Emotional Well-Being Dimension Exercise #3

Active Constructive Responding: *"That's awesome! Tell me more!"*

To hone our ACR skills, let's **first** begin to listen to, and notice, how our friends, family members, work colleagues, and strangers respond to our efforts at capitalization—sharing our good news with them. What emotions do we feel when others use different communication styles—**active constructive, passive constructive, active destructive, passive destructive**—in reacting to our capitalization efforts?

Start by recalling a piece of positive news you recently shared with each of these categories of communication partners below.

Communication Partner	Your Capitalization Disclosure	The Communication Partner's Response	Response Style	What Emotions Did You Feel in Receiving this Response?	How Does This Response Style Affect the Health of this Relationship?
Name of friend: ________					
Name of family member: ________					
Name of work colleague: ________					
A stranger					

Next, let's notice how *we* respond to capitalization efforts by our friends, family members, work colleagues, and strangers. In doing so, we can discern our own productive and unproductive response patterns. In the chart below, recall a recent example of capitalization—an effort to share a piece of positive news with you—by individuals from each of the identified relationship categories.

Communication Partner	The Communication Partner's Capitalization Attempt (i.e., piece of positive news)	Your Response Style
Name of friend: _______		
Name of family member: __________		
Name of work colleague: __________		
A stranger		

Could we adjust our response style to:

- Actively focus on the positive in the disclosure?
- Celebrate how the disclosure showcases a signature character strength, or use the conversation to spark a discussion about character strengths generally (for more on character strengths, see Chapter 3)?
- Emphasize how the disclosure evidences our dialogue partner's personal power and growth?
- Highlight the disclosure as an expansion of future possibility and potential?
- Use the disclosure to deepen our connection with the person?

Additionally, we can activate our character strengths to amplify positivity from another person's capitalization efforts. Recall your signature character strengths from your VIA Survey of Character Strengths (Chapter 3) and list them here: ______________

____

Which of your signature strengths might be most helpful in exercising **active constructive responding** to a positive disclosure by a friend, family member, work colleague, or stranger? ____

To awaken human emotion is the highest level of art.

Isadora Duncan

Chapter 7

Our Artistic/Creative Dimension

Every artist was first an amateur.

Ralph Waldo Emerson

Art is a line around your thoughts.

Gustav Klimt

In this chapter, we will learn about:

- Immersion
- Embeddedness
- Acquisition
- Socialization
- Reflection
- Expression
- Meaning-Making

You might be thinking, "I don't have an artistic bone in my body, and besides, what does art have to do with my role as a member of the legal profession? Who has time for creative pursuits?" Author Meera Lee Patel wrote a masterful book called *My Friend Fear: Finding Magic in the Unknown.* In her book, she says, "[W]e are all artists ourselves. Living is art. Taking chances is art. Being present for ourselves and others is art."[754]

Just as we can analogize ourselves to athletes and other performers, we can (and should) consider ourselves artists. Remember my story about Bono introducing U2's song *Iris* in the 2015 iNNOCENCE + eXPERIENCE tour by thanking his mother and whispering into the microphone, "She left me an *artist*"? I invite us to take a pause from the intellectual arena of lawyering, and regard *ourselves* as artists. Let's cultivate our creative dimension to activate different functions of our brains, minds, and bodies. As part of our prehabilitation training, we can strengthen our (artistic) muscles *around* vulnerable (occupational/intellectual) joints that may later encounter pain points. Dabbling in painting, molding clay, sketching, sculpting, playing instruments, writing song lyrics, singing, taking photographs, landscaping, gardening, even constructing something physical—these activities might relax us, but also can help clear mental and emotional space for us to see legal problems more clearly. Additionally, we can carve out moments to immerse ourselves in art created by other people. In this dimension, we will explore how nurturing our inner artist can be therapeutic and calming, but also helpful in kickstarting our imagination and igniting our problem-solving skills.

Lawyering is a creative act. As thinkers, researchers, writers, collaborators, and solution-generators, we often need to be imaginative when the "right" answer is not readily available in the statutes, case law, regulations, policies, or contracts. While cultivating our physical well-being dimension in Chapter 5, it might have felt strange at first to regard ourselves as athletes or performers in the same ranks as NFL quarterback Patrick Mahomes or singer Billie Eilish. Similarly, here, we also might never have considered that we have anything in common with street artist Banksy, or photographers Anton Corbijn or Annie Leibovitz, or tattooers like Jessica Valentine. But we do.

I love hearing about athletes and performers who step into unfamiliar artistic arenas to activate different parts of their bodies and brains, to make them better at their day jobs. I mentioned in the Introduction to this book that NFL athletes Steve McLendon and Lynn Swann took ballet lessons to become better football players. Boxer Vasyl Lomachenko credits Ukrainian dance lessons for his fierce footwork. U2 bass guitarist Adam Clayton wanders the hallways of art galleries in cities where the band is playing, to calm his mind before shows. What if we, as law students and lawyers, hand our inner artist a paintbrush, a blob of clay, a set of fingerpaints, a disposable camera, and say, "Go experiment"? We just might unleash a wildly creative spirit within us, one that will help us solve stubborn legal problems. Also, apparently art-making is good for our health, and our work.

TAPPING INTO OUR INNER ARTIST TO ENHANCE OUR CREATIVE PROBLEM-SOLVING AND WELL-BEING

According to journalist Malaka Gharib, "making art is good for your mind and body."[755] Dr. Girija Kaimal, a professor at Drexel University and a leading researcher in art therapy, similarly reports that "[t]he act of creation can reduce stress and anxiety and improve your mood."[756] Further, "flexing our creative side can give us a stronger sense of agency—the ability to solve problems by imagining possible solutions."[757] Why? Creativity stirs *divergent* (rather than convergent) thinking, that is, the act of generating a bunch of alternative solutions to problems.[758] When we allow ourselves the gift of creative exploration, we get to focus on *quantity* and *range* of ideas, not perfection or idealization of *one correct path*. Creativity spurs us to conceptualize ideas differently and act in fresh and novel ways.[759] When we tap into our creative side, we activate a sense of freedom to tinker, take risks, make mistakes, and start again.

The exciting part is, we don't have to be "real" artists for this to happen. Merriam-Webster defines an artist as "a person who creates art (such as painting, sculpture, music, or writing) using conscious skill and creative imagination."[760] We just need to give ourselves permission to *consciously* play with new skills and unleash our imagination. Professor Kaimal states, "There are no differences in health outcomes between those who identify as experienced artists and those who don't."[761] It is the act of getting our hands dirty and making art "that induces those feelings of stress relief and positive energy—not what you make or how you make it."[762] Acts of creativity "boost mood and reduce anxiety."[763]

CREATIVITY AS PREHABILITATION

Creativity can (and should) play an important role in our prehabilitation training to be great performers. Phil Jackson injected creativity into training the Chicago Bulls, rejecting business-as-usual coaching and incorporating developmental activities that—on the surface—had little, if anything, to do with the sport of basketball. He explained, "On a deeper level, I believe that focusing on something other than the business at hand can be the most effective way to solve complex problems. When the mind is allowed to relax, inspiration often follows."[764] He "pushed the envelope" by having "experts come in and teach the players yoga, tai chi, and other mind-body techniques. [He] also invited guest speakers—including a nutritionist, an undercover detective, and a prison warden—to show them new ways of thinking about difficult problems."[765] Taking a page from Coach Jackson's playbook, let's explore new inner personas—in this case, through art—and observe if, and how, doing so invigorates our day jobs.

As law students and lawyers, we might still be thinking, *There is no room in my life for creativity or artistry. The law is rule-based. Right versus wrong. The answers to problems are right there in the statutes, cases, and contracts.* Not always. And writing powerfully about the law, crafting briefs and contracts, influencing others—clients, opposing counsel, juries, judges—*demands* creativity. Michael F. Melcher wrote a cool book called *The Creative Lawyer: A Practical Guide to*

Authentic Professional Satisfaction in which he identifies four aspects of being a creative lawyer:[766]

- Identifying and defining our interests, values, nature, and character
- Surveying whether and how our work meshes with our interests, values, nature, and character
- Crafting pathways to further integrate our work with our interests, values, nature, and character
- Identifying tools and resources to move us from *thinking* about our interests, values, nature, and character toward *infusing* them into our work

These tenets echo our Socrates-inspired theme of "know thyself." If we intentionally allocate some time in our schedules, even just 15 or 30 minutes, to periodically play around with some acrylic paints on a canvas; make a collage of ticket stubs and travel memorabilia (postcards, train receipts, restaurant matchbooks); experiment with yarn, chalk, a disposable camera; rearrange words we like into a poem or haiku—our brains and minds can't help but shift gears. Different sparks, jolts, and connections will ignite. If Phil Jackson can convince elite athletes like Michael Jordan and Scottie Pippen to sit down and listen to speakers like undercover detectives and prison wardens, to expand their problem-solving skills, certainly we can take a few moments to rest our intellectual muscles—and notice what interesting stuff blooms.

Over the years, I am grateful to have had several law students appear in my office doorway at the end of an academic year and offer me hand-made gifts that embody their artistic personas. Beautiful pieces of pottery—two cobalt-blue plates and a bowl in a shade of raspberry, a coffee tumbler painted with the word *writing* in different languages, a watercolor self-portrait. Each of these students took time out of their overpacked extracurricular and class schedules to tend to their art. Their introspective, creative dimension also showed in their legal writing—in the phrasing, analogies, imagery, and metaphors they carefully chose to illustrate complex legal concepts.

Sasha Phillips, a former associate at the law firm of Reed Smith (and who was a professional artist before shifting careers to law), highlights the role art and creative pursuits can, and should, play in a committed plan to cultivate our well-being. In describing an Arts for Wellness program—part of Reed Smith's Wellness Works initiative—she emphasized, "Art should be as much a part of anyone's wellness program as a proper diet and exercise."[767]

BE YOUR OWN MUSE

Sometimes when I am feeling particularly in need of a jolt of artistic rebellion, I remind myself of a quote often attributed (some say erroneously) to artist Frida Kahlo: "I am my own muse." I adjust it slightly to spur myself into creative action: *Be your own [insert F-bomb] muse.* I also like Twyla Tharp's emboldening statement, "Creativity is an act of *defiance.* You're challenging the status quo. You're questioning accepted truths and principles."[768]

Consider this an invitation to be your own muse, to invite your inner artist to come out and play, to experiment, to get messy. I've always liked the French words *dilettante* (one who dabbles in an art form purely for the sake of enjoyment) and *flâneur* (a person who wanders or strolls without restriction, exploring and observing, to better understand oneself). These might sound like derogatory or "lazy" terms but, to me, it feels exciting and liberating to engage in an artistic endeavor merely for amusement at first, then seeing what emerges, noticing what we discover about ourselves.

I'm a huge fan of author Steven Pressfield's books on the creative process: *The War of Art, Do the Work, Turning Pro,* and *The Artist's Journey.*[769] (I also love that his publishing logo is a boxing glove!) His books are not intimidating; they are accessible and relatable. Pressfield says that when we decide to be an artist (however we define that term), our life changes in purpose; it becomes about "finding [our] voice" and "becoming who [we] really [are]."[770] He acknowledges that, yes, making art (like being a law student and lawyer) can feel scary at times. We inevitably will encounter internal and external resistance. But Pressfield urges, "The artist, like the test pilot, learns to stay cool and keep flying the plane."[771]

Pressfield does us a huge favor and distinguishes the drudgery of making art *for other people,* which he calls "hierarchical," from the cherished gift of making art for ourselves, which he deems "territorial" in a good way.[772] When we worry about what other people think of our art, we hobble its ability to nurture our soul and our health. Pressfield says, "When the artist acts hierarchically, she short-circuits the Muse. She insults her and pisses her off."[773] Conversely, when we nurture our inner artist for the primary purpose of becoming a healthier, happier human, we get our "sustenance . . . from the act itself, not from the impression it makes on others."[774] (This reminds me of the "autotelic" nature of activities in which we find *flow.* Such endeavors serve a purpose in themselves; we don't need external reinforcement to reap rewards from engaging in them.[775])

Pressfield also differentiates between amateurs and pros, flipping the concepts in an inspiring way. Pressfield notes that amateur artists "focus exclusively on the product and the payoff."[776] Pros focus on the *process.* In Pressfield's potent words, "The amateur tweets. The pro works."[777] In this context, we are aspiring to be the best "pro" version of ourselves. I know that at my current glorious age, I am never going to be a "pro" boxer, or a genius artist like Picasso, or an uber-famous and cool author like Erica Jong or Julia Cameron. But I sure am going to be the best "pro" version of myself—as teacher, writer, public speaker, novice fighter, friend.

So, my fellow pros, let's get to work.

AN EMERGING FIELD CALLED THE "POSITIVE HUMANITIES"

There is an interesting emerging field of scientific study called the "positive humanities," a collaboration between positive psychology researchers and scholars in the humanities.[778] The humanities include creative domains such as music, art, writing, literature, and poetry (and also culture, religion, languages, philosophy, history, and law). Researchers in the positive humanities have begun identifying and measuring connections and correlations between engagement in creative pathways such as music, art, writing, and literature and enhanced well-being.[779] Studies are showing that spending time in activities that nurture our creativity can help us generate positive ideas, feelings, and behaviors, which in turn can facilitate flourishing.[780] It appears that creativity can fuel positive emotions, and reciprocally, positive emotions can ignite creativity.[781]

Let's explore the science of this concept a bit further.

Researchers have identified six mechanisms through which engagement with humanities like music, art, writing, and reading literature or poetry can change us: immersion, embeddedness, acquisition, socialization, reflectiveness, and expression.[782]

Immersion

When we immerse or engross in music, art, writing, or reading literature or poetry, we momentarily release our tight grip on the throttle of our lives. This shift in attention and temporary relinquishment of control rekindles our senses and emotions.[783] The novelty of hearing a new song, or stumbling upon a colorful street mural, or reading an amazing excerpt in a travel memoir disrupts the day-to-day mundanity of our lives; these moments can jolt us out of *habituation*, or our natural acclimatization to our surroundings.

Embeddedness and Acquisition

Embeddedness and acquisition are internal processes through which we adopt new perspectives, habits, and skills when experimenting with the arts.[784] As we pick up a guitar to learn a different chord, or grab a paintbrush to attempt a self-portrait, or grip a favorite pen to write a journal entry in loopy handwriting, we amp up "socio-cognitive processes," or the ways we influence and are influenced by our environment.[785] We start to recognize that we are getting better at performing particular tasks (strumming the guitar, mixing paint colors, capturing orange sunsets in photographs); we might even eventually develop a sense of mastery along the way.[786] Further, embedding in art, music, writing, and reading literature or poetry affords us opportunities to enrich our character strengths such as curiosity, creativity, love of learning, appreciation of beauty, zest, and more.

Socialization

Engaging with music, art, writing, and reading literature or poetry can foster our growth by deepening our understanding of our existing and desired roles and identities in our communities. This mechanism is called socialization. When we step into interactive activities such as music festivals, painting classes, museum tours, writing groups, or book clubs, we broaden our interpersonal networks and add layers to our personas.[787] Connecting with others, we better comprehend who we are, who we want to be, and how we want to fit into society and the world.[788]

Reflectiveness

Art, music, writing, and reading literature or poetry also invite self-expansion through reflectiveness; artistic experiences often nudge us to pause, take perspective, and think critically about our views and actions.[789] The process of contemplation during or after an encounter with art, music, writing, or reading can prompt us to challenge our existing thoughts, feelings, behaviors, and perspectives.[790] Through the act of reflection, we can notice and fortify good or constructive habits, values, and viewpoints.[791] We also can take note of, and be inspired to improve, maladaptive ones.[792]

After I listen to a new song, stare at a painting by Italian artist Morandi, read a cool travel essay, notice hip graffiti, or linger with an artsy photograph on Instagram, I often find myself reflecting on it through journaling (or strangely, while I am exercising) and get inspired to tap into my own creative spirit. Street art and graffiti prod me to broaden my thinking on what constitutes "art." The National Geographic television series *Genius: Picasso* challenged me to ponder how often we conflate extraordinary individuals' talents with their character. Can we separate art from the artist?

Expression

Further, the humanities invite us to eventually share our thoughts and emotions about art, music, writing, and literature with others through the act of expression.[793] We might find ourselves externalizing our ideas and feelings about what we saw, felt, touched, or experienced—through museum postcards, Instagram snapshots of our travels, sketches, blogs, a spoken word poem. The process of expression also can help us expand our self-awareness.[794] Putting our thoughts into words helps us comprehend.

MEASURABLE LINKS BETWEEN ENGAGEMENT WITH THE HUMANITIES AND HUMAN FLOURISHING

On the well-being front, researchers are identifying measurable links between engagement within the humanities and:

- Positive neurological, emotional, and physiological changes
- Enhanced psychological competencies
- Augmented general psychological and physical well-being
- Societal benefits like increased civic involvement and volunteering[795]

Studies indicate that encounters with art, music, and literature, for example, can incite real-time neurological, emotional, and physiological changes; researchers determine this by testing somatic arousal levels, the amounts of cortisol present in our saliva, and galvanic skin responses.[796] Engagement with the humanities is also linked to enhanced psychological competencies such as short- and long-term memory capacity, creative problem-solving, and reflectiveness.[797] Even desirable physical outcomes—longevity, better sleep, healthy diets, and heightened physical activity—may ensue![798] Further, researchers are investigating connections between our immersion in the humanities and "altruism and civic action."[799]

Let's delve deeper into how engagement with art, music, writing, and reading literature or poetry can affect us in positive ways.

Two Junes ago, I sat at a bistro table on the cobblestones of Via dei Coronari, a shopping street in Rome, sipping a glass of Chianti, savoring a bite of avocado dipped in olive oil so tangy it tickled my throat. Businesswomen strutted by on stilettos, their voices a stream of animated Italian. Tourists meandered past, licking gelato dripping from cones. I stared across the cobblestones at a wall holding my favorite piece of graffiti in the world: thick blue lines outlining a curvaceous female reclining on a divan, a she-wolf (Rome's symbol) standing guard at her elbow, an ellipsis and the capital letters "ART" emerging from the woman's mouth. Below the letters, someone else had scribbled, "or vandalism?" No piece of art in any fancy museum has ever lit my soul on fire as much as this graffiti. Why? The authors of the book *Art as Therapy*, Alain de Botton and John Armstrong, write that art is so formidable because it can seem to reach out, grab us by both shoulders, and say "this is [you]."[800] This graffiti does that for me. It jars my system, stalls my racing brain, and forces me to sit there and appreciate my nomad female soul. It also fires up my character strengths of zest, curiosity, creativity, love of learning, and appreciation of beauty.

Is there a piece of art that has gripped you this way?

HOW ENGAGEMENT WITH ART CAN ENHANCE OUR WELL-BEING

de Botton and Armstrong suggest that art can augment our well-being by optimizing our relationship with seven aspects of the human experience:

- Memory
- Hope
- Sorrow
- Balance
- Self-identity
- Appreciation
- Growth[801]

Let's start with *memory*. Constantly bombarded with new information and data each day, we naturally can forget details of cherished moments: the smell of grass after rain, a romantic partner's wistful look, the taste of mascarpone cream in a bite of tiramisu, the feel of cool sheets on a hot summer night. Art can *revive* memories.[802] An unusual shade of green in a painting, for example, might ignite a memory of the color of the carpet in a hotel we stayed in on a fun trip to a city we forgot we visited.

Of course, at times, life's frustrations, disappointments, and misunderstandings can eclipse our hope. Enveloped in temporary clouds of gloom, we can lose sight of the reality that life has normal ups and downs, ebbs and flows. Art's colors and hues can infuse fresh brightness and light into our lives, nudging us to place inevitable rejections and defeats in healthy perspective, resuscitating *hope.*[803]

Art also recognizes *sorrow* as a necessary component of an enriched and *balanced* life, helping us reframe struggles as stepping-stones to eventual joys.[804] For example, feeling adrift amid the trauma of my divorce and 9/11 aftermath, I visited a museum, seeking a quiet escape from the raucous opera in my head. There, I encountered a glass case holding a paint palette and spectacles once owned by Claude Monet. Staring at these vintage artistic artifacts, I suddenly felt a visceral urge to create. I ran home, grabbed my neglected paint box out of a closet, squeezed magenta acrylic paint onto a wooden cutting board, thrust my hands into it, and smeared pink swirls onto a canvas. Every handprint became a defiant assertion to the world: *I matter.* Suddenly, I remembered a quote from the Roman poet Ovid that inspired the title of a novel I read by Peter Cameron: *Perfer et obdura, dolor hic tibi proderit olim.*[805] It means: *Be patient and tough; someday this pain will be useful to you.* I painted those words in Latin on my magenta canvas in glistening white letters. Seeing art, and creating it, helped me tap into resources of resilience I didn't realize I had accrued.[806] *Everything is going to be okay.*

Further, to meet societal expectations, we often compartmentalize dimensions of our lives; some of us tend to stow away aspects of our persona that do not fit neatly into work, family, or relationship boxes. To blend, we don mask after mask, suppressing our true interests, values, nature, and character. Before long, we can become mysteries to ourselves and others. Art helps us rebalance and reconnect with neglected, treasured layers of our *self-identity,* steering us toward self-integration and wholeness.[807] When I traveled to Venice with one of my friends, she arranged for us to paint carnival masks at an art studio; as I decorated my mask with pink, black, and white swirls and dots, I thought about which masks of my persona I finally could discard. Art invites rediscovery of our *self.*[808] Art whispers—sometimes even shouts—Socrates's maxim, "Know thyself." As de Botton and Armstrong urge, art prompts us to sift and discern until we see something and exclaim, "This is me!"[809] I love when I *see* myself in an alleyway mural of a rebellious blonde in a leather jacket adorned with pink roses in Bondi Beach, Australia, or in graffiti of a ponytailed girl brandishing boxing gloves on a garage door in Puerto Rico.

Additionally, fears we harbor—of failure, mistake-making, rejection, loss—can manifest in resistance, disconnection, and inauthenticity. On the flip side though, addiction to safety can breed boredom. We habituate to familiar surroundings, desensitizing to both the beauty and the trash around us. When I lived in Laguna Beach for five years, picturesque Pacific views and cascading bougainvillea morphed into mundane wallpaper that I didn't even notice after a while. Now in New York City, I step over garbage like it is part of the pavement. Art snaps us back to attention, re-igniting *appreciation* of our habitats.[810]

Finally, art invites us to linger with taboo and strangeness.[811] It can help us learn how to feel again, trust that we can handle discomfort, *grow*, and safely expand our horizons.

What type of art prompts you to say, "This is me!"?

HOW ENGAGEMENT WITH MUSIC CAN ENHANCE OUR WELL-BEING

Like art, researchers indicate that engagement with music—listening to songs or performances, playing instruments, singing, composing—can augment our well-being. Scientists have studied how music can enhance our mood, emotions, and energy levels, and reduce tension.[812] Music can help us adopt helpful well-being strategies of "distraction, relaxation, and active coping."[813] Studies reveal that "music is a successful tool for modulating overwhelming negative emotion, fostering hope and resilience, and circumventing self-destructive impulses."[814] Further, interaction with music has been linked to increases in empathy.[815]

Interestingly, researchers can measure music's effect on our emotions through an instrument called the Music in Mood Regulation scale (MMR).[816] The MMR looks at seven factors to assess how music functions as a mood regulator:

- Entertainment—fostering positive atmospheres and feelings
- Revival—reinvigorating us with new energy; refreshing and relaxing us
- Strong sensation—igniting intense emotions
- Diversion—distracting us from undesirable thoughts or feelings
- Discharge—helping us release emotions like sadness, grief, anger
- Mental work—making space for contemplating and reappraising emotions
- Solace—aiding us in accepting and understanding emotions[817]

Notably, researchers recently used this assessment scale in a study analyzing the effect of music as a mood regulator in response to lockdown during the pandemic in the United Kingdom.[818]

Music gives us the opportunity to experiment with six mechanisms of the humanities we learned earlier: immersion, embeddedness, acquisition, socialization, reflectiveness, and expression. When we immerse in music by writing songs, singing, memorizing lyrics, playing an instrument, or attending concerts, for example, we momentarily step away from the cacophony of our daily lives. We can gain a sense of mastery and confidence as we develop new skills. Sharing music with others, we can feel part of something bigger than ourselves. We can reflect on what music means to us and then express how it makes us feel.

HOW ENGAGEMENT WITH WRITING CAN ENHANCE OUR WELL-BEING

Okay, now let's talk about one of my favorite subjects—besides U2, boxing, travel, and introversion, of course—the impactful and healing power of writing. In my positive psychology studies, I was thrilled to learn about measurable links between writing and well-being.

To me, writing is a perfect embodiment of personal *agency*, which means acting out of our own volition and exercising free choice. The conscious act of picking up a pen and transmitting an idea, a phrase, or a memory from our brain to our hand, ink imprinting the paper like a tattoo, is so potent. When we write, we bring the invisible into view. Our writing does not need to reach the heights of published literature or renowned poetry or award-winning journalism to influence our life or the lives of others. A simple thank you note, a love letter, a post card, a recollection scribbled in a spiral-bound journal, a text message—they all matter. The most basic configurations of nouns, verbs, adjectives, and adverbs can connect us to ourselves and others.

Writing invites us to make ourselves and others seen. Writing is an act of bravery, an exposition of our raw self on the page. It can help transform chaos into meaning. As we convert thoughts, emotions, and behaviors into letters, punctuation, and symbols, writing amplifies our authentic voices. Writing yields truths. It bares the beauty within us. Writing can be a formidable tool for personal transformation—starting with its utility in meaning-making.

Writing Is a Tool for Meaning-Making

The M in Seligman's PERMA well-being construct stands for *meaning*—feeling like we are part of something larger than ourselves.[819] **Meaning-making** is a method of making sense of life's ups-and-downs and ambiguities through exercising curiosity, creativity, imagination, and analysis.[820] Writing can help us explore four pillars of meaning identified by author Emily Esfahani Smith:[821]

- **Belonging:** feeling connected to others as we share stories
- **Purpose:** identifying our contribution(s) to the world
- **Storytelling:** placing past experiences in context as we craft a coherent narrative about our life
- **Transcendence:** stepping into a world beyond ourselves

Writing can be a vibrant source of meaning-making because it gives us a conduit to choose language and symbols that help us connect the dots of our life experiences.[822]

According to Dr. James W. Pennebaker and Dr. Joshua M. Smyth, who wrote a book called *Opening Up by Writing it Down: How Expressive Writing Improves Health and Eases Emotional Pain,* "putting our deeply emotional experiences into language and words facilitates our brain's capacity to help us manage our emotional states."[823] Writing about scenes and snippets of our lives helps us integrate isolated events into a broader structure, illuminating who we are and who we want to be.[824] Writing can spotlight patterns woven through relationships and life events that we hadn't previously recognized. As Pennebaker and Smyth point out:

> *When people write about important events, they begin to organize and understand them. Writing about the thoughts and feelings connected with unexpected experiences forces us to bring together their many facets. Once we can distill complex experiences into more understandable packages, we can begin to move beyond them.*[825]

Battered by relentless waves of grief, guilt, and shame during my divorce trauma and 9/11 distress, I discovered Julia Cameron's Morning Pages practice.[826] She suggests three pages of long-hand journal-writing every morning: no editing, no re-reading, no judgment, no stopping-and-starting. Just uninterrupted pen strokes on paper for 15 to 20 minutes. Even if we feel like we have nothing to say, we can simply write, "I have nothing to say, I have nothing to say . . ." until, boom, something spills onto the page. For 20 years, almost without skipping a day, I have awakened, brewed a pot of coffee, lit a candle, grabbed a funky-looking journal and a blue-ink pen, and watched as fear, frustration, loneliness, shame, guilt, and worry transformed into hopes, ideas, dreams, renewal, rebelliousness, and motivation on the page. Cameron's powerful and healing writing practice has served as a constant confidante and unconditional friend—the kind who will gently call me out on my nonsense while at the same time urging, *Keep going! This rocks! OMG, you're a goddess warrior queen!* Morning Pages have revealed important themes in my relationships. They have supercharged my creativity, inspiring my various book projects. Wherever I am on my day-to-day emotion continuum from adrift to ecstatic, I start each day with this ritual. It provides a sense of security and safety. It helps me extract meaning from murk.

Research Studies Support Writing as an Amplifier of Well-Being

As a legal writing professor, I've heard a bounty of excuses about why people resist the practice of writing: *I'm not good at it. It's boring. I struggle with English grammar. I feel stifled by structure.* If we can find a way to gently set aside perceived obstacles to this simple yet powerful action, anyone can access the basic instrument of writing as part of our conscious endeavor to augment our well-being.

In fact, Pennebaker and Smyth refer to writing as "preventative maintenance."[827] They indicate:

> *The value of writing or talking about our thoughts and feelings lies in reducing the work of inhibition and in organizing our complicated and messy mental and emotional lives. Writing helps us to keep our psychological compass oriented. Writing can be an inexpensive, simple, albeit sometimes painful way to help maintain our health.*[828]

Researchers (such as Pennebaker and Smyth) indicate that writing about impactful life events—a form called disclosive writing—can positively affect one's health and well-being in the long term.[829] Originally, scientific studies about the power of writing focused on disclosure and processing of *traumatic* life experiences.[830] An initial expressive writing intervention created by Pennebaker, a social psychologist, prompted individuals to write about personal traumatic experiences for approximately 15 minutes for three to five consecutive days.[831] Since then, however, studies have explored numerous health benefits associated with writing about positive topics.[832] Researchers suggest that the act of expressive or disclosive writing has healing properties; crafting a coherent personal narrative helps us make sense out of life.[833]

A writing practice does not have to be complicated or high-level to affect our well-being. For example, studies of undergraduates who wrote about intensely positive emotional experiences for a mere 20 minutes a day for three days reported augmented positive mood and *buffering* effects—a building of inner resources to reduce the impact of future life stressors.[834] Another study showed connections between writing three letters of gratitude over a period of eight weeks and increases in happiness and gratitude.[835] Other studies yielded links between writing in gratitude journals once a week over a 10-week period and heightened well-being in the form of greater positive emotions.[836] Participants in a different study who wrote narrative descriptions of their best possible future selves—in 20-minute writing sessions for four consecutive days—reported a significant increase in positive mood.[837] Writing about positive topics can generate positive emotions that can amplify our attention and perspective.[838]

When friends or students confide they are struggling mentally or emotionally, I try to reiterate (in a non-pushy way) how Cameron's Morning Pages writing practice helps me garner a sense of control and empowerment. I feel better when I start my day that way; I feel all over the place when I don't. Nonetheless, I'm often met with more resistance: *I don't like my handwriting. Journaling seems cheesy. I'll feel like I have to edit every sentence. What if someone reads it?* As Cameron urges, the act of writing Morning Pages is designed to get mental and emotional debris out of our heads; it's actually best if we don't re-read them, edit them, or hem and haw over words. The point is to just keep the pen moving across the page. Be sloppy, messy, even incoherent. Sometimes I write my Morning Pages *diagonally* across each journal page; my handwriting changes and evolves; I feel no compulsion to care about how it sounds; if I make a mistake or a spelling error, I just write a new word right next to the "wrong" word. This ejection of language out of my brain and onto paper is incredibly liberating and freeing. Also, there is minimal chance of anyone reading these entries; my best friend Clay knows that if anything ever happens to me, his number one priority is to break into my apartment and burn all my journals—ha! If you need to buy a locked vault in which to protect your Morning Pages journal from potentially prying eyes, do it.

Anyone who can hold a pen or press fingertips to laptop keys can write. If we give ourselves permission to relinquish judgment and self-doubt, we can let the words on the page reveal themselves, stare back at us, and murmur, *I see you. I hear you. Please, go on. I want to know more. Take all the time you need.* Writing is our personal embodiment of active constructive responding (the communication style we learned in Chapter 6). *Keep going. Tell me more.*

Like fingerprints or footprints, writing helps us leave a trace in the world. We are not invisible. We are here.

HOW ENGAGEMENT WITH THE WRITING OF OTHERS CAN ENHANCE OUR WELL-BEING

Separate from our own writing, reading the written work of *others*—literature, memoirs, poetry—also can help us situate our own ups and downs within a lifelong trajectory. Literature and personal narratives offer new prisms through which to view the world and our life experiences.[839]

Narrative transportation theory is the study of the "phenomenological" experience of immersion in a world of shared stories.[840] (*Phenomenological* means the actual or perceived lived experience of individuals, rather than a theoretical or abstract interpretation of human experience.) Interestingly, researchers have developed an instrument called the Transportation Scale to measure changes in our emotions, attention, awareness, and capacity for mental imagery when we engross in other people's stories.[841] Restorative narratives in particular, that is, personal accounts of recovery from trauma or adversity, can help us translate life's challenges into emblems of hope.[842] The vicarious experience of immersing in another writer's story invites us to experiment with new personas and envision positive future identities.[843]

As an avid reader in my twenties, I felt transported by John Grisham's crime novels and Clive Cussler's adventure stories. But navigating my relationship troubles, I somehow lost all thirst for fiction. Instead, I craved the comfort and reassurance I found in restorative narratives about other people's recovery from trauma. Now, two decades later, my bookshelves bend under the weight of beautiful memoirs about buoyant growth after loss or heartbreak and true stories of personal redemption. I also fully immerse in nonfiction travel memoirs, connecting with fellow solo voyagers. I feel a bond with these writers as they bare their souls so vulnerably. *Keep going*, they press.

As we step into cultivating our artistic and creative dimension, let's craft opportunities to experiment with and immerse in art, music, writing, and reading. What piques your interest first?

> *I am my own experiment. I am my own work of art.*
>
> Madonna

Creative Well-Being Dimension Exercise #1

Cultivating Character Strengths through Positive Art and Writing

In this positive art and writing exercise, let's focus on exploring our character strengths. We've talked about two tools suggested by Julia Cameron in her book, *The Artist's Way*:[844]

- **Morning Pages:** three pages of longhand writing each morning, to shift memories, ideas, hopes, and sorrows *outward*
- **Artist Dates:** solo weekly excursions with our inner artist, receiving insights and inspirations from the universe *inward*

If you haven't already, consider taking the VIA assessment surveying twenty-four character strengths, found at www.VIAcharacter.org.[845] In doing so, you'll discover your top 5 "signature strengths." (You can find more information about the VIA assessment in Chapter 3. Also, a book by Ryan Niemiec and Robert E. McGrath called *The Power of Character Strengths: Appreciate and Ignite Your Positive Personality*, describes each of the twenty-four strengths and offers reflection exercises and activities to nurture each one.)

Next, consider choosing one of your signature strengths and letting it launch your Morning Pages each day for a week. Each morning, before you start your Morning Pages, take a moment to think about why that particular signature strength excites, energizes, or comes easily for you. You might ponder how you recently used the signature strength in your relationships or work. You might contemplate how the signature character strength bolsters your intellectual, emotional, spiritual, physical, or social fitness to practice law, or aspects of your personal life. You might muse about how the signature strength helps illuminate your interests, values, goals, and true nature.

As you do your Morning Pages, notice any themes, patterns, surprises, or interesting threads that pop up. You could consider committing to this exercise for five weeks (exploring one of your Top 5 signature strengths per week through Morning Pages).

Next, once a week, take yourself on a live or virtual Cameron-inspired Artist Date. Look for a piece of art—this could be anything from street art to fine art in a museum—that inspires you or ignites your creative spirit. OR, create your own piece of art through drawing, sketching, painting, playing with clay, knitting, taking photographs. Sit with the piece of art for a bit, and reflect on how the work's themes, images, textures, and colors energize one or more of your signature character strengths. Notice if you feel any creativity fireworks. What emotions do you feel? Does the piece of art help illuminate your interests, values, goals, or true nature?

If you need an idea to get your pen moving across the page of the next day's Morning Pages, consider reflecting on your Artist Date.

Creative Well-Being Dimension Exercise #2

A Positive Music Exercise

One idea for using music to cultivate our creative dimension is a mash-up between Fredrickson's Positivity Portfolio[846] activity (described in Chapter 6) and a "Serotonin Playlist" idea inspired by my friend Kelly.

In this exercise, let's first choose a positive emotion (the P in PERMA) from the list in Fredrickson's book: joy, gratitude, serenity, interest, hope, pride, amusement, inspiration, love, or awe.[847] Next, let's ask ourselves: What pieces of music spark this emotional state in us? Engaging *awe*, for instance, what songs or tracks make our skin tingle, jar our senses, or invoke excitement along with perhaps a few backflips in our stomach?

Next, like our Positivity Portfolio activity, let's create a "Serotonin Playlist." My friend Kelly originally created a playlist of songs to help quell anxiety that sometimes would pop up in the mornings. Now, she plays some or all of the songs in the mornings "regardless of anxiety status." She constantly adds to the playlist. Let's curate a playlist based on our chosen positive emotion. If we are feeling ambitious, we could create different playlists for several different positive emotional states. Like our Positivity Portfolio, let's experiment with listening to the playlist every day for a week, perhaps in the mornings as we are getting ready for our day.

Activating the reflection/expression mechanisms of the humanities we learned earlier, can we extract a positive or empowering lyric from one of the songs to carry with us through our day? (My U2 girlfriends and I found a leather-goods store in Dublin called ThunderSolas where we like to have bracelets made with short lines of lyrics translated into Gaelic. One time, we were trying to convert the word "surrender" from U2's song *Bad* into Gaelic, but the direct translation was *Give up*. Not exactly the zen message we were going for!)

A NOTE ON BEGINNING TO GIVE OURSELVES *REGARD* AS ARTISTS

If you'd like to dig a little deeper into giving yourself *regard* as an artist, and perhaps developing a creative practice around writing, music, or art as you nurture your creative dimension, here are some tips that have helped me.

Tip #1: Experiment with Self-Identifying as an Artist, or a Writer, or a Musician

Say *I'm an artist,* or *I'm a writer,* or *I'm a musician* out loud to strangers who ask you what you do. (A few years ago, when prompted to list my profession on various forms, I stopped defaulting to labels like "attorney" or "law professor" and started inserting "writer." In many circumstances, it's perfectly fine for you to say, "I'm a law student AND I'm an artist" or "I'm a lawyer AND I'm an artist.")

Tip #2: Create a Protected Artist Space

I've always romanticized cool, bohemian writers sitting in Parisian cafés, sipping coffee, smoking Gauloises cigarettes, and penning profound literature. However, I can't write in public spaces. Loud conversations, dogs barking, any genre of music, and people who don't mute their phone alert chimes rile my inner writer into an enraged misanthrope. (Also, obviously smoking = bad!) To write, I need a quiet space with a positive, artsy vibe and zero human intrusions. A designated artist space can be small. We only need room for our bodies, our tools, and a few talismans to remind us we are *artists.* I like curating a writing space with a candle, a journal, and a few travel treasures: sea glass I collected in Sicily, a postcard from a Picasso museum in Barcelona, a rock from a volcanic black-sand beach in the Canary Islands. Create your personalized artist space vibe. If you share living accommodations with other humans, gently let them know that this space needs to be as protected as an environmental habitat, a UNESCO historical site, or Fort Knox. Because majorly important things are going to happen here.

Tip #3: Nurture Seeds of Ideas

Tom Sturges wrote a book called *Every Idea Is a Good Idea: Be Creative Anytime, Anywhere.*[848] In the idea germination phase of our artistic process, *there are no bad ideas.* Write that down on a colorful Post-it® Note and stick it in a prominent place in your artist space. There. Are. No. Bad. Ideas.

Speaking of Post-it Notes, when a nugget of a new idea pops into my head and I feel a little jolt of, *Oh, THAT would be kinda cool to write about,* I jot the idea on a large (6- by 8-inch) orange or pink Post-it and stick it on a window in my Manhattan apartment. In the mornings, after I've finished writing my Morning Pages,[849] I sip coffee and stare at the lone Post-it. The singular idea usually percolates and transmutes from there. One idea captured on a colorful Post-it leads to another Post-it and yet another. I now know and trust that when I have ten to twelve major Post-it ideas dotting my Manhattan window (and smaller ones capturing sub-ideas beneath the major ones), I'm looking at the arc of a new book's Table of Contents. This process works.

Tip #4: Oust the Critics

Our artist space needs to be a no-critics zone. Right before the pandemic, during my tenure application process, I self-imposed a rule: *Under no circumstances are you allowed to read the scholarship reviews in your tenure packet.* ("Scholarship reviews" are memos that law professors around the country write in which they evaluate the published written work of junior faculty applying for promotion.)

And then what did I go do?

I slumped into a shame spiral when I read that one law professor had referred to a component of my written work as "pablum." Honestly, I had to Google the word to make sure I fully grasped the insult. (Technically, "pablum" is a processed cereal for infants.) Ouch. Over the past decade, I've also received less-than-pleasant typewritten letters from readers of some of my *ABA Journal* articles, critiquing my ideas, grammar choices, and so on. Some also like to Tweet (without seeming to have fully read the article they're bashing.) Worrying about criticism is natural, but to get actual writing work done, I like to invoke novelist Paulo Coelho's ethos: "Haters are confused admirers."[850] I also like to tell myself, *If you reach literally one person with this piece of writing, you've done your job.* Our artist space is a no-critics zone.

Tip #5: Be You

Don't worry about what everyone else is doing, or working on, or creating. Start with what you know. Start with what you enjoy. Write, sing about, paint, shape, or build what excites you, not what you think will impress people or sell. Who cares if someone has already written on a similar topic or has created a comparable sound or look? Your art will be different because it is infused with your voice and perspective.

Tip #6: Set Up a Realistic System for Doing the Work

Ritual and routine, for me at least, are the key to *regarding* myself as an artist. I've mentioned that choreographer Twyla Tharp emphasizes the importance of ritual for setting aside hesitation or trepidation about starting a new project. She says that establishing a creative habit reminds us, "I've done it before. It was good. I'll do it again."[851] I also love author Steven Pressfield's advice from his motivating book on the creative process, *Do the Work*: "Get the first version of your project done from A to Z as fast as you can. Don't stop. Don't look down. Don't think."[852]

I can't write for more than two hours or I get a migraine. So, when I'm working on my art and launching a new writing project, I commit to a routine of waking up, brewing a pot of coffee, doing my Morning Pages, and then writing for two straight hours. At the end of the two hours, I close the laptop and go about my day. I do my two hours every single day, including weekends, for as many days in a row as it takes to get the first (horrifyingly bad) draft done. And then I start from the beginning again and set a daily page quota for editing. And then I start from the beginning yet again and set another daily page quota for editing.

Every artist is different, obviously. You might find you do your best work late at night or at midday, instead of mornings like me. You might be more motivated by word counts or page tallies (or some other quantifiable goal for your art) than time blocks. The important thing is to discern the right time of day and establish a realistic daily practice that works best for you. And when you are just beginning to regard yourself as an artist, your daily practice can be with the mindset of a *dilettante* (one who dabbles in an art form purely for the sake of enjoyment) or *flâneur* (a person who wanders or strolls without restriction, exploring and observing, to better understand the self).

Establish your system, set reasonable and realistic boundaries against intrusions (family, email, social media). Give yourself the gift of routine and watch your art emerge.

Tip #7: Reward Yourself for Sticking to Your System

Let's face it: creating art can be mentally, emotionally, and physically exhausting. When I emerge from a two-hour writing groove, I look like I've just hiked Mount Etna. My hair looks like I stuck my finger in a light socket; my eyes are wild; I'm starving. I also often realize that I've just experienced Csikszentmihalyi's *flow*.[853] Each time we follow through with our routine, I believe we deserve a reward. Julia Cameron's Artist Dates are marvelous rewards. Establish your own creativity reward system. What post-art-creation activity sounds fun to you? What types of Artist Dates would replenish your creative soul: Making a collage? Baking? A virtual gallery visit? A walk in a botanical garden? Emerge from your artist groove and take your inner artist on a well-deserved date.

Tip #8: Trust Your System, *Hear* and Absorb Positivity, and Lift One Another Up

Creating art can be simultaneously exhilarating and terrifying. One of U2's lyrics describes how I feel when I pour my soul onto the page: *Where poets speak their heart then bleed for it.* We are in a tough profession chock full of (often gratuitous) critique and judgment. But cultivating our creative dimension can help us notice messages within us that we feel are important to share. Here's the best advice I can give on how to give yourself artistic *regard*:

- Establish your individualized art-creation system, and then trust your system.
- Forget trying to please everyone; it's impossible. When I stress out about so-and-so smart person thinking my writing is too touchy-feely or not

intellectual enough, I remind myself: *They are not your audience!* Think about who you might want to eventually reach through your art; your audience may just be you, and that's great! I know my audience consists of anxious and fearful law students and lawyers (and other members of the profession), so I write for them (for you!) and myself.

- When you receive positive feedback from someone, immediately stop everything else you are doing and listen to or read that priceless gem again. Like, really hear it and let it sink in. Keep a positivity folder. Respond to every single piece of written communication from someone telling you that your work spoke to them. Those moments and connections are impactful.
- Let's lift each other up. Let's help each other create our art.

If you need a nudge to set up your protected artist's space or establish a workable routine or brainstorm Artist Dates, I've got your back. I can't wait to see what you create.

HELPFUL BOOKS TO SPARK A CREATIVE PROCESS

These are my favorite go-to books to give ourselves *regard* as artists:

- Julia Cameron, *The Artist's Way: A Spiritual Path to Higher Creativity* (New York: Jeremy P. Tarcher/Putnam, 2002).
- Steven Pressfield, *Do the Work* (New York: The Domino Project, 2011).
- Steven Pressfield, *The Artist's Journey* (Egremont: Black Irish Entertainment LLC, 2018).
- Steven Pressfield, *The War of Art* (New York: Black Irish Entertainment LLC, 2002).
- Steven Pressfield, *Turning Pro* (New York: Black Irish Entertainment LLC, 2012).
- Tom Sturges, *Every Idea Is a Good Idea: Be Creative Anytime, Anywhere* (New York: Jeremy P. Tarcher/Penguin, 2014).
- Twyla Tharp, *The Creative Habit: Learn It and Use It for Life* (New York: Simon & Schuster, 2006).

THERAPEUTIC RESOURCES INVOLVING THE ARTS

Sasha Phillips (a lawyer at the law firm, Meyer, Unkovic & Scott, LLP) and other attorneys have highlighted art therapy—a collaboration between the disciplines of art and psychology—as an impactful option for members of the legal profession grappling with stress and anxiety.[854] Art therapy is an accredited field grounded in the understanding that creative expression can enhance well-being and nurture healing.[855]

The term "art therapy" is originally attributed to Adrian Hill, an artist who painted while convalescing from tuberculosis in the mid-1900s.[856] Margaret Naumberg and Edith Kramer pioneered the field of art therapy in the United States. Art therapists emphasize the healing properties of the creative *process* rather than the quality of the artwork produced. One of my fellow graduates of the Master of Applied Positive Psychology program at the University of Pennsylvania, Sophia Heiser, generously compiled these links to find credentialed art therapists:

- **The Art Therapy Credentials Board**: www.atcb.org/find-a-credentialed-art-therapist/
- **The Art Therapy Alliance** (with international resources): www.arttherapyalliance.org/GlobalArtTherapyResources.html
- **Expressive arts therapists** (therapy incorporating elements of art, music, poetry, dance/movement, and drama): www.psychologytoday.com/us/therapists/expressive-arts/
- **Drama therapists** (in North America): www.nadta.org/membership/member-search.html
- **Drama therapists** (outside North America): www.worldallianceofdramatherapy.com/collaborating-members
- **Music therapists:** https://my.cbmt.org/cbmtssa/f?p=CRTSSA:17800:6639804424619:::17800::
- **Dance/movement therapists:** https://www.adta.org/find-a-dancemovement-therapist
- **Biblio/poetry therapists:** https://ifbpt.org/find-a-professional/find-a-credentialed-professional/

Further, Leah Guzman, a board-certified art therapist, wrote a book called *Essential Art Therapy Exercises,* with prompts and exercises for self-expression.

Sophia Heiser also generously compiled a helpful list of information about the intersection of positive psychology and art therapy:

- Rebecca Ann Wilkinson and Gioia Chilton are the visionaries behind positive psychology-based art therapy. Their website, www.creativewellbeingworkshops.com, offers workshops, trainings, worksheets, and blogs.
- This podcast—www.safeharbourtherapy.com/positive-psychology-and-art-therapy-with-jess-winnicki/—discusses positive art therapy and positive interventions.
- The Health Arts Research Centre offers art-based worksheets and positive interventions: www.healtharts.ca/category/recent-work/art-worksheets/.
- The Foundation for Arts & Healing offers exercises for individuals: www.artandhealing.org/creative-relief/.

> *Creativity is like crabgrass—it springs back with the simplest bit of care.*
>
> Julia Cameron

Chapter 8

Our Social Dimension

Invisible threads are the strongest ties.

Friedrich Nietzsche

In this chapter, we will learn about:

- **Positivity resonance**
- **Capitalization**
- **Active constructive responding (ACR)**
- **Constructivist listening**
- **Perspective-giving and perspective-taking**
- **The hive switch**
- **Defusing bullies**

As an introvert currently nestled on my couch in my apartment, happily clacking away on my laptop, sipping coffee and writing solo, I admit I am feeling *resistance* to the alert on my iPhone reminding me to log into a Zoom meeting at noon, and another at 1:30, and another at 4:00 p.m. I am loving the fact that after today's virtual appointments, I have zero social engagements for the next two glorious days. I can work at my own pace, go for runs or walks in my neighborhood, meet my (introverted) boxing trainer for a one-on-one outdoor session, read positive psychology books in the afternoons, grade some papers, and enjoy my quiet and productive zone of solitude. But, I also know it's important for me to cultivate my social life and social well-being dimension.

I love texting my friends. I love sending "old school" letters and cards and pressing cool U.S. Post Office stamps onto the envelope corners. (I recently ordered a set of greeting cards from a company called Summer Soul that read, "You are absolutely gorgeous and that is the least interesting thing about you." I sent them to my ten closest friends and mailed them with Hip-Hop graffiti stamps.) I love getting together one on one or in small groups for drinks and dinner.

I do NOT love networking events, blind dates, or breakout rooms on Zoom. Anything called "speed-networking," or "speed-dating," or "speed-mentoring" makes me speed in the opposite direction.

This does not mean I am antisocial. Yet because I am so comfortable being, traveling, living, and working alone, it takes a conscious effort for me to nurture social connections, networks, groups, and communities.

When I was a law student in my early twenties, I focused all my attention on my long-term boyfriend (who became my husband)—fearful he would reject or discard me—to the exclusion of developing more than a handful of lifelong friends and colleagues at school. Later, as a young lawyer, I had no clear vision about which networks or communities were genuinely valuable, so I threw myself into everything. I overextended trying to attend *every* networking event and conference in the construction industry, which ran wholly contrary to my introverted personality. Ultimately, I did develop my own (small) portfolio of clients. But I exhausted and depleted myself, sacrificing meaningful relationships along the way.

Here, in our social dimension, let's examine the R in PERMA: positive relationships. Let's explore healthy approaches to developing a sense of belonging and to contributing to groups and communities that stir meaning for us as individuals. In reading Seligman's book, *Flourish,* I paused when I read his assertion, "Very little that is positive is solitary."[857] At first, I thought, *No, I honestly* love *being alone.* I crave solitude. I thrive in it. My writing and well-being depend on it. But I also cherish my closest friends: their hilarious texts and witty pandemic memes, their Instagram posts, the laughs we share over margaritas and tacos.

A Note on Introversion

Introversion at times seems to get a bad rap or be somewhat misdescribed by the really smart people in positive psychology. For example, in Seligman's book, he wrote, "introverts are much less cheery than extroverts."[858] I consider myself and my introverted friends and students plenty cheery! Further, Dr. Stephen M. Schueller asserts that introverts "shy away from social interaction."[859] No, we are just choosy about it. Fredrickson cites a study that apparently says, "if you simply pretend to be extraverted when you're with others—that is, if you act bold, talkative, energetic, active, assertive, and adventurous—no matter what your inclinations are, you'll extract more positivity from those exchanges."[860] Dr. Jonathan Haidt cites the same study, and states (to my chagrin), "It's not just that extroverts are naturally happier and healthier; when introverts are *forced* to be more outgoing, they usually enjoy it and find that it boosts their mood."[861] Well . . . While I obviously have the utmost respect for these trailblazers in the field, I *wholeheartedly disagree* with the premise that introverts should ever have to fake anything or be *forced* to act like something we categorically are not. There are better ways for us to nurture our well-being.

I'm happy that Dr. Isaac Prilleltensky (also a positive psychology groundbreaker) offers a different perspective, noting, "Introverted kids prefer solitary play. If we push them to interact with others, just because we think it's good for them, we're not in tune with their constitution."[862] As I wrote in my *Introverted Lawyer* book, introverts value authenticity. Yes, we can learn to amplify our voices when we need to make ourselves heard, but we don't need to "fake it till we make it." We are vibrantly interactive in the right circumstances.

If you are introverted like me, please feel free to resist societal pressure to fake or force extroversion. *Be you.* We can cultivate plenty of positivity in our lives in ways that align authentically and best with our interests, values, nature, and character.

In nurturing our social dimension, let's assess what genres of interpersonal connections feel most valuable to us. This likely will differ for each of us. Let's get to know our personality types and understand what modes of social engagements help us thrive, and identify those that sap our energy. Let's analyze different communication styles, and how we can best contribute to groups and communities in ways that feel meaningful to us in our lawyering and personal lives. Here, we'll reprise some communication techniques we discussed in the context of our emotional dimension in Chapter 6:

- **Positivity resonance**
- **Capitalization**
- **Active constructive responding (ACR)**

We'll add two more communication techniques that emphasize the art of listening:

- **Constructivist listening**
- **Perspective-giving and perspective-taking**

Further, we'll explore a community-bonding concept called the "hive switch,"[863] suggested by Haidt, a social psychologist. And finally, we'll delve into how to pull the plug on two obstacles that can impede healthy social connections: bullying and some versions of cancel culture.

POSITIVE PEOPLE POWER

Three types of high-quality relationships can help amplify our well-being:

- Our relationship with ourselves (which we are working on by cultivating multiple well-being dimensions and getting to know ourselves more deeply)
- Our relationships within mindfully selected positivity partnerships (also called dyads, that is, one-on-one relationships)
- Our relationships within positive groups

Healthy relationships can help us flourish.[864] Researchers link good health and well-being with high-quality close relationships and effective social support—defined as a human network of assistance and care.[865] Importantly, the ability of dyads and groups to magnify our well-being depends on *quality*, not *quantity*, of contacts. *More* social connections do not necessarily equate to *better* social support.

POSITIVITY RESONANCE

Chapter 6, which focuses on our emotional dimension, introduces the concept of **positivity resonance**, advanced by Fredrickson.[866] Because you may be diving into our well-being dimensions in a different order than the way these chapters are chronologically sequenced (which I highly encourage—b*e you!*), I'll briefly repeat the definition of positivity resonance here, as it relates to our social dimension. Relationship partners can ignite *positivity resonance* through:

- Mutual exchange of positive emotions
- Moments of biobehavioral synchrony (mirroring one another's behavior —such as eye contact, facial expressions, and body language)
- Investment in one another's well-being[867]

When we interact with another human being in a dyad, we can spark *emotional contagion*—a transfer of emotions.[868] It is wild to think how, by fruitfully investing in our own emotional well-being and working on cultivating healthy emotions, we can positively affect our relationship partners, our friends, our colleagues, our clients, and so on, and vice versa.

In nurturing our social dimension, let's give thought to how we speak, listen, and engage in one-on-one interactions. Do we naturally amplify one another's positive emotions? Are we unconsciously mirroring each other's body language and facial expressions, that is, making eye contact, nodding, smiling, leaning in? Are we genuinely invested in each other's happiness and well-being?

As an introvert, I'm pretty tuned into one-on-one interactions with people who amp up my energy and zest for life. My best friend Clay—a fellow introvert—is an energy amplifier. I feel positivity resonance bouncing off the walls of restaurants, buildings, and street signs of New York when Clay and I hang out. We laugh a lot, smile, banter back and forth about positive daily highlights, and when we part, we both feel energized and uplifted. My boxing trainer Lou—also an introvert—is another energy amplifier. He constantly highlights the positive in life. My travel friend Jenna likewise exudes enthusiasm and adventure. We ask each other a lot of questions when we are together, and our collective energy reverberates off one another. Who in your life ignites positivity resonance when you spend time together?

And then, there are those conversation partners who, unfortunately, do the opposite. They siphon precious energy and zest out of us. We often leave those encounters feeling like an empty balloon.

There are two communication techniques we can use to shape one-on-one encounters in a positively resonant way: **capitalization** and **active constructive responding** (which we'll reprise here from Chapter 6). Let's consider speaking openly about these techniques with our conversation partners so together we can share the benefits.

CAPITALIZATION AND ACTIVE CONSTRUCTIVE RESPONDING

As we first encountered in Chapter 6, when we interact in pairs, we have an awesome opportunity to practice and facilitate *capitalization*—when we magnify the effect of a positive experience by describing it to another person.[869] In disclosing a positive event to someone else (e.g., a good grade, a fun first date, a successful negotiation, a sense of accomplishment in a new exercise class), the positive emotion can resound beyond the occurrence itself.[870] Research indicates that the act of capitalization correlates to greater well-being and self-esteem, and reduced loneliness.[871]

The success of capitalization, however, depends on the response of the recipient of the good news disclosure. Researchers created a measure called Perceived Responses to Capitalization Attempts (PRCA) to characterize four reactions to positive disclosures.[872] In PRCA, an *active-constructive* respondent expresses eagerness or delight about a disclosed event, and actively follows up with positive probing questions or reflections.[873] *That's amazing! Tell me more! What's your first step?*

A *passive-constructive* respondent reacts supportively but in a subdued and succinct manner, halting engagement.[874] *Cool.* Then stares into their Instagram feed.

An *active-destructive* respondent accentuates negative implications of the disclosed event.[875] *Wow, that sounds like a ton of work and really expensive. Are you sure you want to put yourself through that? And aren't you worried about the cost? Why didn't you consider a different route?*

A *passive-destructive* respondent ignores the disclosure altogether.[876] *I'm thinking I'll order the pasta for dinner.*

Research indicates that relationship pairs who practice an active-constructive communication style share heightened levels of satisfaction, trust, and intimacy.[877] In addition to amplifying positivity, positive relationship pairs can help *buffer* each other from negativity, building resources to help one another transform future threats or stressors into possibilities or opportunities.[878]

There is another really interesting psychology term called the Michelangelo phenomenon: like a sculptor liberating an ideal figure from stone, healthy one-on-one relationships can move each partner closer to their ideal self.[879]

LET'S BE BETTER LISTENERS

During the pandemic, I noticed two communication arenas in which decision makers sought to improve the act of listening. (Both involve controversial figures, and when I wrote about these observations in an *ABA Journal* article,[880] I received a couple emails about how I "shouldn't" give either of these guys airtime. I get it, but the character of these two men was not at all my point.) First, in New York's daily pandemic press briefings, the clamor of reporters seeking to ask Governor Andrew Cuomo a question prompted him one day to suggest that, instead of yelling over each other, the journalists should ask their questions one at a time and he would make sure everyone's questions were heard. I have wondered—for 27 years—why we don't conduct lawyering activities such as depositions, negotiations, and oral arguments in a similarly less disruptive fashion, rather than the usual riot of interruptions in which the loudest voices often reign. Our listening skills could use an upgrade.

Interestingly, the U.S. Supreme Court presented a prime example of such a communication boost. In October 2019, prior to the pandemic, the Court started affording each advocate two minutes to present initial statements without the traditional interruption by the justices. Then, mid-pandemic, it announced a new protocol for its first-ever telephonic arguments: The justices would ask questions in order of seniority rather than the usual free-for-all.

Some folks on Twitter and cable news seemed surprised that Justice Clarence Thomas—historically quiet in oral arguments—unmuted his microphone and actively questioned advocates in the Court's new format of telephonic hearings. When I started hearing the buzz about Justice Thomas's invigoration in this new platform, I immediately thought, "He must be an introvert." Introverts resist interruption—to themselves and others. I Googled Justice Thomas to see if there was any information about where he fit along the introversion/extroversion continuum. Sure enough, Justice Thomas spoke at the University of Kentucky in 2012, during which he shared his views on the traditional format of justices interrupting advocates with questions. He remarked, "Maybe it's the introvert in me, I don't know. I think that when somebody's talking, somebody ought to listen."[881] Thus, it made sense to me why he would speak up more readily under the new pandemic protocols, without the expectation to speak over an advocate or a colleague to be heard.

One respondent to my *ABA Journal* article about the change to the Supreme Court protocol countered that appellate lawyers actually enjoy and welcome justices' interruptions. I'm sure that many, maybe even most, do. However, as we train new lawyers, we will foster a more inclusive community if we consider how some traditional styles of communication in our profession intimidate and silence many nascent voices. I've observed numerous oral arguments (law school moot court tryouts and real-life courtroom appearances) in which judges and justices are not exactly polite or respectful in the way they interrupt advocates; some have been downright rude and unnecessarily aggressive or demeaning. We can do a much better job of training law students and novice attorneys (especially the naturally quiet ones) in how to handle the valid role of questioning in oral arguments, so the hard work they invested in researching and writing their briefs can shine. We can make space for them to gain their footing in training and find their powerful advocacy voices.

In tending to our social dimension, let's consider how we can facilitate opportunities for diverse voices to be heard. Two interesting communication techniques might aid in this endeavor: **constructivist listening** and **perspective-giving/perspective-taking**.

Constructivist Listening

Education professor Dr. Julian Weissglass boils the act of listening down to two fundamental requirements: "Listening requires that one person, the talker, sends a message and one (or more) listener(s) receives that message."[882]

He describes seven forms of listening, some being more productive and effective than others:

- **Conversational listening:** alternating between talking and listening, with the expectation of interruption and mutual exchange of viewpoints
- **Informational listening:** seeking to obtain information from another person
- **Active listening:** the listener paraphrasing or echoing back the content of the talker's communication
- **Argumentative listening:** a form of conversational listening but peppered with disagreement and challenges to ideas
- **Passive listening:** the listener staying quiet but conveying interest and attention through eye contact and body language like nodding and smiling
- **Pretend listening:** thinking about something else while showing an interested facial expression
- **Inattentive listening:** hearing the sounds of someone's communication but simultaneously doing something else like staring at a phone or reading, making little or no effort or attempt to understand or react[883]

An eighth form of listening, called *constructivist listening*, is designed to benefit the speaker rather than the listener. In constructivist listening, we create space for a person to "reflect on the meaning of events and ideas; express and work through feelings that are interfering with clearer thinking; construct new meanings; and make decisions."[884] Constructivism is a learning theory based on the premise that we each actively construct our own foundation of knowledge by integrating and synthesizing new information and concepts into our unique amalgam of prior life experiences.[885]

In the context of the profession of teaching, Weissglass describes how many educators communicate:

> *The profession promotes conversational or argumentative listening. Advice and opinions are freely given. Interruptions are commonplace. Even educators who are good listeners, and there are many, rarely listen carefully to each [other's] feelings or the expression of emotions.*[886]

This sounds similar to the legal profession (and legal academia). Lots of talking; not typically a lot of deep, quiet listening—especially when it comes to emotions and feelings.

Weissglass draws linkages between *unresolved emotions* and behavior that thwarts learning and caring for one another as humans. He says that distress, which he defines as "the accumulation of emotions left from hurtful experiences," is a driving force of "unintelligent and uncaring behavior."[887] (In our physical well-being dimension, which we explore in Chapter 5, we investigate how to notice when stress might potentially catapult us into *distress.* With enhanced awareness, we can consciously strive to toggle into, and linger in, *eustress* instead.)

The process of expressing emotions can help us recover from past distress, understand and synthesize our past and present experiences, and gain clarity as we look ahead to the future.[888] To encourage healthy processing of emotions, Weissglass suggests we facilitate opportunities to practice constructivist listening.

The National Equity Project, an education reform organization, provides a helpful description of the purpose of constructivist listening:

> *Constructivist listening is an effective strategy for engaging in conversations that are both intellectually demanding and emotionally challenging. It is distinct from most forms of listening in that its purpose is for the benefit of the speaker, not the listener.*[889]

Shane Safir, a leadership coach in educational equity, outlines four assumptions that ideally should serve as the foundation for any constructivist listening exercise:[890]

- Emotions are a natural and integral part of living and must play a role in our personal and professional lives.
- Emotional distress hinders intelligent thinking and caring behavior toward one another.
- When afforded adequate reflection time, individuals are capable of resolving their own dilemmas and problems.
- Because we are social beings, the act of speaking and having people listen to us helps us make meaning of our feelings (as we convert feelings to language).

The potential upsides of constructivist listening are threefold:

- For the speaker, self-expression and emotional release
- For the listener, insight into the speaker's lens, experience, and perspective
- Mutual relationship-building through exchange of trust, care, vulnerability, and authenticity[891]

So, how does constructivist listening work?

Constructivist listening involves affording each speaker an allotted time period for uninterrupted sharing.[892] Weissglass describes an episode of constructivist listening between two individuals as follows:

> *[T]wo people (a dyad) take turns listening to each other for a fixed amount of time. In a dyad, the talker has the opportunity, indeed, the responsibility, to talk authentically about his or her thoughts and feelings. The person might talk about problems or successes, situations that one would like to handle better, one's thoughts about an . . . issue, feelings about one's job or prior experiences that may be affecting her or his present functioning.*[893]

Importantly, the listener does not translate, evaluate, paraphrase, analyze, render advice, or interrupt with personal viewpoints or anecdotes.[894]

The National Equity Project suggests these guidelines for structuring a constructivist listening activity among members of a group:

- Each speaker is allotted a set number of minutes to talk. (Even two minutes can work!)
- The speaker talks without interruption.
- Listeners refrain from reacting or responding *in any way*. No nods, gestures, or murmurs; no interpreting, paraphrasing, advising, or countering.
- The speaker does not criticize or complain about the listener(s) or other colleagues during their allotted time period.
- Participants refrain from distractions like eating, drinking, or glancing at cell phones.
- The constructivist listening experience must be kept confidential.

According to Weissglass, constructivist listening can serve as a vehicle for self-empowerment, community-building, and change because it enables individuals to gain self-understanding, extract meaning from prior experiences, and process emotions in a healthy manner.[895]

Safir suggests prompts like these to get a constructivist listening session started:

- What is it like to be you today?
- What thoughts and feelings are you carrying today?
- What's "up" for you today?[896]

Is there a scenario in your personal or professional life in which you or others could cultivate social well-being by engaging in a constructivist listening session?

Perspective-Giving and Perspective-Taking

Researchers have explored another communication exercise to help ameliorate attitudes and empathy in members of groups in *conflict* due to a perceived or actual power differential: perspective-giving and perspective-taking.[897] In this exercise, one member of a disempowered (or disadvantaged or nondominant) group is paired with a member of an empowered (or advantaged or dominant) group. The member of the disempowered group shares their perspective on challenges experienced by their group (perspective-giving). Then, the member of the empowered group summarizes the disclosure back to the speaker (perspective-taking).

This exercise could alternatively be performed as a writing activity. For example, one research study set up a perspective-giving and perspective-taking exchange between members of dominant and nondominant groups like this:[898]

- Members of a nondominant group were assigned the role of sender, that is, perspective-giving.
- Members of a dominant group were assigned the role of responder, that is, perspective-taking.
- Each sender wrote a short description of difficulties and challenges experienced by members of their group.
- Each responder summarized the sender's statement in writing, in the responder's own words, without infusing any of their own assessments, evaluations, beliefs, or experiences.

Researchers report that this type of exchange can broaden the perspective of both groups.[899] Responders are prompted to see situations from the senders' standpoint, and senders have the experience of being listened to and heard by the responders.[900]

Are there interpersonal dynamics in your personal or professional life that might benefit from a perspective-giving and perspective-taking exercise?

THE HIVE SWITCH

Now that we have delved into how to improve some of our *one-on-one* interactions with other individuals, let's ponder how purposeful engagement in *groups* can enhance our well-being.

It's fun to consider the possibility that shared experiences like rock concerts, group exercise classes, and sporting events serve a purpose far beyond entertainment or physical fitness; research indicates that the self-transcendent nature of such experiences can magnify well-being.[901] Haidt, a social psychologist, offers us the concept of the **hive switch**. A hive switch is a phenomenon that occurs when individuals realize they have become part of and fused within a positive collective; we transcend self-interest and merge with something larger than ourselves.[902]

Recurring Theme Alert!

Transcendence is one of the six virtues identified by the VIA Institute on Character (as noted in Chapter 3). In Chapter 6 (our emotional dimension), we talk about how the positive emotions of inspiration and awe can help us experience transcendence. Further, transcendence is one of Emily Esfahani Smith's four pillars of meaning-making (described in Chapter 7, our artistic/creative dimension).

For millennia, groups that have figured out how to operate in synchrony—rather than in isolated silos—have achieved greatness.[903] Psychologists such as Haidt have studied phenomena like "muscular bonding"—how armies, for example, forge bonds by moving physically together in time.[904] When humans engage in synchronous or rhythmic movements (like flash mob dances, for instance), we temporarily dissolve many of our hierarchies, borders, and rigid delineations.[905] Other group rituals like parades, festivals, and carnivals incite "collective effervescence"—a feeling of electricity and elation that can make us less selfish, more caring, and increasingly focused on communal fusion rather than individuality.[906] When these experiences of "interlocking" flip our hive switch, we can momentarily forget ourselves, trust others more, and coalesce.[907]

Haidt emphasizes that too much self-focus can hinder happiness.[908] To really thrive, he urges us to intermittently lose ourselves in a hive.[909] A hive switch can transform a group of people from a loose assortment of detached individuals into a healthier collective social organism.[910]

What Does a Hive Switch Moment Look Like?

I recall three poignant hive switch moments in my life. First, at a U2 concert in Rome's Olympic Stadium, fans coordinated a surprise for the band. During the song *With or Without You*, thousands of fans held up colored pieces of paper (taped beneath our seats) forming a massive image of a Joshua tree (the icon invoking the band's 1987 album). Bono paused on stage in the middle of the song, seemingly gripped when he saw the visual.

Second, I felt a hive switch in a spinning class on Thanksgiving morning in New York a few years ago: with music blasting, pedals pumping, and muscles exerting, every person in the room became collectively emotional as we united in the spirit of physical and social well-being.

Third, an Italian guy I was dating took me to a Rome-Bologna soccer match. Ten minutes into the game, the crowd began swaying back and forth arm-in-arm, singing a Roman anthem and waving burgundy and gold flags. Pure magic.

In those moments, all my seemingly urgent, self-focused concerns evaporated. I felt intense human connection. I felt motivated and inspired to make a positive impact in the world.

So, how does this relate to the legal profession?

Happily, hive switches are not limited to entertaining distractions like U2 shows, spinning classes, and Italian soccer matches. Haidt says we can capitalize on the power of the hive switch to fuel the successes of many different types of groups.[911] Haidt notes that this concept has profound implications for how leaders should craft and manage organizations.[912] He distinguishes between organizations run by *transactional* leaders who motivate through "institutionalized carrots-and-sticks" and *transformational* leaders who generate social capital and bonds of trust among employees.[913]

According to Haidt, members of hives work harder, experience more joy and exuberance while doing so, and are less likely to abandon the hive for shinier opportunities.[914] Further, he reports that hives outperform less cohesive groups. In contrast, "pitting individuals against each other in a competition for scarce resources (such as bonuses) will destroy hivishness, trust, and morale."[915]

Unfortunately, traditional legal education and practice models do not tend to cultivate synchrony, unity, and collective trust. Instead, we often *do* feel pitted against one another in fierce, unhealthy, survival-of-the-fittest competition. Outdated educational traditions that reinforce the myth of one path to success in law school—the Socratic method used in an intimidating way, exams worth 100% of semester grades, strict grading curves, class rankings, selection mechanisms for accolades like membership on law review editorial boards and advocacy teams—entrench a scarcity mindset. Similarly, many law firms rely on the same metrics every year to recruit new talent, and thereafter default to compensation systems that can reinforce self-interest rather than regard for the health of the collective. Likewise, legal academia is notoriously hierarchical; elitism and exclusion remain alive and (not) well.

Obviously, some tiered structures are natural and necessary in professions like the law in which we evolve in substantive expertise, mature into leadership and mentorship roles, and supervise newer practitioners with less experience. Teams and groups can benefit, however, from temporarily setting aside pecking orders and seniority. Anthropologist Victor Turner explains that periodic collective experiences of "anti-structure"—through group rituals in which boundaries and hierarchies provisionally melt away—enhance the humaneness and stability of such structures when community members return to them.[916]

How Do We Flip the Hive Switch?

Haidt suggests three pathways for heightening our hivishness:[917]

- Identifying and celebrating shared values and a common identity
- Facilitating experiences that foster synchrony in physical movement
- Nurturing healthy and friendly intergroup team rivalry

Indeed, the pandemic has spotlighted the importance of connection and community, and the health (and societal) risks of remaining too isolated and siloed. Haidt reiterates that synchronous physical movement and team-based activities can activate the hive switch, fostering collective bonds.[918] He offers the example of Toyota starting each day with companywide, coordinated calisthenics.[919] I had a similar experience in an all-weekend Zoom conference during my Penn master's program. Organizers invited a leader of an online dance community called Daybreaker to give us a 45-minute movement-dance break on Zoom. I felt incredibly awkward and cheesy dancing on screen at first (and turned off my video), but then decided to set aside my hang-ups, turn my video back on, and participate. By the end, I felt more closely bonded to my fellow participants.

If group movement (such as coordinated stretching in the middle of the day) feels unrealistic or awkward in a legal setting—and, of course, being mindful of the reality that not everyone can participate in physical movement—we can get creative. Haidt notes alternative ways of flipping the hive switch, such as healthy team activities/rivalries, and collective moments of awe:[920]

- Can we explore hivishness by undertaking activities in departmental groups or established work teams, engendering healthy and friendly intergroup team rivalry?
- Can we connect with group members in virtual or live musical performances or artistic showcases, and seek to tap into collective awe?

- Can we inspire one another to get outside and appreciate an awe-inspiring aspect of nature and then exchange our reflections on those experiences?
- Can we team up to work on humanitarian initiatives and charitable projects in our communities?

Our profession could use some hivishness. We are in this together; we learn together; we grow together; we build together; we hive together; and we thrive together.

DEFUSING BULLIES

Many individuals in our profession—attorneys, judges, clients, law professors, law students—have high expectations of themselves, others, and the profession.[921] They are intelligent and hardworking, yet they also are kind, considerate, and respectful in interpersonal interactions. Engaging in intellectual debates with these folks—even tough negotiations, oral arguments, disagreements over legal strategy or policy—feels fulfilling, motivating even. It is not mutually exclusive to be a successful, assertive, and ambitious member of our profession yet also be nice.

Contrast this with the bullying or uncivil behavior that unfortunately happens in some law offices, courtrooms, deposition rooms, boardrooms, conference rooms, and classrooms across the country. Law students, lawyers, paralegals, legal assistants, support staff, court reporters, and even judges endure bullying from individuals who often are excused as "strong personalities," "eccentric rainmakers," "results-driven," or "just under a lot of pressure."

When I encountered such characters in law practice, I erroneously assumed their behavior was the direct result of me making some sort of mistake. Like, I should have been tougher, louder, better, quicker on my feet, clairvoyant, meaner. After a decade of reflection, studying myself and how law practice affected my mental and physical health and that of my colleagues, I realize, *no.* These people were bullies, plain and simple.

We rarely talk about how to effectively stand up to or *defuse* bullies in the legal profession. We lament a continuing decline in civility. We reaccentuate standards of professionalism. But when do we teach law students and junior attorneys (and other members of our profession) how to mentally and physically recalibrate in a bullying moment, and if, when, and how to substantively respond to the perpetrator? We can do more than just talk about civility problems or advise targets of bad behavior to "just toughen up" or "just stand up for yourself."

Taking a hard look at bullying does not mean we are going to reduce the intellectual rigor of our profession or lower standards of excellence in our work environments. Working in a legal environment obviously takes grit and stamina. Some cases are fast-paced; others require slogging through months of discovery; genuine last-minute crises arise. The law can be equally exhilarating and frustrating, and emotions naturally heighten. But there is a marked difference between a person in a position of strength, power, or authority seeking to motivate an individual to do the best job they can, and using that influence as a weapon to cut someone down or make someone feel weak or inferior.

What Is the Definition of Bullying?

Merriam-Webster defines bullying as "abuse and mistreatment of someone vulnerable by someone stronger, more powerful."[922] Perceived power differentials can derive from variations in physical stature, employment status, social demographics, depth of legal experience, wealth, and even personality type (e.g., an aggressive, extroverted, quick-to-speak individual versus a naturally quiet introvert who might need time to process a rapid-fire Socratic dialogue).

Lynne Curry, author of *Beating the Workplace Bully: A Tactical Guide to Taking Charge*, defines workplace bullying as "psychological violence and aggressive manipulation in the form of *repeated* humiliation or intimidation."[923] Of course, we all can have bad days, and not every episode of snark in a meeting, rude outburst, or temper flare-up constitutes bullying. The key here is the repetition, or the pattern. As columnist Elizabeth Bernstein wrote, "A bully is someone who tries to intimidate another person, often repeatedly, whom he or she sees as weak or vulnerable."[924] Further, the Workplace Bullying Institute defines bullying as "repeated, health-harming mistreatment of one or more persons (the targets) by one or more perpetrators."[925]

Catherine Mattice Zundel, CEO of Civility Partners, distinguishes bullying from "a minor disruption or small annoyance."[926] Bullying behavior is persistent and lingering. It "creates a psychological power imbalance between the person doing the bullying and their target or targets to a point where that person at the receiving end develops [a] feeling of helplessness."[927]

What Type of Behavior Constitutes Bullying?

Author Fran Hauser characterizes a bully as "someone who makes consistent personal attacks or comments that are degrading, demeaning, insulting or offensive."[928] Bullying conduct "is intimidating, threatening, or humiliating to the target. It can, and often does, interfere with the target's ability to get their work done."[929]

Writer Stav Ziv describes four different types of workplace bullies:[930]

- **The aggressive screamer:** someone who yells, fires off nasty emails, is verbally hostile in meetings (possibly accompanied by intimidating body language)
- **The "constant critic":** someone who (unjustifiably) relentlessly nitpicks and harps on the work of another
- **The "gatekeeper":** someone who intentionally withholds information—such as deadlines, project parameters, clear direction, assistance—about work assignments
- **The behind-the-scenes meddler:** someone who acts friendly face to face but secretly undercuts another person

LawCare, an online well-being hub for the British legal community, provides additional examples of bullying behavior, such as excessive monitoring of work, social exclusion and silent treatment, repeated manipulation of responsibilities and assignment objectives, and blame for outcomes beyond the target's control.[931] Sabotaging or interfering with assignments, or misappropriating credit for ideas, can also constitute bullying.[932] More obvious forms of bullying include verbal mistreatment such as mocking jokes.[933]

Of course, as an article in Healthline (a health and well-being website) points out, criticism in the workplace "isn't always bullying. For example, objective and constructive criticism and disciplinary action directly related to workplace behavior or job performance aren't considered bullying."[934] However, "criticism meant to intimidate, humiliate, or single someone out without reason would be considered bullying."[935]

In the legal profession, bullying can lurk in different forms. Perhaps a more senior opposing counsel mistreats a junior lawyer by constantly interrupting her deposition, speaking over her on conference calls, or using sarcasm to call attention to her purported lack of experience. Or a supervising attorney yells and slams doors around law office interns, junior attorneys, and support staff, intentionally fueling a volatile office atmosphere. More subtle bullying in the form of manipulation might involve a boss persistently keeping employees completely in the dark until the last minute about whether they need to work late again, all weekend, or through holidays. It can include purposely withholding feedback about whether employees are meeting the supervisor's expectations. It can entail cultivating an atmosphere in which employees constantly feel they have done something wrong, but they don't know what that "something" is. People in positions of authority might routinely demand meetings or conference calls only to show up late or fail to appear. Bullies also might engage in gaslighting—manipulative behavior designed to push or keep an individual off-kilter, repeatedly render a person confused, and make them distrust their own thought processes. Bullies gaslight by flip-flopping on opinions or decisions and making more vulnerable people question their own memories or judgment after acting in reliance upon the bully's initial position.

Dr. Lilia Cortana, a leading expert in workplace incivility, and her colleagues developed a Workplace Incivility Scale with questions that can help measure incivility in our work environments.[936]

What Are Some of the Harmful Effects of Bullying?

Curry explains that the bully's intent is to weaken us through derisive language and intimidation.[937] She vividly describes the process: "[B]ullies gnaw away at your vulnerabilities until you crack wide open, humiliated and demeaned."[938]

LawCare articulates some of the detrimental effects of bullying on the target:[939]

- Feelings of anxiety, humiliation, and fear
- Decline in motivation, performance, and productivity
- Deterioration of office relationships
- Physical illness
- Anxiety about going to the office
- Thoughts about leaving the organization or company

Broader ripple effects can include staff turnover, reduced morale, and difficulty hiring new employees.[940]

How Do We Defuse Bullies?

Much of the discourse about handling bullies uses phrasing like "beating bullies"—even the title of Curry's (helpful) book.[941] As a legal profession already mired in "win-lose" dynamics though, let's consider methods to *defuse* bullies—cutting off their power source—rather than *beating* them.

As a junior attorney, I mistakenly thought that just keeping my head down, getting my work done, or focusing on my deposition/negotiation strategy and avoiding engaging with a bully was the wisest move. I wish I could go back and have a do-over. Well, numerous do-overs.

As Curry points out, many of us distrust our feelings, so we're not exactly sure whether someone is indeed bullying us, whether we did something to deserve it (we didn't), or how best to address it. Curry explains, "If, when you were growing up, someone taught you not to trust your feelings, the lesson you derived was that other people could disregard how you felt. This led you to believe you had no right to protest a bully's taunts. *Bullies love victims who distrust their own feelings.*"[942] Hauser similarly notes, "Often, we 'nice girls' carry around a tiny seed of doubt that a conflict is somehow our fault. When a bully spots that doubt, he or she will be very likely to prey on it."[943] Thus, if you feel like you are being bullied, a huge first step is: Trust your feelings. Curry reminds us that we did not create the bully, and we did not invite the bullying behavior.[944] LawCare emphasizes that bullying is not a personality conflict, an exercise in building character, an acceptable style of leadership, or the result of anything we did to invite or "provoke" it.[945] We can reassert our power by refusing to participate in the bully's dance or game; we get to decide what we will and won't permit.[946]

Next, Curry recommends we avoid reacting right away but instead briefly assess the situation and plan a response.[947] In a bullying moment—whether it's in a deposition or the office or even the courtroom—we can pause to process what just happened. We should not just look the other way though, even if we think that would be taking the high road. Curry explains that "if a bully insults you and you don't counter it, the bully pokes a second time, testing your boundaries."[948] As Ziv notes, "Once that power imbalance has been cemented, it can be virtually impossible for the target to fix."[949] Indeed, "ignoring bullying contributes to a toxic work environment."[950] Workplace culture consultant, Heidi Lynne Kurter, advises "addressing the situation on the spot. Sometimes this is exactly what the bully needs to realize they've overstepped boundaries."[951] Of course, this might take some *prehabilitation* work and *practice*—so we are more readily capable of doing this in the heat of a stressful moment. As Kurter states, "As uncomfortable as it may be, practicing courage will show the bully you're not as easy as a target as they initially thought."[952]

The bottom line with bullies is: we cannot remain silent. Curry explains, "bullies interpret silence as a concession and behave as badly as you let them."[953] She urges that we "have to speak up in a manner that says, 'I stand up to you. I stand up for me.'"[954] Here are some suggestions on how to do that.

Step 1: Let's Do a Mental Reboot

If we feel we just experienced a moment of aggression, abuse, mistreatment, destructive manipulation, humiliation, or intimidation, let's first catch ourselves if we start to self-blame. Let's notice the launch of any negative mental soundtrack and stop. Let's pause and take a realistic stock of what just happened: "No, this feels like underhanded manipulation. No, this feels like inappropriate aggression. No, this feels like intentional undermining." Then, we can mentally reboot and launch our new internal soundtrack (our appraisal script from Chapters 5 and 6): "I worked hard to be in this professional moment. I did the work. I prepared as much as humanly possible based on my level of experience and expertise. I exercised my best judgment. I deserve to be here."

Step 2: Let's Channel Our Inner Athlete or Performer

Bullying behavior is intended to make us feel weak and small. Often, when we feel verbally attacked or physically intimidated, our bodies automatically launch self-protective mechanisms.

In reflecting on the way my body physically reacts when I feel blitzed by a bully, I realize that I subconsciously cross my arms and legs, hunch my shoulders, and fold inward—as if bracing for a blow. Unfortunately, as I shared in Chapter 5, my body's natural effort to protect me only exacerbates my anxiety and fear symptoms; the contraction of my physical frame blocks my energy, blood, and air flow. My heart begins to race. I blush. I sweat.

So, instead of caving inward, let's channel our inner athlete or performer. In a bullying moment, let's pause and notice if our bodies have shifted toward self-protection. Then, let's recalibrate with intention. Let's stand or sit in a balanced stance like an athlete or performer primed to move in any direction. Let's open our physical frame—both feet on the floor, shoulders back, hands and arms open, spine tall—allowing energy, blood, and air to flow in a productive way, calm our minds, and power our brains.

Step 3: Let's Cut the Bully's Power Source

Curry acknowledges that bullying problems often do not have simple solutions.[955] But she cautions, "Remain silent, and you collude with bullies."[956]

To defuse bullies, to cut their power source, we must *assert*, and we can do so concisely and deftly. We're not going to engage in a debate. We are not going to get defensive or make excuses. We are not going to try to bond with them. We're going to deliver a short, concrete assertion that reestablishes our power internally and transmits it outward.

Curry recommends we "[b]uild and memorize an arsenal of statements and questions that swiftly neutralize verbal attacks."[957] Let's consider combinations or variations of these:

- "I perceive that you are trying to [*intimidate/confuse/rattle/manipulate/embarrass/humiliate/demean/test*] me."

- "I worked hard to be here. I'm working hard right now."
- "Raising your voice at me is the opposite of motivation."
- "Demeaning me is not conducive to moving this case forward."
- "My goal is to do a great job for you, but respectfully, I can't read your mind."
- "Your body language feels aggressive to me right now and I'd like you to take a step back."

Curry suggests we practice asserting short phrases like: "Let me finish."[958] "I don't agree."[959] "I don't allow that."[960] "I'm not playing."[961] Alternatively, she proposes posing a question like, "Does it make you feel good to try to make me feel bad?"[962]

I know it might feel scary to try to cut the power source of a bully, especially if we work directly for one, and we want and need our job. But it's quite possible that no one has ever stood up to this person. Although I've never loved hearing this kind of advice, in the end, deep down, the bully likely is more afraid of us (or the situation) than we are of them. Kurter indicates that the bully might feel threatened by our persona or achievements.[963] Clinical psychologist Dr. Craig Malkin notes that "[b]ullies are motivated by fear—fear of feeling insecure, fear of being unconfident, fear of being exposed."[964] Curry emphasizes, "Bullies rarely examine their own behavior."[965] Well, that's unfortunate, but it's about time for them to work on themselves. Let's demand they start doing so. Let's honor the hard work we invested in our legal education and training. Let's make our profession better.

How Can We Stand Up for Others?

If we see something, let's *say something*. Zundel advises that, if we witness a bully trying to push someone else around, we should "state the problem, state the consequences, and offer a solution."[966] Let's not perpetuate institutional bullying, which "happens when a workplace accepts, allows, and even encourages bullying to take place."[967] Let's be part of the solution, creating a workplace culture that says no to this behavior—in a civil but unequivocally strong way.

When I reflect on the bullies in my professional and personal life, I wish I had stood up to them. I wish I had valued myself enough at the time to stop cowering, stand up, look them in the eye, and say, "Enough. You do not get to speak to me that way anymore." I also wish I had contested their enablers, observers in positions of authority who sat there mute, not saying a word, or worse, dismissed the bad behavior with quips like, "Oh you know him, he's just in a mood," or "That's just her version of intellectual candor."

No. These are not valid justifications for disrespectful or abusive treatment of individuals in vulnerable employment situations or hierarchical relationship dynamics.

Of course, our jobs are demanding and we're all going to encounter intense moments in which everyone is stressed. Naturally we're all going to have bad days when our emotions get the best of us and we say things less artfully than we should. But when that behavior becomes a pattern, the norm rather than the exception, we must stand up for ourselves and others.

Back then, I mistakenly thought my work situations were all-or-nothing. That if I couldn't handle the screaming, the belittling, the condescension, that it was *my* weakness and I probably needed to leave. I'd lie in bed at 3:00 a.m. worrying—about not having enough money, about starting over, about my reputation. And then, ultimately, I did leave. I changed firms twice and left the third firm to teach full-time.

Instead of erroneously viewing ourselves as weak in the face of domineering bullies, let's pause and recalibrate. Let's mentally reboot. Let's remind ourselves that we have worked hard to be here. That *their unchecked behavior* is the problem. Let's channel our inner athlete or performer, stand or sit taller, balance our physical frames, and remember our power. Then let's step up and say—calmly, yet forcefully—that this behavior is inappropriate and demeaning, and will stop *now*.

If you are struggling with a bully at law school or in the workplace, I see you. I'm here to listen to you. Together we will stand up.

For a great podcast episode discussing bullying in the law firm environment, check out LegalSpeak's (Leigh Jones and Vanessa Blum's) conversation with Kathleen Pearson (Chief Human Resources Officer at Pillsbury Winthrop Shaw Pittman) and Patrick Krill (of Krill Strategies), titled "Jerk Partners Beget Jerk Partners: Ending Big Law's Cycle of Dysfunction."[968]

WE HAVE THE POWER TO CHANGE THE TONE IN OUR PROFESSION

Sometimes I sit in meetings and am flabbergasted at the way members of our profession talk to each other, and about other people. Healthy disagreement is one thing, but snarky, elitist mockery is another. As attorney James Goodnow writes, "In short, the practice of law teaches us to be jerks."[969] Indeed, "the norms of the legal world are not normal, pro-social human behavior."[970] Attorney Trent Collier echoes this sentiment, saying "[a]buse is the default setting for many lawyers."[971] But abuse also is merely "noise and distraction."[972] As Goodnow encourages, "The legal mindset is a tool, one that can be used for good or for ill. We can choose to use it well."[973]

Attorney Paul Kiernan wrote an article that I love called "'Being Nice' and Finishing First."[974] He explained, "being nice gives a lawyer an edge. I do not mean nice-timid or nice-enabling. I mean nice-smart."[975] He elaborates:

> *In the field of commercial and corporate litigation where I work, the best lawyers are also nice people. They are confident and self-aware. They have colleagues and protégés who like working with them. They respect the rules. They serve their communities. They don't pick stupid fights or deny reasonable requests or play hide-the-ball.*[976]

Often at law conferences when we talk about civility and shutting down bullies, someone inevitably will ask, "But when clients are in legal trouble, don't they want a tough, strong lawyer—a pitbull?"[977] Kiernan counters:

> *I'm not sure they do if it means they want an aggressive jerk. Aren't clients really saying they want someone who is tough intellectually; thorough; always playing offense; knows how to write and argue; someone who will drive the client's agenda—not someone who can write snippier emails than the other lawyer?*[978]

I like how Kiernan frames this conversation in grammatical terms:

> *Clients yearn for action verbs from their trial lawyers, not adverbs and interjections. Nice people—polite, reasonable, confident, professional, laser-focused on* [the] *client's goals—can be tougher to litigate against than the growliest, snarkiest, high-handed sanctions-threatener that ever refused to pick up the phone to resolve something.*[979]

Kiernan's words remind me of one of the most intellectually challenging yet rewarding cases I ever worked on: a litigation between a cruise line and a shipyard. The Virginia lawyers representing the opposing party in the case were smart guys, amazing writers, incredible strategists—and profoundly nice people. The level of civility in that case gave us the room to up our collective intellectual game. On both sides of the case, our briefs were better, our arguments had more depth, the judge and jury seemed thoroughly engaged in a contract-based case that could have come across as mind-numbingly boring, and most importantly, the clients and all the lawyers on the respective teams felt good about the process.

I have a t-shirt that says: *Work Hard. Be Nice.*[980]

Let's do it.

A WORD ABOUT CANCEL CULTURE

I have to admit that scrolling Law Twitter often depresses me. With several notable exceptions (including many legal research and writing professors I follow, and legal innovators like Professor Cat Moon who spread smart positivity), a constant theme seems to be: *cancel culture is cool.* Cancel culture, also referred to as "callout culture," is "the removal ('canceling') of support for individuals and their work due to an opinion or action on their part deemed objectionable to the parties 'calling' them out."[981] Social media—especially Twitter—is a popular forum for campaigns to "cancel" people or businesses. While of course we want to foster healthy individual, community, and institutional accountability (which can be the well-meaning driver behind a cancel/callout campaign), we should also push back when a different form of bullying emerges masked as something else.[982]

Dr. Arthur C. Brooks wrote an interesting article in the *New York Times* called "Our Culture of Contempt."[983] He describes our "outrage industrial complex."[984] He calls attention to the current "noxious brew of anger and disgust," noting how we don't just exhibit "contempt for other people's ideas, but also for other people."[985] He deems this state of affairs to be worse than incivility. Brooks notes, "Disagreement helps us innovate, improve, and find the truth."[986] He emphasizes that "what we need is not to disagree less, but to disagree better."[987]

We are all capable of making a statement or asserting an opinion about something, and later changing our minds as we study, investigate, and learn more. In my master's program at Penn, one of my teachers, Dr. Karen Reivich, made a thought-provoking comment about our tendency to call politicians and leaders who change their minds "flip-floppers." Reivich noted, "When a person changes their view on a subject, we shouldn't assume it's flip-flopping. Changing one's view is often out of a commitment to learn and understand and shows an openness to continue to question one's own perspective and challenge one's beliefs. That strikes me as critical thinking, and humility."[988]

To me, this echoes a quote by actor Joaquin Phoenix:

> *And I think that's when we're at our best, when we support each other. Not when we cancel each other out for past mistakes, but when we help each other to grow, when we educate each other, when we guide each other towards redemption. That is the best of humanity.*[989]

Brooks invites us to "make a commitment never to treat others with contempt, even if we believe they deserve it."[990] He points out the simplicity of it all: "This is a chance to change at least one heart—yours."[991]

Social Well-Being Dimension Exercise #1

Enhancing One-on-One Communication through Art

As we move through our different well-being dimensions, we might start intertwining two or three dimensions together, layering our learnings. In this exercise, we can nurture our artistic, emotional, and social dimensions at the same time.

Art can teach us how to love and be loved,[992] and help us articulate how we wish to be understood and imagined.[993] An ex-boyfriend once told me he loved the poem *Ithaka* by Greek poet, Constantine P. Cavafy.[994] I created a collage for this guy, weaving the poem's words into a menu saved from a meal we shared at Locanda Verde, one of my favorite New York restaurants. Before I gave him the gift, he dumped me—pretty abruptly. Savoring the collage now hanging on *my* wall, I wish I had used art to convey what *I* needed in a healthy relationship.

Shared art experiences—collages, pottery classes, painting, gallery visits—could generate **positivity resonance** (bidirectional emotional exchange, synchronous sensory connections, mutual regard).[995] A shared art practice could help us reciprocally articulate what we need to feel safe in relationships so that we can take risks: comfortably expressing and being our true selves.[996]

Is there someone in your life with whom you want to improve your communication style? Do you have difficulty expressing what you need? Consider using artistic expression to open up a dialogue. Can you paint a picture together? Make a collage? Write a song? A poem? Build something? Talk about what the piece of art, or the creative project, means to each of you. As you converse, practice an active constructive style of responding to one another.

Relationship Resources

For what it's worth, and if you are like me and struggle with healthy attachment, here are two books that have helped me:

- Dr. Amir Levine and Rachel S. F. Heller, *Attached* (London: Bluebird, 2019).
- Amy Chan, *Breakup Bootcamp: The Science of Rewiring Your Heart* (New York: Dey Street Books, 2020).

Social Well-Being Dimension Exercise #2

Constructivist Listening

Is there someone in your professional or personal life with whom you'd like to cultivate healthier listening skills? Consider setting aside some time to engage in constructivist listening with one another. You could set these parameters similar to those suggested by Weissglass and the National Equity Project (or create your own):[997]

- Give each speaker two minutes to speak about how they are feeling.
- The listeners do not react or respond *in any way*. No nods, no gestures, no murmurs. No interrupting, interpreting, paraphrasing, advising, or countering.
- The speaker does not criticize or complain about the listener(s) during their allotted time period.
- Participants should refrain from distractions like eating, drinking, or glancing at cell phones.
- The constructivist listening experience must be kept confidential.

After all participants have had their turn to speak without interruption, each person could reflect on the experience in writing for ten minutes. Then, participants could have the opportunity to share their reflections, but without pressure to do so.

Social Well-Being Dimension Exercise #3

Perspective-Giving and Perspective-Taking

If you are observing or experiencing a conflict between members of a disempowered (or disadvantaged or nondominant) group and an empowered (or advantaged or dominant) group, consider engaging in a dyadic, perspective-based, writing-oriented exercise. You could set these parameters (or create your own):[998]

- Create pairs comprised of one member of the disempowered group and one member of the empowered group.
- Ask each member of the disempowered group to write a one-page essay about their perspective (perspective-giving).
- Afterward, the member of the empowered group can meet in person with their pair-partner and verbally summarize the pair-partner's statements (perspective-taking). Alternatively, the member of the empowered group could write a summary of the pair-partner's statements (perspective-taking).

Social Well-Being Dimension Exercise #4

The Hive Switch

Consider identifying and then engaging in potential hive switch activities:

- Opportunities for group rhythmic movement involving physical synchrony: Dance? Marching in a parade? A spinning class? A rock concert?
- Healthy team rivalry
- Collective awe experiences: hikes in nature, artistic outings

Afterward, take a moment to reflect on emotions that arise when we temporarily set aside our own concerns to become part of a collective.

You and I are artists and creators constantly meeting and greeting each other.

Helen Edwards

CHAPTER 9

The Dimension of Culture

Adventure is worthwhile.

Aesop

In this chapter, we will learn about:

- Immersion
- Embeddedness
- Acquisition
- Socialization
- Reflection
- Expression
- Cultural humility

In the movie *Chocolat*, a story set in a small town in France, the character played by actor Juliette Binoche often feels tugged by a mysterious "north wind" to move, to explore, to roam. I can relate.

One morning in June 2018, I woke up in my Rome Airbnb, wrote five pages of my *Untangling Fear* book manuscript, cleared my head with a midday jog in the sweltering summer heat along the Tiber River, then set off to explore historical and cultural artifacts all afternoon. Seeking to escape the throngs of humanity near the Colosseum, I meandered past the Teatro Marcello (an ancient theater), aiming for the Portico d'Ottavia, a structure once used as a library and a fish market. Three ancient columns—standing alone amid crumbling ruins—stopped me in my tracks. These columns shot high into the sky, connected by a lingering cornice, vestiges of a temple. Standing in a nondescript triangular plot of soil, grass, and pebbles, staring up at the trio of columns, I felt a jolt of electric current—like I had stepped on a live wire. These columns made me feel tiny but expansive at the same time. I sensed the massiveness of the universe and the reality that I'm just one blip in a timeline of literally millennia of humans standing in that same cross-section of longitude and latitude. But I also felt a supercharge of motivation that I can, and must, do something worthwhile and big. When I returned to my apartment, sweaty and dusty, I settled into the couch, turned on the TV, and learned that Anthony Bourdain—chef and explorer of international culture and the human condition—had taken his life. I didn't know him personally, yet grief sucked the air from my lungs. My dog-eared copy of his book, *Medium Raw: A Bloody Valentine to the World of Food and the People Who Cook,*[999] stared at me from the coffee table. Through his prose, he had seemed to reach out, grab me by the shoulders, and urge, *Heidi, go. Go now. Go explore the world.* Though Bourdain's pain became too burdensome to bear, he modeled how to plumb the wellsprings of history and culture to find meaning and purpose. He seemed to roam the earth in a perpetual state of awe. I aspire to do that too.

Dictionaries define awe as "a feeling of reverential respect mixed with fear or wonder."[1000] Awe is a multistep experience. First, we perceive something profound, stunning, vast, or epic. It could be:

- Physical—my three columns in Rome, a lightning storm, an iceberg, a cascading waterfall, a black volcanic sand beach, a street mural, a rainbow, a sculpture
- Interactive—a rock concert, a Broadway show, a sporting event, a dance-off in a subway station
- Conceptual—a peaceful protest, a moving political speech, a poetry reading

Suddenly, we feel small, insignificant, temporarily immobilized. As author Emily Esfahani Smith writes, "[A]we challenges the mental models that we use to make sense of the world. Our mind must then update those models to accommodate what we just experienced."[1001] As we vibrate from the electrical charge of awe, our minds sift and sort past memories, striving to incorporate and integrate this new source of information.

Fredrickson explains that awe is so impactful because it teeters on the precipice of safety; it blends positive emotions like inspiration with less pleasant sensations like fear.[1002] For me, sometimes awe (while it's my favorite emotion) can resonate, in part, as a fear of being forgotten or left out. In the end, awe is self-transcendent. Riding the waves of an awe experience, ultimately, we can merge with something much larger than ourselves.

Immersing ourselves in cultural experiences can ignite awe, which in turn can spark positive change in the way we view the world, how we fit into it, and how we aspire to fit into it. I suggest we approach our cultural well-being dimension by cultivating an open-minded yearning to seek awe experiences. Let's dive into learning how exposing ourselves to different cultures and ways of life—through perhaps travel, food, music, architecture, art, languages, and ritual—can expand our thinking and help us flourish. Here, we'll also enhance our understanding of the concept of **cultural humility** and its role in individual and community well-being.

RESEARCHERS LINK CULTURAL ENGAGEMENT WITH HUMAN FLOURISHING

Chapter 7 (which focuses on our artistic/creative dimension) explores how engagement with the humanities—such as art, music, writing, and literature—can enhance our well-being through the mechanisms of immersion, embeddedness, acquisition, socialization, reflection, and expression.[1003] Researchers indicate that we can activate similar processes when we explore culture.

Immersion

When we immerse in culture, through travel, food, fashion, architecture, cartography, films, books, art, or rituals, for example, we temporarily detach from everyday concerns.[1004] Cultural encounters can re-ignite senses and emotions that may have been dulled or tamped down by our daily routine.[1005]

As an introvert who craves quietude to get anything accomplished, I savored the imperative to work from home during the initial year of the pandemic. However, the inability to travel (a huge part of my identity, and an important calibrator of my well-being) challenged my ability to unplug the whirring treadmill in my brain. One of the few activities besides exercise that shocks my mental, emotional, and physical systems enough to interrupt my brain's preoccupation with work is travel. Flying to another region or time zone, perking up to the melody of accents or other languages, touching unfamiliar currency, and tasting unusual food combinations draw me out of my head into the world. We don't need to jump on a plane to make this happen though; we can immerse ourselves in the richness of cultural tableaux in our own communities.

Acquisition and Embeddedness

Culture can enrich us through the mechanisms of acquisition and embeddedness. As we steep in cultural experiences, we acquire new insights, habits, and skills.[1006] We might learn new languages or vocabulary, improve our facility with reading maps, memorize historical timelines, or partake in interesting rituals. (Studies indicate that individuals can reap well-being benefits from learning new languages, specifically from increased social ties and boosts in subjective feelings when mastering new words and phrases.)[1007] As we practice using fresh knowledge, behaviors, and talents, our socio-cognitive processes (the ways we influence and are influenced by our environment) become hardier; we develop confidence that we can successfully perform tasks, and we learn how to notice and regulate emerging emotions in healthy ways.[1008]

Further, engaging with culture fosters opportunities to nurture character strengths identified by the VIA Institute on Character, such as curiosity, creativity, love of learning, appreciation of beauty, zest, and more. When we intentionally step into other cultures with open minds, we can't help but add layers to our personas.

When I traveled to Tenerife in the Canary Islands to work on this book, I needed to rent a car to get to my remote Airbnb nestled in hills flecked with hundreds, possibly even thousands, of banana trees. Feeling obligated to get my money's worth out of the rental car (even though driving on the one-lane, two-directional roads was nerve-wracking—a **hormesis** activity!), every other afternoon or so, I set out to explore different villages, hiking trails, and seaside coves. As I bought gas and groceries, ordered food in restaurants, and figured out traffic signs, I learned new vocabulary: Spanish words for different tapas foods, geographical directions, friendly modes of communication with locals. I boosted my confidence navigating the stick-shift car on the twisty roads. I expanded my knowledge about nature: volcanos that created the black-sand beaches, weather patterns that carried dust to the island all the way from the Sahara Desert, the agricultural conditions that made the bananas taste so good.

Anthony Bourdain summarized this phenomenon perfectly: *Travel changes you. As you move through this life and this world, you change things slightly, you leave marks behind, however small. And in return, life—and travel—leaves marks on you.*[1009]

Socialization

The socialization mechanism of culture also fosters growth. When we step into unfamiliar activities and experiment with cultural traditions alongside other human beings (e.g., ceremonial meals, seasonal festivals, religious rituals), we add more layers to our personas.[1010] We connect with other people in deep and impactful ways.[1011] This process can help us better understand ourselves and how we fit, and would like to fit, into society and the world.[1012]

Cultural experiences can invite us to get to know, and possibly expand the richness of, our individuality but also make us feel part of a collective—the important sense of belonging. Walking with strangers in an Easter parade called Vasa Vasa (*kiss, kiss*) in Modica, Sicily, one year on my birthday, I pondered my own tumultuous relationship with religion, yet at the same time felt connected to the spirituality of the ritual. (Also, the rhythm of the crowd's movement through the cobblestone streets swept me into a hive switch moment, explored in Chapter 8!) Visiting Paris with my best friend Clay, we stumbled upon the Yellow Vest economic political protests, and later the French version of the Gay Pride Parade. Instead of standing on the periphery as tourists, we were folded into both moving montages. The cultural moments became part of us, and we became part of them. Others' points of views and perspectives seeped into our psyche.

Reflection and Expression

Cultural experiences also invite self-expansion through reflection.[1013] During or after a cultural immersion, for example, a visit to a mind-blowing Greek ruin, a simple yet extraordinary meal at an authentic Irish pub, a vibrant linguistic exchange with a Sicilian fishmonger, a book festival in Brooklyn, an art fair in Miami, a music festival in Wisconsin, we contemplate. This pondering process nudges us to challenge existing thoughts, habits, feelings, behaviors, and perspectives.[1014] Through reflection, we can notice and fortify constructive habits, values, and viewpoints.[1015] We also can recognize, and feel inspired to improve, maladaptive ones.[1016]

The self-awareness gleaned through reflection, in turn, can prompt us to want to share our thoughts and emotions with others, expressing ourselves.[1017] Similar to Anthony Bourdain's show *Parts Unknown*, actor Stanley Tucci's CNN show, *Searching for Italy*, chronicles his culinary adventures through twenty regions of Italy. In each episode, Tucci models the activities of reflection and expression. First, he educates himself and viewers on Italian politics and the origin of gastronomic traditions such as pasta, pizza, polenta, balsamic vinegar, and ricotta. Then he reflects on how these new experiences stoke memories of his childhood and early adulthood as the son of Italian American parents. Next, he articulates the different positive emotions that these surprises and adventures, intertwined with past recollections, invoke—like the P in PERMA! For me, his show was a pandemic positive intervention.

Reflective expression after a cultural foray may take diverse forms for each of us: postcards, snapshots of cultural experiences shared on Instagram, travel memoirs, blogs, even a t-shirt with a phrase in a different language, or other expressive fashion. When we convey emotion through sharing our cultural experiences with others, we can enrich our own personas and forge deeper connections with other human beings.

The challenges of day-to-day life may sometimes leave us feeling invisible—to relationship partners, work colleagues, family members, friends, strangers, the world. When we engage with culture, we gain opportunities to leave our fingerprints and footprints behind, as evidence that we were, and are, *here* sharing space with other humans. In turn, the air we breathe in cultural spaces leaves imprints in our bodies, minds, and souls, like ornate stamps in our biological passports. We are an amalgamation of our cultural experiences. We are not invisible. We are *here*, together.

CULTURAL HUMILITY

I like the concept of *humility*. Some dictionaries (mis)define the word as "a modest or low view of one's own importance." That's not how I view humility at all. Socrates was basically the brand ambassador for intellectual humility, but he didn't have a low view of himself. He simply didn't act like he was the smartest person in the room; instead, he savored the joy of learning from others. We can be badass and exercise humility at the same time. There is nothing sexier to me than someone who owns their power yet is not afraid to say, "I don't know much about that. Please tell me more."

The VIA Institute on Character provides a helpful exploration of humility:[1018]

> *A common misconception is that humility involves having a low self-esteem, a sense of unworthiness, and/or a lack of self-focus. However, true humility involves an accurate self-assessment, recognition of limitations, keeping accomplishments in perspective, and forgetting of the self.*

The VIA Institute reiterates that humility doesn't make us doormats:[1019]

> *[Humility] is not bowing to every wish or demand of another person and it is not being highly self-critical. Truly humble people think well of themselves and have a good sense of who they are, but they also are aware of their mistakes, gaps in their knowledge, and imperfections.*

As we nurture our cultural dimension, let's take a look at how the terminology of **cultural competence** has shifted toward championing **cultural humility** instead.

Approximately two decades ago, the medical field began incorporating the concept of cultural competence into the training of doctors, nurses, and other medical professionals. In 2008, the American Association of Colleges of Nursing defined cultural competence as "the attitudes, knowledge, and skills necessary for providing quality care to diverse populations."[1020] As the study of cultural competence evolved though, many individuals in the health care profession began to express concerns that the term *competency* suggested mastery or achievement of a skill; they pointed out the presumptuousness of intimating, implying, or assuming we can ever master another person's culture.[1021] Accordingly, the medical profession began shifting toward studying and teaching the concept of *cultural humility* (a term originated by Dr. Melanie Tervalon and Dr. Jann Murray-García in 1998).[1022]

A learning endeavor grounded in cultural humility emphasizes the importance of considering a person's culture from that individual's viewpoint, and developing and exercising the self-awareness, sincerity, and grace to say "I don't know" when we lack knowledge or understanding.[1023] As we learn and practice cultural humility, we:

- Take responsibility for how we engage with other people.
- Educate ourselves.
- Commit to improving our active listening skills.
- Notice and give *regard* to our thoughts, feelings, assumptions, and presumptions regarding culture.
- Reflect.
- Continuously remain open to learning.[1024]

Importantly, cultural humility is a lifelong educational pursuit, not a degree or accolade with a definitive end point.[1025] We don't receive a certificate that says, "I'm culturally competent now!" or "I've passed the cultural humility exam!" Instead, as health care scholars eloquently state, "Cultural humility incorporates a lifelong commitment to self-evaluation and self-critique, [and] to redressing the power imbalances in the patient-physician dynamic."[1026] Similarly, in the social work context, researchers indicate that the concept of cultural humility encourages us to recognize power differentials and enhance our personal accountability to dismantle institutional obstacles that marginalize groups of individuals.[1027]

Dr. Josepha Campinha-Bacote, an expert in transcultural health care, proffered another interesting term: *cultural competemility*.[1028] Campinha-Bacote defines cultural competemility as a "synergistic process between cultural humility and cultural competence."[1029] Her concept suggests we can achieve interim degrees of improved competence in certain skills (better listening, for example), but then we move forward and keep learning, practicing, and growing. This reminds me of our interplay between the deliberate practice aspect of **grit**, and episodes of **flow**, explored in Chapter 4. In deliberate practice, our challenge exceeds our skill level. Eventually, we improve the particular skill; when the challenge and skill ultimately meet in equipoise, we can experience flow. But because we are gritty, we don't stop there. We identify a new skill to hone and the next challenge to embrace. Lifelong learning.

Campinha-Bacote outlines five components of cultural competence (which we can apply to lawyering):[1030]

- Cultural awareness
  - Examining and exploring our own cultural background
  - Noticing and acknowledging our own biases, prejudices, and assumptions about people from different cultures and backgrounds
- Cultural knowledge—educating ourselves about diverse cultural and ethnic groups
- Cultural skill—learning how to gather pertinent and necessary information about a client's circumstances while respecting variations in individuals' characteristics and backgrounds
- Cultural desire—a genuine passion for and commitment to becoming culturally knowledgeable, aware, skillful, caring, open, and flexible
- Cultural encounters—regarding others as helpful "cultural informants," and embracing opportunities to step into and learn from cross-cultural interactions[1031]

Campinha-Bacote emphasizes that cultural humility should permeate each of the five domains of cultural competence. She describes this as "both a process of becoming and the process of being."[1032] In other words, we "must engage in the process of *becoming* culturally competent while synchronously *being* engaged in the process of cultural humility."[1033]

> *Humility is not thinking less of yourself, it's thinking of yourself less.*
>
> C. S. Lewis

Cultural Well-Being Dimension Exercise #1

A Cultural Outing

Like Julia Cameron's Artist Dates which we discussed in the context of our artistic/creative dimension in Chapter 7, we can design Culture Dates to nourish our cultural dimension *and* deepen our cultural humility. We can do this right in our own communities if transport to a different city, state, or country is not realistic. Choose a location or destination in which you can explore food, fashion, architecture, cartography, films, books, art, or rituals that are different from your everyday experience. Consider activating the six mechanisms we discussed in this chapter:

- Immersion—give yourself time away from your daily obligations to soak up the experience, letting your senses and emotions stir, noticing and savoring any moments of awe
- Embeddedness and acquisition—notice whether you are acquiring, learning, or practicing new knowledge or skills; consider how the experience is enriching your persona or helping you make sense of your role (or the role you would like to have) in the world
- Socialization—pay attention to positive emotions you experience in your encounters with other human beings
- Reflection—carve out some time to reflect on the experience; observe emotions that emerge; note any learnings
- Expression—consider sharing your reflections, for example, through conversations, writing, art

RESOURCES FOR CULTURAL HUMILITY EDUCATION

Many helpful educational resources and programs exist for us to nurture our cultural humility. Here is a nonexhaustive list to get us started.

- Microaggression worksheet: https://academicaffairs.ucsc.edu/events/documents/Microaggressions_Examples_Arial_2014_11_12.pdf
- Anti-racism education resources:
    - https://www.bridgew.edu/racial-justice/resources
    - Reading resource list: https://blog.fracturedatlas.org/resources-for-white-people-to-learn-and-talk-about-race-and-racism-5b207fff4fc7

- LGBTQ education resources:
    - https://www.youtube.com/watch?v=XEKqnVyroBk
    - Reading resource list: https://www.glaad.org/resourcelist
    - Trevor project resource guide: https://www.thetrevorproject.org/resources/black-and-lgbtq-approaching-intersectional-conversations/
    - https://unerased.org/ (mission: "putting LGBTQ history in its rightful place—the classroom")
- Disability education resources: https://projectlets.org/disability-justice
- Communication resources:
    - Vernā A. Myers, *What If I Say the Wrong Thing? 26 Habits for Culturally Effective People* (Chicago: ABA Publishing, 2013).
    - Marshall B. Rosenberg, *Nonviolent Communication: A Language of Life* (Encinitas: PuddleDancer Press, 2015).

As we engage in our cultural humility education, we also might structure opportunities to practice constructivist listening and perspective-giving/perspective-taking to learn from individuals with backgrounds different from ours—for example, in activities like Exercises #2 and #3 suggested at the end of Chapter 8 (in the context of our social well-being dimension).

You can't use an old map to explore a new world.

Albert Einstein

Chapter 10

Our Spiritual Dimension

Spirituality lies in what you do and how you do it and not what result you get.

Kapil Dev

In this chapter, we will explore:

- Meaning
- Transcendence
- Purpose

Growing up as the daughter of an Episcopal minister, my adolescent life revolved around church. Multiple services on Sundays and weekdays, summer vacation Bible schools, mountain spiritual retreats. When I went off to college and began meeting and dating guys who weren't raised in religious households, I struggled to figure out my identity. I tried to keep my feet in both worlds—religious and secular—but my church-going dwindled, to the extreme displeasure of my parents. Over the years, we've had many difficult conversations about our differences in approaches toward organized religion. This tension has often left me (and likely them, as well) feeling alienated. At times, I've felt *unsafe*, not physically, but emotionally. I grapple with misplaced shame. I'm happy that the pandemic brought my parents and me much closer together; though physically and geographically separated, we became more spiritually connected through weekly dialogues on Zoom, and vastly improved the openness of our communication flow. We've taken the time to *listen* to how we individually define spirituality.

I think it's interesting, and notable, that the Task Force on Lawyer Well-Being included spiritual well-being as a dimension for us to examine as members of the legal profession. Distinct from (or perhaps supplemental to) practicing a particular religion, here we can explore what *spirituality* means to each of us.

The Oxford English Dictionary defines *spiritual* as "relating to or affecting the human spirit or soul as opposed to material or physical things."[1034] I like the Task Force's definition: "Developing a sense of meaningfulness and purpose in all aspects of life."[1035]

What does *spiritual* mean to you? Have you ever had those moments when the world seems to stand still for a second and you feel both huge and small in the expanse of the universe at the same time? Have you felt an overwhelming sense of joy that had nothing to do with a physical possession, or another human, but just your connection with nature, the ocean, a mountain, a sunset or sunrise, something bigger than you? Where were you? What were you doing? What was around you?

In early September 2001, I sat on the balcony of a hotel called Homeric Poems in Santorini, Greece. A fierce wind whipped strands of my hair against my cheeks. Wrapped in a blanket, I stared at the dark Aegean Sea, finally feeling the vise of guilt, shame, and fear beginning to loosen its grip on my heart and lungs. A week earlier, I had traveled to Greece as part of what I thought would be a short mental health leave from my law firm in Tower Two of the World Trade Center. Processing the finality of my divorce, I needed a break to figure out a new life plan.

I will never forget sitting on that balcony, breathing in the salt air, each strong gust of wind seeming to lash away strata of pain and regret. I felt like the universe, God, nature, every force greater than me, was enveloping me in care, whispering, *You are absolutely going to be okay, I promise.* The next day, I flew to Athens, spent the night in the Athens airport, flew to Frankfurt, and boarded a Lufthansa plane bound for the United States. A few hours into the flight, our pilot diverted the plane to Gander, Newfoundland, Canada.

9/11 happened during my flight home.

I was tremendously lucky that my visceral and urgent need to tend to my well-being for the first time in my life—prompting the leave of absence from my law firm job—kept me out of the towers that day. I was profoundly fortunate to be on a different plane that day.

When I ponder what spirituality means to me, I think of that moment on that balcony in Greece when I felt loved and taken care of, even though I was totally alone. Even though my world had imploded and I had no clue yet how to put it back together, I felt for the first time that I was going to be okay, that I would live again. When our collective world fell apart two days later, I couldn't stop thinking about that wind.

As we dive into our spiritual dimension, let's investigate sources of **meaning** in our lawyering and personal lives. *Meaning* serves as the M in positive psychology's PERMA construct; Seligman defines meaning as "belonging to and serving something that you believe is bigger than the self."[1036] The VIA Institute on Character provides a framework for exploring character strengths that can help us cultivate *meaning*. One of the six virtues identified by the VIA Institute is **transcendence—**finding meaning through connecting with something greater than ourselves.[1037] The character strengths housed within the virtue of transcendence include:[1038]

- **Appreciation of beauty and excellence:** perhaps we marvel at something or someone that is physically or tangibly beautiful to us (a piece of art, a person, a song), or a skill (an amazing performance by an Olympic athlete or a friend who plays the piano), or a demonstration of moral beauty (an act of giving)
- **Gratitude:** being thankful, showing appreciation
- **Hope:** being optimistic and buoyant about the future
- **Humor:** being cheerful, amused, amusing, lighthearted
- **Spirituality:** believing that there are aspects of life that are beyond our comprehension but which we can treasure, revere, and hold sacred

As we explore our spiritual dimension, let's consider opportunities to activate these character strengths in our daily lives.

Reminder: A book by Ryan Niemiec and Robert E. McGrath, called *The Power of Character Strengths: Appreciate and Ignite Your Positive Personality*, describes each of the twenty-four strengths and offers reflection exercises and activities to nurture each one.

MINING OUR LIVES FOR MEANING

Dr. Isaac Prilleltensky, a funny and brilliant teacher and writer, and one of the lecturers in my positive psychology program at Penn, says that true, sustainable well-being requires a strong sense of *meaning* and *mattering*.[1039] He defines meaning as "devotion to a worthy cause" and "making a difference in the world through passion, devotion, dedication, achievement, and commitment to a set of values and beliefs."[1040] He defines mattering as "feeling that we count, that we are important, and that we can make a difference."[1041] While we'll focus more on *mattering* when we study our occupational dimension in Chapter 11, let's explore what gives our lives *meaning*, here in our spiritual dimension.

Chapter 7, which focuses on our artistic/creative dimension, mentions four channels offered by Smith in her book, *The Power of Meaning: Finding*

Fulfillment in a World Obsessed with Happiness, for understanding what infuses our lives with meaning:[1042]

- **Belonging:** feeling connected to others
- **Purpose:** contributing to the world
- **Storytelling:** placing past experiences in context through crafting a life narrative
- **Transcendence:** stepping into a world beyond ourselves

Belonging

Regarding a sense of belonging, Smith says that each of us "need[s] to feel understood, recognized, and affirmed" by the people with whom we spend time.[1043] This happens when we cultivate relationships based on mutual care and which are characterized by frequent positive interactions; in this type of relationship, each person "feels loved and valued by the other."[1044] Smith cautions that "social exclusion . . . is a threat to meaning."[1045] This brings to mind Fredrickson's concept of *positivity resonance,* when two individuals generate and augment positive energy in one another through three intertwined actions: a two-way exchange of positive emotions (warmth and openness); synchronous moments (mirroring one another's behavior, such as smiles, body language, and other verbal and nonverbal expressions); and mutual investment in one another's well-being.[1046]

Who in our lives helps us feel understood, recognized, and affirmed? Who do *we* help feel understood, recognized, and affirmed? With whom do we feel a sense of belonging? With whom do we feel a sense of safety to be ourselves, safe enough to take risks and embark on self-discovery adventures? How do these individuals contribute to our broader understanding of our purpose in our lives?

Purpose

Purpose, Smith says, "is a goal toward which we are always working" through which we make "a contribution to the world."[1047] Psychologists Dr. Todd Kashdan and Dr. Patrick McKnight describe purpose as "a predominant theme of a person's identity."[1048] Interestingly, they state that "a purpose cannot be achieved"; rather, our purpose is a set of "continual targets," driving us "to dedicate resources in particular directions and toward particular goals and not others."[1049] I love this notion that our purpose is not actually an ascertainable end target, but rather a set of constantly updating new aims and objectives. (This reminds me of the definition of cultural humility from Chapter 9—that learning about other cultures is a lifelong pursuit, not an accolade we can achieve or for which we can check a box of finality. This also reminds me of our gritty deliberate practice; we articulate overarching goals, but on a day-to-day basis, we work on sub-goals that move us along a life continuum toward the broader objectives.)

Kashdan and McKnight describe how purpose offers us a supportive frame for the "big picture" of our life. They encourage, "It is easier to confront long lasting, difficult challenges with the knowledge that there is a larger mission in the background."[1050]

To tap into our true purpose, let's channel our friend Socrates again and engage in self-reflection.[1051] Let's take the time to unearth our authentic selves and figure out what we want our life's purpose to be.[1052] How do we want to contribute to the world? How would we most like to connect with something larger than ourselves?

In one of my positive psychology courses at Penn called Introduction to Positive Psychology, Seligman and his assistant instructors asked us to craft a ten-word purpose statement. I hemmed and hawed, and ultimately wrote: *Inspire vulnerability, authenticity, courage, perseverance, adventure through writing, teaching, traveling.* Later, I wrote another one: *Introverted writer, traveler, novice boxer, U2 fanatic, Italian language student.* What adjectives, nouns, or action verbs might your ten-word purpose statement include?

Personal Narrative and Storytelling

Of Smith's four pillars of meaning, storytelling is my favorite. Smith talks about how French philosopher and author Albert Camus's source of meaning was his writing.[1053] (I can relate!) Smith explains how storytelling—journaling, writing, talking about our life experiences perhaps through the spoken word or even through a simple medium like our Instagram posts—helps us connect the dots of our life events.[1054] By paying attention to and noticing patterns and links, we can gain profound insights and lessons about who we are, who we want to be, and the persons, things, and experiences that stir meaning in our lives. When we piece together pivotal life events through personal narrative, the meaning and purpose of our existence can emerge like holograms. We might finally observe shapes, themes, and threads that illuminate how we want to spend the next year, five years, ten years of our lives.

Transcendence

The final pillar of Smith's meaning framework is transcendence.[1055] We touch on the concept of transcendence in our discussion of the emotion of awe in Chapter 6, and our contemplation of the hive switch in Chapter 8. Smith describes transcendence as moments when we experience "the abject humility [of realizing] we are nothing but tiny flecks in a vast and incomprehensible universe" but at the same time, we become filled "with a deep and powerful sense of meaning."[1056] When we intentionally step into transcendent experiences—whether through nature, music, art, peaceful protests, literature—we let go of our intense self-focus and feel connected to humanity and the world.[1057]

This is why I love the emotion of awe. As Smith (and psychologists such as Haidt[1058] and Fredrickson[1059]) explains, awe moments occur when we encounter a grandness or vastness that rattles our existing mental models. Our brains and minds are jolted into sifting and synthesizing this new information and innovating new mental frameworks. We are nudged, or forced, to reconfigure our understanding of the world and our role in it (and the role we *want* to have in it).[1060] Awe shocks our systems out of complacency and doldrums.

When did you last feel a sense of *awe*? Remember that awe can be a confusing sensation combining positive emotions with less pleasant ones (like fear, loneliness, worry). That's okay. We can learn to discern, feel, and synthesize both.

When I step into encounters with nature that feel a tad dangerous, a sense of awe begins to ripple through me. One day while working on this book manuscript in Tenerife, I woke up to canaries chirping outside my window. I brewed a pot of coffee and opened the sliding glass doors dividing my writing room and a terrace. Lizards scooted along the stones. I wrote my three Morning Pages, hunkered down to write for my two-hour daily quota, and then prepped myself for a driving adventure in my rental car.

I maneuvered the stick-shift Citroën through the gated entryway to the property of the house I rented, peered both ways up and down the one-lane serpentine street, shifted the car into first gear, and prayed I would not encounter another vehicle before I veered onto a larger two-lane road. Translating the Spanish road signs, I drove to the Anaga Forest, a protected biosphere with beautiful mossy tree canopies. The roads twisted and curved; I downshifted and upshifted. Eventually, sunshine and blue sky broke through the treetops. I pulled the car into a small half-moon lookout area on the side of the road. A gasoline truck careened around the bend, honking hello before disappearing in a blur. I checked the parking brake on the car three times, then opened the door. The smell of eucalyptus trees enveloped me. I gazed toward the Atlantic Ocean below. I observed how the twisty road descended down, down, down toward volcanic lava formations and black-sand beaches. I hesitated. To get down to sea level would require me to continue guiding the car around countless switchbacks in the road. Eventually, to get home, I'd need to do the whole thing again in reverse.

I stared at the miles of hills covered in yellow and green vegetation. Pillows of fog hung over knoll after knoll. Whitecapped waves smacked against volcanic rocks far, far below. In that moment, I felt tiny, but also like I wanted every person I'd ever met to experience this view. I felt awe. I was scared to get back in the car, nervous that one slip of my foot would send the Citroën plummeting through the flimsy guard rail. I took one last whiff of eucalyptus. *Keep going. You've got this. And you've got colossal things to accomplish in this life.*

What inspires us to keep going in our personal and professional pursuits? What gives our lives meaning? What are we passionate about? What are we devoted, dedicated, or committed to? In what situations or circumstances do we feel part of something bigger than ourselves? And if we don't know yet, that's okay too. Psychologists Dr. Roy F. Baumeister and Dr. Kathleen D. Vohs define meaning as "an imposition of a stable conception onto a changing biological process."[1061] (This definition reminds me of allostasis: our body's ability to restore constancy or stability through change!) Our lives, including our legal careers, inevitably evolve and transform. Articulating and trying to capture what gives our lives meaning now in the present can help provide a sense of stability throughout the natural oscillation and fluctuation of our personal and professional journeys.[1062]

Baumeister and Vohs offer four pathways to guide us in designing our meaningful life's mission:[1063]

- **Purpose** (echoing one of Smith's four pillars of meaning): establishing goals for the future and crafting courses of action to move toward them
- **Values:** articulating what we *treasure* as "good" in life to help us shape such chosen courses of action
- **Efficacy:** believing we are capable of making a difference in the world through our actions, reinforcing a sense of control
- **Self-worth:** realizing we are valuable and *worthy*

It's exciting to know that, even if we are unclear about or unsure of the meaning of our lives right now, we can take the time to ponder. Each of us can find meaning through different pursuits that resonate within us as individuals. What gives my life meaning likely will be different from what infuses meaning into yours.

Dr. Michael Steger, who runs a laboratory for the study of meaning and purpose at Colorado State University, emphasizes the inner power that derives from identifying our purpose, that is, declaring long-term goals that invoke our passion, commitment, and motivation.[1064] He indicates we can tap into our purpose through *comprehension*: seeking to notice "patterns, consistency, and significance" in our life experiences, and then spending time "synthesizing and distilling" themes and motivating factors.[1065] If we devote time to contemplating the sights, sounds, aromas, interactions, experiences, and achievements that thrill, amaze, and inspire our brains, bodies, minds, and souls, we'll begin to identify what matters to us and where we want to channel the precious commodity of our energy in the future.[1066] We honor "where we've been, where we are, and where we're going."[1067]

MEANING-MAKING THROUGH WRITING

I liked reading in Smith's book about how French philosopher and author, Albert Camus, derived his meaning through writing. Writing about my difficult experiences has led me to discover the meaning of my life. It started with *storytelling* (one of Smith's four pillars of meaning).

When I was going through my rough times in my early thirties, I felt compelled to write. I couldn't *not* write. I had so much pain inside me, it needed to bubble out somewhere. Pen, paper, journals, and my laptop offered the best troughs imaginable for capturing and distilling an overwhelming tsunami of emotions. First, shame, guilt, grief, sadness, regret spilled onto the page. But then, empowerment, authenticity, triumph surfaced. At first, I wrote for an audience of one. Telling myself my own stories helped me piece together events. Relationship patterns emerged. I began to understand myself. I started to hear my needs. I finally began to like myself, and care about myself, for the first time.

Storytelling led to savoring memories of *transcendence*. I relived moments of sheer awe: my pre-9/11 moment on that balcony in Greece; my 9/11 experience in Gander, Newfoundland; travel adventures; rock concerts. Exhuming the unpretty truths of my personal life led me to write about my struggles as a law student and lawyer, eventually revealing my *purpose*: to write books that aim to help anxious or fearful law students and lawyers untangle pain and self-doubt so they can soar. I began to self-identify as a writer, over and above being a lawyer or law professor. I now know my purpose for the rest of my life is to write.

My purpose also has led to finally feeling a sense of *belonging*: I love connecting with readers who reach out over LinkedIn, Instagram, or email, sharing stories of vulnerability and victory. This long overdue feeling of belonging has solidified my *values*: authenticity, vulnerability, humility, truthtelling, adventure, courage. I now realize I have the power to make a difference—I have *efficacy*. I finally like who I am. I know my *worth*.

Writing can unleash our superpower. It's like Vitamin C. A booster shot. For me, and *to* me, the physical act of writing is so powerful because it's like an endless current of water or wind that no one else can control or manipulate. When we write, we are the ones moving the pen across the page or pressing our unique fingerprints to laptop keys. If we write about our own experiences (even for an audience of one: ourselves), it's impossible for us to run out of material. Also, we can write wherever, whenever, however—it transcends all borders and boundaries.[1068]

Just like you may never have considered yourself an athlete or a performer or an artist, you may not (yet) consider yourself a writer. You may be feeling all sorts of resistance at the suggestion that you try to let your life's meaning and purpose emerge through writing. But Baumeister and Vohs validate that the act of writing helps us find meaning both in negative and positive life experiences.[1069] We can write to discern themes. We can write to extract humor from challenges. Or we can write simply to clear out our brain clutter, making space for meaning to bloom in other ways.

Adopting a writing practice does not have to be time consuming. I know I sound like a broken record heralding the potential impact of Julia Cameron's Morning Pages—three pages of longhand, stream-of-consciousness writing.[1070] But trust me, they work!

Cameron urges that we deem this morning ritual "non-negotiable."[1071] Mine take approximately 10 to 15 minutes max. Even if we feel we have nothing to say, it's okay to write "I have nothing to say. I have nothing to say . . ." then BOOM. *Something* that has been percolating often tumbles onto the page. Morning Pages are not elegant or eloquent. They are messy, sloppy, and real. They help unearth stressors, wishes, hopes, ideas, themes, and patterns.

I once met Cameron at a book-signing in Manhattan. I told her, "Your book saved my life." She wrote an inscription on the inside cover of my dog-eared copy of her book: *To Heidi, For your heart.* The piles of spiral-bound journals stacked on my bookshelves and under my nightstand hold decades of Morning Pages. Just this morning, I ran out of pages in my latest journal. I'm excited to go explore a bookstore or stationery shop and choose a new one.

Spirituality is not a formula; it is not a test. It is a relationship.
Spirituality is not about competency; it is about intimacy.
Spirituality is not about perfection; it is about connection.

Mike Yaconelli

Spiritual Well-Being Dimension Exercise #1
A Meaning-Making Writing Practice

Would it feel do-able to try a meaning-making writing practice for seven days to explore our spiritual dimension? As you navigate your day, try to notice moments when you tap into the character strengths situated within the virtue of transcendence:[1072]

- Appreciation of beauty and excellence
- Gratitude
- Hope
- Humor
- Spirituality

Consider exploring these strengths as you write in a journal each morning for seven days. If three pages of Julia Cameron's Morning Pages (10 to 15 minutes each morning) sounds daunting (I promise it goes by quickly!), let's start with one page each morning. Did you notice anything intensely beautiful or excellent yesterday? Are you thankful for something in particular today? What are you optimistic about for tomorrow? What made you laugh yesterday? Did you make someone else laugh? Are you feeling part of something bigger than yourself right now? Write about whatever pops into your mind—the good, the bad, the ugly, the pretty. If your mind feels blank, write, "My mind feels blank. My mind feels blank . . ." until a thought blossoms.

If you feel you might need a tad more structure, consider ordering a journal like the one called *Nude Gratitude*[1073] that my friend Lizzy Bunker created. Lizzy's journal (available on Amazon) prompts us—in one page per day—to write (1) two things we love about ourselves, (2) things/events/people/feelings we are grateful for *today*, and (3) things/events/people/feelings we are grateful for in the *future*.

Over 7 days (and hopefully longer!), notice if themes, threads, and patterns emerge. Get curious. Any stories? Nuggets of your life's meaning? Your life's purpose? In what environments do you feel a sense of belonging? Moments of awe? The lightbulb meaning moment doesn't need to happen right away. Over time, writing helps us synthesize our life experiences and gain clarity about the future we want to create for ourselves (and others).

Spiritual Well-Being Dimension Exercise #2

Discerning Themes of Meaning and Purpose

Let's use the pillars and pathways of meaning and purpose identified by Smith and Baumeister and Vohs to discern if any themes emerge.

Smith's Pillars	Baumeister and Vohs' Pathways
Belonging: When/how do we feel connected to other individuals?	**Values:** What do we treasure as "good" and "important"?
Purpose: How do we feel we contribute to others and the world?	**Purpose:** What are some of our long-term goals?
Storytelling: As we express or share our life narrative with others, do any patterns appear?	**Efficacy:** What capabilities do we possess that will enable us to achieve our long-term goals?
Transcendence: When do we feel connected to something bigger than ourselves?	**Self-Worth:** What makes us feel worthy of love and appreciation?

When you're ready, think about crafting a ten-word meaning/purpose statement like the one I was asked to construct in my master's program at Penn. What adjectives, nouns, or action verbs might your ten-word purpose statement include? Write your statement on a Post-it® and tack it to your laptop so you can look at it every day!

If you are interested in exploring the concept of meaning further, consider reading Smith's book, *The Power of Meaning.*

The meaning of life is to find your gift.
The purpose of life is to give it away.

Pablo Picasso

Chapter 11

Our Occupational Dimension

Think not of yourself as the architect of your career
but as the sculptor.
Expect to have to do a lot of hard hammering
and chiseling and scraping and polishing.

B. C. Forbes

In this chapter, we will learn about:

- Meaning, purpose, discretion, autonomy, variety, and engagement in our work
- Job v. career v. calling
- Mattering
- Occupational fitness
- Self-determination theory
- Deliberate practice and grit
- Flow and engagement

About a decade ago, on a trip to Mexico, while filling out a travel form, I paused at the box marked "Occupation." Instead of writing "lawyer" or "law professor," I wrote "writer." Doing so made me happy and feel a bit rebellious. Instead of listing the role that the institution writing my paycheck or the public uses to label or define me, I couched my occupation as the *activity* I perform every day that gives me a jolt and makes me feel most alive. I chose the occupational pursuit that I *deliberately practice* (activating my *grit*), which often leads me into a state of *flow*.

WHY DO WE WORK?

As we nurture our occupational well-being dimension, let's dig into *why* we work. Why *do* we work? Obviously, we work to earn a living. We have mouths to feed and bills to pay. We also work to finance trips, experiences, investments, charity donations, and "stuff" we "need." (Instagram really needs to stop reading my mind and sending me ads for cool exercise clothes and edgy camouflaged handbags.) Additionally, though, many of us honestly enjoy working. Why?

Dr. Barry Schwartz, a lecturer in one of my positive psychology classes, wrote a book called *Why We Work*. In his book, Schwartz points out nonmonetary reasons why we work:

- We feel like our work is meaningful (i.e., that we make a difference in other people's lives or in the world).[1074]
- When we perceive we are in control of our actions (i.e., we have a reasonable measure of autonomy and discretion in how we perform our jobs), we develop mastery and we gain expertise—which feels rewarding.[1075]
- We feel a sense of engagement that is so immersive, we periodically lose ourselves in our projects (i.e., flow).[1076]

Schwartz identifies aspects of work that, if present, are conducive to our well-being:[1077]

- We feel like we can do our best.
- Our supervisors or employers encourage us to grow, learn, and develop.
- We feel appreciated and valued.
- Our voices, opinions, and ideas matter.
- We feel like our work is important.
- We are able to foster friendships and relationships with our colleagues.

Throughout his book, Schwartz reiterates six factors that drive occupational thriving: **meaning**, **purpose**, **discretion**, **autonomy**, **variety**, and **engagement**.[1078]

Schwartz poses an interesting (long-term) question: Do we regard our work as a **job**, a **career**, or a **calling**?[1079] When we view our work as a *job*, we likely feel somewhat limited in the levels of meaning, discretion, and engagement yielded in our daily professional activities; fundamentally, we work to pay the bills.[1080] When we regard our work as a *career*, we experience increased degrees of meaning, discretion, engagement, and enjoyment, but our focus tends to be on advancement.[1081] When we ultimately are able to characterize our work as a *calling*, we feel happy and satisfied; our work forms part of our identity; we sense we make an impact.[1082] Of course, it can take time to find our calling. (It took me nearly two decades to identify as an introverted writer and teacher instead of trying to fake and force an extroverted litigator persona!) But when we eventually get there, watch out!

As we delve into our occupational well-being dimension, let's first ponder what components of our work make us feel electrified, happy, motivated, or inspired. Which aspects of our work activate our character strength of *zest* (a boost of energy, enthusiasm, and vitality when approaching tasks)?[1083] Using the National Task Force's definition of occupational well-being, what part(s) of our jobs ignites a sense of satisfaction or enriches us?[1084] At what time of day do those moments occur most often? Is it early morning? Late at night? What exactly are we doing? Are we in the physical office, or do we do our best work from home? What items surround us? What's the lighting like? How about the noise level? What are we wearing? (That's a serious question; I get much more work done in sweatpants than I ever did in my stuffy suit.) What tasks do we perform that make us feel engaged and in *flow* (the E in PERMA)? What types of projects give us a sense of achievement or accomplishment—the A in PERMA? What words would we use to describe our occupation if the terms "law student," "lawyer," "attorney," "paralegal," "court reporter," or "judge" evaporated from our vocabulary? (My hair stylist Thom describes himself as a "cranial follicular specialist.")

As a noun, *occupation* refers to our vocation or profession, yet also to "a way of spending time."[1085] As a verb, to *occupy* means to fill or take up time or space, or to seize control.[1086] In this dimension, let's ask ourselves: how do we—as individuals and workers—want to fill space in a room? Let's *occupy* with intention. What purpose do we want our *act* of occupying time and space to serve? Can we make internal and external shifts to occupy space and time more thoughtfully? Are there environmental factors we can change or enhance to maximize how we occupy time and space at work?

DEVELOPING A SENSE OF MATTERING IN OUR WORK

Prilleltensky wrote an article called "Wellness as Fairness" in which he identified objective and subjective indicators of occupational well-being:[1087]

- **Objective:**
  - Access to resources to perform our work
  - A clear description of our responsibilities
  - Good communication channels
  - Positive reinforcement
  - Recognition of contributions

- **Subjective:**
  - Feeling appreciated
  - Feeling engaged
  - Having a positive view of our working climate
  - Perceiving opportunities for meaning-making
  - Having a healthy and positive working relationship with our supervisors[1088]

Prilleltensky also identified indicators of lack of occupational well-being, including instances of conflict and absenteeism.

The objective and subjective indicators of well-being echo themes of support, clarity, communication, recognition, appreciation, purpose, and healthy relationships. Obviously, unless we run our own businesses, we may not have the ability to control some of these factors. But in fostering occupational well-being, we can start paying attention to what elements of our work environments energize, stimulate, and motivate us, and which do not. And then we get to discern and decide what we can change for the better.

Prilleltensky teaches that well-being requires a sense of both meaning *and* mattering. We explored *meaning-making* in the context of nurturing our spiritual dimension in Chapter 10. Let's delve into *mattering* now as we cultivate our occupational dimension.

Prilleltensky says mattering is about "*feeling* valued and *adding* value."[1089] He notes that "mattering is a fundamental psychological need."[1090] Mattering involves *recognition* from others and *impact* on others.[1091] It requires a balance of self-affirmation and (healthy doses of) external validation. It derives from having voice, choice, and respect.[1092]

In What Environments Do We *Feel* Valued?

To gauge whether we *feel* valued, Prilleltensky prompts us to ask ourselves two questions:

- Am I appreciated, respected, and recognized?
- Do I feel a sense of belonging, inclusion, and fairness?[1093]

Prilleltensky warns that "[j]ust as belonging is a powerful tonic for well-being, exclusion is toxic for health."[1094] Prilleltensky says that when we do not feel valued, we default to either a sense of invisibility or entitlement, helplessness or ruthlessness.[1095]

What is your default emotion or behavior when your sense of *mattering* or feeling valued at work is challenged? Invisibility? Or entitlement? Helplessness? Or ruthlessness? I lean toward invisibility—feeling unseen or ignored. Interestingly though, my self-protection response is not helplessness; in this context, I veer toward ruthlessness (*fight*, not flight or freeze).

In What Environments Do We *Add* Value?

To assess how we *add* value, Prilleltensky encourages us to consider five questions:

- Do I make a contribution or difference?
- Do I exercise my skills when presented with opportunities?
- Do I feel a sense of empowerment, autonomy, control over my life, mastery, self-efficacy (ability to handle tasks), and self-determination?
- Do I have voice and visibility?
- Am I physically and psychologically present when I am performing my work?[1096]

A lack of a sense of mattering for us at work can lead to personal devaluation, disconnection in relationships, disengagement, and, on a broader level, disintegration of communities.[1097] What can we do about this? First, Prilleltensky suggests we consider the concept of occupational fitness.[1098]

OCCUPATIONAL FITNESS

In Chapter 5, we explore *fitness* from the perspective of bolstering our physicality to practice law, learning how to toggle into eustress and hormesis, optimizing our allostatic load. Prilleltensky invites us to think about fitness in terms of occupational fit. He defines a "good person-environment fit" as a space in which our needs are met and we can flourish and thrive.[1099] He says "[a] good fit builds on people's strengths."[1100]

Channeling Socrates, let's continue getting to know ourselves with the aim of seeking and cultivating work dynamics that *fit* our strengths, talents, personalities, values, and dreams.[1101] Prilleltensky encourages, "A good fit between your temperament, preferences, and environment is a wonderful thing."[1102] A sound occupational fit enhances our engagement and creativity—our industrious spark.[1103] It's important for us to find and seek to foster work environments in which we have healthy doses of recognition for our efforts and "opportunities for growth and flow."[1104] Work cultures that encourage individual and collective progress—that "study their processes, reflect on their mission, and offer instrumental and emotional support"—help workers tap into occupational fit.[1105]

Tending to our occupational fitness, this is another great opportunity to review our character strengths identified in the VIA Survey. (See Exercise #1 in Chapter 3.) Which of our signature strengths connect to the work activities we perform each day? What aspects of our work contribute to the purpose statement we crafted in Exercise #2 at the end of Chapter 10 (our spiritual dimension)?

Daily Work Activities	**Character Strengths (from Exercise #1 in Chapter 3)**	**Words in Our 10-Word Purpose Statement (Exercise #2 in Chapter 10)**

SELF-DETERMINATION: UNDERSTANDING OUR NEED TO FEEL A SENSE OF COMPETENCE, AUTONOMY, AND RELATEDNESS AT WORK

Psychologists Dr. Richard M. Ryan and Dr. Edward L. Deci developed an approach to well-being called **self-determination theory.**[1106] They identify three psychological needs each of us possesses:

- **Competence:** knowledge that we can handle tasks and our environment, and that we can direct outcomes
- **Autonomy:** a sense that we have the power to make choices and exercise control
- **Relatedness:** a feeling of meaningful connection to other human beings[1107]

As we cultivate our occupational well-being, let's assess how we fare with these three basic needs in our work environments.

Enhancing Our Sense of Competence

In our discussion of the stress-eustress-distress continuum in Chapter 5, we learned that the key to stepping into and lingering in productive eustress rather than catapulting into distress is remembering that we have the coping mechanisms to deal with stimuli in our environment. There were many times during my years of law practice that I worried about my level of competence—on the substantive level, but more urgently, on the mental, emotional, and physical levels—to handle particular lawyering scenarios. As law students and lawyers, we can hone our substantive, procedural, and logistical skills—enhancing our occupational and intellectual competence—through engaging in *deliberate practice* of various lawyering techniques. Our deliberate practice reflects our *grit* to achieve our long-term professional and personal goals. Further, the work we are doing here to nurture multiple dimensions of our well-being can bolster our sense of mental, emotional, and physical competence to handle lawyering challenges.

If our employers (or law schools) are not offering or encouraging competence training to the degree or in the occupational areas we need it, let's request it or seek it out. Schwartz cites an alarming statistic that, in the automobile industry for example, Japan invests an average of 364 hours in training new hires, compared with Europe's 178 hours, and the United States' paltry 21 hours.[1108] In the legal realm, let's amp up our multi-dimensional competence by enrolling in workshops, continuing legal education courses, and seminars on various lawyering skills and substantive topics. If a training opportunity does not seem to exist on a skill set we seek to obtain, let's create one. Further, let's keep diving into cultivating our ten well-being dimensions as part of our prehabilitation program.

Fostering Our Sense of Autonomy

Schwartz writes about the importance of having a reasonable measure of discretion in how we do our jobs.[1109] Anne Brafford (editor-in-chief of the National Task Force report, and a fellow graduate of Penn's MAPP program) asserts that "autonomy fuels well-being."[1110] Psychology experts define autonomy as "a sense of being self-governed and of being able to engage in volitional behaviors that are congruent with one's true beliefs, values and interests."[1111] Law professor Larry Krieger wrote, "Autonomy support is defined as a person's sense that she is *respected for her needs and preferences rather than controlled* regardless of her needs and preferences."[1112] In contrast, "[a] high level of responsibility with little control is a toxic combination that often characterizes junior attorneys' work."[1113] Brafford candidly shares memories of her own lawyering experience: "[W]hen I was practicing law, things that brought me to the brink of quitting on so many occasions were most often related to leaders infringing on my autonomy and triggering feelings of disrespect. I have fat catalogues of examples."[1114] I can relate.

In one law firm where I worked, the glaring fluorescent light over my desk gave me migraines. It buzzed all day and night. Also, the constant noise of partners vociferously debating nuances of case strategy in the hallway just outside my office door made it nearly impossible for me to concentrate. My introverted brain needs quietude to function at its peak. One day, I finally asked the maintenance team to please disconnect the fluorescent bulbs in the ceiling over my desk. I brought a lamp from home and placed it on my desk. I closed my office door. I wrote better briefs. My productivity increased exponentially. But the dim lighting and closed office door infuriated one of the partners. He wanted to be able to see his employees cranking away. It didn't seem to matter to him what I needed in order to do my best work.

Of course, law students and novice attorneys need a reasonable level of supervision and guidance, and often, we'll obviously need to defer to schedules, deadlines, expectations, and preferences imposed by decision makers and other people in positions of authority and who bear responsibility for outcomes.

However, we all need to have a sensible measure of control over our working style and methods (and our personal lives, for that matter).[1115] Brafford advocates that supervisors should afford junior attorneys "as much independence and discretion as lawyers' level of experience and competence allow."[1116]

As a junior associate, it was not the long hours that took a toll on me; I actually loved the substantive work, researching, writing, and reviewing documents and strategizing about our cases. It was the utter lack of control over my schedule. I never knew whether the senior partner would stop by my office thirty seconds after I finally decided to go home to tend to my disintegrating marriage, or whether he would decree at the eleventh hour that he wanted something done or written by the next morning. It also became nearly impossible to plan vacations, for fear I would have to cancel at the last minute and irritate my travel partners. As Brafford notes, "poor supervisor support" and "lack of autonomy" can be worse than "excessive hours."[1117]

How can we construct healthy quantities of discretion and autonomy? Perhaps the third component of self-determination theory offers a key: relatedness. We can work on communicating with our teammates, colleagues, and supervisors about how we deliver our best work, and what a reasonable extent of control looks like for each of us. We can endeavor to identify and articulate—in a respectful way—the environment and parameters in which we perform at our peak. We can discuss—out loud—our individual zones of optimal functioning, our IZOF.

I completely understand supervising attorneys' desire for "face-time"—seeing junior attorneys and legal support staff physically in the office. However, it's important for us also to acknowledge that many of us deliver much higher levels of performance if we can curate working environments that are conducive to our optimal functioning. As an introvert (who lives alone), I can be incredibly productive working at home in my exercise clothes, surrounded by all my favorite possessions, lights off, not a single sound other than the occasional New York City ambulance siren in the distance. I'm motivated, inspired, driven. I don't stop writing, creating, strategizing, organizing until I look up from my laptop and realize that hours have passed and I really need to give my brain and body a break and go outside for a run. But, on the days that I need to go to the office, or answer nonstop phone calls, or "hop on a Zoom" every other hour, my productivity plummets. I'm not saying we introverts should all be able to work in solitude forever, and I certainly recognize that not everyone is productive at home, but it's important for employers to understand differences in working styles and make space for diverse preferences that will lead to enhanced collective performance, productivity, and positive emotions toward our work.

SETTING (REASONABLE) BOUNDARIES TO HELP PREVENT OCCUPATIONAL BURNOUT

In an article entitled, "The Enlightened Lawyer," Dr. Geralyn Datz explains that the erosion of boundaries that normally would protect our personal, relational, and spiritual lives from being overrun by work intrusions can tax our well-being, resulting in burnout.[1118] She defines burnout as "a state of overwhelming, long-term exhaustion and diminished interest in work."[1119] Similarly, John Hollway, Associate Dean and Executive Director of the Quattrone Center for the Fair Administration of Justice at the University of Pennsylvania Carey Law School, defines burnout as "a toxic blend of physical and emotional exhaustion, cynicism, and a lack of control or ability to change things."[1120]

Datz highlights two antidotes to burnout:

- Reasonable down time away from the stress of work
- Engagement within our work

She urges:

> *In the same way that we need air, water, and food to survive, our minds need certain conditions to feel as if we have accomplished something, that we have a purpose, that we are loved and understood, and that we have "down" time away from intense stress. When we do not have these, we become out of balance. When we are out of balance, we often try to create balance in ways that will never achieve it.*[1121]

Datz and Hollway both point out that the polar opposite of burnout is engagement (the E in PERMA!).[1122] Datz defines engagement as "the state of feeling energized, effective, and connected to one's life, career, and surroundings."[1123] Likewise, Hollway explains:

> *Where burnout is cynical, exhausted, and overwhelmed, engagement is energetic, dedicated, and absorbed. Engaged lawyers have a sense of pride in their work and their organization, and puff out their chests a little when they say where they work.*[1124]

What activities make you feel most engaged at work? What activities drain your energy? What environmental conditions contribute to your engagement, and which ones sap it?

ACTIVATING GRIT AND FLOW IN OUR WORK

Considering how to help more individuals tap into *flow*, Csikszentmihalyi wrote:

> *Perhaps the most powerful effect flow theory could have in the public sector is in providing a blueprint for how institutions may be reformed so as to make them more conducive to optimal experience.*[1125]

Our legal academic and training environments certainly could use such a blueprint, to construct occupational frameworks that first *teach* how flow works, and then help more individuals tap into flow to optimize engagement with our work, ultimately enhancing performance. However, in the meantime, let's ponder how to foster our own flow to enhance our occupational well-being.

Remember that in Chapter 4, we investigated the interplay between *deliberate practice* (an element of our *grit*—defined by Duckworth and her colleagues as perseverance and passion for long-term goals[1126]) and *flow*. As a starting point, let's consider the character strengths that fall into the virtue category of *courage*—defined as the exercise of will to accomplish goals—identified by the VIA Institute on Character:

- **Bravery**: treasuring a goal or belief and taking action on it even in the face of challenges
- **Perseverance**: organizing oneself to strive toward identified goals and continuing to pursue such objectives even when encountering obstacles
- **Honesty**: exhibiting genuineness, sincerity, and integrity; assuming responsibility for our thoughts, emotions, and behavior
- **Zest**: enthusiastically jumping into projects, situations, and life

Zest is my personal favorite (and one of my top five signature strengths). Let's get zesty together!

Remember from Chapter 4 that a flow state involves nine components:[1127]

- A balance between the present challenge and our skill level
- A clear goal for the activity or work session
- A sense of control over the interim steps needed to accomplish the task
- Unambiguous and immediate feedback (self-generated or external)
- An ability to tune out the world and concentrate on the task at hand

- A melting away of boundaries between action and awareness
- A loss of self-consciousness or self-judgment
- Transformation of time
- An "autotelic" experience, that is, the activity serves a purpose in itself (and does not require an external reward to feel worthwhile)

To cultivate our occupational dimension (and ideally, to foster flow more often in our work and personal lives), let's start by paying closer attention to circumstances in which challenges and skills shift into alignment and equilibrium. Conversely, let's identify which challenges currently exceed our skill level. Let's notice the internal and environmental conditions that enable us to enter a state of flow, and those that disrupt or impede flow. Can we adjust such conditions to foster flow more regularly?

When a specific challenge exceeds our degree of skill, let's activate our *grit.*[1128] Let's step into *deliberate practice.* Remember that deliberate practice involves five elements:

- We deconstruct larger performance goals into smaller components
- We select one stretch sub-goal at a time
- We invest focused attention and effort on sub-goal tasks
- We welcome feedback
- Then we repeat the sequence[1129]

Through deliberate practice, we improve our skills. Challenge and skill will meet in equipoise again; then we can notice if we have experienced flow. Eventually, new challenges will present themselves, requiring us to attain new or more sophisticated skills. Grit. Deliberate practice. Flow. Repeat.

> *We are what we repeatedly do. Excellence, then, is not an act, but a habit.*
>
> Aristotle

Occupational Well-Being Dimension Exercise #1

Let's Occupy Our Occupational Dimension with Intention

How do we want to occupy space in our work?

Right now, is your work: • a **job**: not a ton of discretion, engagement, or meaning—primarily focused on earning an income? • a **career**: a bit more discretion, engagement, and meaning—currently aspiring toward advancement? • a **calling**: lots of discretion, engagement, and meaning—intertwined with self-identity?[1130] ***Note: It's okay if right now your work is a job. It can take time to find our calling.*	
Feeling **valued** (a component of mattering):[1131] • Do you have a voice at work? Is your voice heard? • Do supervisors recognize your contribution(s)? • Do you feel appreciated?	
Adding **value** (a component of mattering): • Take a look at the 10-word purpose statement you created in Exercise #2 in Chapter 10 (our spiritual dimension). • Does your work tie into what gives your life **meaning**? How? Why? Do you feel you impact the lives of others? • What is your work's (long-term) **purpose**?	
Tapping into **flow**: • At work, do you ever lose sense of time and space when you are performing a task you enjoy (even, or especially, if the task is difficult)? In other words, is there ever a time at work when you feel completely "in the zone" and the outside world just seems to temporarily disappear? If so, what are you doing? • How does it feel when you're in your "zone"? • What are the environmental conditions around you (What time of day is it? Where are you located? What sounds (if any) do you hear? What's the lighting like?)	

• What skills are you deploying to meet the present challenge? • How are you deriving instant feedback to motivate you to keep going? (Feedback can be internal, an inner recognition that you are doing a good job or making progress. Feedback does not need to come from an external source during a flow state.) • Is the activity enjoyable in itself, regardless of any external rewards? Why?	
Nurturing our **competence** (skills to meet challenges): • What skills would you like to develop further (these could be intellectual, substantive, procedural, logistical, mental, emotional, physical, social)? • At work, are you encouraged to grow and evolve? • What resources can you access to develop competence in identified areas of potential growth? • Can you exercise **grit** (perseverance and passion for long-term goals) and establish a **deliberate practice** (like a **prehabilitation** program!) to enhance competence in particular skills?	
Nurturing our **discretion, autonomy, and control**: • Do you have a reasonable degree of freedom in how you perform your work? • Are there aspects of your work in which you would prefer more discretion, autonomy, and control? • If you feel limited in your discretion, autonomy, and control, does this affect your emotional or physical well-being (or other well-being dimensions)? How? • Can you (respectfully and reasonably) articulate to your supervisors or mentors what conditions might help you feel more in control of your actions—so you can perform more optimally? Perhaps you can identify your character strengths (Chapter 3) and (using positive communication channels discussed in Chapter 8) share how you might deploy them more often in your day-to-day work. • Can you experiment with identifying your IZOF and (respectfully and reasonably) explore with supervisors or mentors how to step into your IZOF more often? (See Chapter 5 for an explanation of IZOF.)	

Fostering **relatedness**: • Are you able to connect with coworkers, colleagues, supervisors, and clients in a healthy and meaningful way? • Are healthy communication channels present in your work environment? • Can you respectfully and reasonably explore ways to enhance communication channels? (See Chapter 8 for a discussion of active-constructive responding, constructivist listening, and perspective-giving and perspective-taking.) • Do you seek and receive clear guidance regarding expectations for your work? • Do you seek and receive helpful feedback?	

We can use these prompts to highlight strengths of our occupational well-being dimension and identify areas for growth. As we hone our communication skills (perhaps through cultivating our social dimension in Chapter 8), we can engage in healthy dialogue with colleagues, coworkers, mentors, and supervisors about how to foster conditions that will help all of us thrive occupationally.

Inspired by the work of the Center for Positive Organizations, three professors (Justin M. Berg, Jane E. Dutton, and Amy Wrzesniewski) developed a "Job Crafting Exercise," available for a fee at www.jobcrafting.com. The exercise encourages us to articulate our values, strengths, and passions and consider how we might adjust our approach to work tasks, our interactions with other people, and the way we think about our work—to align with our authentically powerful selves.

If you ask me what I came to do in this world,
I, an artist, will answer you:
I am here to live out loud.

Émile Zola

CHAPTER 12

Our Intellectual Dimension

Inspiration pushes me out of my tight intellectual comfort zone
and into humility, the wonderous state of not knowing.
From this place of zero, limitless possibilities seem to arise.

Sharon Gannon

In this chapter, we will learn a bit about:

- Intellectual humility
- Metacognition
- Critical thinking

In cultivating our intellectual dimension, let's channel Socrates yet again—in two ways. First, let's emulate his intellectual humility. Remember, Socrates didn't walk around Athens acting like he knew it all or was the smartest person in the city square. On the contrary, he constantly sought to learn and discover. Second, let's continue embracing his call to action to "know thyself."

LET'S BE INTELLECTUALLY HUMBLE SO WE CAN BE INTELLECTUAL ROCKSTARS

When I first started teaching law, I thought I had to know the answer to every student's question in the heat of the moment in the classroom or they would think I was a giant professorial fraud and demand their tuition money back. But to be honest, students periodically stumped me; they asked awesome questions about nuances of the law I had never encountered in two decades of law practice, often because their queries addressed aspects of criminal procedure (and I only handled civil cases) or involved "cases of first impression" due to ever-developing areas of law like social media, for example. After a couple months of fumbling answers (my face flushing with a fiery blush), I changed tactics and started saying out loud, "Hmmm, good question. Let's look it up." Then, together as a class, we'd hop onto an electronic legal research platform and use the question as a collaborative learning exercise. I discovered that being intellectually humble in those moments, rather than pretending I knew the answer, bonded me closer to my students. We also learned more about *how* we learn.

Obviously, in many lawyering performance moments, we need to project competence, showing that we did our homework, researched appropriate statutes and cases, spent time writing high-quality legal documents, and honed our substantive and procedural strategies *before* walking into the room. But there is nothing more impressive to me than a law student, lawyer, law professor, or judge who, though clearly prepared for a legal scenario, is confident enough to say, "Hmmm, I don't know the answer to that and I need to look it up," or "I need to think about that for a minute," or "Interesting, can you tell me more?"

Conversely, it can be colossally annoying when members of our profession obviously have limited knowledge about a topic but either act like an expert, or perhaps worse, show little or no curiosity to learn from someone clearly excited and more knowledgeable about the subject matter. This scenario reminds me of the four types of dialogue responses we delved into in the context of cultivating our social dimension in Chapter 8: active-constructive responding (ACR), passive-constructive responding, active-destructive responding, and passive-destructive responding. Let's tailor ACR to intellectual engagement:

Active-constructive engagement	Expressing eagerness, enthusiasm, or delight about a subject, and actively following up with positive probing questions or reflections	Example: "That is SO interesting. I'd love to know more about that. Can you explain a bit further?"
Passive-constructive (dis)engagement	Reacting supportively but in a quiet, subdued, understated, and succinct manner, halting engagement	Example: "Nice." *Then stares at iPhone.*
Active-destructive (dis)engagement	Accentuating negative implications of the proposed subject (without having researched it); demeaning the subject	Example: "I wouldn't waste time pursuing that angle. That sounds boring/pointless/too labor-intensive."
Passive-destructive (dis)engagement	Ignoring the subject altogether; changing the subject	Example: "Ugh, my emails are blowing up today."

By adopting an intellectually humble mindset, we'll become better listeners and responders. We can attune to sparks of ideas that emerge in conversations. We can pay attention to terms, words, and phrases we don't know, and look them up or ask questions about them. We can investigate unfamiliar processes, systems, and procedures. Of course, we might discover that new ideas, concepts, or notions don't ultimately resonate with us. That's fine too. But intellectual curiosity can lead us down paths that broaden into fresh thinking and teach us lots about ourselves, other people, new subject matter, the law, and the world.

THINKING ABOUT HOW WE THINK

In understanding our intellectual dimension, let's think about how we *think*. Metacognition is the act of thinking (and learning) about our own thought processes. The president and dean of Mitchell Hamline School of Law, Anthony Niedwiecki, writes about metacognition in the context of legal education. He explains:

> *Metacognition refers to the self-monitoring by an individual of his own unique cognitive processes. Generally, metacognition refers to having both awareness and control over one's learning and thinking.*[1132]

Niedwiecki urges us to become self-regulated expert learners.[1133] We can do this by studying:[1134]

- How we learn.
- What skills we already possess and which new ones we can and should acquire.
- How to craft effective strategies to obtain the new skills we need (*this reminds me of our deliberate practice and grit!*).
- How to manage, monitor, and assess the progress of our learning.

Niedwiecki outlines two parallel metacognitive pathways: (1) enhancing our knowledge about *how* our cognitive processes work, and (2) improving how we *use* that knowledge to regulate our cognitive processes.[1135]

First, to become *knowledgeable* about our cognitive processes when we are learning something new or performing an activity that requires thinking, we can start by: (1) naming the interim steps and ultimate goal of an intellectual task, (2) paying attention to, and noticing, how and when our skills, abilities, strengths, weaknesses, learning styles, and preferences are activated in each interim step on the path toward the end goal, and (3) determining how to use such heightened awareness in a helpful way.[1136] Next, we can *regulate* our cognition through three actions:

- **Planning:** consciously choosing strategies and activating internal and external resources to accomplish the task, such as blocking out time on our calendar, removing distractions, and setting ourselves up for a session of *deliberate practice*
- **Monitoring:** paying attention—as we go—to whether we comprehend what we are doing, learning, or working on, and how our performance is going
- **Evaluating:** assessing the final outcome of the task, comparing our work product against established goals or benchmarks, and determining whether our intentional approach to learning or performance worked or whether we should adjust our planning and monitoring going forward[1137]

For a deeper dive into cognitive strategies for success in law school and practice, consider checking out my friend Professor Shailini Jandial George's book, *The Law Student's Guide to Doing Well and Being Well*, published by Carolina Academic Press.

INVESTIGATING HOW WE THINK, LEARN, AND ENGAGE

In nurturing our intellectual dimension, let's get curious about how our individual brains and minds work. Each of us likely have markedly different methods of approaching intellectual challenges and the process of learning. How do you learn best? Do you find that you process new material best by *reading* it, or *hearing* someone explain it, or *talking* about the concepts with others, or *seeing* information presented in a colorful chart, or *sketching* your own "mind map" to make sense of unfamiliar content? Are you introverted (like me) and do you perhaps need a quiet space to read, write, think, and work in peace? Or are you extroverted? Do you gain intellectual energy by bouncing ideas off colleagues or listening to music while reviewing or drafting documents?

Let's also get vulnerable and transparent about situations that hinder our learning or our ability to focus when solving problems. How do we handle ourselves when we don't know the answer to a difficult legal question? How can we cultivate or contribute to professional and personal environments in which we feel comfortable admitting what we don't know? How can we foster conditions in which continuing to learn and develop feels good, and not embarrassing, scary, overwhelming, or defeating?

Some resources that might be helpful within our "know thyself" endeavor include:

- **Learning styles or preferences:** A website called https://vark-learn.com/the-vark-questionnaire/ helps us assess whether our learning style or preference is:[1138]
  - **Verbal:** we prefer learning through written text; that is, we like absorbing information through reading and writing
  - **Visual:** graphics, maps, and charts help us process information as we learn
  - **Oral:** we learn through discussing subject matter with others
  - **Aural:** we learn by listening to and absorbing instruction
  - **Kinesthetic:** we learn by doing
  - **A combination of these styles or preferences**
- **Personality types**: A website called www.16personalities.com adapts the Myers-Briggs Type Indicator®, offering insights into our personalities and linkages to:
  - How we interact with our surroundings (**mind**)
  - How we see the world and process stimuli and information (**energy**)
  - How we make decisions and cope with emotions (**nature**)
  - How we approach work, planning, and decision-making (**tactics**)
  - How we appraise and integrate our abilities and decisions (**identity**)
- **How we "negotiate" life**: Erica Ariel Fox's book *Winning from Within*[1139] identifies four inner aspects we all have, and helps discern which one(s) tends to govern our interactions with others:
  - **Our inner dreamer**: we foster possibility, establish a definitive vision, administer direction
  - **Our inner thinker**: we clearly articulate perspectives, analyze information and data, assess and manage risks
  - **Our inner lover**: we recognize emotions, care about other people's viewpoints, prioritize managing relationships in decision-making
  - **Our inner warrior**: we initiate action, make performance happen, get things done, achieve goals and objectives

Additionally, in a team-building exercise at a fun retreat with my fellow Penn MAPP graduates, I learned about four different leadership styles framed by the National Outdoor Leadership School:

- **Analyst and architect**: we prioritize examining concepts and their meaning
- **Driver**: we embody action and direction
- **Relationship master**: we concentrate on bringing human beings together and caring for others
- **Spontaneous motivator**: we infuse emotional stimulation, energy, and passion into projects[1140]

Further, our intellectual dimension offers another great opportunity to explore different character strengths, particularly those situated within the virtue of *wisdom*—defined by the VIA Institute on Character as "cognitive strengths that entail the acquisition and use of knowledge."[1141] These character strengths include creativity, curiosity, judgment (also called critical thinking), love of learning, and perspective.[1142] Do any of these strengths appear in your signature strengths, or do they comprise middle or lower strengths that we can work on cultivating?

Ryan Niemiec and Robert E. McGrath's book, *The Power of Character Strengths: Appreciate and Ignite Your Positive Personality*, describes each of these strengths and offers reflection exercises and activities to nurture each one.

THE CHARACTER STRENGTH OF JUDGMENT OR CRITICAL THINKING

Law professors often evaluate students based on their "critical thinking skills" yet, in my opinion, we could do a better job of defining and teaching what critical thinking actually is. When we activate the character strength of judgment and critical thinking, we contemplate issues from multiple angles, question assumptions, synthesize evidence, and practice intellectual flexibility.[1143] Critical thinking is not a fixed skill we either have or don't. We absolutely can learn it, practice it, and develop it.[1144] To do so, we can engage in metacognition.

Interestingly, researchers created an assessment called the Metacognition Awareness Inventory (MAI) to help us understand our current level of awareness of our metacognitive processes, and also discern how we can grow.[1145]

Dr. Roberta Golinkoff and Dr. Kathy Hirsh-Pasek wrote a book called *Becoming Brilliant,* in which they outline four developmental levels of critical thinking skills.[1146] They point out that we don't start off—as kids—as critical thinkers.[1147] In Level 1 of our development as critical thinkers, we believe what we see and hear.[1148] However, as we mature, we begin to recognize the existence of multiple points of view on issues; we begin comparing what we see and hear.[1149] As we move into Level 2 though, we still somewhat parrot the assertions of others.[1150] As we further evolve into Level 3, developing our own ideas, we tend to over-rely on opinion rather than evidence.[1151] Finally, we enter Level 4 in which we question opinions, critique premises, and synthesize evidence.[1152] Golinkoff and Hirsh-Pasek summarize:

> *[C]ritical thinkers are open-minded and consider different points of view. Critical thinkers use evidence. They will even be open to changing their position when they learn new things.*[1153]

Professors Brett Brosseit, Elizabeth Mortenson, and Sarah Murphy wrote a book called *Applied Critical Thinking and Legal Analysis: Performance Optimization for Law Students and Professionals,* offering exercises and activities for exploring critical thinking as law students and lawyers. The book is available through Carolina Academic Press.

LET'S GET GRITTY AGAIN, AND STEP INTO DELIBERATE PRACTICE

To be intellectually humble, it's important that we set aside any pride or embarrassment about being a novice in learning new skills and stepping into unfamiliar experiences. On my trip to the Canary Islands to work on this book, I decided to start nearly every conversation with, "Lo siento, no hablo español muy bien." *I'm sorry, I don't speak Spanish very well.* I spent decades in school studying French, and I've studied Italian on my own over the past decade, but other than a few Spanish phrases I picked up from binge-watching Netflix shows set in Spain or South America throughout the pandemic, I barely speak the language. But I definitely wanted to try.

Each morning in Tenerife, I practiced basic Spanish phrases on my Duo Lingo app. At meals in local restaurants, I requested menus in Spanish instead of defaulting to English (and ultimately ate seven different versions of octopus and squid because I constantly ordered the wrong thing). Rather than stoking self-consciousness about my lack of comprehension and communication skills, language-learning added zest to my adventure. (Remember from Chapter 9 that studies show individuals can reap well-being benefits from studying new languages!) I made closer connections with strangers. Waiters helped me pronounce the words properly and laughed *with* me as we exchanged funny phrases in our native tongues. The temporary cognitive shift away from hyper-focusing on book-writing fired up new sparks in my brain.

The same thing happens in my boxing lessons. I have no choice but to admit I am a complete novice fighter. My trainer Lou teaches me the nuances of boxing physics: balance, energy conservation, power, breath, angles. I learn new terminology. I have a habit of holding my breath a lot; when I'm not getting optimal air, I overthink and become easily frustrated when I can't execute punch combinations. Lou notices. He pauses the lesson and says, "Relax for a minute. Stop trying to force things. Let's get out of your head. Just flow. Watch like an outside observer as your brain and body begin to make interesting new connections." *Metacognition.* It's fun when a new boxing maneuver finally clicks. My brain and body work in tandem as I learn. I can almost see it happening in slow motion: I re-assume boxer's stance. *Grounded and balanced. Gloves up.* At Lou's instruction, I start the next punch by rotating my hips instead of broadcasting my next move with my shoulders or fist. The momentum carries my body in the right direction. My arm is the last thing to move. *Slap-crack.* My glove hits Lou's mitt. I do it again. *Deliberate practice. Grit. Eventually, flow.*

Our intellectual dimension presents a prime opportunity to experiment with grit (perseverance and passion for long-term, high-level goals),[1154] deliberate practice, and flow. I believe that gritty people like us are not self-conscious about looking completely foolish when we set off on our trek to learn a new skill. When I speak Spanish, I'm sure I sound ridiculous. When I box, I *know* I look absurd: red-faced, sweaty, wild-eyed. But to me, our willingness to get messy as we step into deliberate practice—with intellectual humility, ready to learn—is absolutely beautiful.

In deliberate practice, each challenge posed exceeds our skill level—at first. We're intellectually humble; we practice; we train; we increase our multi-dimensional fitness; we improve; and eventually, our skill level elevates, settling into a state of equipoise with the challenge. If the conditions are right, we can enter a state of *flow.* When we emerge from a glorious state of flow, we realize, *OMG, that was amazing!* And then, because we are gritty, we don't sit back and eat red velvet cupcakes (for very long). We establish the next challenge. We identify the next skill set or level we want to achieve. We adopt our humble mindset again. We put on our gear for another round of deliberate practice.

The only true wisdom is in knowing you know nothing.

Socrates

Intellectual Well-Being Dimension Exercise #1

Let's Get Ready to . . . Humble

As part of our continuing effort to "know thyself," let's dig into some intellectual humility exploration.

Metacognition: Enhancing Our Awareness of Our Skills, Abilities, Strengths, Learning Styles, and Preferences

There are myriad ways for us to increase our awareness of our skills, abilities, strengths, learning styles, and preferences, but here are a few suggestions for getting started:

- Consider taking the free VARK Questionnaire (on learning styles or preferences) found on the www.vark-learn.com website.
- Consider taking the free NERIS Type Explorer® personalities assessment on the 16personalities.com website.
- If you haven't already, consider taking the free VIA Character Strengths Survey found on the VIA Institute on Character website—www.VIAcharacter.org—and noting where your wisdom-oriented character strengths (creativity, curiosity, judgment, love of learning, and perspective) fall in your list of twenty-four strengths.
- Consider reading Erica Ariel Fox's book *Winning from Within*,[1155] and discerning which inner aspect(s) governs your interactions with others:
    - **Inner dreamer**: we foster possibility, establish a definitive vision, administer direction
    - **Inner thinker**: we clearly articulate perspectives, analyze information and data, assess and manage risk
    - **Inner lover**: we recognize emotions, care about other people's viewpoints, prioritize managing relationships in decision-making
    - **Inner warrior**: we initiate action, make performance happen, get things done, achieve goals and objectives
- Check out the four different leadership styles framed by the National Outdoor Leadership School:[1156]
    - **Analyst and architect**: we prioritize examining concepts and their meaning
    - **Driver**: we embody action and direction
    - **Relationship master**: we concentrate on bringing human beings together and caring for others
    - **Spontaneous motivator**: we infuse emotional stimulation, energy, and passion into projects

Next, armed with this enhanced knowledge, let's explore thinking about how we *think*. The next time you initiate a work-related task or a new activity in your personal life, ponder the following as you proceed:[1157]

How much time am I going to devote to completing this task or performing this activity?	
What is the end goal of my performance of this task or activity today?	
What are the interim steps I need to take to achieve that end goal today?	
Which skills, abilities, character strengths, learning styles, and preferences can I activate while I complete this task or perform this activity?	
What "lesser strengths" (from our list of VIA character strengths) might pose a challenge to my completion or performance of this task or activity? How can I begin to nurture those strengths? **Ryan Niemiec and Robert E. McGrath's book, *The Power of Character Strengths: Appreciate and Ignite Your Positive Personality*, describes all 24 VIA character strengths and offers reflection exercises and activities to nurture each one.	
Planning: How can I plan my **deliberate practice** today to get the most out of my task completion or performance of this activity?	
Monitoring: At various intervals along the way during the task or activity, ask: • How am I doing? • What's working? • Can or should I adjust my approach? • What skills, abilities, character strengths, learning styles, and preferences am I activating?	
Evaluation: At the end of the time allotted to the task or activity, assess: • How did it go? • What worked? • What skills, abilities, character strengths, learning styles, and preferences did I activate? • What skills or strengths could I hone or research further?	

Consider taking the Metacognitive Awareness Inventory (MAI)[1158] to enhance your awareness of *your thinking process* while you complete tasks and perform activities.

Also, for practice in honing critical thinking skills, consider checking out Brett Brosseit, Elizabeth Mortenson, and Sarah Murphy's book called *Applied Critical Thinking and Legal Analysis: Performance Optimization for Law Students and Professionals*, available at Carolina Academic Press.

Intellectual Well-Being Dimension Exercise #2

Let's Double-Dip Dimensions

Throughout this self-discovery adventure, some of our well-being dimensions might begin to overlap or intertwine, especially as we *deliberately practice* new skills in each domain. For example, nurturing our physical dimension through exercise or bodily movement (Chapter 5) can generate cognitive and intellectual benefits, generating brain-derived neurotrophic factor or BDNF (which Ratey calls "Miracle-Gro for the brain"![1159]). Or, tending to our creative dimension through experimenting with art, music, or writing (in Chapter 7) might concurrently augment our emotional and spiritual well-being. Cultivating positive emotions (in our emotional dimension; Chapter 6) can broaden our peripheral vision (Fredrickson's broaden-and-build theory), opening our minds to a wider range of ideas and solutions to problems—which could then enhance our occupational, intellectual, and creative dimensions.

Over the next month, consider engaging in an activity that requires learning a new skill. Notice any positive emotions that arise. Ponder how engaging in a task situated in one well-being dimension might intertwine with another well-being dimension.

New Activity	New Skill to (Humbly) Learn?	Resulting Positive Emotion?	Does This Activity Help Enhance Another Well-Being Dimension?
Physical: A new exercise? A new type of bodily movement?			
Emotional: Engaging with self-transcendent emotions like awe or inspiration?			
Creative: Experimenting with art? Music? Writing?			
Social: A new social activity? A hive switch experience? A new communication technique or approach?			

New Activity	New Skill to (Humbly) Learn?	Resulting Positive Emotion?	Does This Activity Help Enhance Another Well-Being Dimension?
Cultural: A trip? A new language? A museum? A class? A food or type of cuisine or restaurant?			
Spiritual: An exercise in meaning-making?			
Occupational: A new work-related skill?			

Those who are best at thinking outside the box do it
not to puff themselves up,
but to see how small they really are.

Criss Jami

Chapter 13

Our Moral/Ethical Dimension

The stars don't matter. How I get there does.

P. S. Scott, *Angel Land*

In this chapter, we will learn about:

- **Six forms of justice:**
  - **Distributive**
  - **Procedural**
  - **Intrapersonal**
  - **Relational/interpersonal**
  - **Organizational**
  - **Cultural/community**
- **Virtues and character strengths that can help us navigate moral and ethical challenges**

The law might seem—on its face—as a dualism of "right" and "wrong," or "yes" and "no," or "win" and "lose." But it has an abundance of gray areas. Dilemmas posed by the gray areas can affect our well-being. Scholars distinguish morality (our *personal* set of beliefs that help us make decisions) from ethics (codes of behavior adopted and accepted by a *group* or *community*). In writing *Untangling Fear,* I spent some time digging into how fear can affect our moral and ethical decision-making. Fear of making a mistake, of disappointing a supervisor or client, of looking less than competent if we don't readily know the answer to every legal question, can take a toll on us. Unfortunately, our profession tends to perpetuate the "myth of infallibility" of the "good" lawyer. The truth is: lawyers don't know everything about everything (remember Socrates's urging that we practice intellectual humility?). We don't have all the answers at the tips of our tongues. The law is complicated—procedurally and substantively—and the right approach or solution is not always apparent from the statutes, regulations, case law, contracts, or client documents. Often, we need time to research and think before delivering an answer. Sometimes the conclusion is not what our supervisor or our client wants to hear. Despite our utmost diligence, mistakes periodically happen. In fact, even the most esteemed lawyers make mistakes.

When I was a junior attorney, I often felt adrift in a sea of uncertainty. I felt unsure about the scope and parameters of some of my high-stakes assignments. Tentative about my answers to difficult legal questions. Concerned I might miss something in my extensive research. Unclear whether some of the directives doled out by supervising attorneys were ethically sound. Hesitant about how to handle bullies and bad behavior. Indecisive about my role and purpose in the grander scheme of things. But I suppressed all those genuine and valid feelings and kept forcing myself to "fake it till I make it." Fake confidence. Fake bravado. Fake fulfillment. Fake smile. If I could go back and do it all over again, I would have allotted some time to tend to my moral and ethical dimension, and sought out help in doing so. Instead, at times I sold my soul.

Sometimes I feel like our profession assumes "good" morals and ethics are obvious. We take the required Professional Responsibility course in law school. We sit for the Multistate Professional Responsibility Exam. We're expected to know our state bars' Rules of Professional Conduct. But in real life, many of us will encounter gray areas that have the potential—if we are not paying close attention—to erode our moral and ethical well-being. Perhaps someone will seek to nudge or pressure us into cutting a slight corner, or glossing over a minor (or major) mistake, or not being entirely forthcoming with information, all under the veneer of zealous advocacy. The "little" things can add up.

Let's take some time to nurture our moral and ethical well-being dimension. Let's start by considering a concept proposed by Prilleltensky: "wellness as fairness."[1160]

"WELLNESS AS FAIRNESS"

Prilleltensky's article, "Wellness as Fairness," outlines concepts that might be helpful as we attend to our moral and ethical well-being.[1161] Prilleltensky describes six avenues of justice in our personal and professional lives:

- Distributive
- Procedural
- Intrapersonal
- Relational/interpersonal
- Organizational
- Cultural/community

Prilleltensky describes *distributive* justice as "the fair and equitable allocation of burdens and privileges, rights and responsibilities, and pains and gains in society."[1162] He suggests we consider how to balance *merit*, in which we reward individuals "based on effort and capacity," with *need*, distributing resources "based on what individuals require to survive and to thrive."[1163]

Next, he explains *procedural* justice as fostering "fair, transparent, informative, respectful, and . . . participatory decision-making processes."[1164] Procedural justice begets "trust, respect, control, and empowerment."[1165]

I love that Prilleltensky includes *intrapersonal* justice in his list, that is, justice in our relationship with ourselves.[1166] He emphasizes two prongs of intrapersonal justice: psychological and physical. We promote psychological intrapersonal justice by refraining from unduly demeaning ourselves, or deeming ourselves unworthy of love, care, and regard.[1167] We advance physical intrapersonal justice by avoiding self-injurious behavior and the infliction of undue pain and suffering on ourselves.[1168]

Interpersonal justice relates to our interactions with other people, that is, treating one another with consideration and regard.[1169] This realm calls to mind some of the interactive techniques we learned in the context of our social well-being dimension (Chapter 8)—to make more voices heard. For example, we can activate communication pathways like constructivist listening, perspective-giving and -taking, and active-constructive responding to amplify others' voices.

Regarding *organizational* justice, Prilleltensky highlights the need for informational fairness—fostering transparency in decision-making and clear communication channels—within institutions.[1170] Good communication systems help members of organizations and institutions feel included and part of the participatory process.

Finally, *cultural* and *community* justice govern interactions between and among groups.[1171] Within groups and collectives, we can strive to fuel multiple forms of justice, such as distributive, procedural, and interpersonal.

As we investigate our moral and ethical well-being dimension, let's consider how we can appropriately engender these six forms of justice in our day-to-day interactions and decision-making processes.

MORAL AND ETHICAL DECISION-MAKING APPRAISAL SCRIPTS

In my experience, one of the most difficult aspects of practicing law was grappling with identifying the right course of action when a situation made me morally or ethically uncomfortable or confused—especially as a junior attorney. It's easy for us to say in law school, or in the early years of law practice, *Oh, I'd never do that [borderline questionable act].* At several junctures in my legal practice career though, I lacked trust in my own judgment and my own voice. I let the more dominant personalities and powerful authority figures in my life dictate decisions and behavior. I wish I hadn't.

When we face situations in our professional life that stir moral or ethical discomfort or confusion, let's first practice Prilleltensky's *intrapersonal justice.* Let's promote psychological intrapersonal justice by refraining from unfairly putting ourselves down, or deeming ourselves weak or unworthy.[1172] Next, let's advance physical intrapersonal justice by avoiding self-injurious behavior that causes unwarranted internal pain and suffering.[1173]

Like the appraisal scripts we developed in the context of our physical and emotional dimensions in Chapters 5 and 6, it might be helpful to develop a personal script or a checklist of character-strength-based questions to ask ourselves when we encounter a moral or ethical challenge in our lawyering lives. (Employing a script or action-based checklist can be especially helpful when we are dealing with a strong or domineering personality, or even perhaps a bully, who is clouding our sense of clarity about which direction to take.) Instead of hemming and hawing, or letting self-doubt creep in, we can adopt and practice routines and rituals like these as part of our prehabilitation program:

- **First, we can notice our discomfort or confusion**: Instead of barreling into making a decision, we can recognize and honor mental, emotional, and physical sensations of unease or uncertainty.
- **Next, we can mentally reboot**: We can remind ourselves that we have done the work to nurture our multi-dimensional well-being and have constructed good coping systems to handle situations like these.
- **We can physically recalibrate**: We can stand or sit in a balanced athlete's or performer's stance and engage in calm breathing (using the physical techniques we learned in Chapter 5, activating our vagus nerve).
- **We can realistically, optimistically appraise**: Rather than overinflating the stakes of the situation—in our minds—to rival the Super Bowl halftime show or an Olympic performance or a life-or-death situation, we can activate a realistic and optimistic explanatory style: "This is today, not permanent," "This is one situation I can handle; this is not my entire life or career," and "This situation is not all on me, but rather I have a plethora of external resources I can access to handle it."
- **We can activate a decision-making script or a moral/ethical action checklist:** We can deploy justice-based and character-strength-based questions to work through the problem or dilemma.

- **We can ask for appropriate help from trustworthy individuals**: We can call upon others (who we view as having solid moral and ethical well-being) for guidance.

Dr. Robert Biswas-Diener, my teacher in a positive-psychology-based coaching certification program called Positive Acorn, defines ethics as a decision-making *process* rather than a static set of rules. And we don't need to navigate the process alone.

FLEXING CHARACTER STRENGTHS TO ENHANCE OUR MORAL AND ETHICAL WELL-BEING DIMENSION

The six overarching virtues identified by the VIA Institute on Character—wisdom, courage, humanity, transcendence, justice, and temperance—and the twenty-four character strengths situated therein can serve as helpful resources to guide us in moral and ethical decision-making, especially in confusing or difficult situations.

Calling upon our virtue of wisdom, we can activate our character strengths of curiosity, creativity, judgment, love of learning, and perspective, and ask ourselves, *What cognitive strengths can I use to solve this problem? How can I be sure to adequately think through a range of wise options, examining the situation from multiple angles and perspectives, before making a decision?*[1174] We can tap into our virtue of courage, using character strengths like bravery, perseverance, honesty, and zest, and ask ourselves, *What energy resources within me can I amp up to break this challenge into manageable, action-oriented steps, leading me to make the right decision?*[1175] We can access the virtue of humanity, amplifying character strengths of kindness and social intelligence (and even love), asking ourselves, *How can I use this dilemma to serve others in need of connection, care, or support?*[1176] We could focus on the virtue of transcendence, using character strengths like gratitude and hope, and ask ourselves, *What is the meaning and purpose of my lawyering life? What do I want it to be? How will my response to this moral/ethical scenario reflect my life's meaning and purpose?*[1177]

The virtues of justice and temperance might be particularly helpful as we nurture our moral and ethical well-being dimension. Three character strengths reside within the virtue of justice: teamwork, fairness, and leadership.[1178] The VIA Institute defines teamwork as "being committed to the success of the team or group you are part of. It extends to being a good citizen in your community and partnering with others to get things done."[1179] The VIA Institute describes fairness as "treating people justly without favoritism or bias. This strength focuses on giving people a chance and seeking equal opportunity for all."[1180] The VIA Institute explains leadership in the context of character strengths as "the inclination to organize and encourage a group to get things done for the benefit of the system, team, or organization. The best leadership starts with self-awareness."[1181] (I have to admit that all three of these justice-oriented character strengths appear in the "lesser strengths" category of my VIA Total 24 Character Strengths Report.) When grappling with a moral or ethical challenge, we can activate our virtue of justice and ask ourselves, *How can I be community-focused, or serve as an advocate or supporter of others, in this moral/ethical scenario?*[1182]

The VIA Institute defines the virtue of temperance as a grouping of strengths that guard against excess.[1183] These include:

- **Forgiveness**: accepting the humanness of others and offering second chances
- **Humility**: letting our accomplishments speak for themselves, and also acknowledging what we don't know
- **Prudence**: deploying caution and avoiding unnecessary risks
- **Self-regulation**: exercising discipline, and calibrating emotions and desires

Accessing our virtue of temperance to help us resolve a moral or ethical quandary, we can ask ourselves, *How can I exercise intellectual humility and prudence, regulating my emotions while I methodically research options and make a disciplined decision?*

Ryan Niemiec and Robert E. McGrath's book, *The Power of Character Strengths: Appreciate and Ignite Your Positive Personality*, describes all twenty-four character strengths and offers reflection exercises and activities to nurture each one.

Character, like a photograph, develops in darkness.

Yousuf Karsh

Character, like a silhouette, also develops in light.

HKB

Moral/Ethical Well-Being Dimension Exercise #1

Shaping Our Personal Sense of Justice

Let's refresh and shape our personal sense of justice. What do each of the six domains of justice (identified by Prilleltensky) mean to you? Consider writing a short "mission statement" for each one in the chart on page 246, articulating your approach to cultivating that type of justice. It's okay if you are not quite sure yet how you define each justice ambit. This might take us some time. Additionally, sometimes we may experience conflict between our *personal* sense of justice and the demands of our *professional* roles.

- **Distributive justice**: "the fair and equitable allocation of burdens and privileges, rights and responsibilities, and pains and gains in society"; balancing merit (rewarding individuals "based on effort and capacity") with need (distributing resources "based on what individuals require to survive and to thrive")[1184]
- **Procedural justice**: fostering "fair, transparent, informative, respectful, and . . . participatory decision-making process[es]"[1185]
- **Intrapersonal justice**: justice in our relationship with ourselves, including psychological intrapersonal justice (refraining from unfairly putting ourselves down, or deeming ourselves unworthy) and physical intrapersonal justice (avoiding self-injurious behavior and infliction of undue pain and suffering on ourselves)[1186]
- **Relational and interpersonal justice**: justice in our interactions with other people
- **Organizational justice**: cultivating open channels of communication and information transparency in institutions
- **Cultural and community justice**: justice in interactions between and among groups

---

Giving some thought to these six spheres of justice may help illuminate our mission, meaning, and purpose in our personal and professional lives. In turn, our mission, meaning, and purpose may help guide us when we inevitably encounter moral and ethical challenges in our work.

Do any of these six forms of justice reflect words you included in your ten-word purpose statement from Exercise #2 in Chapter 10? Or vice versa—does your interpretation of any of the forms of justice inspire words to include in, or add to, your purpose statement?

Prilleltensky's Six Realms of Justice	Words in Your Purpose Statement
Distributive	
Procedural	
Intrapersonal	
Relational and interpersonal	
Organizational	
Cultural/community	

Moral/Ethical Well-Being Dimension Exercise #2

Developing a Moral/Ethical Dilemma Script and Action Checklist

We're all likely going to face moments in our lawyering (and personal) lives that pose moral and ethical dilemmas. The "right" course of action is not always clear. Especially as law students and junior attorneys, we may face situations in which supervisors or authority figures ask us to do something that stirs a bit of moral or ethical discomfort, confusion, or unease. It might be helpful to develop a script or action checklist to work through moral/ethical problems. Over time, we can tweak and hone our script and checklist to find a process that works best for each of us.

Ponder a recent scenario at work or in your personal life that stoked a bit of inner conflict related to your morals or ethics. Refer back to your responses to Exercise #1 in this chapter, and then consider these questions:

Can my sense of **distributive justice** help guide my actions in this situation? Why or why not?	
Can my sense of **procedural justice** help guide my actions in this situation? Why or why not?	
Can my sense of **intrapersonal justice** help guide my actions in this situation? Why or why not?	
Can my sense of **relational/ interpersonal justice** help guide my actions in this situation? Why or why not?	
Can my sense of **organizational justice** help guide my actions in this situation? Why or why not?	
Can my sense of **cultural/community justice** help guide my actions in this situation? Why or why not?	

Next, let's consider which virtues and character strengths we might activate to help us chart a path toward moral and ethical decision-making. If you haven't already done so, consider taking the free VIA Character Strengths Survey found on the VIA Institute on Character website—www.VIAcharacter.org. Take a look at the six virtues, and also your "signature strengths." Which of your virtues and strengths might help guide you in making moral and ethical decisions that align with your values and nature?

Virtues and Character Strengths Identified by the VIA Institute on Character	**Circle your "signature strengths" (or other strengths that resonate with you) in the left-hand column, and consider how each strength might help guide your moral and ethical decision-making in a given situation**
The virtue of **wisdom** includes these character strengths: • Creativity • Curiosity • Judgment • Love of learning • Perspective	
The virtue of **courage** includes these character strengths: • Bravery • Perseverance • Honesty • Zest	
The virtue of **humanity** includes these character strengths: • Love • Kindness • Social intelligence	
The virtue of **justice** includes these character strengths: • Teamwork • Fairness • Leadership	
The virtue of **temperance** includes these character strengths: • Forgiveness • Humility • Prudence • Self-regulation	
The virtue of **transcendence** includes these character strengths: • Appreciation of beauty and excellence • Gratitude • Hope • Humor • Spirituality	

Based on your responses above, consider crafting a script or action checklist that you can practice and hone each time you encounter a scenario that requires moral and ethical decision-making. Obviously, as law students and lawyers, we must honor and comply with ethical rules that govern our profession and areas of law practice. In scenarios in which the "right" response or action still seems unclear, we can use our checklists to supplement our professional code(s) of conduct, especially as we discuss our decision-making processes appropriately with others we trust. We can encourage other individuals to ponder the six realms of justice (identified by Prilleltensky), in addition to the VIA virtues and our respective character strengths invoked by the pressing situation. We can help one another make moral and ethical decisions that align with our individual and collective values, nature, and character.

Sample Action Checklist

This situation invokes a question of:

- **Distributive justice** because ______________________________
- **Procedural justice** because ______________________________
- **Intrapersonal justice** because ______________________________
- **Relational/interpersonal justice** because ______________________
- **Organizational justice** because ____________________________
- **Cultural/community justice** because _________________________

This situation invites me to activate my VIA character strengths of:

- Strength #1: ________________ (corresponding virtue:____________)
- Strength #2: ________________ (corresponding virtue:____________)
- Strength #3: ________________ (corresponding virtue:____________)
- Strength #4: ________________ (corresponding virtue:____________)
- Strength #5: ________________ (corresponding virtue:____________)

I feel comfortable talking openly about this moral/ethical scenario with one or more of these three individuals:

(1)__________________ (2)__________________ (3)__________________

Next, consider the following steps:

- Choose one person with whom you feel comfortable talking through the scenario (keeping in mind confidentiality parameters). This person might be a mentor, an approachable supervisor, or an advisor on a confidential ethics hotline.

  - The key is to find someone who will (a) listen to you, (b) not minimize or dismiss the concern, (c) exhibit appropriate empathy, and (d) provide (or connect you with someone who can provide) trustworthy guidance.
- Try to name and be as specific as possible (within the bounds of client confidentiality) about your concern or your inner conflict.

> *Character isn't something you were born with and can't change, like your fingerprints. It's something you weren't born with and must take responsibility for forming.*
>
> Jim Rohn

CHAPTER 14

Our "Caring" or Caregiving Dimension

Compassion is a verb.

Thích Nhất Hạnh

In this chapter, we will learn about:

- **The differences among sympathy, empathy, and compassion**
- **Trauma awareness (direct and vicarious trauma)**

To round out our self-discovery journey, I've included a tenth and final dimension: our "caring" or caregiving dimension. Though this dimension relates to our interactions and relationships with other human beings, I consider the study of this aspect of our well-being to have a different emphasis than our social and cultural dimensions. To start, let's explore the differences among sympathy, empathy, and compassion.

When we feel sympathy for someone, we share their emotions. If our best friend is sad, sympathy manifests in our coextensive feelings of gloom or despondency. Empathy is different; in empathy, we can kindly understand the feelings of someone else without necessarily processing the same emotion. For example, we can comprehend why our friend is bummed out (and care deeply about them), but we do not simultaneously feel down ourselves. In empathy, we maintain a degree of detachment. Dr. Christopher Kukk wrote a great book called *The Compassionate Achiever: How Helping Others Fuels Success.*[1187] Kukk defines empathy as "understanding what another person is experiencing."[1188] He differentiates empathy from compassion: "Compassion is a holistic understanding of a problem or the suffering of another with a commitment to act to solve the problem or the alleviation of the suffering."[1189] The action in compassion is the distinction.

Kukk makes an interesting (albeit slightly confusing) observation: "When we think compassionately, we use the same neural pathways as love, but when we think empathically we use the brain regions associated with pain."[1190] He says, "The constant use of the brain's pain neural pathways leads to feelings of burnout; empathy is not sustainable. Because compassion is connected to feelings of love, we are nourished and the brain is primed for achievement."[1191] As a compassion advocate, Kukk reports connections between compassion and (1) greater self-esteem and health,[1192] (2) productivity boosts at work,[1193] (3) improved academic performance,[1194] and (4) healthier communities.[1195] Kukk suggests a four-step approach to being what he calls "a compassionate achiever," using the acronym LUCA:[1196]

- Listening
- Understanding
- Connecting people to resources
- Acting

Dr. Paul Bloom, who wrote a book (with a controversial title) called *Against Empathy*, defines empathy as "*the act of coming to experience the world as you think someone else does*."[1197] Bloom cautions that empathy can serve as a "spotlight" with too narrow a focus; he says empathy shines light only on what we point it at, and thus can reflect our personal biases.[1198] He warns that empathy can be a flawed ethos because we think "we understand other people by using ourselves as a model."[1199] Bloom acknowledges the obvious importance of compassion and kindness, but emphasizes that they too can be misguided at times.[1200] He says we need to blend empathy and compassion with "smarts and more self-control."[1201] In somewhat of a tough-love fashion, Bloom urges, "You can't act to make the world better if you aren't smart enough to know which action will achieve that goal."[1202] Tying this back to Kukk's action-oriented definition of compassion, perhaps we need to learn when to act and not act, or what constitutes truly helpful action. When is compassionate action healthy, and when is it not?

As we explore our caring and caregiving dimension, let's investigate how we can cultivate healthy (and wise) sympathy, empathy, and compassion.

NURTURING CHARACTER STRENGTHS TO BOLSTER OUR CARING AND CAREGIVING DIMENSION

In exploring our caring and caregiving dimension, the virtue of *humanity*—included in the VIA Institute on Character's list of six virtues—comes to mind.[1203] The three VIA character strengths situated within the virtue of humanity include love, kindness, and social intelligence. In this context, love is defined as caring about someone else's feelings and well-being, genuinely enjoying putting that person's needs above our own at appropriate times, and expressing warmth and affection toward that person.[1204] When we exhibit kindness, we listen, nurture others, and demonstrate consideration for others' well-being.[1205] When we activate the character strength of social intelligence, we are aware of, and understand, our own thoughts and feelings, and sense those of people around us.[1206] Echoing Prilleltensky's concept of *mattering*, the character strengths within the virtue of humanity can guide us in making others *feel* valued and in spotlighting their strengths to show how they *add* value.[1207]

Positive psychologist Dr. Chris Peterson is renowned for asserting, "Other people matter."[1208] In cultivating our caregiving dimension, let's practice showing other people that they matter.

Caring/Caregiving Dimension Exercise #1
Artifacts of Meaning and Mattering

Recently, at my neighborhood park, a new acquaintance gently put a hand on my shoulder to nudge me out of the way of a gardener's leaf blower. Later, I checked my mailbox; a friend sent me a card in which she paraphrased a cool U2 lyric, "She's a wave, she's a tide." An attendee of a presentation I recently gave wrote me a follow-up email saying, "Thank you . . . I felt heard." All three gestures boosted my mood. These were not just momentary jolts of joy in my day that glimmered and fizzled out. They constituted tangible artifacts of meaning and mattering that help me build a body of evidence toward a life of well-being.

This week, can we undertake one gesture (or more) to make others feel valued? Can we reach out and say, *Thank you for being you, for being brave, for writing that truth, for taking that risk, for suggesting that idea, for working so hard. You matter. You help me understand the meaning of my own life too.*

What artifacts of meaning and mattering will you notice this week? What footprints of meaning and mattering will you stamp into the soil for yourself and others?

HOLDING SPACE FOR TRAUMA PROCESSING

In cultivating the dimension of caring and caregiving, it is essential that we understand the power of *trauma*—in ourselves and others—and that we make space to untangle and process it with wisdom and humanity. Trauma is commonly defined as "a psychological, emotional, and/or bodily response to a deeply disturbing event or series of events."[1209] Williams states that "[a]n event, or series of events, counts as traumatic if it exceeds a person's ability to return to a baseline of calm afterwards."[1210] She emphasizes that trauma can derive from a "life-or-death emergency," or from a "not necessarily life-threatening but socially and emotionally painful experience of being repeatedly criticized or humiliated by someone who has power over you."[1211]

Over the course of our legal careers, no matter what type of law we practice, we likely will encounter clients (and colleagues) who are dealing with, or have dealt with, trauma from profoundly disturbing past events or ongoing experiences. Judge David T. Suntag poignantly wrote, "it is an unusual day when someone who has experienced trauma is *not* in the courtroom."[1212] Of course, some areas of law practice, such as domestic relations, immigration, and criminal law, involve overt trauma to a greater degree than other practice arenas. But invisible trauma can loiter where we least expect it.

It is important for us to comprehend that trauma is not a compartmentalizable experience that occurred to someone in the past that is necessarily over and complete. As Bessel van der Kolk, author of the helpful book, *The Body Keeps the Score: Brain, Mind, and Body in the Healing of Trauma*, points out, trauma is "the imprint left by that experience on mind, brain, and body."[1213] Trauma can tattoo memories into our physiology; it can change the way our brain perceives present danger and how our body filters new stressors.[1214] Many traumatized individuals navigate life as if the trauma is ongoing, rather than something that happened in the past.[1215] Unless the traumatized individual learns how to process the trauma and separate new experiences from the past event, the brain, body, and mind will repeatedly activate the fight-flight-or-freeze response. (Remember we learned in Chapter 5 how an overactive nervous system can contribute to allostatic overload, chipping away at our well-being?) Professor Jean Koh Peters explains that "trauma disrupts and attacks the self. It disintegrates your sense of who you are, what you hold dear, and what you believe."[1216]

Additionally, the repeated or extreme exposure of law students, lawyers, judges, and other members of our profession to details of clients' trauma can lead to a condition called *secondary* or *vicarious trauma.*[1217] Alternatively, this may be referred to as *compassion fatigue* or *secondary traumatic stress.*[1218] Experts indicate that individuals can experience secondary trauma simply by working in a professional environment in which *coworkers* grapple with secondary trauma—a domino or ripple effect.[1219] Canadian attorney Crystal Tomusiak indicates that members of our profession have a particular "susceptibility to vicarious trauma, which comes as a result of the horrifying and disturbing cases to which many of us are routinely exposed."[1220]

And let's not gloss over the fact that many of us have sustained our own *primary* trauma. Tomusiak points out the vivid reality that many members of our profession have experienced personal trauma prior to going to law school or entering the profession. We may never have fully understood, realized, or processed the resulting physiological and psychological imprint.

Ending my 12-year relationship—six years of dating during college and law school, plus six years of marriage—the year I turned thirty was *trauma*. Leaving the person I loved most in the world, the home we built together, all our friends, a secure law firm job, the approval and acceptance of my parents, then moving to New York toting bags of shame, embarrassment, and guilt, starting completely over—felt like hacking off a limb with a rusty saw. The occurrence of 9/11 a year later compounded my trauma, especially because I had worked in Tower Two of the World Trade Center, yet was on a plane diverted to Gander, Newfoundland, Canada, on that tragic day. Over the past 20 years, I have done an immense amount of personal exploratory work—through therapy, reading, writing, studying—to plumb and expel entrenched fears, regret, shame, and guilt. Still, my trauma response reappears at surprising and unexpected moments: in particularly invasive medical appointments, episodes of interpersonal conflict at work or in relationships, and chaotic and loud ambient environments. Trauma speaks to us. It seeks our attention and *regard.*

Tomusiak points out the oft-mistaken supposition that lawyers "start out in this profession in a factory-fresh state without any significant pre-existing wounds or vulnerabilities."[1221] She highlights the importance of recognizing that many law students and lawyers (and others in our profession) "survived the kinds of adversity that the clients and justice system participants and stakeholders whom we serve may also have endured."[1222] Trauma we experienced prior to our entry to the profession can "shape how our mental health is impacted by the pressures of the profession,"[1223] exacerbating other well-being issues.[1224] Dr. Erika Tullberg, an expert on secondary trauma, indicates that individuals who experienced personal trauma themselves "can be more vulnerable to developing secondary traumatic stress—especially if the individual is working with clients who have suffered a similar kind of trauma."[1225]

Because law students, lawyers, and other members of our profession are not often trained to recognize or address trauma, sudden eruptions of confusing emotions may become overwhelming.[1226] Secondary trauma can affect our decision-making processes, listening skills, ability to assert and maintain appropriate and effective boundaries, and performance.[1227] Fortunately, we can educate ourselves on how to discern and process symptoms (and roots) of primary and secondary trauma, and seek guidance from appropriately knowledgeable individuals in doing so.

Symptoms of Primary and Vicarious Trauma

Experts indicate that symptoms of primary or vicarious trauma include irritability, disturbing dreams, headaches, stomachaches, tiredness, overactive guilt, memory issues, numbness, concentration problems, anger, fear, and detachment from friends and family.[1228] Additional symptoms of vicarious trauma can include:

- Hypervigilance, that is, perceiving colleagues and clients as threatening, or considering all clients to be in danger
- Hopelessness
- Problems handling complexity or ambiguity
- Inability to maintain attention while listening

- Avoidance, for example, arriving late or leaving early, missing meetings, evading clients, skirting certain subject matter during conversations
- Argumentativeness or cynicism
- Sleeplessness
- Chronic exhaustion
- Physical ailments
- Minimizing issues
- Shutting down or numbing out[1229]

Enhancing Trauma Awareness

To ensure that we process our own trauma and potential vicarious trauma in a healthy way, we can start by enhancing our awareness of the foregoing signs, signals, and symptoms. Next, we can identify work-related, client-related, or personal-life scenarios that might trigger trauma symptoms, develop protocols for talking with appropriate individuals (such as trained therapists) about situations that launch trauma-related thoughts or feelings, and establish self-care routines (including setting and maintaining healthy boundaries).[1230]

Deborah Wood Smith, Senior Knowledge and Information Services Analyst at the National Center for State Courts, describes a three-part process for working through vicarious trauma based on the acronym A-B-C:[1231]

- **Awareness**: learning how to spot the signs and symptoms of vicarious trauma in ourselves and others, and honoring the fact that "these types of reactions to trauma [are] part of being human and not a sign of weakness"
- **Balance**: establishing healthy boundaries in work and personal life, and committing to routines of self-care
- **Connection**: talking openly about vicarious trauma with supportive individuals, such as colleagues or trained therapists

Further, in healing from trauma, we can build on the work we did in exploring our emotional well-being dimension in Chapter 6. Encouraging research indicates that investing time in cultivating positive emotions as we process crises and trauma can "pay off both in the short term, by improving subjective experiences, undoing physiological arousal, and enhancing broadminded coping, and in the long term, by minimizing depression and building enduring resources, the hallmark of thriving."[1232]

Additional resources for recognizing, assessing, and processing primary and vicarious trauma include:

- Bruce D. Perry and Oprah Winfrey, *What Happened to You? Conversations on Trauma, Resilience, and Healing* (New York: Flatiron Books, 2021).
- Bessel van der Kolk, *The Body Keeps the Score: Brain, Mind, and Body in the Healing of Trauma* (New York: Penguin Books, 2014).
- Laura Van Dernoot-Lipsky, *Trauma Stewardship: An Everyday Guide to Caring for Self While Caring for Others* (Oakland: Berrett-Koehler Publishers, 2009).
- A measurement tool called the Professional Quality of Life Scale (ProQOL), available online, helps evaluate an individual's compassion satisfaction, compassion fatigue, burnout, and secondary traumatic stress. The website https://proqol.org/ provides information about using the scale and obtaining permissions as appropriate.
- Websites with trauma resources for members of the legal profession include:
    - www.americanbar.org/groups/lawyer_assistance/resources/compassion_fatigue/
    - www.traumainformedlaw.org/resources/
    - https://www.livingabovethebar.org/trauma-and-burnout

Further, a book by Dr. James W. Pennebaker and Dr. Joshua M. Smyth called *Opening Up by Writing it Down: How Expressive Writing Improves Health and Eases Emotional Pain*, discusses how "expressive writing"—writing about upsetting experiences for 15 to 20 minutes a day for three to four days—"has been found to improve people's physical and mental health for weeks, months, and even years when compared to individuals who write about emotionally neutral topics (or other comparison groups)."[1233] Pennebaker and Smyth emphasize that "[w]riting about traumas helps us to organize the traumas."[1234] They further indicate that, in research studies, "[p]eople who wrote about their deepest thoughts and feelings surrounding traumatic experiences evidenced enhanced immune function compared with those who wrote about superficial topics."[1235] They caution that "writing about feelings associated with traumatic experiences [can be] painful in the short term."[1236] But research shows that expressive writing has positive long-term effects in helping us process trauma.[1237]

Additionally, a list of therapeutic resources involving the arts is included at the end of Chapter 7 (Our Artistic/Creative Dimension).

If your compassion does not include yourself, it is incomplete.

Jack Kornfield

Caring/Caregiving Dimension Exercise #2

Exploring Our Sympathy-Empathy-Compassion Continuum

As we nurture our caring and caregiving dimension, let's explore our sympathy-empathy-compassion continuum.

- **Sympathy**: sharing emotions with other individuals; feeling the same emotion that another person is feeling (e.g., sadness, grief, anxiety, pain)
- **Empathy**: understanding and caring about how another person feels, but not taking on that emotion
- **Compassion**: understanding the suffering of another and taking action to quell the person's suffering

As we navigate interactions with others during our day or week, let's notice:

- When we feel emotions that others are feeling (discerning whether we feel these emotions in a healthy way, or in a way that is not so conducive to our own and others' well-being) ____________________
- When we exhibit care for others *without* necessarily taking on emotions that might not be conducive to our own and others' well-being ____________________
- When we exhibit care for others and feel compelled to *act* to alleviate their pain or suffering, or alternatively when we might necessarily need to hold back from "fixing" another person's perceived problem or intervening to relieve their suffering ______

____

The foregoing scenarios offer opportunities to practice some of the techniques we learned in the context of other well-being dimensions:

- Positivity resonance (Chapters 6 and 8)
- Active constructive responding (Chapters 6 and 8)
- Constructivist listening (Chapter 8)
- Perspective-giving and perspective-taking (Chapter 8)

Helpful Resources for Exploring Sympathy, Empathy, and Compassion

- Book: Paul Bloom, *Against Empathy: The Case for Rational Compassion* (New York: Harper Collins, 2016).

- Book: Christopher Kukk, *The Compassionate Achiever: How Helping Others Fuels Success* (San Francisco: HarperOne, 2017).

Be kinder to yourself and then let your kindness flood the world.

Pema Chödrön

Conclusion

When I teach my legal writing students how to reference the litigants in the legal cases we analyze when drafting our memoranda and briefs, I urge them not to default to boring (and often unclear) terminology like "plaintiff/defendant" or "appellate/appellee" or "petitioner/respondent." I encourage my students to use more interesting and illustrative terms for the "roles" the individuals play in society. I suggest they use vivid descriptors, such as pilot, police officer, gymnast, teacher, plumber, sister, politician, celebrity, author, guitarist, shop owner, fingerprint expert. In my view, using vibrant language to identify the key players in each case enlivens the facts for the reader; the reader is more likely to be able to envision what happened on an airplane between a passenger and a flight attendant, or what transpired in a hospital between a doctor and a patient, rather than trying to keep track of who was the "plaintiff" or the "defendant." In the same vein, let's not sell ourselves short by limiting how we define and describe ourselves.

We are not *just* law students or lawyers or law professors or judges or paralegals or court reporters or legal staff. We are scholar-athletes, performers, artists, creators, muses, puzzle-solvers, friends, teachers, learners, caregivers, confidantes, writers, readers, builders, listeners, motivational speakers, fighters, advocates, champions.

Prior to that trip to Mexico when the travel form prompted me to rethink *who* or *what I am*, I described myself in one (boring) phrase: "I'm a litigator." Now, I define myself as a writer, a fighter (my boxing lessons), a passionate U2 fan, a world traveler, a proud introvert, and of course, a teacher to awesome law students. We are much more than "just" the label of "law student" or "lawyer" or "legal professional." We are multi-dimensional. Multi-faceted. Multi-layered. Multi-nuanced. Let's nurture our myriad dimensions, facets, layers, and nuances. Let's appreciate our complexity, our intricate tapestry. Let's fortify *all* our well-being dimensions so when we inevitably encounter challenges in one area, our other stanchions will solidify and hold us up. Let's strengthen the muscles around all our potentially vulnerable joints—as *pre*habilitation. Let's cultivate a sense of personal safety so we can step into healthy risk and adventure.

Let's make the next five, ten, twenty, thirty years of our legal careers wildly interesting, enriched, and full of wonder and awe. Just like us.

Let's thrill, amaze, and inspire. I'm rooting for you.

Epilogue

In the Preface, I included a quote I liked from Ratey and Manning's book, *Go Wild*: "There is no reason to write a book unless the process of doing so changes the author's life."

As I type this paragraph, I'm sitting in an airport, sipping coffee, excited about the next adventure. I began researching and crafting this book just before the pandemic hit New York. For the first time in my book-writing life, I tossed my original chapter-by-chapter proposal in the trash and started over—with no roadmap. I commenced the drafting process without a concrete idea or image of what the end product would or should look like. It was a new creative experience, just being patient, observing, letting this book tell me, show me, what it wanted to be.

Writing was my friend and companion during lockdown.

After lockdown, I moved from Brooklyn to Chelsea to be geographically closer to my best friend Clay. I began training with my boxing coach Lou outside in my neighborhood park. I embarked on a new academic year, taught my students online, and simultaneously pursued my master's degree in applied positive psychology at Penn (also online). I tended to, mended, and nurtured my relationship with my parents—who live in Florida—through Sunday zooms. When writing, teaching, learning, and zooming in my tiny apartment felt claustrophobic, the park beckoned. I met a guy there during one of my daily 2-mile jogs. Uncharacteristically, after working out together a few times, I mustered up the courage to ask him out. He entered my life like a tornado, jarred a numbed aspect of my soul awake, ripped open forgotten wounds I thought had healed, and whirled away just as turbulently. He reappeared, vanished—again and again. Throughout all this, I wrote every day. I scribbled Morning Pages in journals. I drafted dozens of papers for my master's program. I read piles of scholarly articles and psychology books. As soon as I got the Moderna vaccine and finished teaching, I bought a one-way ticket to Croatia and hopped on a plane.

I wrote this book in Split, Dubrovnik, Barcelona, Tenerife, Rome, Colorado, North Carolina, Virginia, Bologna, Milan, Miami, and of course New York City. Every day, two hours a day, for 169 days in a row without taking a day off—to get the initial draft manuscript ready to submit. And then many more months of editing.

Choosing words one at a time, seeing them shape into ideas on the page, makes me happy. This book invited me to treat myself like a scholar-athlete. To give myself *regard* as an artist. It nurtured my PERMA:

Positive emotions: Even on the days when the work progressed more slowly than I desired or I felt rudderless, I experienced *joy* in the act of connecting word to word. I felt *inspired* when themes budded. I felt *electrified* watching art emerge. I felt *hope* that this thing could possibly help at least one person feel better about life and lawyering. I felt *amused* reflecting on my rambunctious adventures. I felt *awe* at the writer life I get to live. I felt *love* for the people who encourage me, and even for the ones who never "got me" or are afraid to try.

Engagement: I don't even know how to adequately describe how appreciative I am of the episodes of *flow* this book gifted me. It was like being a little drunk. Inebriated, sipping on words. I want to feel this way every day for the rest of my life.

Relationships: Writing is being in love . . .

Meaning: This book insisted that I look my raw self in the mirror and define the meaning and purpose of my life. Ten words: *Writer, muse, artist, traveler, teacher, impactful introvert, friend, lover, fighter.*

Achievement: I'm excited and proud that, once again, I trusted *my* system, *my* process. I designed and stuck to my *prehabilitation* regimen. I hung in there in *eustress* and *hormesis* moments. I found my IZOF. I earned a master's degree, improved as a novice boxer, patiently awaited the freedom to travel again and then explored a bunch of new destinations solo, and wrote this book (my seventh)—all during a global pandemic.

So, how did this book change my life? *I really like being me now.* I liked learning that my signature character strengths are perseverance, curiosity, zest, creativity, and love of learning. I love that I'm introverted and thrive being alone. I love realizing that when I love someone, I do it unabashedly, all-in, and intensely, and if that means I end up being "too much" for those that can't handle it and I have to bushwhack through tangles of sadness and loss again until I get my groove back, that's just fine too.

In the end, writing this book inspired me to imagine and sculpt *my own* well-being framework (see Appendix D)—one that captures the essence of what *eudaimonia* means to *me.*

This book changed my life because it showed me exactly how I want to live the next week, month, year, five years, twenty years, fifty years of my time on earth. Being real.

Writing this book was a pandemic positive intervention for me.

Thank you for accompanying me on this writing trip. If you ever want to share your adventures of discovering yourself in life and lawyering, I'd love to hear your stories.

We carry each other.

U2

www.theflourishinglawyer.org
heidi@theintrovertedlawyer.com

Appendix A PERMA Well-Being Components Tracker

Consider referring to this chart if you wish to focus on, or keep track of, specific PERMA components as we work through our ten well-being dimensions. Opportunities to nurture each PERMA component permeate *multiple* dimensions; the chart below simply offers a few suggestions for each.

Introduction to PERMA	Chapter 1
Positive emotions (P in PERMA)	Chapter 6 (Emotional Well-Being Dimension) Chapter 8 (Social Well-Being Dimension)
Engagement (E in PERMA)	Chapter 4 (Flow) Chapter 5 (Physical Dimension) Chapter 7 (Artistic/Creative Dimension) Chapter 11 (Occupational Dimension)
Relationships (R in PERMA)	Chapter 8 (Social Well-Being Dimension) Chapter 9 (Dimension of Culture) Chapter 14 (Caring or Caregiving Dimension)
Meaning (M in PERMA)	Chapter 7 (Artistic/Creative Dimension) Chapter 10 (Spiritual Dimension) Chapter 13 (Moral/Ethical Dimension)
Achievement/ accomplishment (A in PERMA)	Chapter 5 (Physical Dimension) Chapter 7 (Artistic/Creative Dimension) Chapter 11 (Occupational Dimension) Chapter 12 (Intellectual Dimension)

Appendix B VIA Character Strengths and Virtues Tracker

Consider referring to this chart if you wish to focus on, or keep track of, specific character strengths identified by the VIA Institute on Character as we work through various well-being dimensions. Opportunities to nurture each strength and corresponding virtue permeate *multiple* dimensions; the chart below simply offers a few suggestions for each.

Introduction to the VIA character strengths and virtues	Chapter 3 (and Exercise #1, Exercise #2, Exercise #3 in Chapter 3)
Activating character strengths when developing emotional appraisal scripts	Chapter 6 (Emotional Well-Being Dimension)
Activating character strengths when engaging in active constructive responding (ACR)	Chapter 6 (Emotional Well-Being Dimension) and Chapter 8 (Social Well-Being Dimension)
Cultivating character strengths through positive art and writing	Chapter 7 (Artistic/Creative Dimension, Exercise #1)
Nurturing character strengths through cultural engagement	Chapter 9 (The Dimension of Culture)
Considering which signature character strengths connect to the work we do every day	Chapter 11 (Occupational Dimension)

TRACKER FOR CULTIVATING SPECIFIC VIA VIRTUES AND STRENGTHS

Opportunities to nurture VIA virtues and character strengths permeate *multiple* dimensions; the chart below simply offers a few suggestions for each.

VIA Virtue	VIA Character Strengths	Book Chapter
Wisdom	Creativity Curiosity Judgment Love of learning Perspective	• Chapter 5 (Physical Dimension) • Chapter 12 (Intellectual Dimension) • Chapter 13 (Moral/Ethical Dimension) • Some of these strengths can be activated through the Artistic/Creative Dimension (Chapter 7) • Some of these strengths can be activated through the Dimension of Culture (Chapter 9)
Courage	Bravery Honesty Perseverance Zest	• Chapter 5 (Physical Dimension) • Chapter 11 (Occupational Dimension) • Chapter 13 (Moral/Ethical Dimension)
Humanity	Kindness Love Social intelligence	• Chapter 6 (Emotional Dimension) • Chapter 8 (Social Dimension) • Chapter 9 (Dimension of Culture) • Chapter 13 (Moral/Ethical Dimension) • Chapter 14 (Caring or Caregiving Dimension)
Justice	Fairness Leadership Teamwork	• Chapter 11 (Occupational Dimension) • Chapter 13 (Moral/Ethical Dimension)
Temperance	Forgiveness Humility Prudence Self-regulation	• Chapter 6 (Emotional Dimension) • Chapter 13 (Moral/Ethical Dimension) • Chapter 14 (Caring or Caregiving Dimension) • Humility can be activated through the Dimension of Culture (Chapter 9) and the Intellectual Dimension (Chapter 12)

VIA Virtue	VIA Character Strengths	Book Chapter
Transcendence	Appreciation of beauty and excellence Gratitude Hope Humor Spirituality	• Chapter 6 (Emotional Dimension) • Chapter 7 (Artistic/Creative Dimension) • Chapter 8 (Social Well-Being Dimension; discussion of transcendence in conjunction with the "hive switch") • Chapter 10 (Spiritual Dimension; discussion of connecting with something greater than ourselves) • Chapter 13 (Moral/Ethical Dimension) • Appreciation of beauty and excellence can be activated through the Dimension of Culture (Chapter 9)

Appendix C
Proposed "Flourishing Lawyer Project" Curriculum

Unit 1: Beginning to Regard Ourselves as Scholar-Athletes or Scholar-Performers

- Reading: Introduction to *The Flourishing Lawyer*
- (Shorter) Reading: "Let's Mend Our Profession by Exploring the Mental and the Physical," *ABA Journal* (April 1, 2020), https://www.abajournal.com/magazine/article/lets-mend-our-profession-by-exploring-the-mental-and-the-physical
- (Shorter) Reading: "What Elite Athletes Like Naomi Osaka and Simone Biles Can Teach Lawyers About Performance Anxiety," *ABA Journal* (December 1, 2021), https://www.abajournal.com/magazine/article/what-elite-athletes-like-naomi-osaka-and-simone-biles-can-teach-lawyers-about-performance-anxiety
- (Shorter Reading) "Athletic Performance Training Isn't One-Size-Fits-All, Lawyer Training Shouldn't Be Either," *Attorney at Law Magazine* (January 28, 2022), https://attorneyatlawmagazine.com/athletic-performance-training-isnt-one-size-fits-all-lawyer-training-shouldnt-be-either
- "Know Thyself" Reflection (end of Introduction to *The Flourishing Lawyer*)

Unit 2: Introduction to Positive Psychology

- Reading: Chapter 1 of *The Flourishing Lawyer*
- (Shorter) Reading: "The Eudaimonic Turn: How We Can Help Lawyers Flourish," *ABA Journal* (September 7, 2021), https://www.abajournal.com/columns/article/the-eudaimonic-turn-how-we-can-help-lawyers-flourish
- Supplemental Resources for Teachers and Students
    - Jacolyn Norrish, *Positive Education: The Geelong Grammar School Journey* (Oxford: Oxford University Press, 2015)
    - R. Lisle Baker, "Designing a Positive Psychology Course for Lawyers," *Suffolk University Law Review* 51, no. 2 (2018): 207–288

Unit 3: Let's Get to Work Cultivating Multiple Well-Being Dimensions

- Reading: Chapter 2 of *The Flourishing Lawyer*

Unit 4: Cultivating Character Strengths

- Reading: Chapter 3 of *The Flourishing Lawyer*
- Assign the free VIA Character Strengths Survey (www.VIAcharacter.org)
- Exercises #1, #2, #3 in Chapter 3 of *The Flourishing Lawyer*
- Supplemental Resources for Teachers and Students
  - Deborah L. Rhode, "Moral Character as a Professional Credential," *The Yale Law Journal* 94, no. 3 (1985): 491–603
  - R. Lisle Baker, "Character and Fitness for Leadership: Learning Interpersonal Skills," *Santa Clara Law Review* 58 (2018): 101–124
  - R. Lisle Baker, "Character and Fitness for Leadership: Educating Lawyers for Compassion and Courage as Well as Brains—The Wizard of Oz Was Right," *Tennessee Journal of Law and Policy* 14, no. 2 (2020): 287–338
  - Ryan M. Niemiec, *Character Strengths Interventions: A Field Guide for Practitioners* (Boston: Hogrefe Publishing, 2018)
  - Ryan Niemiec and Robert McGrath, *The Power of Character Strengths: Appreciate and Ignite Your Positive Personality* (Cincinnati: VIA Institute on Character, 2019)

Unit 5: Deliberate Practice, Grit, and Flow

- Reading: Chapter 4 of *The Flourishing Lawyer*
- Reading: "How Can Lawyers Find Flow?," *ABA Journal* (December 1, 2020), https://www.abajournal.com/magazine/article/from-drinking-from-a-fire-hose-to-achieving-our-peak-state
- Exercise: When Are You in Flow? (from Chapter 4 of *The Flourishing Lawyer*)
- Supplemental Resources for Teachers and Students
  - Angela L. Duckworth, *Grit: The Power of Passion and Perseverance* (New York: Scribner, 2016)
  - Mihaly Csikszentmihalyi, *Flow: The Psychology of Optimal Experience* (New York: Harper Perennial, 1990)

Unit 6: The Physicality of Fitness to Practice Law (Our Physical Dimension)

- Reading: Chapter 5 of *The Flourishing Lawyer* (Note: This is the longest chapter of the book, so this unit could be broken into sub-parts)

- Exercises #1 to #7 (from Chapter 5 of *The Flourishing Lawyer*)
- Supplemental Resources for Teachers and Students
    - Daniel Lieberman, *Exercised: The Science of Physical Activity, Rest and Health* (London: Penguin Books, 2021)
    - John J. Ratey and Eric Hagerman, *Spark: The Revolutionary New Science of Exercise and the Brain* (New York: Little, Brown & Company, 2008)
    - John J. Ratey and Richard Manning, *Go Wild: Eat Fat, Run Free, Be Social, and Follow Evolution's Other Rules for Total Health and Well-Being* (New York: Little, Brown & Company, 2014)
    - Stanley Rosenberg, *Accessing the Healing Power of the Vagus Nerve: Self-Help Exercises for Anxiety, Depression, Trauma, and Autism* (Berkeley, CA: North Atlantic Books, 2017)
    - Robert M. Sapolsky, *Why Zebras Don't Get Ulcers: The Acclaimed Guide to Stress, Stress-Related Diseases, and Coping* (New York: St. Martin's Griffin, 2004)
    - Bessel van der Kolk, *The Body Keeps the Score: Brain, Mind, and Body in the Healing of Trauma* (London: Penguin Books, 2014)
    - Caroline Williams, *Move! The New Science of Body Over Mind* (London: Profile Books, 2021)
    - Jim Loehr and Jack Groppel, *The Corporate Athlete Advantage: The Science of Deepening Engagement* (Orlando, FL: Human Performance Institute, 2008)

Unit 7: Our Emotional Well-Being Dimension

- Reading: Chapter 6 of *The Flourishing Lawyer*
- Exercise #1 (from Chapter 6 of *The Flourishing Lawyer*): Dr. Barbara Fredrickson's Positivity Portfolio
- Exercise #2 (from Chapter 6 of *The Flourishing Lawyer*): Oxygenating Our Optimism
- Exercise #3 (from Chapter 6 of *The Flourishing Lawyer*): Active Constructive Responding
- Supplemental Resources for Teachers and Students
    - Barbara Fredrickson, *Positivity: Discover the Upward Spiral That Will Change Your Life* (New York: Harmony, 2009)
    - Todd Kashdan and Robert Biswas-Diener, *The Upside of Your Darkside* (New York: Plume, 2014)

Unit 8: Our Artistic/Creative Dimension

- Reading: Chapter 7 of *The Flourishing Lawyer*
- Exercise #1 (from Chapter 7 of *The Flourishing Lawyer*): Positive Art and Writing
- Exercise #2 (from Chapter 7 of *The Flourishing Lawyer*): A Positive Music Exercise
- Supplemental Resources for Teachers and Students
    - Alain de Botton and John Armstrong, *Art as Therapy* (London: Phaidon Press, 2013)
    - Julia Cameron, *The Artist's Way: A Spiritual Path to Higher Creativity* (New York: Jeremy P. Tarcher/Putnam, 2002)
    - Michael F. Melcher, *The Creative Lawyer: A Practical Guide to Authentic Professional Satisfaction* (2d ed.) (Chicago: American Bar Association, 2014)
    - Steven Pressfield, *Do the Work* (New York: The Domino Project, 2011)
    - Steven Pressfield, *The Artist's Journey* (Egremont: Black Irish Entertainment, 2018)
    - Steven Pressfield, *The War of Art* (New York: Black Irish Entertainment, 2002)
    - Steven Pressfield, *Turning Pro* (New York: Black Irish Entertainment, 2012)
    - Tom Sturges, *Every Idea Is a Good Idea: Be Creative Anytime, Anywhere* (New York: Jeremy P. Tarcher/Penguin, 2014)
    - Twyla Tharp, *The Creative Habit: Learn It and Use It for Life* (New York: Simon & Schuster, 2006)
    - Kathleen Elliott Vinson, Samantha A. Moppett, and Shailini Shandial George, *Mindful Lawyering: The Key to Creative Problem Solving* (Durham, NC: Carolina Academic Press, 2018)

Unit 9: Our Social Dimension

- Reading: Chapter 8 of *The Flourishing Lawyer*
- Exercise #1 (from Chapter 8 of *The Flourishing Lawyer*): Enhancing One-on-One Communication Through Art
- Exercise #2 (from Chapter 8 of *The Flourishing Lawyer*): Constructivist Listening

- Exercise #3 (from Chapter 8 of *The Flourishing Lawyer*): Perspective-Giving and Perspective-Taking
- Exercise #4: The Hive Switch
- Supplemental Resources for Teachers and Students
    - Relationship/Attachment Resources:
        - Amy Chan, *Breakup Bootcamp: The Science of Rewiring Your Heart* (New York: Dey Street Books, 2020)
        - Barbara L. Fredrickson, *Love 2.0: Creating Happiness and Health in Moments of Connection* (New York: Penguin Group, 2013)
        - Dr. Amir Levine and Rachel S. F. Heller, *Attached* (London: Bluebird, 2019)
    - Bullying Resource: "We Can Be Smart, Ambitious and Accomplished Members of the Legal Profession Without Being Jerks," *ABA Journal* (November 1, 2019), https://www.abajournal.com/magazine/article/we-can-be-smart-ambitious-and-accomplished-members-of-the-legal-profession-without-being-jerks
    - Communication Resources:
        - Vernā A. Myers, *What If I Say the Wrong Thing? 26 Habits for Culturally Effective People* (Chicago: ABA Publishing, 2013)
        - Marshall B. Rosenberg, *Nonviolent Communication: A Language of Life* (Encinitas, CA: PuddleDancer Press, 2015)

Unit 10: The Dimension of Culture

- Reading: Chapter 9 of *The Flourishing Lawyer*
- Exercise (from Chapter 9 of *The Flourishing Lawyer*): A Cultural Outing
- Supplemental Resources for Teachers and Students
    - Vernā A. Myers, *What If I Say the Wrong Thing? 26 Habits for Culturally Effective People* (Chicago: ABA Publishing, 2013)
    - Marshall B. Rosenberg, *Nonviolent Communication: A Language of Life* (Encinitas, CA: PuddleDancer Press, 2015)

Unit 11: Our Spiritual Dimension

- Reading: Chapter 10 of *The Flourishing Lawyer*
- Exercise #1 (from Chapter 10 of *The Flourishing Lawyer*): A Meaning-Making Writing Practice

- Exercise #2 (from Chapter 10 of *The Flourishing Lawyer*): Discerning Themes of Meaning and Purpose
- Supplemental Resources for Teachers and Students
    - Benjamin Sells, *The Soul of the Law* (Chicago: ABA Publishing, 2013)
    - Emily Esfahani Smith, *The Power of Meaning: Finding Fulfillment in a World Obsessed with Happiness* (New York: Crown, 2017)

Unit 12: Our Occupational Dimension

- Reading: Chapter 11 of *The Flourishing Lawyer*
- Exercise (from Chapter 11 of *The Flourishing Lawyer*): Let's Occupy Our Occupational Dimension with Intention
- Supplemental Resources for Teachers and Students
    - Barry Schwartz, *Why We Work* (New York: Simon & Schuster, 2015)
    - Justin M. Berg, Jane E. Dutton, and Amy Wrzesniewski, "Job Crafting Exercise," available for a fee at www.jobcrafting.com

Unit 13: Our Intellectual Dimension

- Reading: Chapter 12 of *The Flourishing Lawyer*
- Exercise #1 (from Chapter 12 of *The Flourishing Lawyer*): Let's Get Ready to . . . Humble
- Exercise #2 (from Chapter 12 of *The Flourishing Lawyer*): Let's Double-Dip Dimensions
- Supplemental Resources for Teachers and Students
    - Brett Brosseit, Elizabeth Mortenson, and Sarah Murphy, *Applied Critical Thinking and Legal Analysis: Performance Optimization for Law Students and Professionals* (Durham, NC: Carolina Academic Press, 2017)
    - Erica Ariel Fox, *Winning from Within: A Breakthrough Method for Leading, Living, and Lasting Change* (New York: Harper Business, 2013)
    - Shailini Jandial George, *The Law Student's Guide to Doing Well and Being Well* (Durham, NC: Carolina Academic Press, 2021)
    - Anthony Niedwiecki, "Lawyers and Learning: A Metacognitive Approach to Legal Education," *Widener Law Review* 13, no. 33 (2006): 33–72
    - Kathleen Elliott Vinson, Samantha A. Moppett, and Shailini Shandial George, *Mindful Lawyering: The Key to Creative Problem Solving* (Durham, NC: Carolina Academic Press, 2018)
    - Metacognitive Awareness Inventory (available at https://advising.lafayette.edu/wp-content/uploads/sites/247/2021/10/metacognitive_awareness_inventory.pdf)

  - VARK Learning Styles: https://vark-learn.com/the-vark-questionnaire/
  - NERIS Type Explorer® personalities assessment: www.16personalities.com

Unit 14: Our Moral/Ethical Dimension

- Reading: Chapter 13 of *The Flourishing Lawyer*
- Exercise #1 (from Chapter 13 of *The Flourishing Lawyer*): Shaping Our Personal Sense of Justice
- Exercise #2 (from Chapter 13 of *The Flourishing Lawyer*): Developing a Moral/Ethical Dilemma Script and Action Checklist
- Supplemental Resources for Teachers and Students
  - Benjamin Sells, *The Soul of the Law* (Chicago: ABA Publishing, 2013)
  - Isaac Prilleltensky, "Wellness as Fairness," *American Journal of Community Psychology* 49 (2012): 1–21
  - Bernard A. Burk, Veronica J. Finkelstein, and Nancy B. Rapoport, "Why Smart People Do Stupid Things: Cognitive Biases and the Stresses of Practice," Chapter 4 in *Ethical Lawyering: A Guide for the Well-Intentioned* (New York: Wolters Kluwer, 2022)

Unit 15: Our Caring/Caregiving Dimension

- Reading: Chapter 14 of *The Flourishing Lawyer*
- Exercise #1 (from Chapter 14 of *The Flourishing Lawyer*): Artifacts of Meaning and Mattering
- Exercise #2 (from Chapter 14 of *The Flourishing Lawyer*): Exploring Our Sympathy-Empathy-Compassion Continuum
- Supplemental Resources for Teachers and Students
  - Paul Bloom, *Against Empathy: The Case for Rational Compassion* (New York: Harper Collins, 2016)
  - Christopher Kukk, *The Compassionate Achiever: How Helping Others Fuels Success* (San Francisco: HarperOne, 2017)
  - Trauma Processing Resources:
    - Bruce D. Perry and Oprah Winfrey, *What Happened to You? Conversations on Trauma, Resilience, and Healing* (New York: Flatiron Books, 2021)
    - Bessel van der Kolk, *The Body Keeps the Score: Brain, Mind, and Body in the Healing of Trauma* (New York: Penguin Books, 2014)
    - Laura Van Dernoot-Lipsky, *Trauma Stewardship: An Everyday Guide to Caring for Self While Caring for Others* (Oakland: Berrett-Koehler Publishers, 2009)

- Websites:
  - www.americanbar.org/groups/lawyer_assistance/resources/compassion_fatigue/
  - www.traumainformedlaw.org/resources/
  - https://www.livingabovethebar.org/trauma-and-burnout

Unit 16: Reflection Questions

- How can I begin and continue to treat myself like a scholar-athlete or scholar-performer?
- How can I begin and continue to give myself *regard* as an "artist"?
- What are my Top 5 "signature" character strengths (as identified by the VIA Institute on Character)? How can I embody my signature strengths daily/weekly?
- When do I feel like I am in *flow*? How can I cultivate flow more often in my personal and professional life?
- What is my ten-word purpose statement? How can I live my purpose daily/weekly? (See Exercise #2 in Chapter 10 of *The Flourishing Lawyer.*)
- How have I cultivated my PERMA (**p**ositive emotions, **e**ngagement, **r**elationships, **m**eaning, **a**chievement/accomplishment) through this self-discovery adventure? How can I continue to do so?
- If I were to create my own well-being framework, what elements or components would I include? (See Appendix D to *The Flourishing Lawyer.*) What does *eudaimonia* mean to me?
- How can I help *others* cultivate both hedonic (feeling good) and eudaimonic (functioning well) well-being?

Special Unit for Law Students Grappling with Grades and Identity: Multiple Pathways to Success

- Reading: "Finals Don't Finalize Who We Are," https://abaforlawstudents.com/2019/12/04/finals-dont-finalize-who-we-are-defining-success-in-law-school/
- Reading: "Law School Grades Are Not Your Story; You Are Your Story," https://abaforlawstudents.com/2020/01/09/law-school-grades-are-not-your-story-you-are-your-story/

Special Unit for Members of Our Profession Grappling with Fear

- Reading: Heidi K. Brown, *Untangling Fear in Lawyering: A Four-Step Journey Toward Powerful Advocacy* (Chicago: ABA Publishing, 2019)

- (Shorter) Reading: "Fear and Lawyering: Create a Work Culture of 'Psychological Safety' That Encourages Taking Intellectual and Creative Risks," *ABA Journal* (May 1, 2019), https://www.abajournal.com/magazine/article/fear-lawyering-psychological-safety
- (Shorter) Reading: "What Elite Athletes Like Naomi Osaka and Simone Biles Can Teach Lawyers About Performance Anxiety," *ABA Journal* (December 1, 2021), https://www.abajournal.com/magazine/article/what-elite-athletes-like-naomi-osaka-and-simone-biles-can-teach-lawyers-about-performance-anxiety

Special Unit for Members of Our Profession Grappling with Public Speaking Anxiety

- Reading: Heidi K. Brown, *The Introverted Lawyer: A Seven-Step Journey Toward Authentically Empowered Advocacy* (Chicago: ABA Publishing, 2017)
- Reading: Heidi K. Brown, *Untangling Fear in Lawyering: A Four-Step Journey Toward Powerful Advocacy* (Chicago: ABA Publishing, 2019)
- (Shorter) Reading: "Are You a Lawyer with Public Speaking Anxiety? You Are Not Alone," *ABA Journal* (March 1, 2019), https://www.abajournal.com/magazine/article/face-fear-dont-fake-it
- (Shorter) Reading: "What Elite Athletes Like Naomi Osaka and Simone Biles Can Teach Lawyers About Performance Anxiety," *ABA Journal* (December 1, 2021), https://www.abajournal.com/magazine/article/what-elite-athletes-like-naomi-osaka-and-simone-biles-can-teach-lawyers-about-performance-anxiety
- (Shorter) Reading: "Untangling Students' Fears about 1L Oral Arguments," https://teachlawbetter.com/2019/03/18/untangling-students-fears-about-1l-oral-arguments/

Special Unit on the Power of Introversion in Lawyering

- Reading: Heidi K. Brown, *The Introverted Lawyer: A Seven-Step Journey Toward Authentically Empowered Advocacy* (Chicago: ABA Publishing, 2017)
- (Shorter) Reading: "Talented but Overlooked: We Should Transform Hiring and Mentoring of Introverted Lawyers," *ABA Journal* (August 1, 2018), https://www.abajournal.com/magazine/article/talented_overlooked_introverted_lawyers
- (Shorter) Reading: "Navigating 'Introvert Hell': You Don't Have to Be Hard-Charging to Be an Impactful Legal Networker," *ABA Journal* (July 1, 2019), https://www.abajournal.com/magazine/article/navigating-introvert-hell-legal-networker

Additional Resources for Developing a Well-Being Curriculum

- Jarrod Reich, "Capitalizing on Healthy Lawyers: The Business Case for Law Firms to Promote and Prioritize Lawyer Well-Being," *Villanova Law Review* 65 (2020): 361–418
- The Association of American Law Schools (AALS) Section on Balance in Legal Education and the Mindfulness in Law Society maintain a list of courses on well-being and mindfulness taught at US law schools.
- Resources and contacts for incorporating positive psychology into legal education and practice training:
    - R. Lisle Baker, MAPP, "Designing a Positive Psychology Course for Lawyers," *Suffolk University Law Review* 51, no. 2 (2018): 207–288
    - Anne Brafford, MAPP, *Positive Professionals: Creating High-Performing Profitable Firms Through the Science of Engagement* (Chicago: American Bar Association, 2017)
    - Jordana A. Confino, CAPP, "Where Are We on the Path to Law Student Well-Being? Report on the ABA CoLAP Law Student Assistance Committee Law School Wellness Survey," *Journal of Legal Education* 68 (Spring 2019): 650–715; the Appendix to this article provides an extraordinary list of well-being programs at law schools throughout the United States
    - Individuals focusing on Positive Psychology curricula in legal education and practice:
        - Professor Heidi K. Brown (MAPP), The Flourishing Lawyer Project, www.theflourishinglawyer.org
        - Professor Lisle Baker (MAPP) and Professor Shailini Jandial George coteach a positive-psychology-based course at Suffolk University Law School called Preparing for Professional Success
        - Professor Lisle Baker (MAPP) teaches Positive Psychology for Lawyers, and an intercession course called Character and Fitness for Professional Success, at Suffolk University Law School
        - Professor Jordana Confino (CAPP) teaches a Positive Lawyering course at Fordham University School of Law
        - Associate Dean John Hollway (MAPP) teaches Positive Psychology in Legal Practice at the University of Pennsylvania Carey Law School
        - Professor Dan Bowling (MAPP) teaches Well-Being and the Practice of Law at Duke University School of Law

- Martha Knudsen (MAPP) is the Executive Director of the Utah State Bar Well-Being Committee for the Legal Profession, and incorporates principles of applied positive psychology into her programming
- Anne Brafford (MAPP) is the Vice President of the Institute for Well-Being in Law, which provides evidence-based education in well-being for members of the legal profession
- **Also, while not solely grounded in positive psychology principles, Professor Rosario Lozada teaches a course called Professional Identity and Well-Being Practices in the Legal Profession at Florida International University College of Law; additionally, Professor Christopher Corts teaches a course called The Happy Lawyer at the University of Richmond School of Law

Positive Podcasts

- Kevin Pratt, *The Human Lawyer*, https://thehuman.lawyer/
- Mike Anderson and Darlene Tonelli, *The Lawyer Life Podcast*, https://www.interalia-law.com/podcast/
- Kaitlyn O'Connor and Laura Manchester, *Mens Sana Podcast*, https://podcasts.apple.com/us/podcast/mens-sana-a-motion-for-mental-health/id1486109928
- Jennifer Leonard, *Law2030 Podcast*, University of Pennsylvania School of Law's Future of the Profession Initiative, https://podcasts.apple.com/us/podcast/law-2030/id1505898171
- Shelley Appleby-Ostroff, *XL Legal*, https://podcasts.apple.com/us/podcast/xl-legal/id1510039293
- Leslie Garfield Tenzer, *Law to Fact*, https://www.lawtofact.com/
- Scott Love, *The Partner Podcast*, https://podcasts.apple.com/us/podcast/the-partner-podcast/id589504175
- Adriana Linares, *New Solo*, https://legaltalknetwork.com/podcasts/new-solo/
- Christina Previte, *Wake Up Call #FEMSQUIRE Podcast*, https://podcasts.apple.com/us/podcast/wake-up-call/id1476019292
- Pamela Deneuve, *Lawyer of the Week*, https://pameladeneuve.com/lawyeroftheweek/
- Jake Sanders and Paul Julius, *Lawsome*, https://www.thelawsomepodcast.com/
- Angela Han, *Fit to Practice*, https://www.angela-han.com/podcast

Appendix D Sample "Personalized Well-Being Framework"

To build upon my master's degree in applied positive psychology, I am pursuing certification in positive-psychology-based coaching through an organization called Positive Acorn led by Dr. Robert Biswas-Diener. As part of our coursework, Dr. Biswas-Diener prompted my classmates and me to imagine and craft our own well-being frameworks. I've shared mine with you here. Consider carving out some time to design your *own* well-being model. What does *your* definition of *eudaimonia* look like? What elements of flourishing might you include?

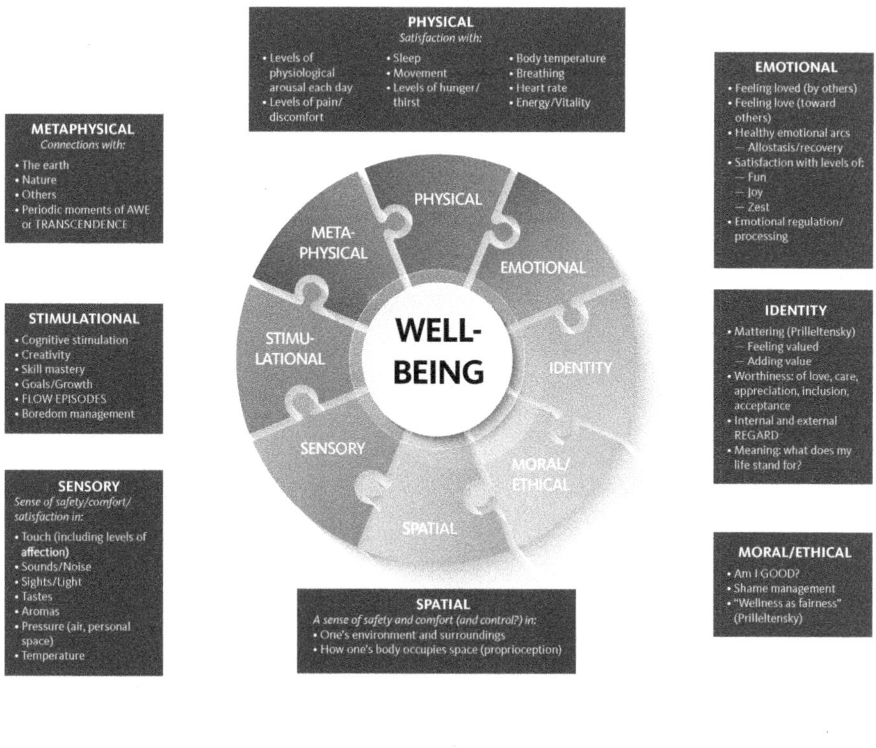

Notes

1. Heidi K. Brown, "Let's Mend Our Profession by Exploring the Mental and the Physical," *ABA Journal* (April 1, 2020), https://www.abajournal.com/magazine/article/lets-mend-our-profession-by-exploring-the-mental-and-the-physical.
2. National Task Force on Lawyer Well-Being, "The Path to Lawyer Well-Being: Practical Recommendations for Positive Change," August 14, 2017, 9, https://lawyerwellbeing.net/wp-content/uploads/2017/11/Lawyer-Wellbeing-Report.pdf.
3. Martin E. P. Seligman, *Flourish: A Visionary New Understanding of Happiness and Well-Being* (New York: Atria Books, 2011).
4. Seligman, *Flourish,* 16.
5. Steven Pressfield, *Do the Work: Overcome Resistance and Get Out of Your Own Way* (New York: Black Irish Entertainment, 2015), 38.
6. Heidi K. Brown, "Get with the Pronoun," *Legal Communication and Rhetoric: JALWD* 17 (2020), https://www.alwd.org/lcr-archives/fall-2020-volume-17/575-get-with-the-pronoun.
7. Lea Waters, Sara B. Algoe, Jane Dutton, Robert Emmons, Barbara L. Fredrickson, Emily Heaphy, Judith T. Moskowitz, Kristin Neff, Ryan Niemiec, Cynthia Pury, and Michael Steger, "Positive Psychology in a Pandemic: Buffering, Bolstering, and Building Mental Health," *The Journal of Positive Psychology* (2021): 1–21, https://doi.org/10.1080/17439760.2021.1871945.
8. Barbara Fredrickson, *Positivity: Discover the Upward Spiral That Will Change Your Life* (New York: Harmony, 2009), 21, 25.
9. "Flourish," in *Lexico Dictionaries* (Oxford Dictionary), accessed September 9, 2021, https://www.lexico.com/definition/flourish.
10. "Flourish," in *Merriam-Webster* (Merriam-Webster Dictionary), accessed September 9, 2021, https://www.merriam-webster.com/dictionary/flourish.
11. "Flourish," in *Lexico Dictionaries* (Oxford Dictionary), accessed September 9, 2021, https://www.lexico.com/definition/flourish.
12. Bruce D. Perry and Oprah Winfrey, *What Happened to You? Conversations on Trauma, Resilience, and Healing* (New York: Flatiron Books, 2021), 196.
13. John J. Ratey and Richard Manning, *Go Wild: Eat Fat, Run Free, Be Social, and Follow Evolution's Other Rules for Total Health and Well-Being* (New York: Little, Brown Spark, 2014), 15.

14. Michelle Tea, *Modern Tarot: Connecting with Your Higher Self Through the Wisdom of the Cards* (New York: HarperOne, 2017), 75.
15. Benjamin Sells, *The Soul of the Law* (Chicago: ABA Publishing, 2013).
16. Leonard Cohen, "Anthem," track 5 on *The Future,* Columbia Records, 1992, compact disc.
17. Mihaly Csikszentmihalyi, *Flow: The Psychology of Optimal Experience* (New York: Harper Perennial, 1990).
18. Csikszentmihalyi, *Flow,* 4.
19. Csikszentmihalyi, *Flow,* 3.
20. U2, "One," track 3 on *Achtung Baby,* Island Records, 1991, compact disc.
21. Julia Cameron, *The Artist's Way: A Spiritual Path to Higher Creativity* (New York: Jeremy P. Tarcher/Putnam, 2002), 9.
22. Alanis Morissette, "That I Would Be Good," track 6 on *Supposed Former Infatuation Junkie,* Maverick, 1998, compact disc.
23. Shelly L. Gable, Harry T. Reis, Emily A. Impett, and Evan R. Asher, "What Do You Do When Things Go Right? The Intrapersonal and Interpersonal Benefits of Sharing Positive Events," *Journal of Personality and Social Psychology* 87 (2004): 228, 233, https:/doi.org/10.1037/0022-3514.87.2.228.
24. Julian Weissglass, "Constructivist Listening for Empowerment and Change," *The Educational Forum* 54, no. 4 (1990): 351–370, http://doi.org/10.1080/00131729009335561.
25. Emile G. Bruneau and Rebecca Saxe, "The Power of Being Heard: The Benefits of 'Perspective-Giving' in the Context of Intergroup Conflict," *Journal of Experimental Social Psychology* 48, no. 4 (2012): 855–866, https://doi.org/10.1016/j.jesp.2012.02.017.
26. For an interesting summary of what happened in each state, see "Bar Exam Modifications During COVID-19: 50-State Resources," *Justia,* https://www.justia.com/covid-19/50-state-covid-19-resources/bar-exam-modifications-during-covid-19-50-state-resources/.
27. Stephanie Francis Ward, "Jurisdictions with COVID-19-Related Diploma Privilege Are Going Back to Bar Exam Admissions," *ABA Journal* (December 10, 2020), https://www.abajournal.com/web/article/jurisdictions-with-covid-related-diploma-privilege-going-back-to-bar-exam-admissions.
28. Sarah Mills, "All the States That Are Allowing Law Graduates to Begin Practicing During the Pandemic," *Lawline* (October 21, 2020), https://blog.lawline.com/all-the-states-that-are-allowing-law-graduates-to-begin-practicing-during-the-pandemic.
29. Natalie Runyon, "Exploring Diploma Privilege and Alternatives for Attorney Licensure," Thomson Reuters (April 13, 2021), https://www.thomsonreuters.com/en-us/posts/legal/diploma-privilege/.

30. Runyon, "Exploring Diploma Privilege and Alternatives for Attorney Licensure."
31. Sam Skolnik, "California Supreme Court OKs Plan for Bar Exam Narrow Failures," *Bloomberg Law* (January 28, 2021), https://news.bloomberglaw.com/business-and-practice/california-supreme-court-oks-plan-for-bar-exam-narrow-failures.
32. Stephanie Francis Ward, "State Supreme Court Asked to Consider New Licensure Paths for Lawyers," *ABA Journal* (July 1, 2021), https://www.abajournal.com/news/article/oregon-supreme-court-asked-to-consider-new-licensure-paths-for-lawyers.
33. "Oregon Supreme Court Opens Door for Alternatives to Bar Exam," *AP* (January 13, 2022), https://apnews.com/article/oregon-oregon-supreme-court-9cb0cc17109f3b5f1d7169cd0b2c2c7d.
34. Josh Verges, "Should New Lawyers Have to Pass the Bar Exam? MN Supreme Court Is Open to Alternatives," *Pioneer Press* (September 30, 2021), https://www.twincities.com/2021/09/30/should-new-lawyers-have-to-pass-the-bar-exam-mn-supreme-court-is-open-to-alternatives/.
35. New York Judiciary Law § 90 (2021), https://newyork.public.law/laws/n.y._judiciary_law_section_90.
36. Deborah L. Rhode, "Moral Character as a Professional Credential," *The Yale Law Journal* 94, no. 3 (Jan. 1985): 491, 518.
37. State Bar of California, "Rules of Professional Conduct," Rule 1.1(b) (2021), https://www.calbar.ca.gov/Portals/0/documents/rules/New-Rules-of-Professional-Conduct-1.pdf; Washington Supreme Court, "Admission and Practice Rules" (2021), http://www.courts.wa.gov/court_rules/?fa=court_rules.rulesPDF&groupName=ga&setName=APR&pdf=1.
38. Texas Board of Law Examiners, "Board of Law Examiners Guidelines for Determining Character and Fitness and Overseeing Probationary License Holder" (2021), https://ble.texas.gov/guidelines-for-determining-c&f-and-overseeing-pls.
39. Derek Davis, "A Higher Bar: Revisiting Character and Fitness in the Profession," *The Practice* 4, no. 3 (March/April 2018), https://thepractice.law.harvard.edu/article/a-higher-bar/.
40. Rhode, "Moral Character."
41. Davis, "A Higher Bar," citing Rhode, 498 n.15.
42. Davis, "A Higher Bar."
43. Davis, "A Higher Bar."
44. American Bar Association, "ABA Timeline," https://www.americanbar.org/about_the_aba/timeline/.
45. Davis, "A Higher Bar."
46. Davis, "A Higher Bar."

47. Davis, "A Higher Bar."
48. Davis, "A Higher Bar."
49. Davis, "A Higher Bar."
50. A 2017 state survey can be found here: "Bar Exam Application Questions Pertaining to Mental Health, School/Criminal History, and Financial Issues," *Yale Law School* (2017), https://law.yale.edu/sites/default/files/area/department/cdo/document/50_state_survey_-_bar_exams_and_mental_health_-_fall_2017.pdf.
51. Davis, "A Higher Bar."
52. Davis, "A Higher Bar."
53. Rhode, "Moral Character," 493.
54. Rhode, "Moral Character," 493–494.
55. Rhode, "Moral Character," 494.
56. Davis, "A Higher Bar."
57. Marilyn Cavicchia, "A New Look at Character and Fitness: Bar Leaders, Lawyers, Others Urge Elimination of Mental Health Questions," *ABA Bar Leader* 44, no. 3 (January 2020), https://www.americanbar.org/groups/bar_services/publications/bar_leader/2019_20/january-february/a-new-look-at-character-and-fitness-bar-leaders-lawyers-others-urge-elimination-of-mental-health-questions/; Elle Jones, "Law Students Helped Remove Mental Health Question from N.H. Bar Exam," *Concord Monitor* (June 27, 2020), https://www.concordmonitor.com/NH-Removes-Questions-on-Mental-Health-Conditions-from-Bar-Admissions-Applications-34922564; Christian Nolan, "Law School Grads in NY Won't Face Mental Health Inquiry," *NYSBA* (March 1, 2020), https://nysba.org/mentalhealthinquiry/; Debra Cassens Weiss, "New York Removes Mental Health Question from State Bar Application," *ABA Journal* (February 28, 2020) (reporting that New York is the 11th state to remove mental health questions from its application for admission to the bar), https://www.abajournal.com/news/article/new-york-removes-mental-health-questions-from-state-bar-application. See also https://www.americanbar.org/content/dam/aba/administrative/commission-disability-rights/mh-provisions-state-bar-exams.pdf; "Changes Coming to Mental Health Questions on Bar Exam Application," *State Bar of Michigan* (March 18, 2020), https://www.michbar.org/News/NewsDetail/nid/5681/Changes-Coming-to-Mental-Health-Questions-on-Bar-Exam-Application.
58. Davis, "A Higher Bar."
59. Benjamin Franklin, *The Autobiography of Benjamin Franklin,* ed. Peter Conn (Philadelphia: Penn Press, 2005).
60. Franklin, *The Autobiography,* 66–67.
61. Franklin, *The Autobiography,* 69.
62. Franklin, *The Autobiography,* 70.

63. Franklin, *The Autobiography*, 70.
64. Franklin, *The Autobiography*, 70.
65. Franklin, *The Autobiography*, 73.
66. Plato, *Apology*, trans. Benjamin Jowett, http://classics.mit.edu//Plato/apology.html.
67. Christopher Phillips, *Socrates Café: A Fresh Taste of Philosophy* (New York: W.W. Norton & Company, 2001).
68. Plato, *Apology*.
69. Plato, *Apology*.
70. Plato, *Apology*.
71. Plato, *Apology*.
72. "Fitness," in *Lexico Dictionaries* (Oxford Dictionary), accessed September 10, 2021, https://www.lexico.com/en/definition/fitness.
73. The next few paragraphs were originally published in Heidi K. Brown, "Let's Mend Our Profession by Exploring the Mental and the Physical," *ABA Journal* (April 2, 2020), https://www.abajournal.com/magazine/article/lets-mend-our-profession-by-exploring-the-mental-and-the-physical.
74. National Task Force on Lawyer Well-Being, 9.
75. Andrew Wood, "Stress in Elite Sports," *BelievePerform*, https://believeperform.com/stress-in-elite-sports/.
76. Wood, "Stress in Elite Sports."
77. Wood, "Stress in Elite Sports."
78. Wood, "Stress in Elite Sports."
79. Wood, "Stress in Elite Sports."
80. Anne Brafford, "Well-Being Toolkit for Lawyers and Legal Employers," 4, https://lawyerwellbeing.net/wp-content/uploads/2020/02/Toolkit-Full_Final_July-30-2018.pdf.
81. Twyla Tharp, *The Creative Habit: Learn It and Use It for Life* (New York: Simon & Schuster, 2006), 15.
82. Csikszentmihalyi, *Flow*, 4, 52.
83. Cameron, *The Artist's Way*, 9.
84. https://www.viacharacter.org/character-strengths/zest.
85. James O. Pawelski, "Introduction: What Is the Eudaimonic Turn?" in *The Eudaimonic Turn: Well-Being in Literary Studies*, ed. James O. Pawelski and D. J. Moores (Teaneck, NJ: Fairleigh Dickinson University Press, 2013), 1–26; Alejandro Adler and Martin E. P. Seligman, "Using Wellbeing for Public Policy: Theory, Measurement, and Recommendations," *International Journal of Wellbeing* 6, no. 1 (2016): 1, 5, https://doi.org/10.5502/ijw.v6i1.1. Portions of this discussion of the "eudaimonic turn"

first appeared in my article, "The Eudaimonic Turn: How We Can Help Lawyers Flourish," *ABA Journal* (September 7, 2021), https://www.abajournal.com/columns/article/the-eudaimonic-turn-how-we-can-help-lawyers-flourish.

86. Pawelski, "Introduction: What Is the Eudaimonic Turn?"; James O. Pawelski, "The Positive Humanities: Culture and Human Flourishing," in *The Oxford Handbook of the Positive Humanities*, ed. Louis Tay and James O. Pawelski (Oxford: Oxford University Press, forthcoming 2022).
87. Pawelski, "The Positive Humanities," 1.
88. Alejandro Adler and Martin E. P. Seligman, "Using Wellbeing for Public Policy: Theory, Measurement, and Recommendations," *International Journal of Wellbeing* 6, no. 1 (2016): 1, 5, https://doi.org/10.5502/ijw.v6i1.1.
89. Martin E. P. Seligman, "The President's Address," *American Psychologist* 53 (1999): 559–562, https://positivepsychologynews.com/ppnd_wp/wp-content/uploads/2018/04/APA-President-Address-1998.pdf.
90. Martin E. P. Seligman and Mihaly Csikszentmihalyi, "Positive Psychology: An Introduction," *American Psychologist* 55, no. 1 (2000): 5–14, https://doi.org/10.1037/0003-066X.55.1.5.
91. James O. Pawelski, "The Elements Model: Toward a New Generation of Positive Interventions," *Journal of Positive Psychology* 15, no. 5 (2020): 675–679, https://doi.org/10.1080/17439760.2020.1789710.
92. John B. Watson, *Behaviorism* (New York: W.W. Norton, 1925).
93. John B. Watson, "Psychology as the Behaviorist Views It," *Psychological Review* 20 (1913): 158, 176, https://resources.saylor.org/wwwresources/archived/site/wp-content/uploads/2012/01/PSYCH305-7.1.pdf.
94. Seligman and Csikszentmihalyi, "Positive Psychology," 6.
95. Seligman and Csikszentmihalyi, "Positive Psychology," 5.
96. Seligman and Csikszentmihalyi, "Positive Psychology," 6.
97. Carl Rogers, *Client-Centered Therapy: Its Current Practice, Implications and Theory* (London: Constable, 1951).
98. Abraham Maslow, *The Farthest Reaches of Human Nature* (New York: Viking, 1971).
99. Christopher Peterson, *A Primer in Positive Psychology* (New York: Oxford University Press, 2006), 8.
100. Peterson, *A Primer in Positive Psychology*, 8.
101. Bo Jacobsen, *Invitation to Existential Psychology* (Hoboken, NJ: Wiley, 2007), cited in Barbara Walker, "The Humanistic/Person-Centered Theoretical Model," in *Routledge Handbook of Applied Sport Psychology: A Comprehensive Guide for Students and Practitioners*, ed. Stephanie Hanrahan and Mark Anderson (London: Routledge, 2012), 123.
102. Carl Rogers, *On Becoming a Person: A Therapist's View of Psychotherapy* (London: Constable, 1961).

103. Seligman, "The President's Address."
104. Seligman, "The President's Address"; Peterson, *A Primer in Positive Psychology,* 5.
105. Peterson, *A Primer in Positive Psychology,* 5.
106. Peterson, *A Primer in Positive Psychology,* 5.
107. Seligman and Csikszentmihalyi, "Positive Psychology," 7.
108. James O. Pawelski, "Defining the 'Positive' in Positive Psychology: Part I. A Descriptive Analysis," *Journal of Positive Psychology* 11, no. 4 (2016): 339, 340, https://doi.org/10.1080/17439760.2015.1137627.
109. William C. Compton, *An Introduction to Positive Psychology* (London: Thomson Wadsworth, 2005), 182.
110. Martin E. P. Seligman, "Positive Psychology: A Personal History," *Annual Review of Clinical Psychology* 15 (2019): 1–23, https://doi.org/10.1146/annurev-clinpsy-050718-095653.
111. Seligman and Csikszentmihalyi, "Positive Psychology," 5–14.
112. Peterson, *A Primer in Positive Psychology,* 8–9; Seligman and Csikszentmihalyi, "Positive Psychology."
113. Seligman and Csikszentmihalyi, "Positive Psychology," 7.
114. Seligman, "Positive Psychology: A Personal History," 18.
115. Seligman and Csikszentmihalyi, "Positive Psychology," 5.
116. Pawelski, "Defining the 'Positive' in Positive Psychology: Part I," 340; Seligman and Csikszentmihalyi, "Positive Psychology," 5.
117. Seligman and Csikszentmihalyi, "Positive Psychology," 7.
118. Seligman and Csikszentmihalyi, "Positive Psychology," 7.
119. Seligman and Csikszentmihalyi, "Positive Psychology," 13.
120. Pawelski, "Defining the 'Positive' in Positive Psychology: Part I," 341.
121. Seligman, "Positive Psychology: A Personal History," 1–23.
122. Pawelski, "Defining the 'Positive' in Positive Psychology: Part I," 340.
123. Martin E. P. Seligman, *Flourish: A Visionary New Understanding of Happiness and Well-Being* (New York: Atria Books, 2011), 11.
124. Peterson, *A Primer in Positive Psychology,* 4.
125. Seligman, *Flourish,* 13.
126. Adler and Seligman, "Using Wellbeing for Public Policy," 5.
127. Adler and Seligman, "Using Wellbeing for Public Policy," 5.
128. Adler and Seligman, "Using Wellbeing for Public Policy," 5.
129. Adler and Seligman, "Using Wellbeing for Public Policy," 5.
130. Peterson, *A Primer in Positive Psychology,* 15.
131. Peterson, *A Primer in Positive Psychology,* 15.

132. Peterson, *A Primer in Positive Psychology*, 16.
133. Barbara Fredrickson, *Positivity: Discover the Upward Spiral That Will Change Your Life* (New York: Harmony, 2009), 33.
134. Pawelski, "Defining the 'Positive' in Positive Psychology: Part I," 350.
135. Tim Lomas, "Positive Psychology—The Second Wave," *The Psychologist* 29 (2016): 536–539.
136. Martin E. P. Seligman, *Authentic Happiness: Using the New Positive Psychology to Realize Your Potential for Lasting Fulfillment* (New York: Free Press, 2002).
137. Seligman, *Flourish*, 16.
138. Fredrickson, *Positivity*, 21, 25, 91.
139. Mihaly Csikszentmihalyi, *Flow: The Psychology of Optimal Experience* (New York: Harper Perennial, 1990), 4.
140. Barbara L. Fredrickson, *Love 2.0: Creating Happiness and Health in Moments of Connection* (New York: Penguin Group, 2013).
141. Seligman, *Flourish*, 17.
142. Seligman, *Flourish*, 18–19.
143. Pawelski, "Defining the 'Positive' in Positive Psychology: Part I," 349.
144. Pawelski, "The Elements Model," 675.
145. Kristin Layous and Sonja Lyubomirsky, "The How, Who, What, When, and Why of Happiness: Mechanisms Underlying the Success of Positive Interventions," in *Positive Emotion: Integrating the Light Sides and Dark Sides*, ed. June Gruber and Judith Tedlie Moskowitz (Oxford: Oxford University Press, 2014), 472–495; Stephen S. Schueller, "Preferences for Positive Psychology Exercises," *The Journal of Positive Psychology* 5, no. 3 (2010): 192, 193.
146. Carmela A. White, Bob Uttl, and Mark D. Holder, "Meta-Analyses of Positive Psychology Interventions: The Effects Are Much Smaller Than Previously Reported," *PLoS ONE 14*, no. 5 (2019), e0216588, 2, https://doi.org/10.1371/journal.pone.0216588.
147. Nancy L. Sin and Sonja Lyubomirsky, "Enhancing Well-Being and Alleviating Depressive Symptoms with Positive Psychology Interventions: A Practice-Friendly Meta-Analysis," *Journal of Clinical Psychology* 65 (2009): 467, 468, http://doi.org/10.1002/jclp.20593.
148. Layous and Lyubomirsky, "The How, Who, What, When, and Why," 487.
149. Pawelski, "The Elements Model," 676.
150. James O. Pawelski, "Defining the 'Positive' in Positive Psychology: Part II. A Normative Analysis," *Journal of Positive Psychology* 11, no. 4 (2016): 357, 358, https://doi.org/10.1080/17439760.2015.1137628.
151. Pawelski, "Defining the 'Positive' in Positive Psychology: Part II," 359.
152. Pawelski, "Defining the 'Positive' in Positive Psychology: Part II," 360.
153. Pawelski, "Defining the 'Positive' in Positive Psychology: Part II," 360.

154. Pawelski, "Defining the 'Positive' in Positive Psychology: Part II," 360.
155. Pawelski, "Defining the 'Positive' in Positive Psychology: Part II," 361.
156. J. Pawelski, personal communication, September 5, 2020.
157. Pawelski, "Defining the 'Positive' in Positive Psychology: Part I," 350.
158. Pawelski, "Defining the 'Positive' in Positive Psychology: Part I," 351.
159. Adler and Seligman, "Using Wellbeing for Public Policy," 6–9.
160. The Emmons Mood Indicator, described in Edward F. Diener and Robert A. Emmons, "The Independence of Positive and Negative Affect," *Journal of Personality and Social Psychology* 47 (1984): 1105–1117; The Positive and Negative Affect Schedule, described in Jeana L. Magyar-Moe, *Therapist Guide to Positive Psychological Interventions* (Waltham, MA: Elsevier Academic Press, 2009).
161. The Satisfaction with Life Scale, described in Edward Diener, Robert A. Emmons, Randy J. Larsen, and Sharon Griffin, "The Satisfaction with Life Scale," *Journal of Personality Assessment* 49, no. 1 (1985): 71–75, http://dx.doi.org/10.1207/s15327752jpa4901_13.
162. The Subjective Happiness Scale, described in Sonja Lyubomirsky and Heidi S. Lepper, "A Measure of Subjective Happiness: Preliminary Reliability and Construct Validation," *Social Indicators Research* 46, no. 2 (1999): 137–155, http://dx.doi.org/10.1023/A:1006824100041.
163. The Well-Being Survey, described in Organisation for Economic Co-operation and Development, *OECD Guidelines on Measuring Subjective Well-Being* (Paris: OECD Publishing, 2013).
164. Ryff's Well-Being Scales, described in Carol D. Ryff and Corey Lee M. Keyes, "The Structure of Psychological Well-Being Revisited," *Journal of Personality and Social Psychology* 69 (1995): 719–727, http://dx.doi.org/10.1037/0022-3514.69.4.719.
165. The Flourishing Scale, described in Edward Diener, Derrick Wirtz, William Tov, Chu Kim-Prieto, Dong-won Choi, Shigehiro Oishi, and Robert Biswas-Diener, "New Well-Being Measures: Short Scales to Assess Flourishing and Positive and Negative Feelings," *Social Indicators Research* 97, no. 2 (2010): 143–156, https://doi.org/10.1007/s11205-009-9493-y; the PERMA-Profiler, described in Julie Butler and Margaret L. Kern, "The PERMA-Profiler: A Brief Multidimensional Measure of Flourishing," *International Journal of Wellbeing* 6, no. 3 (2016): 1–48, https://doi.org/10.5502/ijw.v6i3.526.
166. The Gratitude Questionnaire, found in Michael E. McCullough, Robert A. Emmons, and Jo-Ann Tsang, "The Gratitude Questionnaire–Six Item Form (GQ-6)" (2001), https://ppc.sas.upenn.edu/sites/default/files/gratitudequestionnaire6.pdf.
167. Martin E. P. Seligman, Attributional Style Questionnaire, https://ppc.sas.upenn.edu/resources/questionnaires-researchers/attributional-style-questionnaire.
168. National Task Force on Lawyer Well-Being, "The Path to Lawyer Well-Being: Practical Recommendations for Positive Change," August 14, 2017, 9, https://lawyerwellbeing.net/wp-content/uploads/2017/11/Lawyer-Wellbeing-Report.pdf.
169. Voltaire, *Candide, ou l'optimisme* (Geneva: Cramer, 1759).

170. Stewart Levine, "Well-Being for Attorneys," *ABA Law Practice Today* (Jan. 14, 2019), https://www.lawpracticetoday.org/article/well-being-for-attorneys/.
171. Levine, "Well-Being for Attorneys."
172. Levine, "Well-Being for Attorneys."
173. Jarrod F. Reich, "Capitalizing on Healthy Lawyers: The Business Case for Law Firms to Promote and Prioritize Lawyer Well-Being," *Villanova Law Review* 65 (2020): 361–418.
174. Virginia State Bar, "Rules of Professional Conduct," Rule 1.1 (2021), http://www.vsb.org/pro-guidelines/index.php/rules/client-lawyer-relationship/rule1-1/.
175. Vermont Supreme Court, "Order Promulgating Amendments to Comment to Rule 1.1 of the Vermont Rules of Professional Conduct" (2019), https://www.vermontjudiciary.org/sites/default/files/documents/PROMULGATEDV.R.Pr_.C.%201_0_0.pdf.
176. State Bar of California Rules of Professional Conduct, Rule 1.1(b) (2021), https://www.calbar.ca.gov/Portals/0/documents/rules/New-Rules-of-Professional-Conduct-1.pdf.
177. John J. Ratey and Richard Manning, *Go Wild: Eat Fat, Run Free, Be Social, and Follow Evolution's Other Rules for Total Health and Well-Being* (New York: Little, Brown Spark, 2014), 134, 187, 259.
178. Ratey and Manning, *Go Wild: Eat Fat, Run Free,* 134.
179. Ratey and Manning, *Go Wild: Eat Fat, Run Free,* 187.
180. Ratey and Manning, *Go Wild: Eat Fat, Run Free,* 134, 187, 259.
181. Christopher Phillips, *Socrates Café: A Fresh Taste of Philosophy* (New York: W.W. Norton & Company, 2001), 11.
182. Phillips, *Socrates Café,* 18.
183. Phillips, *Socrates Café,* 13.
184. Phillips, *Socrates Café,* 22.
185. Ryan M. Niemiec, *Character Strengths Interventions: A Field Guide for Practitioners* (Boston: Hogrefe Publishing, 2018), 18; Christopher Peterson and Martin E. P. Seligman, *Character Strengths and Virtues: A Handbook and Classification* (Washington, D.C.: American Psychological Association, 2004), 3.
186. Nansook Park, Christopher Peterson, and Martin E. P. Seligman, "Character Strengths in Fifty-Four Nations and the Fifty US States," *Journal of Positive Psychology* 1, no. 3 (2006): 603, https://doi.org/10.1080/17439760600619567.
187. Park et al., "Character Strengths in Fifty-Four Nations," 603.
188. Niemiec, *Character Strengths Interventions,* 9; Peterson and Seligman, *Character Strengths and Virtues,* 10.
189. Peterson and Seligman, *Character Strengths and Virtues,* 10, 12.

190. Niemiec, *Character Strengths Interventions*, 22.
191. Niemiec, *Character Strengths Interventions*, 22, 36.
192. https://www.viacharacter.org/.
193. https://www.viacharacter.org/.
194. Ryan M. Niemiec, "Finding the Golden Mean: The Overuse, Underuse, and Optimal Use of Character Strengths," *Counselling Psychology Quarterly* 32, nos. 3–4 (2019): 453, 454, https://doi.org/10.1080/09515070.2019.1617674; VIA Institute on Character (2021), https://www.viacharacter.org/.
195. Niemiec, "Finding the Golden Mean," 454; Martin E. P. Seligman, "Positive Psychology: A Personal History," *Annual Review of Clinical Psychology* 15 (2019): 10–11, https://doi.org/10.1146/annurev-clinpsy-050718-095653.
196. Peterson and Seligman, *Character Strengths and Virtues,* 29–30.
197. https://www.viacharacter.org/.
198. Niemiec, *Character Strengths Interventions*, 18.
199. Niemiec, *Character Strengths Interventions*, 18.
200. R. Niemiec, personal communication, February 5, 2021.
201. Peterson and Seligman, *Character Strengths and Virtues,* 28.
202. Niemiec, *Character Strengths Interventions*, 15–16.
203. VIA Institute, "The 24 Character Strengths," Find Your 24 Character Strengths | Personal Strengths List (VIA Institute on Character), accessed September 22, 2021, https://www.viacharacter.org/character-strengths.
204. R. Niemiec, personal communication, February 5, 2021.
205. https://www.viacharacter.org/reports/total-24.
206. R. Niemiec, personal communication, February 5, 2021.
207. Niemiec, *Character Strengths Interventions*, 9.
208. Peterson and Seligman, *Character Strengths and Virtues,* 18.
209. Lucy C. Hone, Aaron Jarden, Scott Duncan, and Grant M. Schofield, "Flourishing in New Zealand Workers: Associations with Lifestyle Behaviors, Physical Health, Psychosocial, and Work-Related Indicators," *Journal of Occupational and Environmental Medicine* 57, no. 9 (2015): 973–983, https://doi.org/10.1097/JOM.0000000000000508.
210. Niemiec, "Finding the Golden Mean," 454.
211. Niemiec, "Finding the Golden Mean," 456.
212. Niemiec, "Finding the Golden Mean," 455.
213. Niemiec, "Finding the Golden Mean," 456.
214. Niemiec, "Finding the Golden Mean," 457, Table 1 and Table 2; https://www.viacharacter.org/topics/articles/the-overuse-underuse-and-optimal-use-of-character-strengths.

215. Stephen M. Schueller, "Person–Activity Fit in Positive Psychological Interventions," in *The Wiley Blackwell Handbook of Positive Psychological Interventions,* ed. Acacia C. Parks and Stephen M. Schueller (Hoboken, NJ: John Wiley & Sons, 2014), 388–389.
216. Niemiec, "Finding the Golden Mean," 466–467.
217. Ryan Niemiec and Robert McGrath, *The Power of Character Strengths: Appreciate and Ignite Your Positive Personality* (Cincinnati: VIA Institute on Character, 2019).
218. Niemiec, *Character Strengths Interventions,* 50.
219. Niemiec, *Character Strengths Interventions,* 48.
220. Niemiec, *Character Strengths Interventions,* 50.
221. Niemiec, *Character Strengths Interventions,* 59.
222. Niemiec, *Character Strengths Interventions,* 60–61.
223. VIA Institute, "Strength Basics: The Strengths that Help You Thrive," *Via Institute on Character* (2021), https://www.viacharacter.org/topics/articles/what-are-your-signature-strengths.
224. Niemiec, *Character Strengths Interventions,* 41–42 (Character Strength Intervention 11).
225. Niemiec, *Character Strengths Interventions,* 51. This model is alternatively described by Niemiec as "Labeling, Explaining, Appreciating."
226. Barbara L. Fredrickson, *Love 2.0: Creating Happiness and Health in Moments of Connection* (New York: Penguin Group, 2013), 17.
227. Fredrickson, *Love 2.0,* 17.
228. VIA Institute on Character; Niemiec, *Character Strengths Interventions,* 44.
229. Mihaly Csikszentmihalyi, *Flow: The Psychology of Optimal Experience* (New York: Harper Perennial, 1990).
230. Angela L. Duckworth, *Grit: The Power of Passion and Perseverance* (New York: Scribner, 2016).
231. Csikszentmihalyi, *Flow,* 49.
232. Christopher Peterson, *A Primer in Positive Psychology* (New York: Oxford University Press, 2006), 67.
233. Peterson, *A Primer in Positive Psychology,* 66.
234. Csikszentmihalyi, *Flow,* 52.
235. Angela L. Duckworth, Christopher Peterson, Michael D. Matthews, and Dennis R. Kelly, "Grit: Perseverance and Passion for Long-Term Goals," *Journal of Personality and Social Psychology* 92 (2007): 1087, https://doi.org/10.1037/0022-3514.92.6.1087.
236. Duckworth, *Grit,* 62.
237. Duckworth, *Grit,* 91.
238. Duckworth, *Grit,* 118.

239. Duckworth, *Grit,* 131.

240. K. Anders Ericsson, Ralf T. Krampe, and Clemens Tesch-Romer, "The Role of Deliberate Practice in the Acquisition of Expert Performance," *Psychological Review* 100, no. 3 (1993): 363–406, https://doi.org/10.1037//0033-295X.100.3.363.

241. William James, *Principles of Psychology: Briefer Course* (Boston: Harvard University Press, 1984) (Original work published 1892), 128; Wendy Wood and David T. Neal, "Healthy Through Habit: Interventions for Initiating and Maintaining Healthy Behavior Change," *Behavioral Science & Policy* 2, no. 1 (2016), 71–83.

242. James, *Principles of Psychology,* 129.

243. James, *Principles of Psychology,* 128.

244. Wood and Neal, "Healthy Through Habit," 73.

245. Wood and Neal, "Healthy Through Habit," 74.

246. James, *Principles of Psychology,* 134.

247. Csikszentmihalyi, *Flow,* 49.

248. Peterson, *A Primer in Positive Psychology,* 67.

249. See, e.g., Sarah Sinnamon, Aidan Moran, and Michael O'Connell, "Flow Among Musicians: Measuring Peak Experiences of Student Performers," *Journal of Research in Music Education* 60, no. 1 (2012): 6–25, https://doi.org/10.1177/0022429411434931; S. Victoria Jaque, Paula Thomson, Jessica Zaragoza, Frances Werner, Jeff Podeszwa, and Kristin Jacobs, "Creative Flow and Physiologic States in Dancers During Performance," *Frontiers in Psychology* 11 (2020): 1000, https://doi.org/10.3389/fpsyg.2020.01000; Christian Swann, "Flow in Sport," in *Flow Experience: Empirical Research and Applications,* ed. László Harmat, Frans Andersen, Fredrik Ullén, Jon Wright, and Gaynor Sadlo (Cham, Switzerland: Springer International Publishing, 2016), 51–64.

250. Peterson, *A Primer in Positive Psychology,* 67.

251. Susan A. Jackson and Mihaly Csikszentmihalyi, *Flow in Sports: The Keys to Optimal Experiences and Performances* (Champaign, IL: Human Kinetics, 1999).

252. Csikszentmihalyi, *Flow,* 54-58.

253. Csikszentmihalyi, *Flow,* 67.

254. Csikszentmihalyi, *Flow,* 67.

255. Christian Swann, Richard J. Keegan, David Piggott, and Lee Crust, "A Systematic Review of the Experience, Occurrence, and Controllability of Flow States in Elite Sport," *Psychology of Sport and Exercise* 13, no. 6 (2012): 807–819, http://doi.org/10.1016/j.psychsport.2012.05.006.

256. Csikszentmihalyi, *Flow,* 54.

257. Jeanne Nakamura and Mihaly Csikszentmihalyi, "The Construction of Meaning Through Vital Engagement," in *Flourishing: Positive Psychology and the Life Well-Lived,* ed. Corey L. M. Keyes and Jonathan Haidt (Washington, D.C.: American Psychological Association, 2003), 83–104, https://doi.org/10.1037/10594-004.

258. Csikszentmihalyi, *Flow,* 37.
259. Csikszentmihalyi, *Flow,* 31.
260. Csikszentmihalyi, *Flow,* 33.
261. Nakamura and Csikszentmihalyi, "Construction of Meaning," 84.
262. Nakamura and Csikszentmihalyi, "Construction of Meaning," 97.
263. Christian Swann, Lee Crust, and Stewart A. Vella, "New Directions for the Psychology of Optimal Performance in Sport: Flow and Clutch States," *Current Opinion in Psychology* 16 (2017): 48, https://doi.org/10.1016/j.copsyc.2017.03.032.
264. Swann et al., "New Directions for the Psychology of Optimal Performance in Sport," 48.
265. Swann et al., "New Directions for the Psychology of Optimal Performance in Sport," 49.
266. Swann et al., "New Directions for the Psychology of Optimal Performance in Sport," 50.
267. Swann et al., "New Directions for the Psychology of Optimal Performance in Sport," 49.
268. Sam M.S., N., "What Is Arousal? Definition of Arousal," *Psychology Dictionary* (Psychology Dictionary Professional Reference, June 23, 2015), https://psychologydictionary.org/arousal/.
269. Gloria Park, personal communication, March 6, 2021.
270. Guy Faulkner, Kate Hefferon, and Nanette Mutrie, "Putting Positive Psychology in Motion Through Physical Activity," in *Positive Psychology in Practice: Promoting Human Flourishing in Work, Health, Education, and Everyday Life,* ed. Stephen Joseph (Hoboken, NJ: Wiley, 2015), 208.
271. Richard Shusterman, "Thinking Through the Body, Educating for the Humanities: A Plea for Somaesthetics," *Journal of Aesthetic Education* 40, no. 1 (2006): 1, 2, https://doi.org/10.1353/jae.2006.0010.
272. Shusterman, "Thinking Through the Body," 10.
273. Shusterman, "Thinking Through the Body," 10.
274. Shusterman, "Thinking Through the Body," 2.
275. Shusterman, "Thinking Through the Body," 12.
276. P. Z. Pearce, "Prehabilitation: Preparing Young Athletes for Sports," *Current Sports Medicine Reports* 5 (2006): 155–160, https://doi.org/10.1097/01.CSMR.0000306306.10697.3e; John J. Ratey and Eric Hagerman, *Spark: The Revolutionary New Science of Exercise and the Brain* (New York: Little, Brown & Company, 2008), 139.
277. Hans Selye, "Stress and Physical Activity," *McGill Journal of Education* 11, no. 1 (1976): 3, 11.

278. Peter Sterling, "Allostasis: A Model of Predictive Regulation," *Physiology & Behavior* 106, no. 1 (2012): 5–15, https://doi.org/10.1016/j.physbeh.2011.06.004.

279. Sterling, "Allostasis," 5-15.

280. Bruce S. McEwen, "Protection and Damage from Acute and Chronic Stress: Allostasis and Allostatic Overload and Relevance to the Pathophysiology of Psychiatric Disorders," *Annals of the New York Academy of Sciences* 1032 (2004): 1–7, https://doi.org/10.1196/annals.1314.001; Elyse R. Park, Lara Traeger, Ana-Maria Vranceanu, Matthew Scult, Jonathan A. Lerner, Herbert Benson, John Denninger, and Gregory L. Fricchione, "The Development of a Patient-Centered Program Based on the Relaxation Response: The Relaxation Response Resiliency Program (3RP)," *Psychosomatics* 54, no. 2 (2013): 165–174, https://doi.org/10.1016/j.psym.2012.09.001.

281. Yuri L. Hanin, "Emotions and Athletic Performance: Individual Zones of Optimal Functioning Model," *European Yearbook of Sport Psychology* 1 (1997): 29–72; Montse C. Ruiz, John S. Raglin, and Yuri L. Hanin, "The Individual Zones of Optimal Functioning (IZOF) Model (1978–2014): Historical Overview of Its Development and Use," *International Journal of Sport and Exercise Psychology* 15, no. 1 (2017): 41–63, https://doi.org/10.1080/1612197X.2015.1041545.

282. Stephen Porges, "Neuroception: A Subconscious System for Detecting Threats and Safety," *Zero to Three* 24, no. 5 (2004): 19–24, https://www.fresnostate.edu/chhs/ccci/documents/07.15.16%20Neuroception%20Porges%202004.pdf; Stanley Rosenberg, *Accessing the Healing Power of the Vagus Nerve: Self-Help Exercises for Anxiety, Depression, Trauma, and Autism* (Berkeley, CA: North Atlantic Books, 2017), 57.

283. Matthew J. Rivera, Zachary K. Winkelmann, Cameron J. Powden, and Kenneth E. Games, "Proprioceptive Training for the Prevention of Ankle Sprains: An Evidence-Based Review," *Journal of Athlete Training* 52, no. 11 (2017): 1065–1067, https://doi.org/10.4085/1062-6050-52.11.16; Charles Sherrington, *The Integrative Action of the Nervous System* (Cambridge: Cambridge University Press, 1906).

284. Sherrington, *Integrative Action of the Nervous System*; John C. Tuthill and Eiman Azim, "Proprioception," *Current Biology* 28, no. 5 (2018): R194–R203, https://doi.org/10.1016/j.cub.2018.01.064.

285. Sherrington, *Integrative Action of the Nervous System;* Tuthill and Azim, "Proprioception," R194–R203.

286. Jonathan M. Peake, James F. Markworth, Kazunori Nosaka, Truls Raastad, Glenn D. Wadley, and Vernon G. Coffey, "Modulating Exercise-Induced Hormesis: Does Less Equal More?" *Journal of Applied Physiology* 119 (2015): 172–189, https://doi.org/10.1152/japplphysiol.01055.2014.

287. Jeremy P. Jamieson, Wendy Berry Mendes, and Matthew K. Nock, "Improving Acute Stress Responses: The Power of Reappraisal," *Current Directions in Psychological Science* 22, no. 1 (2013): 51–56, https://doi.org/10.1177/0963721412461500.

288. "Rehabilitation," in *Lexico Dictionaries* (Oxford Dictionary), accessed September 22, 2021, https://www.lexico.com/en/definition/rehabilitation.
289. Gareth Healy, "Role of Prehabilitation," *Sports Rehabilitation & Fitness* (March 21, 2016), https://sites.marjon.ac.uk/garethhealy/2016/03/21/role-of-prehabilitation/.
290. Carrie MacMillan, "Marathoners: Could 'Prehab' Help You Run Better?" *Yale Medicine* (October 23, 2019), https://www.yalemedicine.org/news/marathoners-prehab.
291. Jonathan N. Myers and Holly Fonda, "The Impact of Fitness on Surgical Outcomes: The Case for Prehabilitation," *Current Sports Medicine Reports* 15, no. 4 (2016): 282–289, https://doi.org/10.1249/jsr.0000000000000274.
292. Pearce, "Prehabilitation," 155.
293. Pearce, "Prehabilitation," 155.
294. Pearce, "Prehabilitation," 155.
295. Pearce, "Prehabilitation," 158.
296. Pearce, "Prehabilitation," 158.
297. Pearce, "Prehabilitation," 158.
298. Pearce, "Prehabilitation," 158.
299. Pearce, "Prehabilitation," 158.
300. Alan Currie and Allan Johnston, "Psychiatric Disorders: The Psychiatrist's Contribution to Sport," *International Review of Psychiatry* 28, no. 6 (2016): 587–594, https://doi.org/10.1080/09540261.2016.1197188.
301. American Psychological Association, *APA Dictionary of Psychology*, (n.d.). Retrieved July 14, 2021, from https://dictionary.apa.org.
302. Currie and Johnston, "Psychiatric Disorders," 588.
303. R. L. Van Niekerk and E. Lynch, "The Relationship Between Anxiety and Shoulder Injuries Among South African University and Club Rugby Players," *South African Sports Medicine Association* 24, no. 4 (2012): 107–111, https://doi.org/10.7196/sajsm.353.
304. Van Niekerk and Lynch, "The Relationship Between Anxiety and Shoulder Injuries," 107.
305. Van Niekerk and Lynch, "The Relationship Between Anxiety and Shoulder Injuries," 107, 111.
306. Van Niekerk and Lynch, "The Relationship Between Anxiety and Shoulder Injuries," 111.
307. Van Niekerk and Lynch, "The Relationship Between Anxiety and Shoulder Injuries," 109.
308. Van Niekerk and Lynch, "The Relationship Between Anxiety and Shoulder Injuries," 111.

309. George Mumford, *The Mindful Athlete: Secrets to Pure Performance* (Berkeley, CA: Parallax Press, 2016).
310. Mumford, *The Mindful Athlete,* 76.
311. Mumford, *The Mindful Athlete,* 165; Selye, "Stress and Physical Activity," 11.
312. Hans Selye, *The Stress of Life* (New York: McGraw-Hill Education, 1956), 64.
313. Selye, *The Stress of Life,* 27; Juliette Tocino-Smith, "What Is Eustress and How Is It Different than Stress?" *PositivePsychology.com* (April 15, 2020), https://positivepsychology.com/what-is-eustress/#eustress-scale.
314. WJEC, "Sports Psychology," http://resource.download.wjec.co.uk.s3.amazonaws.com/vtc/2015-16/15-16_30/eng/05-heat-of-the-moment/Unit5-stress.html, quoting Richard S. Lazarus.
315. Richard S. Lazarus and Susan Folkman, *Stress, Appraisal and Coping* (New York: Springer, 1984), 19.
316. WJEC, "Sports Psychology."
317. Selye, "Stress and Physical Activity," 11; Tocino-Smith, "What Is Eustress."
318. Regina Bailey, "Definition of the Biology Prefix 'eu-,'" *ThoughtCo* (September 10, 2019), https://www.thoughtco.com/biology-prefixes-and-suffixes-eu-373691#:~:text=The%20prefix%20%28eu-%29%20means%20good%2C%20well%2C%20pleasant%20or,be%20%22true%20bacteria%22%2C%20distinguishing%20them%20from%20archaebacteria%20.
319. Mumford, *The Mindful Athlete,* 165.
320. Mumford, *The Mindful Athlete,* 165.
321. Mumford, *The Mindful Athlete,* 165–166.
322. Mumford, *The Mindful Athlete,* 166.
323. Mumford, *The Mindful Athlete,* 166.
324. WJEC, "Sports Psychology."
325. WJEC, "Sports Psychology."
326. "Types of Stressors (Eustress vs. Distress)," Types of Stressors Eustress vs. Distress Comments (Mentalhelp.net), accessed September 22, 2021, https://www.mentalhelp.net/stress/types-of-stressors-eustress-vs-distress/. See also Tocino-Smith, "What Is Eustress," citing Harry Mills, Natalie Reiss, and Mark Dombeck, "Types of Stressors (Eustress vs. Distress)," https://www.wyomentalhealth.org/poc/view_doc.php?type=doc&id=15644&cn=117.
327. Danica Piršl, "Coping With and Managing Stress Styles of Freshmen Physical Education Students at the PE Faculty in NIS," *Sport Mont Journal* 8–9 (2005): 290.
328. https://www.mentalhelp.net/stress/types-of-stressors-eustress-vs-distress/. See also Tocino-Smith, "What Is Eustress," citing Harry Mills, Natalie Reiss, and Mark Dombeck, "Types of Stressors (Eustress vs. Distress)," https://www.wyomentalhealth.org/poc/view_doc.php?type=doc&id=15644&cn=117.

329. Ratey and Hagerman, *Spark: The Revolutionary New Science,* 79.
330. Ratey and Hagerman, *Spark: The Revolutionary New Science,* 79, 107.
331. Ratey and Hagerman, *Spark: The Revolutionary New Science,* 107.
332. Mumford, *The Mindful Athlete,* 166.
333. Mumford, *The Mindful Athlete,* 166.
334. Mumford, *The Mindful Athlete,* 167.
335. Mumford, *The Mindful Athlete,* 167–168.
336. Walter Cannon, *The Wisdom of the Body* (New York: W. W. Norton & Company, 1932).
337. Piršl, "Coping With and Managing Stress Styles," 291; Robert M. Sapolsky, *Why Zebras Don't Get Ulcers: The Acclaimed Guide to Stress, Stress-Related Diseases, and Coping* (New York: Holt Paperbacks, 2004), 6.
338. Kelvin Rodolfo, "What Is Homeostasis?" *Scientific American* (Jan. 3, 2000), https://www.scientificamerican.com/article/what-is-homeostasis/#:~:text=January%203%2C%202000%20Credit%3A%20Garry%20DeLong%20Getty%20Images,coined%20in%201930%20by%20the%20physician%20Walter%20Cannon.
339. John J. Ratey and Richard Manning, *Go Wild: Eat Fat, Run Free, Be Social, and Follow Evolution's Other Rules for Total Health and Well-Being* (New York: Little, Brown Spark, 2014), 232; Sapolsky, *Why Zebras Don't Get Ulcers,* 6.
340. Sapolsky, *Why Zebras Don't Get Ulcers,* 6.
341. Sapolsky, *Why Zebras Don't Get Ulcers,* 6.
342. Sapolsky, *Why Zebras Don't Get Ulcers,* 10.
343. Bruce S. McEwen, "Protective and Damaging Effects of Stress Mediators," *New England Journal of Medicine* 338 (1998): 171, https://doi.org/10.1056/NEJM199801153380307; Bruce S. McEwen, "Stress, Adaptation, and Disease: Allostasis and Allostatic Load," *Annals of the New York Academy of Sciences* 840, no. 1 (1998): 33, https://doi.org/10.1111/j.1749-6632.1998.tb09546.x; Sapolsky, *Why Zebras Don't Get Ulcers,* 9; Peter Sterling and Joseph Eyer, "Allostasis: A New Paradigm to Explain Arousal Pathology," in *Handbook of Life Stress, Cognition and Health,* ed. Shirley Fisher and James Reason (New York: John Wiley & Sons, 1988), 631, 636.
344. Sterling and Eyer, "Allostasis."
345. McEwen, "Stress, Adaptation, and Disease," 37; Park et al., "The Relaxation Response Resiliency Program," 168; Sterling and Eyer, "Allostasis," 637.
346. Hans Selye, "The General-Adaptation-Syndrome," *Annual Review of Medicine* 2, no. 1 (1951): 327–342, https://doi.org/10.1146/annurev.me.02.020151.001551.
347. Hans Selye, "A Syndrome Produced by Diverse Nocuous Agents," *Nature* 138, no. 3479 (1936): 32, https://doi.org/10.1038/138032a0.

348. Sapolsky, *Why Zebras Don't Get Ulcers,* 7.
349. Selye, *The Stress of Life,* 2; Sapolsky, *Why Zebras Don't Get Ulcers,* 12.
350. Sapolsky, *Why Zebras Don't Get Ulcers,* 12.
351. Sapolsky, *Why Zebras Don't Get Ulcers,* 12.
352. Sapolsky, *Why Zebras Don't Get Ulcers,* 12.
353. Sapolsky, *Why Zebras Don't Get Ulcers,* 13.
354. Sapolsky, *Why Zebras Don't Get Ulcers,* 14; McEwen, "Protection and Damage from Acute and Chronic Stress," 3.
355. Gregory L. Fricchione, "The Science of Mind Body Medicine and the Public Health Challenges of Today," *South African Journal of Psychology* 44, no. 4 (2014): 404, 406, https://doi.org/10.1177/0081246314541025; Chiara Ruini, Emanuela Offidani, and Francesca Vescovelli, "Life Stressors, Allostatic Overload, and Their Impact on Posttraumatic Growth," *Journal of Loss and Trauma* 20 (2015): 109, 110, https://doi.org/10.1080/15325024.2013.830530.
356. Ruini et al., "Life Stressors, Allostatic Overload," 111.
357. Fricchione, "The Science of Mind Body Medicine," 406.
358. Sapolsky, *Why Zebras Don't Get Ulcers,* 20.
359. Sapolsky, *Why Zebras Don't Get Ulcers,* 22.
360. Rosenberg, *Accessing the Healing Power,* xix.
361. Erwin H. Ackerknecht, "The History of the Discovery of the Vegetative (Autonomic) Nervous System," *Medical History* 18 (1974): 1, https://www.ncbi.nlm.nih.gov/pmc/articles/PMC1081519/pdf/medhist00120-0005.pdf.
362. Ackerknecht, "The History of the Discovery of the Vegetative (Autonomic) Nervous System," 1.
363. Sapolsky, *Why Zebras Don't Get Ulcers,* 22.
364. Sapolsky, *Why Zebras Don't Get Ulcers,* 30.
365. Sapolsky, *Why Zebras Don't Get Ulcers,* 37.
366. Sapolsky, *Why Zebras Don't Get Ulcers,* 23.
367. Sapolsky, *Why Zebras Don't Get Ulcers,* 41.
368. Sapolsky, *Why Zebras Don't Get Ulcers,* 41.
369. Sapolsky, *Why Zebras Don't Get Ulcers,* 255.
370. Sapolsky, *Why Zebras Don't Get Ulcers,* 213.
371. Sapolsky, *Why Zebras Don't Get Ulcers,* 213.
372. Sapolsky, *Why Zebras Don't Get Ulcers,* 341.
373. Rosenberg, *Accessing the Healing Power,* xxvi.
374. Rosenberg, *Accessing the Healing Power,* 7.
375. Rosenberg, *Accessing the Healing Power,* 7.

376. Rosenberg, *Accessing the Healing Power,* 7–8.

377. Rosenberg, *Accessing the Healing Power,* 8.

378. Rosenberg, *Accessing the Healing Power,* 8.

379. Stephen W. Porges, "Orienting in a Defensive World: Mammalian Modifications of Our Evolutionary Heritage. A Polyvagal Theory," *Psychophysiology* 32, no. 4 (1995): 301, 309, https://doi.org/10.1111/j.1469-8986.1995.tb01213.x; Ratey and Manning, *Go Wild: Eat Fat, Run Free,* 222.

380. Porges, "Orienting in a Defensive World," 301–302.

381. Rosenberg, *Accessing the Healing Power,* 29.

382. Rosenberg, *Accessing the Healing Power,* 29.

383. Porges, "Orienting in a Defensive World," 305; Rosenberg, *Accessing the Healing Power,* 19.

384. Rosenberg, *Accessing the Healing Power,* 29, 52.

385. Rosenberg, *Accessing the Healing Power,* 30, 41.

386. Rosenberg, *Accessing the Healing Power,* 41.

387. Rosenberg, *Accessing the Healing Power,* 53.

388. Rosenberg, *Accessing the Healing Power,* 57.

389. Porges, "Orienting in a Defensive World," 304; Ratey and Manning, *Go Wild: Eat Fat, Run Free,* 222.

390. Porges, "Neuroception," 19; Rosenberg, *Accessing the Healing Power,* 57.

391. Rosenberg, *Accessing the Healing Power,* 63.

392. Rosenberg, *Accessing the Healing Power,* xxxv.

393. Rosenberg, *Accessing the Healing Power,* 69.

394. Rosenberg, *Accessing the Healing Power,* 69.

395. Rosenberg, *Accessing the Healing Power,* 69.

396. Rosenberg, *Accessing the Healing Power,* 69.

397. Caroline Williams, *Move! The New Science of Body Over Mind* (London: Profile Books, Ltd., 2021), 178.

398. Elite HRV, "Heart Rate Variability vs. Heart Rate" (March 10, 2021), https://elitehrv.com/heart-rate-variability-vs-heart-rate.

399. Williams, *Move!,* 178.

400. Williams, *Move!,* 179.

401. Marcelo Campos, "Heart Rate Variability: A New Way to Track Well-Being," *Harvard Health Blog* (October 22, 2019), https://www.health.harvard.edu/blog/heart-rate-variability-new-way-track-well-2017112212789;see,e.g.,https://elitehrv.com/; https://ouraring.com/.

402. Elissa S. Epel, Bruce S. McEwen, and Jeannette R. Ickovics, "Embodying Psychological Thriving: Physical Thriving in Response to Stress," *Journal of Social Issues* 54, no. 2 (1998): 301, 304, http://doi.org/10.1111/0022-4537.671998067.
403. Epel et al., "Embodying Psychological Thriving," 304.
404. Online Etymology Dictionary, "Origin, History and Meaning of English Words," *Online Etymology Dictionary* (Etymonline.com), accessed September 24, 2021, https://www.etymonline.com/.
405. Epel et al., "Embodying Psychological Thriving," 304.
406. Epel et al., "Embodying Psychological Thriving," 304.
407. Online Etymology Dictionary, https://www.etymonline.com/.
408. Epel et al., "Embodying Psychological Thriving," 304.
409. Epel et al., "Embodying Psychological Thriving," 304.
410. Epel et al., "Embodying Psychological Thriving," 304.
411. Epel et al., "Embodying Psychological Thriving," 305.
412. Epel et al., "Embodying Psychological Thriving," 305.
413. Epel et al., "Embodying Psychological Thriving," 305.
414. Epel et al., "Embodying Psychological Thriving," 306.
415. Epel et al., "Embodying Psychological Thriving," 306.
416. Epel et al., "Embodying Psychological Thriving," 306.
417. Epel et al., "Embodying Psychological Thriving," 306.
418. Epel et al., "Embodying Psychological Thriving," 306.
419. Epel et al., "Embodying Psychological Thriving," 306–307.
420. Epel et al., "Embodying Psychological Thriving," 308.
421. Epel et al., "Embodying Psychological Thriving," 308.
422. Epel et al., "Embodying Psychological Thriving," 310.
423. Epel et al., "Embodying Psychological Thriving," 310.
424. "Hormesis," in *Lexico Dictionaries* (Oxford Dictionary), accessed September 22, 2021, https://www.lexico.com/definition/hormesis.
425. Elissa S. Epel, "The Geroscience Agenda: Toxic Stress, Hormetic Stress, and the Rate of Aging," *Ageing Research Reviews* 63, no. 101167 (2020): 1, 2, https://doi.org/10.1016/j.arr.2020.101167.
426. Epel, "The Geroscience Agenda," 3, 6.
427. Epel, "The Geroscience Agenda," 3.
428. Epel, "The Geroscience Agenda," 2.
429. Epel, "The Geroscience Agenda," 1.
430. Ratey and Manning, *Go Wild: Eat Fat, Run Free,* 103.

431. Ratey and Manning, *Go Wild: Eat Fat, Run Free,* 103.
432. Epel, "The Geroscience Agenda," 2.
433. Epel, "The Geroscience Agenda," 3.
434. Hanin, "Emotions and Athletic Performance," 56.
435. Sam M. S., N., "What Is Arousal? Definition of Arousal," *Psychology Dictionary* (Psychology Dictionary Professional Reference, June 23, 2015), https://psychologydictionary.org/arousal/.
436. Hanin, "Emotions and Athletic Performance," 60; Charles D. Spielberger, Richard L. Gorsuch, and Robert E. Lushene, *Manual for the State-Trait Anxiety Inventory* (Sunnyvale, CA: Consulting Psychologists Press, 1970), 56.
437. Gordon W. Allport and Henry S. Odbert, "Trait-Names: A Psycho-Lexical Study," *Psychological Monographs: General and Applied* 47, no. 1 (1936): i, 211; Charles D. Spielberger and Sumner J. Sydeman, "State–Trait Anxiety Inventory and State–Trait Anger Expression Inventory," in *The Use of Psychological Testing for Treatment Planning and Outcome Assessment,* ed. Mark E. Maruish (Mahwah, NJ: Lawrence Erlbaum Associates, 1994), 292–321.
438. Hanin, "Emotions and Athletic Performance," 60.
439. Hanin, "Emotions and Athletic Performance," 55.
440. Hanin, "Emotions and Athletic Performance," 67.
441. Robert Weinberg, "Activation/Arousal Control," in *Routledge Handbook of Applied Sport Psychology: A Comprehensive Guide for Students and Practitioners,* ed. Stephanie Hanrahan and Mark Anderson (London: Routledge, 2012), 472.
442. Weinberg, "Activation/Arousal Control," 473.
443. Ratey and Manning, *Go Wild: Eat Fat, Run Free,* 131.
444. Ratey and Manning, *Go Wild: Eat Fat, Run Free,* 137.
445. Ratey and Manning, *Go Wild: Eat Fat, Run Free,* 146.
446. Ratey and Manning, *Go Wild: Eat Fat, Run Free,* 132.
447. Ratey and Manning, *Go Wild: Eat Fat, Run Free,* 147.
448. Ratey and Manning, *Go Wild: Eat Fat, Run Free,* 150.
449. Daniel Lieberman, *Exercised: The Science of Physical Activity, Rest and Health* (London: Penguin Books, 2021), 76.
450. Lieberman, *Exercised,* 79.
451. Lieberman, *Exercised,* 83.
452. Lieberman, *Exercised,* 76, 94.
453. Rosenberg, *Accessing the Healing Power,* 134.
454. Julienne E. Bower, Carissa A. Low, Judith T. Moskowitz, Saviz Sepah, and Elissa Epel, "Benefit Finding and Physical Health: Positive Psychological Changes and

Enhanced Allostasis," *Social and Personality Psychology Compass* 2, no. 1 (2007): 223, https://doi.org/10.1111/j.1751-9004.2007.00038.x.

455. Bower et al., "Benefit Finding," 231–232.
456. Fricchione, "The Science of Mind Body Medicine," 407.
457. Park et al., "The Relaxation Response Resiliency Program," 168, 170, 171.
458. Kengo Mihara, Hisayoshi Okamura, Yoshihisa Shoji, Kyoko Tashiro, Yukie Kinoshita, and Akira Tsuda, "Personal Growth and Psychobiological Stress Responsiveness to the Trier Social Stress Test in Students," *Sustainability* 12, no. 4497 (2020): 1, 9, https://doi.org/10.3390/su12114497.
459. Porges, "Neuroception," 19.
460. Emma Meehan and Bernie Carter, "Moving With Pain: What Principles from Somatic Practices Can Offer to People Living with Chronic Pain," *Frontiers in Psychology* 11, no. 620381 (2021): 1, 3, https://doi.org/10.3389/fpsyg.2020.620381.
461. Williams, *Move!*, 196.
462. "Proprio," in Dictionary.com, accessed January 11, 2022, https://www.dictionary.com/browse/proprio.
463. Charles Bell, *The Hand: Its Mechanism and Vital Endowments as Evincing Design* (London: William Pickering, 1833); Tuthill and Azim, "Proprioception," R194.
464. Sherrington, *Integrative Action of the Nervous System*; Tuthill and Azim, "Proprioception," R194–R195.
465. Rivera et al., "Proprioceptive Training," 1065.
466. Uwe Proske and Simon C. Gandevia, "The Proprioceptive Senses: Their Roles in Signaling Body Shape, Body Position and Movement, and Muscle Force," *Physiology Review* 92 (2012): 1651, https://doi.org/10.1152/physrev.00048.2011.
467. Proske and Gandevia, "The Proprioceptive Senses," 1652.
468. Williams, *Move!*, 24.
469. Tuthill and Azim, "Proprioception," R198.
470. Tuthill and Azim, "Proprioception," R198.
471. Joshua E. Aman, Naveen Elangovan, I-Ling Yeh, and Jürgen Konczak, "The Effectiveness of Proprioceptive Training for Improving Motor Function: A Systematic Review," *Frontiers in Human Neuroscience* 8, no. 1075 (2015): 1–18, https://doi.org/10.3389/fnhum.2014.01075.
472. Rivera et al., "Proprioceptive Training," 1066.
473. Aman et al., "Effectiveness of Proprioceptive Training."
474. Aman et al., "Effectiveness of Proprioceptive Training," 11.
475. Leython Williams, "Advanced Exercises to Restore Proprioception," *Sports-Health* (June 18, 2018), https://www.sports-health.com/sports-injuries/general-injuries/advanced-exercises-restore-proprioception.

476. Charles Darwin, *The Expression of the Emotions in Man and Animals* (London: John Murray, 1972).
477. William James, "What Is an Emotion?" *Mind* 9, no. 1884: 188–205, https://doi.org/10.1093/mind/os-IX.34.188.
478. António Damásio, *The Feeling of What Happens: Body and Emotion in the Making of Consciousness* (San Diego, CA: Harcourt Brace, 1999), 26.
479. Damásio, *The Feeling of What Happens,* 287.
480. Damásio, *The Feeling of What Happens,* 42; Tal Shafir, "Using Movement to Regulate Emotion: Neurophysiological Findings and Their Application in Psychotherapy," *Frontiers in Psychology* 7, no. 1451 (2016): 1, 2, https://doi.org/10.3389/fpsyg.2016.01451.
481. Damásio, *The Feeling of What Happens,* 8.
482. Damásio, *The Feeling of What Happens,* 25; Shafir, "Using Movement to Regulate Emotion," 2.
483. Damásio, *The Feeling of What Happens,* 303.
484. Shafir, "Using Movement to Regulate Emotion," 1.
485. Shafir, "Using Movement to Regulate Emotion," 2.
486. Shafir, "Using Movement to Regulate Emotion," 2.
487. Shusterman, "Thinking Through the Body," 12.
488. Shusterman, "Thinking Through the Body," 12.
489. Shusterman, "Thinking Through the Body," 12.
490. Shafir, "Using Movement to Regulate Emotion," 2.
491. Shafir, "Using Movement to Regulate Emotion," 4.
492. Shafir, "Using Movement to Regulate Emotion," 4.
493. William James, "Muscular Vigor," *Physical Educator* 6, no. 2 (1949): 21.
494. Debra Ann Fowler, *Proprioception of the Mind: Balancing Science and Spirit Through Emotional Intelligence,* Thesis Paper, School for International Training, Brattleboro, Vermont (August 30, 2006).
495. Fowler, *Proprioception of the Mind.*
496. Fowler, *Proprioception of the Mind.*
497. Fowler, *Proprioception of the Mind.*
498. Fowler, *Proprioception of the Mind.*
499. Fowler, *Proprioception of the Mind.*
500. Cynthia J. Price and Carole Hooven, "Interoceptive Awareness Skills for Emotion Regulation: Theory and Approach of Mindful Awareness in Body-Oriented Therapy (MABT)," *Frontiers in Psychology* 9, no. 798 (2018): 1, 2, https://doi.org/10.3389/fpsyg.2018.00798.

501. Meehan and Carter, "Moving With Pain," 4.
502. Price and Hooven, "Interoceptive Awareness Skills," 3.
503. David Robson, "Interoception: The Hidden Sense that Shapes Wellbeing," *The Guardian* (August 15, 2021), https://www.theguardian.com/science/2021/aug/15/the-hidden-sense-shaping-your-wellbeing-interoception.
504. Price and Hooven, "Interoceptive Awareness Skills," 3.
505. Williams, *Move!*, 25.
506. Sarah N. Garfinkel, Anil K. Seth, Adam B. Barrett, Keisuke Suzuki, and Hugo D. Critchley, "Knowing Your Own Heart: Distinguishing Interoceptive Accuracy from Interoceptive Awareness," *Biological Psychology* 104 (2015): 65–66, https://doi.org/10.1016/j.biopsycho.2014.11.004.
507. Camila Valenzuela-Moguillansky, Alejandro Reyes-Reyes, and María I. Gaete, "Exteroceptive and Interoceptive Body-Self Awareness in Fibromyalgia Patients," *Frontiers in Human Neuroscience* 11, no. 1170 (2017): 1, 4, https://doi.org/10.3389/fnhum.2017.00117.
508. Robson, "Interoception."
509. Wolf E. Mehling, Cynthia Price, Jennifer J. Daubenmier, Mike Acree, Elizabeth Bartmess, and Anita Stewart, "The Multidimensional Assessment of Interoceptive Awareness (MAIA)," *PLoS One* 7, no. 11 (2012): e48230, https://doi.org/10.1371/journal.pone.0048230; Valenzuela-Moguillansky et al., "Exteroceptive and Interoceptive Body-Self Awareness," 5. The University of California, San Francisco makes the MAIA available to the public at this link: https://osher.ucsf.edu/sites/osher.ucsf.edu/files/inline-files/maia1.pdf.
510. Price and Hooven, "Interoceptive Awareness Skills," 4.
511. Meehan and Carter, "Moving With Pain," 4.
512. Meehan and Carter, "Moving With Pain," 5.
513. Meehan and Carter, "Moving With Pain," 5.
514. Nicole Day, "10 Interoception Activities for Kids," *Hes-extraordinary* (October 22, 2020), https://hes-extraordinary.com/9-interoception-activities-for-kids#:~:text=%20Interoception%20Activities%20for%20Kids%20%201%20Use,hand%20and%20counter%20the%20number%20of . . .%20More%20.
515. South Australia Department for Education, "Applying Interoception Skills in the Classroom," https://www.education.sa.gov.au/schools-and-educators/curriculum-and-teaching/curriculum-programs/applying-interoception-skills-classroom.
516. Meehan and Carter, "Moving With Pain," 6.
517. Meehan and Carter, "Moving With Pain," 6.
518. Meehan and Carter, "Moving With Pain," 6.
519. Meehan and Carter, 6–7.

520. Faulkner et al., "Putting Positive Psychology in Motion," 207.
521. Faulkner et al., "Putting Positive Psychology in Motion," 207.
522. Lieberman, *Exercised.*
523. Faulkner et al., "Putting Positive Psychology in Motion," 207, 214.
524. Faulkner et al., "Putting Positive Psychology in Motion," 207.
525. Faulkner et al., "Putting Positive Psychology in Motion," 208.
526. Ratey and Hagerman, *Spark: The Revolutionary New Science.*
527. Ratey and Hagerman *Spark: The Revolutionary New Science,* 3; Ratey and Manning, *Go Wild: Eat Fat, Run Free,* 102.
528. Ratey and Hagerman, *Spark: The Revolutionary New Science,* 5.
529. Ratey and Hagerman, *Spark: The Revolutionary New Science,* 10.
530. Ratey and Hagerman, *Spark: The Revolutionary New Science,* 10.
531. Ratey and Hagerman, *Spark: The Revolutionary New Science,* 5.
532. Ratey and Hagerman, *Spark: The Revolutionary New Science,* 40.
533. Ratey and Manning, *Go Wild: Eat Fat, Run Free,* 103.
534. Ratey and Manning, *Go Wild: Eat Fat, Run Free,* 103.
535. Ratey and Hagerman, *Spark: The Revolutionary New Science,* 47.
536. Ratey and Manning, *Go Wild: Eat Fat, Run Free,* 107.
537. John J. Ratey and James E. Loehr, "The Positive Impact of Physical Activity on Cognition During Adulthood: A Review of Underlying Mechanisms, Evidence and Recommendations," *Reviews in the Neurosciences* 22, no. 2 (2011): 171, https://doi.org/10.1515/RNS.2011.017.
538. Ratey and Loehr, "The Positive Impact of Physical Activity," 171.
539. Ratey and Loehr, "The Positive Impact of Physical Activity," 173.
540. Ratey and Hagerman, *Spark: The Revolutionary New Science,* 78.
541. Ratey and Hagerman, *Spark: The Revolutionary New Science,* 79.
542. Ratey and Hagerman, *Spark: The Revolutionary New Science,* 79.
543. Bob Rotella, *How Champions Think: In Sports and in Life* (New York: Simon & Schuster, 2005), 92.
544. Rotella; *How Champions Think,* 92.
545. Rotella, *How Champions Think,* 92.
546. Ratey and Loehr, "The Positive Impact of Physical Activity," 175.
547. Faulkner et al., "Putting Positive Psychology in Motion," 216.
548. Faulkner et al., "Putting Positive Psychology in Motion," 216.
549. Lieberman, *Exercised,* xii.
550. Lieberman, *Exercised,* xvi.

551. Lieberman, *Exercised*, xix.
552. Lieberman, *Exercised*, 280.
553. Lieberman, *Exercised*, 297.
554. Ratey and Loehr, "The Positive Impact of Physical Activity," 177.
555. Ratey and Manning, *Go Wild: Eat Fat, Run Free*, 187.
556. Ratey and Manning, *Go Wild: Eat Fat, Run Free*, 173.
557. Ratey and Manning, *Go Wild: Eat Fat, Run Free*, 226–227.
558. Julia Cameron, *Walking in this World: The Practical Art of Creativity* (New York: Jeremy P. Tarcher/Penguin, 2003), 2.
559. Cameron, *Walking in this World*, 2.
560. Cameron, *Walking in this World*, 2.
561. Lieberman, *Exercised*, 277.
562. Williams, *Move!*, 44.
563. Williams, *Move!*, 54.
564. Williams, *Move!*, 196.
565. Williams, *Move!*, 196.
566. Ratey and Manning, *Go Wild: Eat Fat, Run Free*, 237.
567. Ratey and Loehr, "The Positive Impact of Physical Activity," 180.
568. Michael Kellmann, "Overtraining and Recovery," in *Routledge Handbook of Applied Sport Psychology: A Comprehensive Guide for Students and Practitioners*, ed. Stephanie Hanrahan and Mark Anderson (London: Routledge, 2012), 295.
569. Kellmann, "Overtraining and Recovery," 295.
570. Kellmann, "Overtraining and Recovery," 294.
571. Kellmann, "Overtraining and Recovery," 293.
572. Michael Kellmann and Konrad Wolfgang Kallus, *The Recovery-Stress Questionnaire for Athletes, User Manual* (Champaign, IL: Human Kinetics, 2001); Kellmann, "Overtraining and Recovery," 297.
573. Lazarus and Folkman, *Stress, Appraisal and Coping*.
574. Richard S. Lazarus, "From Psychological Stress to the Emotions: A History of Changing Outlooks," *Annual Review of Psychology* 44 (1993): 1–22, http://dx.doi.org/10.1146/annurev.ps.44.020193.000245.
575. Lazarus, "From Psychological Stress to the Emotions"; Malgorzata W. Kozusznik, Isabel Rodríguez, and José Maria Peiró, "Eustress and Distress Climates in Teams: Patterns and Outcomes," *International Journal of Stress Management* 22, no. 1 (2015): 1, 2, https://doi.org/10.1037/a0038581.
576. Elissa S. Epel, Jennifer Daubenmier, Judith T. Moskowitz, Susan Folkman, and Elizabeth Blackburn, "Can Meditation Slow Rate of Cellular Aging? Cognitive

Stress, Mindfulness, and Telomeres," *Annals of the New York Academy of Sciences* 1172 (2009): 34, 36, https://doi.org/10.1111/j.1749-6632.2009.04414.x.

577. Lazarus and Folkman, *Stress, Appraisal and Coping,* 32.
578. Epel et al., "Can Meditation Slow Rate of Cellular Aging?" 36.
579. Epel et al., "Can Meditation Slow Rate of Cellular Aging?" 36–37.
580. Lazarus and Folkman, *Stress, Appraisal and Coping,* 35.
581. Epel et al., "Can Meditation Slow Rate of Cellular Aging?" 37.
582. Epel et al., "Can Meditation Slow Rate of Cellular Aging?" 37.
583. Epel et al., "Can Meditation Slow Rate of Cellular Aging?" 37; Lazarus and Folkman, *Stress, Appraisal and Coping,* 44.
584. James Santomier, "The Sport-Stress Connection," *Theory into Practice* 22, no. 1 (1983): 57, 60, citing Alan Monat and Richard S. Lazarus, *Stress and Coping* (New York: Columbia University Press, 1977), http://www.jstor.org/stable/1476241.
585. Santomier, "The Sport-Stress Connection," 60.
586. Epel et al., "Can Meditation Slow Rate of Cellular Aging?" 37.
587. Epel et al., "Can Meditation Slow Rate of Cellular Aging?" 37.
588. Epel et al., "Can Meditation Slow Rate of Cellular Aging?" 37.
589. Epel et al., "Can Meditation Slow Rate of Cellular Aging?" 37.
590. Jeremy P. Jamieson, Wendy Berry Mendes, and Matthew K. Nock, "Improving Acute Stress Responses: The Power of Reappraisal," *Current Directions in Psychological Science* 22, no. 1 (2013): 51–56, https://doi.org/10.1177/0963721412461500.
591. Jamieson et al., "Improving Acute Stress Responses," 52.
592. Epel et al., "Can Meditation Slow Rate of Cellular Aging?" 38.
593. Epel et al., "Can Meditation Slow Rate of Cellular Aging?" 38.
594. Matthew Blake Hargrove, Debra L. Nelson, and Cary L. Cooper, "Generating Eustress by Challenging Employees: Helping People Savor Their Work," *Organizational Dynamics* 42, no. 1 (2013): 61, 62, https://doi.org/10.1016/j.orgdyn.2012.12.008, citing Marcie A. Cavanaugh, Wendy R. Boswell, Mark V. Roehling, and John W. Boudreau, "An Empirical Examination of Self-Reported Work Stress Among U.S. Managers," *Journal of Applied Psychology* 85, no. 1 (2000): 65–74, https://doi.org/10.1037/0021-9010.85.1.65, and Nathan P. Podsakoff, "Challenge and Hindrance Stressors in the Workplace: Tests of Linear, Curvilinear, and Moderated Relationships with Employee Strains, Satisfaction, and Performance," Doctoral Dissertation, University of Florida (University of Florida Digital Collections, 2007), https://ufdc.ufl.edu/UFE0019680/00001.
595. Hargrove et al., "Generating Eustress by Challenging Employees," 62.
596. Hargrove et al., "Generating Eustress by Challenging Employees," 62.

597. Hargrove et al., "Generating Eustress by Challenging Employees," 66, citing Debra L. Nelson and Bret Simmons, "Eustress at Work: Extending the Holistic Stress Model," *Positive Organizational Behavior*, ed. Debra L. Nelson and Cary L. Cooper (Thousand Oaks, CA: Sage Publications, 2007), 40–54.
598. Hargrove et al., "Generating Eustress by Challenging Employees," 66.
599. Hargrove et al., "Generating Eustress by Challenging Employees," 67.
600. Hargrove et al., "Generating Eustress by Challenging Employees," 67.
601. Twyla Tharp, *The Creative Habit: Learn It and Use It for Life* (New York: Simon & Schuster, 2006), 15.
602. Tharp, *The Creative Habit,* 15.
603. Tharp, *The Creative Habit,* 15.
604. Ronnie Lidor, "Pre-Performance Routines," in *Routledge Handbook of Applied Sport Psychology: A Comprehensive Guide for Students and Practitioners,* ed. Stephanie Hanrahan and Mark Anderson (London: Routledge, 2012), 537.
605. Rotella, *How Champions Think,* 141.
606. Rotella, *How Champions Think,* 141.
607. Rotella, *How Champions Think,* 141.
608. Jennie Bricker, "Fit to Practice," *Oregon State Bar Bulletin* (June 2020), 18–23.
609. Bricker, "Fit to Practice," 20.
610. Bricker, "Fit to Practice," 20.
611. Hargrove et al., "Generating Eustress," 67.
612. WJEC, "Sports Psychology."
613. WJEC, "Sports Psychology."
614. Shusterman, "Thinking Through the Body," 2.
615. Shusterman, "Thinking Through the Body," 13.
616. Shusterman, "Thinking Through the Body," 14.
617. Shusterman, "Thinking Through the Body," 16.
618. Shusterman, "Thinking Through the Body," 16.
619. Julia Cameron, *The Listening Path: The Creative Art of Attention* (New York: St. Martin's Essentials, 2021).
620. Sapolsky, *Why Zebras Don't Get Ulcers,* 48.
621. James Nestor, *Breath: The New Science of a Lost Art* (New York: Riverhead Books, 2020), xxii.
622. Nestor, *Breath,* xxi.
623. Nestor, *Breath,* 38.
624. Nestor, *Breath,* 39.

625. Williams, *Move!*, 164.
626. Nestor, *Breath,* 150.
627. Nestor, *Breath,* 41–42.
628. Nestor, *Breath,* 104.
629. Nestor, *Breath,* 206.
630. Williams, *Move!*, 182.
631. Patrick McKeown, *The Oxygen Advantage* (New York: HarperCollins, 2015), 3.
632. McKeown, *The Oxygen Advantage,* 20.
633. McKeown, *The Oxygen Advantage,* 21.
634. McKeown, *The Oxygen Advantage,* 23.
635. McKeown, *The Oxygen Advantage,* 23.
636. McKeown, *The Oxygen Advantage,* 25.
637. McKeown, *The Oxygen Advantage,* 26.
638. McKeown, *The Oxygen Advantage,* 45.
639. McKeown, *The Oxygen Advantage,* 68.
640. McKeown, *The Oxygen Advantage,* 72.
641. Ratey and Manning, *Go Wild: Eat Fat, Run Free,* 187.
642. Bruce D. Perry and Oprah Winfrey, *What Happened to You? Conversations on Trauma, Resilience, and Healing* (New York: Flatiron Books, 2021), 197.
643. Perry and Winfrey, *What Happened to You,* 198.
644. Ratey and Manning, *Go Wild: Eat Fat, Run Free,* 227.
645. Cameron, *Walking in this World,* 2.
646. Cameron, *Walking in this World,* 2.
647. Mumford, *The Mindful Athlete,* 167–168.
648. Erika B. Hilliard, *Living Fully with Shyness and Social Anxiety* (Philadelphia: Da Capo Press, 2005), 64.
649. *A League of Their Own* (Parkway Productions, 1992).
650. Bessel van der Kolk, *The Body Keeps the Score: Brain, Mind, and Body in the Healing of Trauma* (New York: Penguin Books, 2014), 75. See also Williams, *Move!*, 21 (pointing out that "the word 'emotion' comes from the Latin for 'to move away'").
651. van der Kolk, *The Body Keeps the Score,* 75.
652. Barbara Fredrickson, *Positivity: Discover the Upward Spiral That Will Change Your Life* (New York: Harmony, 2009), 21.
653. Fredrickson, *Positivity,* 21.
654. Fredrickson, *Positivity,* 24.

655. Fredrickson, *Positivity*, 6.

656. Fredrickson, *Positivity*, 9, 10.

657. Fredrickson, *Positivity*, 55.

658. Fredrickson, *Positivity*, 59.

659. Fredrickson, *Positivity*, 61.

660. Fredrickson, *Positivity*, 73.

661. Fredrickson, *Positivity*, 62.

662. Patty Van Cappellen, Elise L. Rice, Lahnna I. Catalino, and Barbara L. Fredrickson, "Positive Affective Processes Underlie Positive Health Behaviour Change," *Psychology & Health* 33, no. 1 (2018): 77, 80, https://doi.org/10.1080/08870446.2017.1320798.

663. Barbara L. Fredrickson, Michele M. Tugade, Christian E. Waugh, and Gregory R. Larkin, "What Good Are Positive Emotions in Crises? A Prospective Study of Resilience and Emotions Following the Terrorist Attacks on the United States on September 11th, 2001," *Journal of Personality and Social Psychology* 84, no. 2 (2003): 365, 367, https://doi.org/10.1037//0022-3514.84.2.365.

664. Martin E. P. Seligman, *Flourish: A Visionary New Understanding of Happiness and Well-Being* (New York: Atria Books, 2011), 66, referring to Barbara Fredrickson's "broaden-and-build" theory of positive emotion.

665. Seligman, *Flourish*, 66.

666. Fredrickson, *Positivity*, 33.

667. Fredrickson, *Positivity*, 159.

668. Fredrickson, *Positivity*, 136.

669. Fredrickson, *Positivity*, 159.

670. Garbage, "Only Happy When It Rains," track #3 on *Garbage (20th Anniversary Standard Edition Remastered)*, Mushroom/Almo Sounds, 1995, Vinyl.

671. Robert Nozick, *Anarchy, State, and Utopia* (New York: Basic Books, 1974).

672. Robert Nozick, *The Examined Life: Philosophical Meditations* (New York: Simon & Schuster, 1990), 113.

673. Christopher Peterson, *A Primer in Positive Psychology* (New York: Oxford University Press, 2006), 50; Fredrickson et al., "What Good Are Positive Emotions in Crises?" 373.

674. Fredrickson et al., "What Good Are Positive Emotions in Crises?" 373.

675. Fredrickson, *Positivity*, 230.

676. Fredrickson, *Positivity*, 39.

677. Fredrickson, *Positivity*, 39.

678. Peterson, *A Primer in Positive Psychology*, 49.

679. Fredrickson, *Positivity*, 47.
680. Fredrickson, *Positivity*, 9, 11.
681. Fredrickson, *Positivity*, 9, 11.
682. Grant Parr, *The Next One Up Mindset: How to Prepare for The Unknown* (Charleston: Advantage, 2019), 22.
683. Parr, *The Next One Up Mindset*, 23.
684. Parr, *The Next One Up Mindset*, 35.
685. Steve Koesterman, "Grant Parr: A Sport's Agent Secret Weapon," *Sports Agent Blog* (January 31, 2020), http://sportsagentblog.com/2020/01/31/grant-parr-a-sports-agent-secret-weapon/.
686. Koesterman, "Grant Parr."
687. Koesterman, "Grant Parr."
688. Parr, *The Next One Up Mindset*, 120.
689. Fredrickson, *Positivity*, 214–223.
690. Phil Jackson, *Sacred Hoops: Spiritual Lessons of a Hardwood Warrior* (New York: Hyperion, 1995), 115–116.
691. Jackson, *Sacred Hoops*, 69.
692. Jackson, *Sacred Hoops*, 69.
693. Richard S. Lazarus and Susan Folkman, *Stress, Appraisal and Coping* (New York: Springer, 1984), 32.
694. Elissa S. Epel, Jennifer Daubenmier, Judith T. Moskowitz, Susan Folkman, and Elizabeth Blackburn, "Can Meditation Slow Rate of Cellular Aging? Cognitive Stress, Mindfulness, and Telomeres," *Annals of the New York Academy of Sciences* 1172 (2009): 36, https://doi.org/10.1111/j.1749-6632.2009.04414.x.
695. Epel et al., "Can Meditation Slow Rate of Cellular Aging?" 36–37.
696. Richard S. Lazarus and Susan Folkman, *Stress, Appraisal and Coping* (New York: Springer, 1984), 35.
697. Epel et al., "Can Meditation Slow Rate of Cellular Aging?" 37.
698. Epel et al., "Can Meditation Slow Rate of Cellular Aging?" 37.
699. Epel et al., "Can Meditation Slow Rate of Cellular Aging?" 37; Lazarus and Folkman, *Stress, Appraisal and Coping*, 44.
700. Epel et al., "Can Meditation Slow Rate of Cellular Aging?" 37; Lazarus and Folkman, *Stress, Appraisal and Coping*, 44.
701. Epel et al., "Can Meditation Slow Rate of Cellular Aging?" 37; Lazarus and Folkman, *Stress, Appraisal and Coping*, 44.
702. Epel et al., "Can Meditation Slow Rate of Cellular Aging?" 37; Lazarus and Folkman, *Stress, Appraisal and Coping*, 44.

703. Epel et al., "Can Meditation Slow Rate of Cellular Aging?" 37; Lazarus and Folkman, *Stress, Appraisal and Coping*, 44.

704. Karen Reivich and Andrew Shatté, *The Resilience Factor: 7 Essential Skills for Overcoming Life's Inevitable Obstacles* (New York: Broadway Books, 2002), 11.

705. Charles S. Carver, Michael F. Scheier, and Suzanne C. Segerstrom, "Optimism," *Clinical Psychology Review* 30 (2010): 879, http://doi.org/10.1016/j.cpr.2010.01.006.

706. Carver et al., "Optimism," 879.

707. Carver et al., "Optimism," 881.

708. Michael F. Scheier and Charles S. Carver, "Dispositional Optimism and Physical Health: A Long Look Back, a Quick Look Forward," *American Psychologist* 73, no. 9 (2018): 1082, 1088, http://dx.doi.org/10.1037/amp00003841082.

709. Scheier and Carver, "Dispositional Optimism and Physical Health," 1082, 1083.

710. Carver et al., "Optimism," 880; Charles S. Carver and Michael F. Scheier, "Dispositional Optimism," *Trends in Cognitive Sciences* 18, no. 6 (2014): 293, 296, http://doi.org/10.1016/j.tics.2014.02.003.

711. Carver et al., "Optimism," 880; Scheier and Carver, "Dispositional Optimism and Physical Health," 1090.

712. Carver et al., "Optimism," 886.

713. Carver et al., "Optimism," 883.

714. Scheier and Carver, "Dispositional Optimism and Physical Health," 1088.

715. Carver et al., "Optimism," 883.

716. Carver et al., "Optimism," 883.

717. See, e.g., Martin E. P. Seligman, *Learned Optimism* (New York: Vintage Books, 2006).

718. Wendy Wood and David T. Neal, "Healthy Through Habit: Interventions for Initiating and Maintaining Healthy Behavior Change," *Behavioral Science & Policy* 2, no. 1 (2016), 73.

719. Seligman, *Learned Optimism*, 15.

720. Seligman, *Learned Optimism*, 44.

721. Seligman, *Learned Optimism*, 44.

722. Seligman, *Learned Optimism*, 47.

723. Seligman, *Learned Optimism*, 49.

724. Seligman, *Learned Optimism*, 107.

725. Seligman, *Learned Optimism*, 115.

726. Charts adapted from Karen Reivich and Judy Saltzberg, Positive Psychology and Individuals: MAPP 708 Spring 2021 Course at the University of Pennsylvania (Power Point slides) (2021).

727. Charts adapted from Karen Reivich and Judy Saltzberg, Positive Psychology and Individuals: MAPP 708 Spring 2021 Course at the University of Pennsylvania (Power Point slides) (2021).

728. Koesterman, "Grant Parr."

729. Twyla Tharp, *The Creative Habit: Learn It and Use It for Life* (New York: Simon & Schuster, 2006), 18.

730. Parr, *The Next One Up Mindset,* 22, citing Graham H. Betchart and Shomari Smith, *Play Present: A Mental Skills Training Program for Basketball Players* (San Bernardino: Play Present, 2015).

731. Jackson, *Sacred Hoops,* 174.

732. Fredrickson, *Positivity,* 184.

733. Adapted from Matthew Blake Hargrove, Debra L. Nelson, and Cary L. Cooper, "Generating Eustress by Challenging Employees: Helping People Savor Their Work," *Organizational Dynamics* 42, no. 1 (2013): 67, https://doi.org/10.1016/j.orgdyn.2012.12.008.

734. Barbara L. Fredrickson, *Love 2.0: Creating Happiness and Health in Moments of Connection* (New York: Penguin Group, 2013), 17.

735. Fredrickson, *Love 2.0,* 17–18.

736. Fredrickson, *Love 2.0,* 19.

737. Fredrickson, *Love 2.0,* 20, 22.

738. Fredrickson, *Love 2.0,* 35.

739. Fredrickson, *Love 2.0,* 60.

740. Fredrickson, *Love 2.0,* 82–83.

741. Fredrickson, *Love 2.0,* 101.

742. Fredrickson, *Love 2.0,* 101.

743. Shelly L. Gable, Gian C. Gonzaga, and Amy Strachman, "Will You Be There for Me When Things Go Right? Supportive Responses to Positive Event Disclosures," *Journal of Personality and Social Psychology* 91, no. 5 (2006): 904, https:/doi.org/10.1037/0022-3514.91.5.904.

744. Gable et al., "Will You Be There for Me When Things Go Right?" 904.

745. Gable et al., "Will You Be There for Me When Things Go Right?" 904.

746. Shelly L. Gable and Courtney L. Gosnell, "The Positive Side of Close Relationships," in *Designing Positive Psychology: Taking Stock and Moving Forward,* ed. Kennon M. Sheldon, Todd B. Kashdan, and Michael F. Steger (London: Oxford University Press, 2011), 5–6.

747. Gable et al., "Will You Be There for Me When Things Go Right?" 904.

748. Gable et al., "Will You Be There for Me When Things Go Right?" 907.

749. Gable and Gosnell, "The Positive Side of Close Relationships," 9.

750. Gable et al., "Will You Be There for Me When Things Go Right?" 906, 913.

751. Peterson, *A Primer in Positive Psychology,* 271.

752. Peterson, *A Primer in Positive Psychology,* 272.

753. Karen Reivich and Judy Saltzberg, "Active Constructive Responding" [PowerPoint slides], Penn Positive Psychology Center, University of Pennsylvania (March 27, 2021).

754. Meera Lee Patel, *My Friend Fear: Finding Magic in the Unknown* (New York: Tarcher-Perigree, 2018), 136.

755. Malaka Gharib, "Making Art Is Good for Your Health. Here's How to Start a Habit," *NPR* (National Public Radio, January 7, 2020), https://www.npr.org/2019/12/30/792439555/making-art-is-good-for-your-health-heres-how-to-start-a-habit.

756. Quoted in Gharib, "Making Art Is Good for Your Health."

757. Gharib, "Making Art Is Good for Your Health."

758. Roberta Michnick Golinkoff and Kathy Hirsh-Pasek, *Becoming Brilliant: What Science Tells Us About Raising Successful Children* (Washington, D.C.: American Psychological Association, 2016), 188.

759. Xiaoqian Ding, Yi-Yuan Tang, Rongxiang Tang, and Michael I. Posner, "Improving Creativity Performance by Short-Term Meditation," *Behavioral and Brain Functions* 10 (2014): 9, https://doi.org/10.1186/1744-9081-10-9; Golinkoff and Hirsh-Pasek, *Becoming Brilliant,* 188.

760. "Artist," in *Merriam-Webster.com* (Merriam-Webster, n.d.), https://www.merriam-webster.com/dictionary/artist.

761. Quoted in Gharib, "Making Art Is Good for Your Health."

762. Quoted in Gharib, "Making Art Is Good for Your Health."

763. Anne Brafford, *Positive Professionals: Creating High-Performing Profitable Firms Through the Science of Engagement* (Chicago: American Bar Association, 2017), 135.

764. Phil Jackson, *Eleven Rings* (New York: Penguin Books, 2014), 22.

765. Jackson, *Eleven Rings,* 126.

766. Michael F. Melcher, *The Creative Lawyer: A Practical Guide to Authentic Professional Satisfaction* (2d ed.) (Chicago: American Bar Association, 2014), 6.

767. Stacy Julien, *The Art of Wellness,* Washington Lawyer (Jan/Feb. 2020), 21, https://washingtonlawyer.dcbar.org/january2020/index.php?startid=25#/p/20.

768. Twyla Tharp, *The Creative Habit: Learn It and Use It for Life* (New York: Simon & Schuster, 2006), 133.

769. Steven Pressfield's books on the creative process: *The War of Art* (New York: Black Irish Entertainment, 2002); *Do the Work: Overcome Resistance and Get Out of Your Own Way* (New York: Black Irish Entertainment LLC, 2015); *Turning Pro* (New York: Black Irish Entertainment, 2012); *The Artist's Journey* (Egremont: Black Irish Entertainment, 2018).

770. Pressfield, *The Artist's Journey*, 32.

771. Pressfield, *The Artist's Journey*, 87.

772. Pressfield, *The War of Art*, 151.

773. Pressfield, *The War of Art*, 156.

774. Pressfield, *The War of Art*, 159.

775. Mihaly Csikszentmihalyi, *Flow: The Psychology of Optimal Experience* (New York: Harper Perennial, 1990), 67.

776. Pressfield, *Turning Pro*, 63.

777. Pressfield, *Turning Pro*, 93.

778. Louis Tay and James O. Pawelski, eds., *The Oxford Handbook of the Positive Humanities* (London: Oxford University Press, forthcoming 2022).

779. Louis Tay, James O. Pawelski, and Melissa G. Keith, "The Role of the Arts and Humanities in Human Flourishing: A Conceptual Model," *Journal of Positive Psychology* 13, no. 3 (2018): 215, 217, https://doi.org/10.1080/17439760.2017.1279207.

780. Tay et al., "The Role of the Arts and Humanities," 217.

781. See, e.g., Xiaoqian Ding, Yi-Yuan Tang, Rongxiang Tang, and Michael Posner, "Improving Creativity Performance by Short-Term Meditation," *Behavioral and Brain Functions* 10 (2014): 9, https://doi.org/10.1186/1744-9081-10-9; Cher-Yi Tan, Chun-Qian Chuah, Shwu-Ting Lee, and Chee-Seng Tan, "Being Creative Makes You Happier: The Positive Effect of Creativity on Subjective Well-Being," *International Journal of Environmental Research and Public* 18 (2021): 7244, https://doi.org/10.3390/ijerph18147244; Chee-Seng Tan, Soon-Aun Tan, Intan Hashimah, Mohd Hashim, Mah-Ngee Lee, Anna Wen-Huey Ong, and Siti nor Binti Yaacob, "Problem-Solving Ability and Stress Mediate the Relationship Between Creativity and Happiness," *Creativity Research Journal* 31, no. 1 (2019): 15–25, https://doi.org/10.1080/10400419.2019.1568155.

782. City of Adelaide, "Wellbeing Benefits of Culture Report" (2020), https://d31atr86jnqrq2.cloudfront.net/docs/wellbeing-benefits-of-culture-report-pawelski.pdf?mtime=20200825102631&focal=none; Tay et al., "The Role of the Arts and Humanities," 217.

783. Tay et al., "The Role of the Arts and Humanities," 217.

784. City of Adelaide, "Wellbeing Benefits," 9; Tay et al., "The Role of the Arts and Humanities," 217.

785. Tay et al., "The Role of the Arts and Humanities," 217.

786. Tay et al., "The Role of the Arts and Humanities," 218.

787. Tay et al., "The Role of the Arts and Humanities," 218.

788. City of Adelaide, "Wellbeing Benefits," 9.

789. City of Adelaide, "Wellbeing Benefits," 9; Tay et al., "The Role of the Arts and Humanities," 218.
790. City of Adelaide, "Wellbeing Benefits," 9; Tay et al., "The Role of the Arts and Humanities," 218.
791. City of Adelaide, "Wellbeing Benefits," 9.
792. City of Adelaide, "Wellbeing Benefits," 9.
793. City of Adelaide, "Wellbeing Benefits," 9.
794. City of Adelaide, "Wellbeing Benefits," 9.
795. Tay et al., "The Role of the Arts and Humanities," 216.
796. Tay et al., "The Role of the Arts and Humanities," 220.
797. Erin C. Westgate and Shigehiro Oishi, "Art, Music, and Literature: Do the Humanities Make Our Lives Richer, Happier, and More Meaningful?" in *The Oxford Handbook of the Positive Humanities,* ed. Louis Tay and James O. Pawelski (London: Oxford University Press, forthcoming 2022).
798. Tay et al., "The Role of the Arts and Humanities," 220.
799. Tay et al., "The Role of the Arts and Humanities," 220.
800. Alain de Botton and John Armstrong, *Art as Therapy* (London: Phaidon Press, 2013), 59.
801. de Botton and Armstrong, *Art as Therapy,* 8, 12, 24, 29, 39, 44, 53.
802. de Botton and Armstrong, *Art as Therapy,* 11.
803. de Botton and Armstrong, *Art as Therapy,* 24.
804. de Botton and Armstrong, *Art as Therapy,* 24.
805. Peter Cameron, *Someday This Pain Will Be Useful to You* (New York: Picador, 2007).
806. Claire Schneider and Barbara L. Fredrickson, "Love and Other Positive Emotions in Contemporary Social Practice and Visual Art," in *The Oxford Handbook of the Positive Humanities,* ed. Louis Tay and James O. Pawelski (London: Oxford University Press, forthcoming 2022), 4.
807. de Botton and Armstrong, *Art as Therapy,* 29.
808. de Botton and Armstrong, *Art as Therapy,* 39.
809. de Botton and Armstrong, *Art as Therapy,* 59.
810. de Botton and Armstrong, *Art as Therapy,* 53.
811. de Botton and Armstrong, *Art as Therapy,* 45.
812. Annelies van Goethem and John Sloboda, "The Functions of Music for Affect Regulation," *Musicae Scientiae* 15, no. 2 (2011): 208, 209.
813. van Goethem and Sloboda, "The Functions of Music for Affect Regulation," 223.

814. Diana Christine Hereld, "Music as a Regulator of Emotion: Three Case Studies," *Music & Medicine* 11, no. 3 (2019): 183–194.

815. Penelope Giannopoulou, Evi Makri-Botsari, and Murray Allison, "Relating Musical Intelligence to Empathy and Aggression in Adolescence," *Collective Volume of the Scientific Conference: Determinants and Prospects in Education* 1, no. 1 (2016): 67–76; Tal-Chen Rabinowitch, "How, Rather Than What Type of, Music Increases Empathy," *Empirical Musicology Review* 10, no. 1 (2015): 96–98.

816. Suvi H. Saarikallio, "Music in Mood Regulation: Initial Scale Development," *Musicae Scientiae* 12, no. 2 (2008): 291–309.

817. Noah Henry, Diana Kayser, and Hauke Egermann, "Music in Mood Regulation and Coping Orientations in Response to COVID-19 Lockdown Measures Within the United Kingdom," *Frontiers in Psychology* (May 2021): 3, https://doi.org/10.3389/fpsyg.2021.647879.

818. Henry et al., "Music in Mood Regulation," 3.

819. Seligman, *Flourish*, 17.

820. Yerin Shim, Louis Tay, Michaela Ward, and James O. Pawelski, "Arts and Humanities Engagement: An Integrative Conceptual Framework for Psychological Research," *Review of General Psychology* 23, no. 2 (2019): 159, 160, https://doi.org/10.1177/1089268019832847.

821. Emily Esfahani Smith, *The Power of Meaning: Finding Fulfillment in a World Obsessed with Happiness* (New York: Crown, 2017), 41.

822. Roy F. Baumeister and Kathleen D. Vohs, "The Pursuit of Meaningfulness in Life," in *Handbook of Positive Psychology*, ed. C. R. Snyder and Shane J. Lopez (London: Oxford University Press, 2002), 614; Geoff Lowe, "Health-Related Effects of Creative and Expressive Writing," *Health Education* 106, no. 1 (2006): 60, 62, https://doi.org/10.1108/09654280610637201.

823. James W. Pennebaker and Joshua M. Smyth, *Opening Up by Writing It Down: How Expressive Writing Improves Health and Eases Emotional Pain* (New York: Guilford Press, 2016).

824. Laura A. King and James W. Pennebaker, "Thinking About Goals, Glue, and the Meaning of Life," in *Advances in Social Cognition*, ed. Robert S. Wyer (Mahwah, NJ: Lawrence Erlbaum, 1996), 104.

825. Pennebaker and Smyth, *Opening Up by Writing It Down*, 65.

826. Julia Cameron, *The Artist's Way: A Spiritual Path to Higher Creativity* (New York: Jeremy P. Tarcher/Putnam, 2002), 9.

827. Pennebaker and Smyth, *Opening Up by Writing It Down*, 80.

828. Pennebaker and Smyth, *Opening Up by Writing It Down*, 80.

829. James W. Pennebaker and Sandra K. Beall, "Confronting a Traumatic Event: Toward an Understanding of Inhibition and Disease," *Journal of Abnormal Psychology* 95 (1986): 274, 281, https://doi.org/10.1037/0021-843X.95.3.274.

830. Pennebaker and Beall, "Confronting a Traumatic Event," 274.

831. James W. Pennebaker, "Writing About Emotional Experiences as a Therapeutic Process," *Psychological Science* 8 (1997): 162, https://doi.org/10.1111/j.1467-9280.1997.tb00403.x.

832. Laura A. King, "The Health Benefits of Writing About Life Goals," *Personality and Social Psychology Bulletin* 27 (2001): 798, https://doi.org/10.1177/0146167201277003.

833. Chad M. Burton and Laura A. King, "The Health Benefits of Writing About Intensely Positive Experiences," *Journal of Research in Personality* 38, no. 2 (2004): 150, 152, https://doi.org/10.1016/S0092-6566(03)00058-8.

834. Burton and King, "The Health Benefits of Writing About Intensely Positive Experiences," 159.

835. Steven M. Toepfer and Kathleen Walker, "Letters of Gratitude: Improving Well-Being Through Expressive Writing," *Journal of Writing Research* 1, no. 3 (2009): 181, 188, https://doi.org/10.17239/jowr-2009.01.03.1.

836. Robert A. Emmons and Michael E. McCullough, "Counting Blessings Versus Burdens: An Experimental Investigation of Gratitude and Subjective Well-Being in Daily Life," *Journal of Personality and Social Psychology* 84, no. 2 (2003): 377, 386.

837. King, "The Health Benefits of Writing About Life Goals," 798.

838. Burton and King, "The Health Benefits of Writing About Intensely Positive Experiences," 152, 160.

839. Kaitlin Fitzgerald and Melanie C. Green, "Stories for Good: Transportation into Narrative Worlds," in *The Oxford Handbook of the Positive Humanities*, ed. Louis Tay and James O. Pawelski (Oxford: Oxford University Press, forthcoming 2022).

840. Fitzgerald and Green, "Stories for Good."

841. Melanie C. Green and Timothy C. Brock, "The Role of Transportation in the Persuasiveness of Public Narratives," *Journal of Personality and Social Psychology* 79 (2000): 701–721, https://doi.org/10.1037//0022-3514.79.5.701.

842. Kaitlin Fitzgerald, Elaine Paravati, Melanie C. Green, Melissa M. Moore, and Jeffrey L. Qian, "Restorative Narratives for Health Promotion," *Health Communication* 35, no. 3 (2019): 356, https://doi.org/10.1080/10410236.2018.1563032.

843. Melanie C. Green, "Transportation into Narrative Worlds: Implications for the Self," in *On Building, Defending and Regulating the Self: A Psychological Perspective*, ed. Abraham Tesser, Joanne V. Wood, and Diederik A. Stapel (East Sussex: Psychology Press, 2005), 53–75.

844. Cameron, *The Artist's Way*, 9.

845. "The VIA Character Strengths Survey," (VIA Institute on Character), accessed October 2, 2021, https://www.viacharacter.org/survey/account/register.

846. Fredrickson, *Positivity*, 215–223.

847. Fredrickson, *Positivity*, 39.

848. Tom Sturges, *Every Idea Is a Good Idea: Be Creative Anytime, Anywhere* (New York: Tarcher Perigree, 2014).

849. Cameron, *The Artist's Way*, 9.

850. https://m.facebook.com/paulocoelho/posts/115407808481824?locale2=ko_KR; https://www.pinkvilla.com/entertainment/hollywood/alchemists-paulo-coelho-defends-bts-against-trolls-haters-are-confused-admirers-who-want-be-you-511654.

851. Tharp, *The Creative Habit*, 15.

852. Pressfield, *Do the Work*, 38.

853. Csikszentmihalyi, *Flow*, 4.

854. "A Growing Pittsburgh Movement Promotes Art Therapy for Lawyers Battling Stress," *Law.com* (November 9, 2018), https://www.yahoo.com/now/growing-pittsburgh-movement-promotes-art-145726022.html?guccounter=1.

855. Kendra Cherry, "What Is Art Therapy?" *www.verywellmind.com* (July 4, 2021), https://www.verywellmind.com/what-is-art-therapy-2795755.

856. https://arttherapycentre.com/blog/adrian-hill-uk-founder-art-therapy-morgan-bush-intern/.

857. Martin E. P. Seligman, *Flourish: A Visionary New Understanding of Happiness and Well-Being* (New York: Atria Books, 2011), 20.

858. Seligman, *Flourish*, 14.

859. Stephen M. Schueller, "Person–Activity Fit in Positive Psychological Interventions," in *The Wiley Blackwell Handbook of Positive Psychological Interventions*, ed. Acacia C. Parks and Stephen M. Schueller (Hoboken, NJ: John Wiley & Sons, 2014), 393.

860. Barbara Fredrickson, *Positivity: Discover the Upward Spiral That Will Change Your Life* (New York: Harmony, 2009), 191.

861. Jonathan Haidt, *The Happiness Hypothesis: Finding Modern Truth in Ancient Wisdom* (New York: Basic Books, 2006), 133 (emphasis added).

862. Isaac Prilleltensky, *The Laughing Guide to Well-Being: Using Humor and Science to Become Happier and Healthier* (Lanham, MD: Rowman & Littlefield, 2016), 113.

863. Jonathan Haidt, *The Righteous Mind: Why Good People Are Divided by Politics and Religion* (New York: Pantheon Books, 2012), 221.

864. Jonathan Haidt, J. Patrick Seder, and Selin Kesebir, "Hive Psychology, Happiness, and Public Policy," *Journal of Legal Studies* 37 (2008): S133, S135, https://doi.org/10.1086/529447.

865. Shelly L. Gable and Courtney L. Gosnell, "The Positive Side of Close Relationships," in *Designing Positive Psychology: Taking Stock and Moving Forward*, ed.

Kennon M. Sheldon, Todd B. Kashdan, and Michael F. Steger (London: Oxford University Press, 2011), 1; Sheldon Cohen and Thomas A. Wills, "Stress, Social Support, and the Buffering Hypothesis," *Psychological Bulletin* 98, no. 2 (1985): 310, https://doi.org/10.1037/0033-2909.98.2.310.

866. Barbara L. Fredrickson, *Love 2.0: Creating Happiness and Health in Moments of Connection* (New York: Penguin Group, 2013), 17.
867. Fredrickson, *Love 2.0,* 17.
868. James H. Fowler and Nicholas A. Christakis, "Dynamic Spread of Happiness in a Large Social Network: Longitudinal Analysis over 20 Years in the Framingham Heart Study," *British Medical Journal* 337 (2008): 1, https://dash.harvard.edu/handle/1/3685822.
869. Shelly L. Gable, Gian C. Gonzaga, and Amy Strachman, "Will You Be There for Me When Things Go Right? Supportive Responses to Positive Event Disclosures," *Journal of Personality and Social Psychology* 91, no. 5 (2006): 904, https:/doi.org/10.1037/0022-3514.91.5.904.
870. Gable et al., "Will You Be There for Me When Things Go Right?" 904.
871. Gable and Gosnell, "The Positive Side of Close Relationships," 5–6.
872. Gable et al., "Will You Be There for Me When Things Go Right?" 907.
873. Gable et al., "Will You Be There for Me When Things Go Right?" 905.
874. Gable et al., "Will You Be There for Me When Things Go Right?" 905.
875. Gable et al., "Will You Be There for Me When Things Go Right?" 905.
876. Gable et al., "Will You Be There for Me When Things Go Right?" 905.
877. Gable et al., "Will You Be There for Me When Things Go Right?" 906, 913.
878. Cohen and Willis, "Stress, Social Support, and the Buffering Hypothesis," 310.
879. Stephen M. Drigotas, "The Michelangelo Phenomenon and Personal Well-Being," *Journal of Personality* 70 (2002): 59, https://doi.org/10.1111/1467-6494.00178; Stephen M. Drigotas, Caryl E. Rusbult, Jennifer Wieselquist, and Sarah W. Whitton, "Close Partner as Sculptor of the Ideal Self: Behavioral Affirmation and the Michelangelo Phenomenon," *Journal of Personality and Social Psychology* 77 (1999): 293, https://doi.org/10.1037/0022-3514.77.2.293.
880. Heidi K. Brown, "4 Lessons We Can Learn as a Profession from the Pandemic," *ABA Journal* (August 1, 2020), https://www.abajournal.com/magazine/article/four-lessons-we-can-learn-as-a-profession-from-the-pandemic.
881. "Clarence Thomas Breaks Long Silence During Supreme Court Oral Arguments," *Washington Post* (January 14, 2013), https://www.washingtonpost.com/politics/clarence-thomas-breaks-long-silence-during-supreme-court-oral-arguments/2013/01/14/a7c6023c-5e7a-11e2-9940-6fc488f3fecd_story.html.
882. Julian Weissglass, "Constructivist Listening for Empowerment and Change," *The Educational Forum* 54, no. 4 (1990): 355, http://doi.org/10.1080/00131729009335561.

883. Weissglass, "Constructivist Listening," 355.

884. Weissglass, "Constructivist Listening," 356.

885. "What Is Constructivism?" *Teaching and Education* (blog), Western Governors University, May 27, 2020, https://www.wgu.edu/blog/what-constructivism2005.html#close.

886. Weissglass, "Constructivist Listening," 359.

887. Weissglass, "Constructivist Listening," 356.

888. Weissglass, "Constructivist Listening," 356.

889. National Equity Project, "Constructivist Listening," https://www.nationalequityproject.org/frameworks/constructivist-listening#:~:text=Santa%20Barbara%3A%20The%20National%20Coalition%20for%20Equity%20and,the%20benefit%20of%20the%20speaker%2C%20not%20the%20listener, adapting information from Ana M. Becerra and Julian Weissglass, *Take It Up: Leading for Educational Equity* (Santa Barbara: The National Coalition for Equity and Education, 2004).

890. ShaneSafir, "Listening Dyads Can Transform Your Team," *Edutopia* (December 10, 2014), https://www.edutopia.org/blog/listening-dyads-transform-team-shane-safir.

891. National Equity Project, "Constructivist Listening."

892. National Equity Project, "Constructivist Listening."

893. Weissglass, "Constructivist Listening," 359.

894. Weissglass, "Constructivist Listening," 359.

895. Weissglass, "Constructivist Listening," 359.

896. Safir, "Listening Dyads."

897. Emile G. Bruneau and Rebecca Saxe, "The Power of Being Heard: The Benefits of 'Perspective-Giving' in the Context of Intergroup Conflict," *Journal of Experimental Social Psychology* 48, no. 4 (2012): 855–866, https://doi.org/10.1016/j.jesp.2012.02.017.

898. Bruneau and Saxe, "The Power of Being Heard," 856.

899. Bruneau and Saxe, "The Power of Being Heard," 855.

900. Bruneau and Saxe, "The Power of Being Heard," 855.

901. Portions of this discussion of the hive switch first appeared in my article, "Can Replacing Hierarchies With a Hive Mentality Transform our Profession?" *ABA Journal* (April 1, 2021), https://www.abajournal.com/magazine/article/can-replacing-hierarchies-with-intergroup-teams-transform-our-profession.

902. Haidt et al., "Hive Psychology, Happiness, and Public Policy," S136.

903. Haidt, *The Righteous Mind*, 221–222.

904. Haidt, *The Righteous Mind*, 221.

905. Haidt et al., "Hive Psychology, Happiness, and Public Policy," S136, S140, citing Victor Turner, *The Ritual Process: Structure and Anti-Structure* (Berlin: Aldine De Gruyter, 1995).
906. Haidt et al., "Hive Psychology, Happiness, and Public Policy," S140.
907. Haidt et al., "Hive Psychology, Happiness, and Public Policy," S139.
908. Haidt et al., "Hive Psychology, Happiness, and Public Policy," S136.
909. Haidt et al., "Hive Psychology, Happiness, and Public Policy," S133.
910. Haidt et al., "Hive Psychology, Happiness, and Public Policy," S133.
911. Haidt, *The Righteous Mind*, 223.
912. Haidt, *The Righteous Mind*, 223.
913. Haidt, *The Righteous Mind*, 237.
914. Haidt, *The Righteous Mind*, 237–238.
915. Haidt, *The Righteous Mind*, 240.
916. Haidt et al., "Hive Psychology, Happiness, and Public Policy," S140, citing Turner.
917. Haidt, *The Righteous Mind*, 239–240.
918. Haidt et al., "Hive Psychology, Happiness, and Public Policy," S142.
919. Haidt, *The Righteous Mind*, 239.
920. Haidt, *The Righteous Mind*, 227, 239–240.
921. Portions of this discussion about defusing bullies first appeared in my article, "We Can Be Smart, Ambitious and Accomplished Members of the Legal Profession Without Being Jerks," *ABA Journal* (November 1, 2019), https://www.abajournal.com/magazine/article/we-can-be-smart-ambitious-and-accomplished-members-of-the-legal-profession-without-being-jerks.
922. "Bullying," in *Merriam-Webster* (Merriam-Webster Dictionary), accessed September 30th, 2021, https://www.merriam-webster.com/dictionary/bullying.
923. Lynne Curry, *Beating the Workplace Bully: A Tactical Guide to Taking Charge* (New York: Amacom, 2016), 11 (emphasis added).
924. Elizabeth Bernstein, "Why It Seems Like Bullies Are Everywhere—And How to Stop Them," *Wall Street Journal* (July 14, 2020), https://www.wsj.com/articles/why-it-seems-like-bullies-are-everywhereand-how-to-stop-them-11594743348.
925. Stav Ziv, "Don't Let Workplace Bullies Win—Here's How to Spot Them and Stop Them," *The Muse*, https://www.themuse.com/advice/how-to-deal-with-workplace-bullies, citing the Workplace Bullying Institute.
926. Ziv, "Don't Let Workplace Bullies Win," citing Catherine Mattice Zundel, CEO of Civility Partners.
927. Ziv, "Don't Let Workplace Bullies Win."

928. Fran Hauser, "How to Cope When You're Being Bullied at Work," *Time* (April 23, 2018), https://time.com/5247289/workplace-bullying/.
929. Ziv, "Don't Let Workplace Bullies Win."
930. Ziv, "Don't Let Workplace Bullies Win."
931. LawCare, "Bullying in the Workplace," www.LawCare.org.uk, https://www.lawcare.org.uk/get-information/articles/bullying-in-the-workplace/.
932. Crystal Raypole, "How to Identify and Manage Workplace Bullying," *Healthline*, https://www.healthline.com/health/workplace-bullying.
933. Raypole, "How to Identify and Manage Workplace Bullying."
934. Raypole, "How to Identify and Manage Workplace Bullying."
935. Raypole, "How to Identify and Manage Workplace Bullying."
936. Tricia Emerson, "Is Your Team Uncivilized?" *Forbes* (April 26, 2020), https://www.forbes.com/sites/triciaemerson/2020/04/26/is-your-team-uncivilized/?sh=4425ed481261.
937. Curry, *Beating the Workplace Bully*, 63.
938. Curry, *Beating the Workplace Bully*, 93.
939. LawCare, "Bullying in the Workplace."
940. LawCare, "Bullying in the Workplace."
941. Curry, *Beating the Workplace Bully*.
942. Curry, *Beating the Workplace Bully*, 70.
943. Hauser, "How to Cope When You're Being Bullied at Work."
944. Curry, *Beating the Workplace Bully*, 112.
945. LawCare, "Bullying in the Workplace."
946. Curry, *Beating the Workplace Bully*, 63–64.
947. Curry, *Beating the Workplace Bully*, 48, 50.
948. Curry, *Beating the Workplace Bully*, 22.
949. Ziv, "Don't Let Workplace Bullies Win."
950. Raypole, "How to Identify and Manage Workplace Bullying."
951. Heidi Lynne Kurter, "Workplace Bullying: 4 Steps to Overcome It and Fight Back," *Forbes* (July 5, 2018), https://www.forbes.com/sites/heidilynnekurter/2019/07/05/workplace-bullying-4-steps-to-overcome-it-and-fight-back/#7824fdf94a50.
952. Kurter, "Workplace Bullying."
953. Curry, *Beating the Workplace Bully*, 118.
954. Curry, *Beating the Workplace Bully*, 63.
955. Curry, *Beating the Workplace Bully*, ix.

956. Curry, *Beating the Workplace Bully,* 63.
957. Curry, *Beating the Workplace Bully,* 93.
958. Curry, *Beating the Workplace Bully,* 65.
959. Curry, *Beating the Workplace Bully,* 65.
960. Curry, *Beating the Workplace Bully,* 66.
961. Curry, *Beating the Workplace Bully,* 90.
962. Curry, *Beating the Workplace Bully,* 97.
963. Kurter, "Workplace Bullying."
964. Bernstein, "Why It Seems Like Bullies Are Everywhere," quoting Dr. Craig Malkin.
965. Curry, *Beating the Workplace Bully,* 33.
966. Ziv, "Don't Let Workplace Bullies Win," citing Zundel.
967. Raypole, "How to Identify and Manage Workplace Bullying."
968. https://www.law.com/2019/07/19/jerk-partners-beget-jerk-partners-ending-big-laws-cycle-of-dysfunction/.
969. James Goodnow, "Don't Let the Law Suck Out Your Soul," *Above the Law* (January 10, 2020), https://abovethelaw.com/2020/01/dont-let-the-law-suck-out-your-soul/.
970. Goodnow, "Don't Let the Law Suck Out Your Soul."
971. Trent Collier, "The Argument Clinic," *Michigan Bar Journal* (March 2020): 18, 19, (originally appeared in *Oakland County Bar Association Journal*).
972. Collier, "The Argument Clinic."
973. Goodnow, "Don't Let the Law Suck Out Your Soul."
974. Paul Kiernan, "'Being Nice' and Finishing First," *Litigation Daily* (January 6, 2018), https://www.law.com/litigationdaily/sites/litigationdaily/2018/01/06/being-nice-and-finishing-first/?et=&bu=&cn=&src=&pt=.
975. Kiernan, "'Being Nice' and Finishing First."
976. Kiernan, "'Being Nice' and Finishing First."
977. Kiernan, "'Being Nice' and Finishing First."
978. Kiernan, "'Being Nice' and Finishing First."
979. Kiernan, "'Being Nice' and Finishing First."
980. www.suburbanriot.com.
981. "Is Cancel Culture (or 'Callout Culture') Good for Society?" *Procon*.org (August 5, 2020), https://www.procon.org/headlines/is-cancel-culture-or-callout-culture-good-for-society/.
982. "Is Cancel Culture (or 'Callout Culture') Good for Society?"

983. Arthur C. Brooks, "Our Culture of Contempt," *The New York Times* (March 2, 2019), https://www.nytimes.com/2019/03/02/opinion/sunday/political-polarization.html.
984. Brooks, "Our Culture of Contempt."
985. Brooks, "Our Culture of Contempt."
986. Brooks, "Our Culture of Contempt."
987. Brooks, "Our Culture of Contempt."
988. K. Reivich, personal communication, August 16, 2021.
989. Helen Murphy and Joelle Goldstein, "Joaquin Phoenix Recites Late Brother River's Song Lyrics in Emotional Oscars Speech for *Joker*," *People* (February 9, 2020), https://people.com/movies/oscars-2020-best-actor-winner-joaquin-phoenix/.
990. Brooks, "Our Culture of Contempt."
991. Brooks, "Our Culture of Contempt."
992. Alain de Botton and John Armstrong, *Art as Therapy* (London: Phaidon Press, 2013), 97.
993. de Botton and Armstrong, 108.
994. Constantine Peter Cavafy, *Ithaka* (1911).
995. Fredrickson, *Love 2.0*, 17.
996. Amy C. Edmondson, *The Fearless Organization: Creating Psychological Safety in the Workplace for Learning, Innovation, and Growth* (Hoboken, NJ: John Wiley & Sons, 2018), xvi.
997. National Equity Project, "Constructivist Listening"; Weissglass, "Constructivist Listening," 359.
998. Bruneau and Saxe, "The Power of Being Heard," 856.
999. Anthony Bourdain, *Medium Raw: A Bloody Valentine to the World of Food and the People Who Cook* (Edinburgh: A&C Black, 2010).
1000. "Awe," in *Lexico Dictionaries* (Oxford Dictionary), accessed September 9, 2021, https://www.lexico.com/en/definition/awe.
1001. Emily Esfahani Smith, *The Power of Meaning: Finding Fulfillment in a World Obsessed with Happiness* (New York: Crown, 2017), 134.
1002. Barbara Fredrickson, *Positivity: Discover the Upward Spiral That Will Change Your Life* (New York: Harmony, 2009), 47.
1003. City of Adelaide, "Wellbeing Benefits of Culture Report" (2020), 9, https://d31atr86jnqrq2.cloudfront.net/docs/wellbeing-benefits-of-culture-report-pawelski.pdf?mtime=20200825102631&focal=none; Louis Tay, James O. Pawelski, and Melissa G. Keith, "The Role of the Arts and Humanities in Human Flourishing: A Conceptual Model," *Journal of Positive Psychology* 13, no. 3 (2018): 217, https://doi.org/10.1080/17439760.2017.1279207.
1004. City of Adelaide, "Wellbeing Benefits," 9.

1005. Tay et al., "Role of the Arts and Humanities," 217.

1006. City of Adelaide, "Wellbeing Benefits," 9.

1007. See, e.g., Blanka Klimova, Gabriela Slaninova, Pavel Prazak, Jaroslav Kacetl, and Martin Valis, "Enhancing Cognitive Performance of Healthy Czech Seniors through Non-Native Language Learning—A Mixed-Methods Pilot Study," *Brain Science* 10 (2020): 573, https:// doi.org/10.3390/brainsci10090573; Simone E. Pfenninger and Sabrina Polz, "Foreign Language Learning in the Third Age: A Pilot Feasibility Study on Cognitive, Socio-Affective and Linguistic Drivers and Benefits in Relation to Previous Bilingualism of the Learner," *Journal of the European Second Language Association* 2, no. 1 (2018): 1–13, https://doi.org/10.22599/jesla.3; Esra Eguz, "Learning a Second Language in Late Adulthood: Benefits and Challenges," *Educational Gerontology* 45, no. 12 (2019): 701–707, https://doi.org/10.1080/03601277.2019.1690273.

1008. Tay et al., "Role of the Arts and Humanities," 217–218.

1009. Anthony Bourdain, *The Nasty Bits* (New York, NY: Bloomsbury Publishing, 2006), xi.

1010. Tay et al., "Role of the Arts and Humanities," 218.

1011. City of Adelaide, "Wellbeing Benefits," 9.

1012. City of Adelaide, "Wellbeing Benefits," 9.

1013. Tay et al., "Role of the Arts and Humanities," 218.

1014. Tay et al., "Role of the Arts and Humanities," 218.

1015. City of Adelaide, "Wellbeing Benefits," 9.

1016. City of Adelaide, "Wellbeing Benefits," 9.

1017. City of Adelaide, "Wellbeing Benefits," 9.

1018. VIA Institute on Character, "Humility," https://www.viacharacter.org/character-strengths/humility.

1019. VIA Institute on Character, "Humility," https://www.viacharacter.org/character-strengths/humility.

1020. American Association of Colleges of Nursing, *Cultural Competency in Baccalaureate Nursing Education* (Washington, D.C.: author, 2008), 1.

1021. Mary Isaacson, "Clarifying Concepts: Cultural Humility or Competency," *Journal of Professional Nursing* 30, no. 3 (2014): 251, 252, https://doi.org/10.1016/j.profnurs.2013.09.011.

1022. Melanie Tervalon and Jann Murray-García, "Cultural Humility Versus Cultural Competence: A Critical Distinction in Defining Physician Training Outcomes in Multicultural Education," *Journal of Health Care for the Poor and Underserved* 9, no. 2 (1998): 117, 119, https://melanietervalon.com/wp-content/uploads/2013/08/CulturalHumility_Tervalon-and-Murray-Garcia-Article.pdf.

1023. Isaacson, "Clarifying Concepts," 252, citing Tervalon and Murray-García, "Cultural Humility Versus Cultural Competence," 119.

1024. Isaacson, "Clarifying Concepts," 252.

1025. Isaacson, "Clarifying Concepts," 252.

1026. Tervalon and Murray-Garcia, "Cultural Humility Versus Cultural Competence," 117.

1027. Marcie Fisher-Borne, Jessie Montana Cain, and Suzanne L. Martin, "From Mastery to Accountability: Cultural Humility as an Alternative to Cultural Competence," *Social Work Education: The International Journal* 34, no. 2 (2015): 165, 169, https://doi.org/10.1080/02615479.2014.977244.

1028. Josepha Campinha-Bacote, "Cultural Competemility: A Paradigm Shift in the Cultural Competence Versus Cultural Humility Debate, Part I," *The Online Journal of Issues in Nursing* 24, no. 1 (2019), https://www.doi.org/10.3912/OJIN.Vol24No01PPT20.

1029. Campinha-Bacote, "Cultural Competemility."

1030. Campinha-Bacote, "Cultural Competemility."

1031. Josepha Campinha-Bacote, "The Process of Cultural Competence in the Delivery of Healthcare Services: A Model of Care," *Journal of Transcultural Nursing* 13, no. 3 (2002): 181, 183.

1032. Campinha-Bacote, "Cultural Competemility."

1033. Campinha-Bacote, "Cultural Competemility" (italics added).

1034. Lexico Dictionaries, "Spiritual," in *Lexico* (Oxford Dictionary, n.d.), https://www.lexico.com/en/definition/spiritual.

1035. National Task Force on Lawyer Well-Being, "The Path to Lawyer Well-Being: Practical Recommendations for Positive Change," August 14, 2017, 9, https://lawyerwellbeing.net/wp-content/uploads/2017/11/Lawyer-Wellbeing-Report.pdf.

1036. Martin E. P. Seligman, *Flourish: A Visionary New Understanding of Happiness and Well-Being* (New York: Atria Books, 2011), 17.

1037. VIA Institute on Character, "Find Your 24 Character Strengths," https://www.viacharacter.org/character-strengths (accessed October 5, 2021).

1038. VIA Institute on Character, "Find Your 24 Character Strengths," https://www.viacharacter.org/character-strengths (accessed October 5, 2021).

1039. Isaac Prilleltensky, *The Laughing Guide to Well-Being: Using Humor and Science to Become Happier and Healthier* (Lanham, MD: Rowman & Littlefield, 2016), 12.

1040. Prilleltensky, *The Laughing Guide,* 12.

1041. Prilleltensky, *The Laughing Guide,* 12.

1042. Emily Esfahani Smith, *The Power of Meaning: Finding Fulfillment in a World Obsessed with Happiness* (New York: Crown, 2017), 41.

1043. Smith, *The Power of Meaning,* 49.

1044. Smith, *The Power of Meaning,* 50.

1045. Smith, *The Power of Meaning*, 66.

1046. Barbara L. Fredrickson, *Love 2.0: Creating Happiness and Health in Moments of Connection* (New York: Penguin Group, 2013), 17.

1047. Smith, *The Power of Meaning*, 78.

1048. Todd B. Kashdan and Patrick E. McKnight, "Origins of Purpose in Life: Refining our Understanding of a Life Well Lived," *Psychological Topics* 18 (2009): 303, 304.

1049. Kashdan and McKnight, "Origins of Purpose in Life," 304.

1050. Kashdan and McKnight, "Origins of Purpose in Life," 304.

1051. Smith, *The Power of Meaning*, 84.

1052. Smith, *The Power of Meaning*, 85.

1053. Smith, *The Power of Meaning*, 34.

1054. Smith, *The Power of Meaning*, 102.

1055. Smith, *The Power of Meaning*, 125.

1056. Smith, *The Power of Meaning*, 131.

1057. Smith, *The Power of Meaning*, 133.

1058. Jonathan Haidt, *The Happiness Hypothesis: Finding Modern Truth in Ancient Wisdom* (New York: Basic Books, 2006), 203.

1059. Barbara Fredrickson, *Positivity, Discover the Upward Spiral That Will Change Your Life* (New York: Harmony, 2009), 46.

1060. Smith, *The Power of Meaning*, 134.

1061. Roy F. Baumeister and Kathleen D. Vohs, "The Pursuit of Meaningfulness in Life," in *Handbook of Positive Psychology*, ed. C. R. Snyder and Shane J. Lopez (London: Oxford University Press, 2002), 609.

1062. Baumeister and Vohs, "The Pursuit of Meaningfulness in Life," 609.

1063. Baumeister and Vohs, "The Pursuit of Meaningfulness in Life," 610.

1064. Michael F. Steger, "Meaning in Life: A Unified Model," in *Oxford Handbook of Positive Psychology*, ed. Shane J. Lopez and C.R. Snyder (Oxford: Oxford University Press, 2009), 679, https://doi.org/10.1093/oxfordhb/9780195187243.013.0064.

1065. Steger, "Meaning in Life," 679.

1066. Steger, "Meaning in Life," 680.

1067. Steger, "Meaning in Life," 682.

1068. Jeanne Nakamura and Mihaly Csikszentmihalyi, "The Construction of Meaning Through Vital Engagement," in *Flourishing: Positive Psychology and the Life Well-Lived*, ed. Corey L. M. Keyes and Jonathan Haidt (Washington, D.C.: American Psychological Association, 2003), 99, citing Creativity in Later Life Project (1994), 9, https://doi.org/10.1037/10594-004.

1069. Baumeister and Vohs, "The Pursuit of Meaningfulness in Life," 613.
1070. Julia Cameron, *The Artist's Way: A Spiritual Path to Higher Creativity* (New York: Jeremy P. Tarcher/Putnam, 2002), 10.
1071. Cameron, *The Artist's Way*, 12.
1072. VIA Institute on Character, "Find Your 24 Character Strengths."
1073. Lizzy Bunker, *Nude Gratitude: Getting Naked with Your Desires* (2019).
1074. Barry Schwartz, *Why We Work* (New York: Simon & Schuster, 2015), 1–2.
1075. Schwartz, *Why We Work*, 1.
1076. Schwartz, *Why We Work*, 1.
1077. Schwartz, *Why We Work*, 3.
1078. Schwartz, *Why We Work*, 8, 11, 16.
1079. Schwartz, *Why We Work*, 16–17.
1080. Schwartz, *Why We Work*, 16.
1081. Schwartz, *Why We Work*, 17.
1082. Schwartz, *Why We Work*, 17.
1083. VIA Institute on Character, "Zest," https://www.viacharacter.org/character-strengths/zest.
1084. National Task Force on Lawyer Well-Being, "The Path to Lawyer Well-Being: Practical Recommendations for Positive Change," August 14, 2017, 9, https://lawyerwellbeing.net/wp-content/uploads/2017/11/Lawyer-Wellbeing-Report.pdf.
1085. Lexico Dictionaries, "Occupation," in *Lexico* (Oxford Dictionary, n.d.), https://www.lexico.com/en/definition/occupation.
1086. Lexico Dictionaries, "Occupy," in *Lexico* (Oxford Dictionary, n.d.), https://www.lexico.com/en/definition/occupy.
1087. Isaac Prilleltensky, "Wellness as Fairness," *American Journal of Community Psychology* 49 (2012): 1–21, http://doi.org/10.1007/s10464-011-9448-8.
1088. Prilleltensky, "Wellness as Fairness," 5–6.
1089. Isaac Prilleltensky, "Mattering at the Intersection of Psychology, Philosophy, and Politics," *American Journal of Community Psychology* (2019): 1, 2, https://doi.org/10.1002/ajcp.12368.
1090. Prilleltensky, "Mattering," 2.
1091. Prilleltensky, "Mattering," 4.
1092. Isaac Prilleltensky, *The Laughing Guide to Well-Being: Using Humor and Science to Become Happier and Healthier* (Lanham: Rowman & Littlefield, 2016), 14–15.
1093. Prilleltensky, "Mattering," 2.
1094. Prilleltensky, "Mattering," 3.

1095. Prilleltensky, "Mattering," 10; Prilleltensky, *The Laughing Guide,* 31.
1096. Prilleltensky, "Mattering," 4.
1097. Prilleltensky, "Mattering," 16.
1098. Prilleltensky, *The Laughing Guide,* 75.
1099. Prilleltensky, *The Laughing Guide,* 30–31.
1100. Prilleltensky, *The Laughing Guide,* 113.
1101. Prilleltensky, *The Laughing Guide,* 75.
1102. Prilleltensky, *The Laughing Guide,* 31.
1103. Prilleltensky, *The Laughing Guide,* 75.
1104. Prilleltensky, *The Laughing Guide,* 75.
1105. Prilleltensky, *The Laughing Guide,* 76.
1106. Richard M. Ryan and Edward L. Deci, "Self-Determination Theory and the Facilitation of Intrinsic Motivation, Social Development, and Well-Being," *American Psychologist* 55, no. 1 (2000): 68–78, https://doi.org/10.1037/0003-066X.55.1.68.
1107. Anneke Ferguson and Stephen Tang, "Determined to be Professional, Ethical, and Well," in *Educating for Well-Being in Law,* ed. Caroline Strevens and Rachael Field (London: Routledge, 2020), 60.
1108. Schwartz, *Why We Work,* 28.
1109. Schwartz, *Why We Work,* 16, 26.
1110. Anne Brafford, "Transform Lawyer Well-Being into a Team Sport," in *The Best Lawyer You Can Be: A Guide to Physical, Mental, Emotional, and Spiritual Wellness,* ed. Stewart Levine (Chicago: American Bar Association, 2018), 47.
1111. Caroline Strevens, Rachael Field, and Nigel Duncan, "Self-Care as a Professional Virtue for Lawyers," in *Educating for Well-Being in Law,* ed. Caroline Strevens and Rachael Field (London: Routledge, 2020), 17.
1112. Larry Krieger, "Being the Happiest, Most Effective Lawyer You Can Be," in *The Best Lawyer You Can Be: A Guide to Physical, Mental, Emotional, and Spiritual Wellness,* ed. Stewart Levine (Chicago: American Bar Association, 2018), 14.
1113. Anne Brafford, *Positive Professionals: Creating High-Performing Profitable Firms Through the Science of Engagement* (Chicago: American Bar Association, 2017), 76.
1114. Brafford, *Positive Professionals,* 75.
1115. Brafford, *Positive Professionals,* 76–77.
1116. Brafford, "Transform Lawyer Well-Being into a Team Sport," 48.
1117. Brafford, *Positive Professionals,* 142.
1118. Geralyn Datz, "The Enlightened Lawyer: Overcoming Stress and Creating Balance," *North Carolina Bar Journal* (2019): 28, https://www.nclap.org/the-enlightened-lawyer-overcoming-stress-and-creating-balance/ (reprinted from *Louisiana Bar Journal* 62 (2014–2015)).

1119. Datz, "The Enlightened Lawyer," 28.
1120. John Hollway, "Lawyer Well-Being at Work: It's a Two-Way Street," *Law.com* (Dec. 11, 2019).
1121. Datz, "The Enlightened Lawyer," 28.
1122. Datz, "The Enlightened Lawyer," 29; Hollway, "Lawyer Well-Being at Work."
1123. Datz, "The Enlightened Lawyer," 29.
1124. Hollway, "Lawyer Well-Being at Work."
1125. Mihaly Csikszentmihalyi, *Flow: The Psychology of Optimal Experience* (New York: Harper Perennial, 1990), 191.
1126. Angela L. Duckworth, Christopher Peterson, Michael D. Matthews, and Dennis R. Kelly, "Grit: Perseverance and Passion for Long-Term Goals," *Journal of Personality and Social Psychology* 92 (2007): 1087, https://doi.org/10.1037/0022-3514.92.6.1087.
1127. Susan A. Jackson and Mihaly Csikszentmihalyi, *Flow in Sports: The Keys to Optimal Experiences and Performances* (Champaign, IL: Human Kinetics, 1999).
1128. Duckworth et al., 1087.
1129. Angela L. Duckworth, *Grit: The Power of Passion and Perseverance* (New York: Scribner, 2016), 137; K. Anders Ericsson, Ralf T. Krampe, and Clemens Tesch-Romer, "The Role of Deliberate Practice in the Acquisition of Expert Performance," *Psychological Review* 100, no. 3 (1993): 367, https://doi.org/10.1037//0033-295X.100.3.363.
1130. Schwartz, *Why We Work,* 16–17.
1131. Prilleltensky, "Mattering," 2.
1132. Anthony Niedwiecki, "Lawyers and Learning: A Metacognitive Approach to Legal Education," *Widener Law Review* 13, no. 33 (2006): 33, 35, https://repository.law.uic.edu/cgi/viewcontent.cgi?article=1102&context=facpubs.
1133. Niedwiecki, "Lawyers and Learning," 42.
1134. Niedwiecki, "Lawyers and Learning," 42.
1135. Niedwiecki, "Lawyers and Learning," 43.
1136. Niedwiecki, "Lawyers and Learning," 44.
1137. Niedwiecki, "Lawyers and Learning," 44.
1138. Niedwiecki, "Lawyers and Learning," 49–50, citing M. H. Sam Jacobson, "A Primer on Learning Styles: Reaching Every Student," *Seattle University Law Review* 25 (2001): 139–177.
1139. Erica Ariel Fox, *Winning from Within: A Breakthrough Method for Leading, Living, and Lasting Change* (New York: Harper Business, 2013), 34.
1140. https://harvardfop.github.io/interpersonal-skills/no-doze.html.
1141. VIA Total 24 Character Strengths Report, 35.

1142. VIA Institute on Character, "Find Your 24 Character Strengths," https://www.viacharacter.org/character-strengths, accessed October 5, 2021.

1143. Roberta Michnick Golinkoff and Kathy Hirsh-Pasek, *Becoming Brilliant: What Science Tells Us About Raising Successful Children* (Washington, D.C.: American Psychological Association, 2016), 161; Ryan M. Niemiec, *Character Strengths Interventions: A Field Guide for Practitioners* (Boston: Hogrefe Publishing, 2018), "Spotlight on Judgment/Critical Thinking."

1144. Golinkoff and Hirsh-Pasek, *Becoming Brilliant,* 160.

1145. Gregory Schraw and Rayne Sperling Dennison, "Assessing Meta-Cognitive Awareness," *Contemporary Educational Psychology* 19 (1994): 460–475, https://doi.org/10.1006/ceps.1994.1033; Metacognitive Awareness Inventory (MAI), https://advising.lafayette.edu/wp-content/uploads/sites/247/2021/10/metacognitive_awareness_inventory.pdf.

1146. Golinkoff and Hirsh-Pasek, *Becoming Brilliant,* 160.

1147. Golinkoff and Hirsh-Pasek, *Becoming Brilliant,* 161.

1148. Golinkoff and Hirsh-Pasek, *Becoming Brilliant,* 162.

1149. Golinkoff and Hirsh-Pasek, *Becoming Brilliant,* 165.

1150. Golinkoff and Hirsh-Pasek, *Becoming Brilliant,* 167.

1151. Golinkoff and Hirsh-Pasek, *Becoming Brilliant,* 170.

1152. Golinkoff and Hirsh-Pasek, *Becoming Brilliant,* 178.

1153. Golinkoff and Hirsh-Pasek, *Becoming Brilliant,* 161.

1154. Angela L. Duckworth, Christopher Peterson, Michael D. Matthews, and Dennis R. Kelly, "Grit: Perseverance and Passion for Long-Term Goals," *Journal of Personality and Social Psychology* 92 (2007): 1087, https://doi.org/10.1037/0022-3514.92.6.1087.

1155. Fox, *Winning from Within,* 34.

1156. https://harvardfop.github.io/interpersonal-skills/no-doze.html.

1157. Some of the steps in this chart are adapted from the recommendations in Niedwiecki, "Lawyers and Learning," 44.

1158. Metacognitive Awareness Inventory (MAI), https://advising.lafayette.edu/wp-content/uploads/sites/247/2021/10/metacognitive_awareness_inventory.pdf.

1159. John J. Ratey and Eric Hagerman, *Spark: The Revolutionary New Science of Exercise and the Brain* (New York: Little, Brown & Company, 2008), 40.

1160. Isaac Prilleltensky, "Wellness as Fairness," *American Journal of Community Psychology* 49 (2012): 1, http://doi.org/10.1007/s10464-011-9448-8.

1161. Prilleltensky, "Wellness as Fairness," 1.

1162. Prilleltensky, "Wellness as Fairness," 6.

1163. Prilleltensky, “Wellness as Fairness,” 6.
1164. Prilleltensky, “Wellness as Fairness,” 7.
1165. Prilleltensky, “Wellness as Fairness,” 7.
1166. Prilleltensky, “Wellness as Fairness,” 8.
1167. Prilleltensky, “Wellness as Fairness,” 8.
1168. Prilleltensky, “Wellness as Fairness,” 8.
1169. Prilleltensky, “Wellness as Fairness,” 8.
1170. Prilleltensky, “Wellness as Fairness,” 8.
1171. Prilleltensky, “Wellness as Fairness,” 8.
1172. Prilleltensky, “Wellness as Fairness,” 8.
1173. Prilleltensky, “Wellness as Fairness,” 8.
1174. VIA Institute on Character, *The VIA Classification of Character Strengths* (2012), www.viacharacter.org.
1175. VIA Institute on Character, *The VIA Classification of Character Strengths* (2012), www.viacharacter.org.
1176. VIA Institute on Character, *The VIA Classification of Character Strengths* (2012), www.viacharacter.org.
1177. VIA Institute on Character, *The VIA Classification of Character Strengths* (2012), www.viacharacter.org.
1178. VIA Institute on Character, “Find Your 24 Character Strengths,” https://www.viacharacter.org/character-strengths, accessed October 5, 2021.
1179. VIA Institute on Character, “Teamwork,” https://www.viacharacter.org/character-strengths/teamwork, accessed October 5, 2021.
1180. VIA Institute on Character, “Fairness,” https://www.viacharacter.org/character-strengths/fairness, accessed October 5, 2021.
1181. VIA Institute on Character, “Leadership,” https://www.viacharacter.org/character-strengths/leadership, accessed October 5, 2021.
1182. VIA Institute on Character, *The VIA Classification of Character Strengths* (2012), www.viacharacter.org.
1183. VIA Institute, “Find Your 24 Character Strengths,” https://www.viacharacter.org/character-strengths, accessed October 5, 2021.
1184. Prilleltensky, “Wellness as Fairness,” 6.
1185. Prilleltensky, “Wellness as Fairness,” 7.
1186. Prilleltensky, “Wellness as Fairness,” 8.
1187. Christopher Kukk, *The Compassionate Achiever: How Helping Others Fuels Success* (San Francisco: HarperOne, 2017).
1188. Kukk, *The Compassionate Achiever*, 2.
1189. Kukk, *The Compassionate Achiever*, 2.

1190. Kukk, *The Compassionate Achiever*, 2.

1191. Kukk, *The Compassionate Achiever*, 2.

1192. Kukk, *The Compassionate Achiever*, 17.

1193. Kukk, *The Compassionate Achiever*, 18.

1194. Kukk, *The Compassionate Achiever*, 18.

1195. Kukk, *The Compassionate Achiever*, 19.

1196. Kukk, *The Compassionate Achiever*, 23–24.

1197. Paul Bloom, *Against Empathy: The Case for Rational Compassion* (New York: Harper Collins, 2016), 16.

1198. Bloom, *Against Empathy*, 31.

1199. Bloom, *Against Empathy*, 66.

1200. Bloom, *Against Empathy*, 234.

1201. Bloom, *Against Empathy*, 234.

1202. Bloom, *Against Empathy*, 235.

1203. VIA Institute on Character, "Find Your 24 Character Strengths," https://www.viacharacter.org/character-strengths, accessed October 5, 2021.

1204. VIA Institute on Character, "Love," https://www.viacharacter.org/character-strengths/love, accessed October 5, 2021.

1205. VIA Institute on Character, "Kindness," https://www.viacharacter.org/character-strengths/kindness, accessed October 5, 2021.

1206. VIA Institute on Character, "Social Intelligence," https://www.viacharacter.org/character-strengths/social-intelligence, accessed October 5, 2021.

1207. Isaac Prilleltensky, "Mattering at the Intersection of Psychology, Philosophy, and Politics," *American Journal of Community Psychology* (2019): 16, https://doi.org/10.1002/ajcp.12368.

1208. Christopher Peterson, "Gratitude: Letting Other People Know They Matter Benefits Us," psychologytoday.com (June 24, 2010), https://www.psychologytoday.com/us/blog/the-good-life/201006/gratitude-letting-other-people-know-they-matter-benefits-us.

1209. Judit Mészáros, "Building Blocks Toward Contemporary Trauma Theory: Ferenczi's Paradigm Shift," *The American Journal of Psychoanalysis* 70, no. 4 (2010): 328–340, https://doi.org/10.1057/ajp.2010.2.

1210. Williams, *Move!*, 72.

1211. Williams, *Move!*, 72.

1212. David T. Suntag, "Reflections from the Bench: Procedural Fairness and Trauma: How Do We Avoid Re-Traumatizing Our Court Users?," *Judicial Edge*, National Judicial College (Dec. 19, 2019), https://www.judges.org/news-and-info/reflection-from-the-bench-procedural-fairness-and-trauma-how-do-we-avoid-re-traumatizing-our-court-users/.

1213. Bessel van der Kolk, *The Body Keeps the Score: Brain, Mind, and Body in the Healing of Trauma* (New York: Penguin Books, 2014), 21.

1214. van der Kolk, *The Body Keeps the Score,* 21.

1215. van der Kolk, *The Body Keeps the Score,* 53.

1216. Marjorie A. Silver, Sanford Portnoy, and Jean Koh Peters, "Stress, Burnout, Vicarious Trauma, and Other Emotional Realities in the Lawyer-Client Relationship: A Panel Discussion," *Touro Law Review* 19 (2004): 847, 854, https://digitalcommons.tourolaw.edu/cgi/viewcontent.cgi?referer=&httpsredir=1&article=1584&context=lawreview.

1217. Deborah Wood Smith, "Secondary or Vicarious Trauma Among Judges and Court Personnel," *Trends in State Courts* (2017), https://www.ncsc.org/trends/monthly-trends-articles/2017/secondary-or-vicarious-trauma-among-judges-and-court-personnel.

1218. Christina Rainville, "Understanding Secondary Trauma: A Guide for Lawyers Working with Child Victims," *American Bar Association* (September 1, 2015), https://www.americanbar.org/groups/public_interest/child_law/resources/child_law_practiceonline/child_law_practice/vol-34/september-2015/understanding-secondary-trauma–a-guide-for-lawyers-working-with/.

1219. Rainville, "Understanding Secondary Trauma."

1220. Crystal Tomusiak, "A More Inclusive Discussion on the Impact of Trauma on Lawyers' Mental Health Is Needed," *Canadian Lawyer* (June 3, 2019), https://www.canadianlawyermag.com/news/opinion/a-more-inclusive-discussion-on-the-impact-of-trauma-on-lawyers-mental-health-is-needed/276166.

1221. Tomusiak, "A More Inclusive Discussion on the Impact of Trauma on Lawyers' Mental Health."

1222. Tomusiak, "A More Inclusive Discussion on the Impact of Trauma on Lawyers' Mental Health."

1223. Tomusiak, "A More Inclusive Discussion on the Impact of Trauma on Lawyers' Mental Health."

1224. Tomusiak, "A More Inclusive Discussion on the Impact of Trauma on Lawyers' Mental Health."

1225. Rainville, "Understanding Secondary Trauma," quoting Dr. Erika Tullberg.

1226. Yael Fischman, "Secondary Trauma in the Legal Professions, A Clinical Perspective," *Torture: Quarterly Journal on Rehabilitation of Torture Victims and Prevention of Torture* 18, no. 2 (2008): 107, 109, https://irct.org/assets/uploads/1018-8185_2008-2_107-115.pdf.

1227. Fischman, "Secondary Trauma in the Legal Professions," 114.

1228. William C. Silverman, "How to Identify and Address Secondary Trauma," *National Law Review* 9, no. 37 (February 6, 2019), https://www.natlawreview.com/article/how-to-identify-and-address-secondary-trauma; Fischman, "Secondary Trauma in the Legal Professions," 108.

1229. Smith, "Secondary or Vicarious Trauma Among Judges and Court Personnel"; Rainville, "Understanding Secondary Trauma."

1230. Fischman, "Secondary Trauma in the Legal Professions," 110.

1231. Smith, "Secondary or Vicarious Trauma Among Judges and Court Personnel."

1232. Barbara L. Fredrickson, Michele M. Tugade, Christian E. Waugh, and Gregory R. Larkin, "What Good Are Positive Emotions in Crises? A Prospective Study of Resilience and Emotions Following the Terrorist Attacks on the United States on September 11th, 2001," *Journal of Personality and Social Psychology* 84, no. 2 (2003): 374, https://doi.org/10.1037//0022-3514.84.2.365.

1233. James W. Pennebaker and Joshua M. Smyth, *Opening Up by Writing It Down: How Expressive Writing Improves Health and Eases Emotional Pain* (New York: Guilford Press, 2016), ix.

1234. Pennebaker and Smyth, *Opening Up by Writing It Down,* 72.

1235. Pennebaker and Smyth, *Opening Up by Writing It Down,* 21.

1236. Pennebaker and Smyth, *Opening Up by Writing It Down,* 21.

1237. Pennebaker and Smyth, *Opening Up by Writing It Down,* 21, 25.

Index